T5-CVG-306

Legal and Ethical Aspects of Treating Critically and Terminally Ill Patients

UNIVERSITY LIBRARY

GOVERNORS STATE UNIVERSITY

PARK FOREST SOUTH, ILL.

UNIVERSITY LIBRARY
GOVERNORS STATE UNIVERSITY
PARK FOREST SOUTH, ILL.

Legal and Ethical Aspects of Treating Critically and Terminally Ill Patients

Edited by

A. Edward Doudera, J.D.
J. Douglas Peters, J.D.

Published in Cooperation with
the American Society of
Law and Medicine

AUPHA Press
Ann Arbor, Michigan   Washington, D.C.
1982

Copyright © 1982 by the Regents of the University of Michigan. Printed in the United States of America. All rights reserved. This book or parts thereof may not be reproduced in any form without written permission of the publisher.

Library of Congress Cataloging in Publication Data
Main entry under title:

Legal and ethical aspects of treating critically and terminally ill patients.

Papers derived from 4 conferences sponsored by the American Society of Law and Medicine, and held in Detroit (Nov. 1979), Los Angeles (Apr. 1980), Minneapolis (May 1980), and Chicago (Oct. 1980)
   Bibliography: p.
   Includes index.
   1. Right to die—Law and legislation—United States—Addresses, essays, lectures. 2. Terminal care—Law and legislation—United States—Addresses, essays, lectures. 3. Right to die—Addresses, essays, lectures. 4. Terminal care—Moral and ethical aspects—Addresses, essays, lectures. I. Doudera, A. Edward, 1949- . II. Peters, J. Douglas, 1948- . III. American Society of Law and Medicine. [DNLM: 1. Euthanasia—Legislation. 2. Ethics, Medical. W 50 L4973]

KF3827.E87L43	344.73'0419	81-20523
ISBN 0-914904-76-0	347.304419	AACR2

AUPHA Press is an imprint of Health Administration Press.

Health Administration Press
School of Public Health
The University of Michigan
Ann Arbor, Michigan 48109
   313-764-1380

Association of University
Programs in Health Administration
One DuPont Circle
Washington, D.C.
   202-659-4354

KF
3827
.E87
L43
1982
c.2

Contents

PART THREE: SPECIAL PROBLEMS WITH NEWBORNS AND CHILDREN

PART FOUR: THE HEALTH CARE TEAM

Contributors

JOHN J. ALLMAN, A.C.S.W., is Director of Social Work at Oakwood Hospital in Dearborn, Michigan.

GEORGE J. ANNAS, J.D., M.P.H., is Associate Professor of Law and Medicine at Boston University Schools of Medicine and Public Health.

NANCY E. ATOR, J.D., is an attorney with Hinshaw, Culbertson, Moelmann, Hoban & Fuller in Chicago and represents hospitals and other health care providers.

CHARLES H. BARON, LL.B., PH.D., is Professor of Law at Boston College, School of Law in Newton, Massachusetts.

CORRINE BAYLEY, C.S.J., M.H.A., is Director of the Bioethics Programs at St. Joseph Hospital in Orange, California.

TERESA A. BROOKS, J.D., is an attorney with Dykema, Gossett, Spencer, Goodnow & Trigg in Detroit, and a former Director of Legal Affairs & Policy Development for the Michigan Hospital Association in Lansing, Michigan.

THE HONORABLE RICHARD P. BYRNE is Presiding Judge of the Los Angeles Superior Court, Juvenile Department.

INGE B. CORLESS, R.N., PH.D., is Program Director at St. Peter's Hospice in Albany, New York.

RONALD E. CRANFORD, M.D., is Associate Physician in Neurology at Hennepin County Medical Center, Minneapolis, Minnesota, and Chairman of the Ethics Committee of the American Academy of Neurology.

LEE J. DUNN, JR., J.D., LL.M., is General Counsel, Northwestern Memorial Hospital in Chicago.

J. KAY FELT, J.D., is an attorney with Dykema, Gossett, Spencer, Goodnow & Trigg in Detroit.

GREGORY R. GINEX, J.D., is Chief of the Municipal Division, Office of the State Attorney in Chicago.

LEONARD H. GLANTZ, J.D., is Assistant Professor of Health Law at Boston University Schools of Medicine and Public Health.

JOAN E. HODGMAN, M.D., is Professor of Pediatrics and Director of Neonatology at Los Angeles County–University of Southern California Medical Center.

ALBERT R. JONSEN, PH.D., is Professor of Ethics in Medicine for the Health Policy Program at the University of California, San Francisco.

JOAN KING, R.N., M.S., works in the Staff Development Office at the University of California Irvine Medical Center in Orange, California.

WALTER A. MARKOWICZ, S.T.L., PH.D., is Assistant Professor of Community Medicine and Coordinator for the Human Values in Medicine Program at Wayne State University School of Medicine in Detroit.

RABBI LEVI MEIER is Chaplain and Psychotherapist at Cedars-Sinai Medical Center in Los Angeles.

GEORGE A. OAKES, J.D., is Deputy District Attorney and Head of the Medicolegal Section for Los Angeles County.

ARNOLD S. RELMAN, M.D., is Editor-in-Chief of the *New England Journal of Medicine* in Boston.

JOHN A. ROBERTSON, J.D., is Professor of Law at the University of Wisconsin-Madison.

SIDNEY D. ROSOFF, J.D., LL.M., is an attorney with Parker, Duryee, Zunino, Malone & Carter in New York City, and President of the Society for the Right to Die.

WILLIAM D. STEIN, J.D., is Deputy Attorney General for the California Department of Justice in San Francisco.

BERNARD TOWERS, M.B., CH.B., is a Professor of Pediatrics and Anatomy and Co-Director of the Program in Medicine, Law and Human Values at the University of California, Los Angeles.

WALTER R. TRINKAUS, J.D., is a Professor of Law at Loyola Law School in Los Angeles.

MICHAEL VAN SCOY-MOSHER, M.D., is a Clinical Assistant Professor of Medical Oncology at the University of Southern California, School of Medicine, Los Angeles.

ROBERT M. VEATCH, PH.D., is a Professor of Medical Ethics at Georgetown University, Kennedy Institute of Ethics in Washington, D.C.

DONNA F. VER STEEG, R.N., PH.D., is Assistant Dean of Student Affairs and Assistant Professor of Nursing at the School of Nursing, University of California, Los Angeles.

SANDRA J. WEISS, D.N.S., is Director of the Collaborative Health Program at the San Francisco Consortium.

C. DICKERMAN WILLIAMS, LL.B., is an attorney and a member of the Board of Directors of Concern for Dying, Inc., in New York City.

Preface

This book investigates the problems associated with deciding whether to withdraw or withhold life-sustaining treatment from terminally or critically ill patients, who should make that decision (the patient or someone else on his or her behalf), and how the decision should be made, e.g., what process should be followed to assure adequate protection of the rights of all involved.

Terminally or critically ill patients may be classified into three groups: competent adults, formerly competent adults, and never competent patients. A competent adult patient, at least in those states whose highest courts have addressed the issue, has the right to refuse life-prolonging medical treatment and to die as naturally as possible. In three states, the right derives from the Constitution, and in New York it is "firmly embodied in the common law." But court decisions have not solved the problem; unanswered questions abound. For example, what about the elderly woman who, once very active, is now confined to bed and is severely depressed, perhaps as a result of the medication her doctor prescribed? Do we acknowledge her pleas to "leave me alone" and "let me die"? Similarly, if we accept the patient's legal right to refuse treatment, how do we rationalize our failure to integrate that right into usual and customary medical and hospital practice? How do we reconcile this right with the view of the medical profession that as physicians, they have an obligation or duty to preserve life and never to do anything that is contrary to that role?

The above questions lead us to the next class of patients, the formerly competent adult—generally a person over 18 who, prior to his or her present incapacity, was a competent, functioning individual. Both Karen Ann Quinlan and Brother Fox fall into this category, and their cases raise the question of who decides. The New Jersey courts let Karen Ann Quinlan's father decide whether or not to exercise Karen's right to refuse treatment. The New York Court of Appeals accepted the "solemn (oral) pronouncements" of Brother Fox as sufficient evidence of what he personally would have decided, and seemingly gave its permission for health care providers to act upon such prior directives. Obviously, the courts ultimately decided in both cases, but the approaches and emphases were different. It is important to mention, however, that problems with the legal system are not just for the lawyers but for all of us. Concepts such as due process, innocent until proven guilty, and the right to redress all wrongs are noble values because they ultimately provide guidance and protection for all in similar cases; they are, nonetheless, difficult to apply to specific cases.

Who decides; or more properly, who decides for what purposes? Courts or legislatures should concern themselves with the governing principles—a search for the fair and just way to assure the rights of all. The fundamental questions are for society and its voice should be heeded, always conscious to protect the rights of the individual. Who decides for a particular patient depends upon whether the patient has provided us with "clear and convincing proof" of his or her desires. In the Brother Fox case, the court left it to the hospitals, the doctors, and the families to settle the question in the specific instance. Elaborate review and approval, a procedure mandated by a lower New York appellate court, was specifically rejected, although the Court of Appeals expressed its willingness to hear cases where uncertainty exists.

In Massachusetts, the *Spring* case made it clear that there are certain factors that should be considered by those involved in making such decisions for a third person. In his chapter, Professor Charles Baron expounds a rigorous role for the court appointed *guardian ad litem*, arguing that only the safeguards of court procedures (albeit specially created expedited procedures) can adequately protect the interests of the incompetent patient. Sister Corrine Bayley, on the other hand, argues that the family is the appropriate party to decide for a loved one without the need of undergoing any court procedure. The key is to give effect to the patients' wishes; the problem of how to accomplish this remains.

This book is composed of 31 chapters, divided among four sections, each derived from one of four conferences sponsored by the American Society of Law & Medicine. The conferences, which took place in Detroit (November 1979), Los Angeles (April 1980), Minneapolis (May 1980), and Chicago (October 1980), provided a novel forum for the multidisciplinary investigation of the legal and ethical aspects of treatment for the critically and terminally ill patient. The participants varied by profession and training but the issues and problems discussed were the same. If there was one aspect of the conferences that impressed attendees more than any other, it was the eye-opening importance of the multidisciplinary search for answers to medical care problems. After all, life and death decisions are not just for doctors or nurses. In many respects, this book is quite similar. Its purpose is to promote a multidisciplinary understanding in all those who have or may ever have to care for terminally ill patients. It is also intended for lawyers who represent health care institutions, providers, and patients, as well as judges asked to decide such cases.

Professionally, the contributors represent physicians, lawyers, nurses, judges, the clergy, ethicists, teachers, and social workers. Although readers will undoubtedly identify with some contributors more than others, the suggestions and comments of those with different perspectives should be considered and evaluated. It is through this process that the value of multidisciplinary analysis becomes apparent.

Because the four conferences were so important to the creation of this book, we would like to thank the chairpersons: J. Kay Felt, J.D., and J. Douglas Peters, J.D. (Detroit); Leslie Steven Rothenberg, J.D. (Los Angeles); Ronald E. Cranford, M.D. (Minneapolis) and Lee J. Dunn, Jr., J.D., LL.M. (Chicago). Each chairperson contributed a significant amount of thought and time to the programs presented. Finally, we would like to thank the conference faculty for their contributions to the conferences and to the book, a collection that represents professionals working together to solve a common problem.

A. EDWARD DOUDERA
J. DOUGLAS PETERS

Note re references: Due to the multidisciplinary nature of this text, the footnote style is the hybrid developed and used by *Law, Medicine & Health Care*—a publication of the American Society of Law & Medicine. The major difference from the *Uniform Systems of Citation* (Cambridge, 1981) is for periodicals. These citations appear in the following order: author, title, vol. number (issue number); pages (date). The only exception is for chapters 5, 11, and 12 which are reprinted from the *American Journal of Law and Medicine* and follow the *Uniform System of Citation*.

Part One

Ethical and Medical Aspects

Chapter 1

Who Should Decide?

Corrine Bayley

In preparing this paper I consulted a number of sources, but one of my primary references turned out to be a book by Lewis Carroll, *Alice's Adventures in Wonderland*. The following is a short section from Chapter 6 of that book:

> Alice went timidly up to the door and knocked. "There's no sort of use in knocking," said the Footman, "and that's for two reasons. First, because I'm on the same side of the door as you are; secondly, because they're making such a noise inside no one could possibly hear you. . . ."
>
> "Please, then," said Alice, "how am I to get in?"
>
> "There might be some sense in your knocking," the Footman went on, without attending to her, "if we had the door between us. For instance, if you were *inside*, you might knock, and I could let you out, you know. . . ."
>
> "But how am I to get in?" she repeated aloud.
>
> "I shall sit here," the Footman remarked, "'til tomorrow—or the next day maybe," he continued, in the same tone.
>
> "How am I to get in?" asked Alice, in a louder voice.
>
> "*Are* you to get in at all?" said the Footman. "That's the first question, you know."[1]

To address a topic such as this, it is important that we ask the first question. I suggest that the first question is not "Who should decide," but rather, "What principles or criteria should guide the decisionmakers?" The question about principles is a philosophical one; the question about decisionmakers is procedural. Grappling with the first should give clues about how to answer the second.

Certain principles and criteria regarding treatment for the terminally ill have emerged over the past several years. Unfortunately, these principles are often ignored in favor of the procedural question of who should decide. This is unfortunate because the procedural question obscures the prior philosophical question, and it suggests that we can simply appoint a decisionmaker and sit back, waiting for the right answer. Some might ask, "Doesn't something like that happen in the Catholic Church?" And I would answer that we need to distinguish our cases.

First, I will identify the class of patients I am addressing, then briefly call attention to some emerging principles on which to base decisions regarding the treatment or nontreatment of these patients. Finally, I will attempt to answer the question of who should decide by identifying various contenders for the office and by evaluating their credentials in light of three questions: 1) What is best for a particular patient? 2) How can we decide in such a way as to promote the interests of other patients in similar situations? 3) How can the decisionmakers be protected from civil or criminal liability?

This chapter concerns only patients with a terminal illness, an irreversible condition which, if untreated, will result in imminent death (a few weeks or months). Various life-support measures may prolong life, but none reverse the underlying condition. I do not refer to patients who have suffered total brain death, since I hope that we are beyond medical, ethical, or legal questions about whether to treat dead persons. Nor do I refer to patients for whom treatment would cure or arrest the disease.

Within the class of terminally ill patients, we need to distinguish between persons who are competent and those who are incompetent. Today, most of us would agree that competent patients have the right to make treatment decisions for themselves, including the right to refuse treatment. The patients with whom I am concerned are minors or incompetent adults who are the victims of terminal illness—patients who are not in a position to decide for themselves.

The task of deciding whether or not life-prolonging medical treatment should be administered to another person is a heavy burden. But, unless we are willing to let the mere presence of our technology compel us to use it, decide we must. Fortunately, whomever the decisionmakers turn out to be, they are not without some principles or criteria to guide them. These principles come from both the moral tradition (which has a long history) and, more recently, from the legal tradition.

For centuries, the Catholic Church has taught that life is a fundamental good that we are obliged to respect and care for, since it comes from God. But there are limits to our duty to preserve life, and these limits are reached when the effort to sustain life becomes an overwhelming burden for the patient (admittedly a subjective evaluation) or when the prognosis is hopeless.[2]

The reasoning behind this principle is that life, while of very great value, is not the ultimate or absolute good. If it were, the corollary would be that death is the ultimate or absolute evil— a position which seriously conflicts with the Judeo-Christian tradition.

There are times when it is more in keeping with respect for life to let it go than to cling to it. When are those times? The moral tradition has given us some guidelines under the rubric of "ordinary" and "extraordinary" means of treatment (an unfortunate choice of words since they are so easily misunderstood, but attempts to find substitutes have, so far, been unsuccessful).[3] Briefly defined, ordinary treatment does not impose an excessive hardship or burden on a patient and offers a reasonable hope of cure or benefit. Persons have a moral obligation to accept such treatment. Extraordinary treatment either imposes excessive hardship or burdens on the patient or does not offer a reasonable hope of cure or benefit. Persons are not obliged to accept such treatment, either for themselves or for others. The emphasis is not on the means themselves, but on what they accomplish for the patient. Thus, antibiotics, respirators, CPR, renal dialysis, cancer therapy, and even intravenous feedings could all be either extraordinary or ordinary, depending upon the condition of the particular patient.

WHEN IS THERE A DUTY TO SUSTAIN LIFE?

This description of the parameters of the duty to sustain life has been discussed frequently with approval in the medical, philosophical and theological literature.[4] The difficulty, of course, is applying it and having the courage to act upon it in a specific situation.

Several of the court cases that have dealt with the question of treatment or nontreatment for the terminally ill have adopted the philosophy behind the ordinary/extraordinary means rubric. For example, in the *Quinlan* case decided by the Supreme Court of New Jersey in 1976, the court noted "that the use of the same respirator or like support could be considered 'ordinary' in the context of the possibly curable patient but 'extraordinary' in the context of the forced sustaining by cardio-respiratory processes of an irreversibly doomed patient."[5] Similarly, the well-known *Saikewicz* case, from Massachusetts, quotes with approval an article that appeared in the *Journal of the American Medical Association:*

> [W]e should not use *extraordinary* means of prolonging life or its semblance when, after careful consideration, consultation, and the application of the most well-conceived therapy it becomes apparent that there is no hope for the recovery of the patient. Recovery should not be defined simply as the ability to remain alive; it should mean life without intolerable suffering.[6]

And, in deciding the case of *Benjamin C.* in Los Angeles, Judge Richard Byrne stated:

> Benjamin suffers from irreversible brain damage and is comatose. There is no possibility of Benjamin's ever emerging from his comatose condition, and there is no treatment or cure for his condition. The respirator performs a maintenance function only, and in view of Benjamin's diagnosis and prognosis, constitutes an extraordinary medical procedure which need not be continued.[7]

It seems fair to say that the medical, ethical and legal communities have explicitly accepted the principle that treatment which merely prolongs life and does nothing to reverse the underlying condition may be discontinued. This principle is certainly supported by the forgotten virtue of common sense, and would seem to be the view of the legal system's "reasonable person."

So, why is there all this confusion concerning appropriate treatment for the terminally ill? Much of it is understandable. It is difficult to watch someone die. It is frightening to face the fact of our own deaths, and all this is complicated by feelings of guilt, failure, anger and ambivalence, which frequently charge the air in Intensive Care Units.

There is, however, another reason for the disturbance—fear of legal liability. Such fear is largely born of confusion and kept alive by ignorance, but it exists nonetheless. It does very little good to tell a physician that no one has ever been prosecuted for withholding or discontinuing medical treatment from an incompetent terminally ill patient. No one wants to be the first example. The situation was difficult enough before the *Quinlan* and *Saikewicz* cases washed like a great wave of anxiety and doubt over the medical and legal communities. The more such cases are interpreted and misinterpreted, the more complicated the problem becomes. Thus, today the nagging question in many hospitals across the country is: Should we get a court order before we discontinue this patient's treatment?

Before I plunge into these turbulent waters, there is a prior question that should be answered—whether the issue of withholding or withdrawing treatment is primarily a medical, a legal, or an ethical question. I believe it is primarily an ethical question.

If we ask, "What type of respirator is the best one in this case?" we are asking a medical question, and medical expertise is required to answer it. If we ask, "Is it a negligent or criminal act to withhold or withdraw this respirator?" we are asking a legal question, and we need to find a lawyer or a judge. But, if we ask, "Should we use a respirator in this case?" we are asking an ethical question because it involves values, rights and obligations. The medical and legal components are necessary, but not sufficient considerations.

I do not mean to imply that this ethical question should be answered by an ethicist, but I do suggest that it should be decided by persons concerned with ethical values and principles.

In the introduction, I mentioned that decisionmakers should be influenced by at least three considerations: what is best for this patient, how this decision might benefit patients in similar situations, and how the decisionmakers can be protected from criminal or civil liability. If all these objectives cannot be met, they should be considered in decreasing order of importance. The first concern must be the patient's best interest. Promoting someone's best interest means, I suggest, doing what the person would do were he or she in a position to decide. If someone can be found who knows what the patient would want, that person should win the title of decisionmaker. I submit that this is most often a family member, or those closest to the patient. It is more likely that they will know the patient's personal history, beliefs and probable wishes. The physicians may also know this if they have communicated with the patient—not because of their medical competence. Rarely, if ever, is a judge in the best position to know what a patient would want, judicial wisdom notwithstanding.

My bias is that appeals to the courts are often motivated by a desire for protection from a charge of negligence or homicide rather than concern for the patient. These are serious charges, and I am in sympathy with those who seek to avoid them. But surely there must be a better way to deal with this situation than by rushing to the courts for absolution. Consider the result: The hospital gets an attorney. Possibly the doctor gets an attorney. The family gets an attorney. The meter starts ticking. A petition is filed in a probate court for someone to be appointed conservator of the patient for the purposes of discontinuing life-prolonging treatment. A temporary guardian is appointed by the judge to look after the best interests of the patient, while clerks and attorneys scramble around looking for pertinent case law. Meanwhile, weeks have passed, and the meter is still ticking. The patient is still lying comatose in an expensive hospital bed, hooked up to tubes and machines. The family is confused, exhausted and besieged by the media. A hearing is finally held, and a week or two later, the judge (hopefully) renders the opinion that there is no need to use extraordinary treatment when there is no hope for recovery of the patient. The hospital and physicians now feel safe. Strictly speaking, however, they are not safe because the trial court cannot grant immunity from criminal prosecution. The district attorney can still step in, though that is most unlikely. Everyone hopes that the opinion of the trial court will not be appealed. If it is, the case could drag on for several more weeks or months.[8]

This scenario has variations, but basically the drama is the same. It is a costly, time-consuming, frustrating and cumbersome procedure. It seems particularly ludicrous for patients in a persistent vegetative state, such as Karen Ann Quinlan in New Jersey, Brother Fox in New York, Vincent Martin Young and Benjamin C. in California.

The *Quinlan* court articulated this "reasonable person" standard: "[T]his decision should be accepted by a society, the overwhelming majority of whose members would, we think, in similar circumstances, exercise such a choice in the same way for themselves or for those closest to them."[9]

In my opinion, appeal to the courts in such cases is not only contrary to the interests of the patient in question but also detrimental to other patients in similar situations. The more that court approval of decisions to withhold or withdraw treatment is sought, the more it will be expected. Once it becomes standard practice, it will be very difficult to reverse the trend.

There are, of course, those who maintain that such decisions do belong in the courts. Professor Charles Baron has some arguments worth our attention.[10] He agrees with the *Saikewicz* court that "such questions of life and death seem . . . to require the process of detached but passionate investigation and decision that forms the ideal on which the judicial branch of government was created."[11] He identifies four qualities possessed by courts which, in his view, qualify them as the best decisionmakers: 1) the proceedings are public; 2) the judge's decision is principled; that is, it is reached according to established legal principles; 3) the judicial process is impartial; and 4) it is adversarial in nature.[12]

Although there are points to be made, pro and con, about each of these qualities, I will spare you that exercise. However, I am bothered by Professor Baron's underlying assumption that these qualities are the sole prerogative of the court. I submit that families, physicians, nurses and moral advisors, consulting together, could also be capable of principled decisionmaking. I do not think that there is evidence to support Baron's contention that "'closet' decision making by physicians and family might lead to treatment of incompetents, which was different from that which would emanate from principled public decision making by the court."[13] Even if the decisions were different, there is no evidence to show that they would be less desirable.

Further, Professor Baron cannot realistically argue that every decision concerning treatment or nontreatment for incompetent terminally ill patients should be made or even reviewed by the courts, although he seems to do precisely that. He further draws the battle-lines between doctors and lawyers by observing:

> [Physicians'] decision-making processes show none of the qualities of process that characterize a court system. There are no institutional frameworks that require doctors to develop principles of decision making that are consistent from one doctor to another and from one time to another. As a result, few doctors have worked out principles of decision making that will survive even the most rudimentary criticism, and decisions which are made on the same set of facts will differ from day to day and from doctor to doctor. Hence, whether an incompetent will be allowed to die depends upon who his doctor is and on what day the decision has to be made.[14]

If that is true, the same thing could certainly be said of lawyers and judges. Those of us who were surprised by the decision in the *Becker* case[15] have reason to think that another court may have decided to authorize life-saving heart surgery for a child with Down Syndrome over the parents' objections.

WHO SHOULD DECIDE?

It is not my intention to stand in the crossfire between doctors and lawyers—the weapons on both sides are sharp and occasionally hit their marks.

I do, however, object to setting up the choice between these two groups. I believe that families and those closest to the patient are usually the best decisionmakers. To decide effectively, they need good medical information and support from the physicians. Ideally, these decisions will be made jointly by physicians and family, although sometimes a family may elect to let the physician decide. If that is clearly their choice, I think it is a reasonable one. Many physicians are willing to take on this responsibility, particularly if it spares the family further anguish.

Another alternative that has been suggested speaks to Professor Baron's complaint concerning the lack of an institutional framework for the process of developing and refining principles on which to make such decisions. Variously referred to as ethics committees, study groups, optimum care committees and the like, these groups can serve as a resource to the physician and family as they make their decision. They approximate some of the qualities of the court system; that is, they are in varying degrees public, principled, impartial, and adversarial. More importantly, they can establish guidelines to help in decisionmaking, both for individual patients and for classes of patients.

I am a member of such a committee at Saint Joseph Hospital in Orange, California, which recently drafted guidelines regarding the treatment of terminally ill patients. These guidelines have been accepted by the medical staff and the hospital's governing board, and begin with the following principles:

> 1) Competent adults have the right to direct the course of their own medical treatment. A patient and his/her family should have access to significant information regarding the patient's condition.

> 2) Questions of when to withhold or withdraw medical treatment are not only medical questions; they involve personal values as well. Therefore, decisions in these matters should not be made by the physician alone, but should involve the patient and those closest to the patient.

> 3) Biological life need not be preserved at all costs. There are times when it is more in keeping with respect for life to let it go than to cling to it.

> 4) A decision to withhold or withdraw treatment which is potentially life-prolonging does not mean the staff has abandoned the patient, but that it is the time for an intensification of efforts to provide physical and emotional comfort.

These principles are followed by specific guidelines for orders not to resuscitate and for the withholding or withdrawing of treatment.[16]

Objections have been raised concerning this method. It is suggested by some that there is a conflict of interests, since it is a hospital committee. I would suggest that if we can only trust those who are disinterested to be impartial, then we are all in trouble. A second objection is that such committees or their guidelines will become mandatory. That need not happen as resort to the courts may always be had.

Of course, there are times when court review is appropriate. Family members do not always agree with each other about what should be done, and in the likely event that no one is the patient's legal guardian, a court proceeding may be required to resolve this conflict. Courts are also useful in cases where there is serious doubt about the first objective, i.e., protecting the best interests of the patient. Judicial review should be the exception rather than the rule.

Before concluding, I would like to touch briefly upon the issue of legislative involvement in this troublesome area. Several states have followed California's lead in drafting Living Will legislation.[17] The intent of this legislation is to provide competent persons with the means of indicating what they would want in the way of treatment, should they become incompetent. To put it bluntly, most of these efforts have not been successful because it is very difficult to define, in statutory language, appropriate responses to the sensitive and unanticipated situations in which people die. Further, if the California experience is any indication, such legislation will be almost unrecognizable to its author by the time it emerges from the legislative machinery.[18] Probably the best thing that can be said about such legislation is that it has served as a symbol of people's unwillingness to have their lives prolonged beyond reasonable limits. It has also been useful in stimulating discussion among patients, families, physicians and lawyers.

Other legislative options have been suggested, including: redefinition of death, to allow a person to be pronounced dead when cognition is irretrievably lost; redefinition of homicide, i.e., the blanket exemption from criminal charges of medical professionals who withdraw treatment from a noncognitive patient; specific authorization for physician and/or family discretion in making treatment decisions; and the mandating of ethics committees or other procedures.[19] If I had to choose, I would say that the redefinition of homicide probably has the most potential for resolving some of our dilemmas. However, my practical sense tells me that such a bill would probably not survive the legislative process.

CONCLUSION

The issues facing us are difficult, and comfortable solutions are elusive. I wish I could offer more concrete answers, but of course that would be foolhardy since each case is different. Instead, I would just like to plead that we return to some of our basic moral convictions about the meaning of human life and death. There are times when prolonging life is an insult to the patient. Unfortunately, our technology and our concern with liability have tended to obscure this truth.

In closing, I would like to read something about decision making from Chapter 8 of *Alice's Adventures*:

> The moment Alice appeared, she was appealed to by all three to settle the question. And they repeated their arguments to her, though as they all spoke at once, she found it very hard indeed to make out exactly what they said.
>
> The executioner's argument was that you couldn't cut off a head unless there was a body to cut it off from; that he never had to do such a thing before, and he wasn't going to begin at *this* time of life.
>
> The king's argument was that anything that had a head could be beheaded, and that you weren't to talk nonsense.
>
> The queen's argument was that if something wasn't done about it in less than no time, she'd have everybody executed all round. (It was this last remark that made the whole party look so grave and anxious).[20]

If there is a message in this that will help in the decision-making process surrounding the terminally ill patient, I think it is that we should not be too grave and anxious, lest we cloud some fundamental truths with our fears.

NOTES

1. L. CARROLL, ALICE'S ADVENTURES IN WONDERLAND (Pan Books, London)(1973) at 54-55 [hereinafter cited as CARROLL].

2. For a good historical survey of the teaching, *see* T. O'DONNELL, MEDICINE AND CHRISTIAN MORALITY (Alba House, New York)(1975) at 46-55; and Kelly, G., *The Duty of Using Artificial Means of Preserving Life*, THEOLOGICAL STUDIES 11:203-20 (March 1950).

3. This tradition was summarized and the terms "ordinary" and "extraordinary" most clearly defined by G. KELLY, MEDICO-MORAL PROBLEMS (Catholic Hospital Association, St. Louis) (1959) at 129. These definitions are often attributed to Pope Pius XII, though his description is more limited and slightly different from Kelly's. *See* Pope Pius XII, *The Prolongation of Life*, THE POPE SPEAKS 3(4):395-96 (February 1958). For a good discussion of both the substance and semantic difficulty of the terms "ordinary" and "extraordinary," *see* McCormick, R.A., *The Quality of Life, The Sanctity of Life*, HASTINGS CENTER REPORT 8(1):30-36 (February 1978). For educational purposes, a (one-page) brochure summarizes Church teachings on the moral duty to preserve life. *See* Connery, J., *The Duty to Preserve Life* (1977). It is available from: Committee for Pro-Life Activities, National Conference of Catholic Bishops, 1312 Massachusetts Ave., N.W., Washington, D.C. 20005.

4. *See, e.g., Proceedings, A.M.A. House of Delegates* (December 1973) *cited in* McCormick, R.A., *The Quality of Life, The Sanctity of Life, supra* note 3, at 30; P. RAMSEY, THE PATIENT AS PERSON (Yale University Press, New Haven) (1970) at 118-12; R. VEATCH, DEATH, DYING AND THE BIOLOGICAL REVOLUTION (Yale University Press, New Haven) (1976) at 105-14.

5. *In re Quinlan*, 355 A.2d 647,668 (N.J. 1976) [hereinafter cited as *Quinlan*].

6. *Superintendent of Belchertown State School v. Saikewicz*, 370 N.E.2d 417, 424 (Mass. 1977) [hereinafter cited as *Saikewicz*], *citing* Lewis, *Machine Medicine and Its Relation to the Fatally Ill*, JOURNAL OF THE AMERICAN MEDICAL ASSOCIATION 206:387(1968).

7. *In re Benjamin C.*, Los Angeles Juvenile Court, No. J914419 (February 15, 1979).

8. Such a situation is evidenced in *In re Spring*, 405N.E.2d115 (Mass. 1980), wherein the Massachusetts Supreme Judicial Court itself noted the delays

that had confronted the family as it attempted to act in Mr. Spring's best interests, at 123.

9. *Quinlan, supra* note 5, at 664.
10. Baron, C., *Medical Paternalism and the Rule of Law: A Reply to Dr. Relman*, AMERICAN JOURNAL OF LAW & MEDICINE 4(4):337-65 (Winter 1979) [hereinafter cited as Baron].
11. *Saikewicz, supra* note 6, at 435.
12. Baron, *supra* note 10, at 347-49.
13. *Id.* at 358.
14. *Id.* at 349.
15. *In re Phillip B.*, 156 Cal. Rptr. 48 (App. Ct. 1979), *cert. denied*, 445 U.S. 949 (1980).
16. The Guidelines are printed in Appendix B.
17. California's law is called the Natural Death Act, and became effective in 1977. *See* CAL. HEALTH & SAFETY CODE §§ 7185-95. Other states with "right to die" laws as of April 1980, are: Arkansas, Idaho, Kansas, Nevada, New Mexico, North Carolina, Oregon, Texas and Washington.
18. Among certain groups in California, there was very active, but unfounded concern that the Natural Death Act was the first step toward "mercy-killing" and other assorted horrors. The Act went through several major revisions, the effect of which was to so limit its application that it is essentially useless. Most of those who are familiar with it have agreed that it too should be allowed to die a "natural death." Its author, Senator Barry Keene, has considered revisions, but feels that the political climate is not conducive at this time.
19. For a good discussion of these and other options, *see* Beresford, H.R., *The Quinlan Decision: Problems and Legislative Alternatives*, ANNALS OF NEUROLOGY 2:74-80 (1977).
20. CARROLL, *supra* note 1, at 84.

Chapter 2

An Oncologist's Case for No-Code Orders

Michael Van Scoy-Mosher

In the absence of law, or of a clear code of medical ethics, each physician must formulate his or her own guidelines for treatment of the terminally ill patient. Since I have been involved in approximately 400 no-code (or DNR—do not resuscitate) orders, my position on this issue is clear, but I will try to define the way I make such decisions.

I view a no-code or DNR order as essentially the last service I can perform for my patient. You have probably heard of a LeBoyer birth; I believe in the concept of a "LeBoyer" death—a peaceful, quiet, undramatic, untechnologic death. I do not favor besetting the last few minutes of a person's life with pumping on the chest, intubation, and all that sort of useless drama.

When we talk about withdrawing or withholding treatment from terminally ill patients, it is important to realize that it is much easier not to start than it is to make a decision about stopping. It is better to "head it off at the pass" than to start procedures or treatments without thinking of their complications. However, life-support is initiated for a variety of reasons. For example, in an emergency situation there is sometimes an attempt to resuscitate before a critical evaluation can be made. This can and often does present problems.

We live in a technical age, and our problems with medical technology are among the most fascinating and troubling ones facing us. We can bypass coronary arteries or even replace whole hearts, we can give chemotherapy to every patient who has cancer, and we can resuscitate or, at least, try to resuscitate most patients. To apply such technologies without concern for the consequences is, I think, the easy—and the wrong—way to practice medicine.

As we develop technologically in medicine, there is a tendency to apply the new technology every time we can. The hard way to practice medicine is with judgment; that is, to try to decide where these technological marvels are really indicated, which patients should and should not get chemotherapy, and which patients should and should not be resuscitated. To a great extent, at least in cancer, resuscitation is almost a false issue, since the chance of resuscitating a person so that he or she will eventually be discharged from the hospital is fairly minimal. One result of our advanced technology is that we are prolonging dying instead of prolonging living. I am not certain whether we must, or even can, make this rather false effort, if the patient does not benefit and our effort is only to satisfy the family's need to feel that everything possible was done, or because of some vague, unfounded legal concern.

Even if we accept the need for DNR orders, or even of passive euthanasia, there are several problems. For example, how do we give this order? Where I was trained, we would write the no-code order in pencil, and then, after the patient died, the order was erased so that there was never any permanent record of it. At several institutions around Los Angeles, the no-code order is only whispered, and there is an understanding between doctors and nurses that a particular patient is not to be resuscitated. Such informal communication assumes, of course, that the "floating" nurse on the 2 a.m. shift has received the information and will react, if need be, in the proper way. In many instances, what has happened is that the physicians have transferred their responsibility to the nurses who are left to make the decisions. If there were any legal difficulties, they would be the nurse's, the physician would argue, because no one wrote a DNR order. Accordingly, I feel strongly that such orders should be written by physicians who must assume the responsibility for them. I think that the no-code order should be viewed as any other medical order. If I can give 30 mg. of morphine by written order, then I think I should be able to write a DNR order.

There are many forms of "codes": slow code, chemical code, partial code. In my opinion, there is a time and a place for a limited code. Recently, I took care of an Hassidic rabbi. Because Hassidic Jews are very uncomfortable with DNR orders or anything that might hasten death,[1] such a course of action was not acceptable to him. We decided that it was reasonable to make some effort to resuscitate, but not necessarily all efforts. Setting such a limit on resuscitative efforts was acceptable to the family. In this case we decided that it would not be acceptable to intubate him nor to leave him on a respirator. So, there is a way of giving what I will call a partial code—some attempt at resuscitation, but not applying everything known to man.

Who makes this decision? Frequently, I find it very difficult to discuss with the patient his or her desires concerning resuscitation. Sometimes it seems cruel and unnecessary. Other times it is just difficult, in the midst of what is usually a very emotional and difficult time, to get around to the question of whether you want us pumping on your chest when you die. Obviously, there are gentler ways to ask, but that is really what it comes down to. I find that very difficult and, quite frankly, have usually shied away from it. Having taken care of someone for some period of time has usually generated prior tacit, if not overt, understanding between the patient and me on these issues.

Another question is the role of the family. The family has no legal right to decide such issues if the patient is competent, and it is foolish to believe that the consent of the family will protect physicians from liability. It is, I suppose, only some sort of medical custom. However, even if we do accept the role of families, many do not agree among themselves on the course of action in such cases. And there are some families, spouses, ex-wives, ex-husbands and separated spouses who should not be trusted, perhaps, to make a decision for the patient.

So, who decides? Personally, I would like to see everyone have a guardian. Under such a system, we would have a trusted friend empowered in advance to make the necessary decisions should we be unable to ourselves. Right now this is not possible, so what I usually wind up doing is suggesting to the family what I think ought to be done. I explain my reasoning, my diagnosis, and my prognosis, but essentially I present them with a decision. I do not like to put the family in the position of feeling that they made the decision because that can cause guilt and depression for them afterwards. I put it to them as my decision, but one with which I want their agreement.

My experience is that this process usually works very well. However, problems do exist, most commonly with other doctors involved who are not comfortable with DNR orders. In one situation, I rewrote a no-code order every morning and every afternoon because the surgeon, who was afraid of the liability, would cancel it during his rounds. The big question among the nurses was on whose shift the patient would die. She died on my shift. Did I want responsibility for this? I am not sure, but someone must take the responsibility, because a "code" is about the only thing that happens automatically in a hospital—it does not require an order. Doing nothing, staying out of it, therefore, requires a decision. Doing nothing is a real step. Someone has to make some sense out of this and be humane, and I think it is the physician who must step in.

I find it interesting that what is thought to be the ultimate in humane care is the hospice. This may well be, but it is as if all rules and debates are suspended if a place calls itself a hospice. One hospital that I know about is developing a so-called hospice unit. It has not even occurred to the hospital administrators that in such a unit, almost by definition, there will be no IVs, no antibiotics, and no resuscitation. It is as if all the usual legal and ethical considerations we might go through on a regular floor do not apply, and I think that has to be dealt with. It is argued that patients volunteer to enter a hospice, but do they really know all the implications of that? Has it been spelled out to them what hospice care means? Most of the patients that I know have not had it fully explained.

In dealing with this issue, I have looked at the situation of rejecting the no-code option if the family disagreed, but I am not sure that is a true option. To whom do I owe my responsibility as a physician? If I really think, after knowing a patient, that I know what he or she would want and what action would be humane and merciful, but the family does not agree, should I go along with the family because I am worried about legal considerations or should I do what I think is responsible in terms of the patient? It is the patient to whom the physician owes responsibility, and sometimes this responsibility may involve making decisions which pose theoretical legal risks. I do not think that the risks are very real.

Although I certainly favor the patient's active role in the decision-making if at all possible, I find a reliance on "prior expression of wishes" a legal convenience. Many people say that if they ever got cancer they would want to jump off a mountain and die. The fact is that patients, when they actually have cancer, rarely feel that way. A lot of patients who may say something at one point in their lives feel very differently when the situation actually occurs. I have heard patients say that they would never have chemotherapy, but when they actually needed the treatment, they were willing to accept it. So this whole business about the prior expression of wishes by the patient may be convenient for judges, but I do not think it valid.

As a closing comment, I can report that in Los Angeles County, we have established a committee to develop guidelines for county–operated facilities regarding when and how to go about writing a no-code order. In these guidelines, it is viewed as any other medical order. It should be discussed with the family and the discussion should be noted in the chart. Certain kinds of doctors should not participate in this decisionmaking process—an intern, for example. The ultimate decision should appear as a written order. To me, such a process legitimizes the no-code order in the county facility, and perhaps presents a model for decisionmaking that can be used elsewhere.

NOTES

1. *See* Rabbi Levi Meier, "Code and No-Code: A Psychological Analysis and the Viewpoint of Jewish Law," Chapter 8.

Chapter 3

A Nurse's View of Treatment Decisions

Joan King

Nursing is a patient-centered profession, and thus nurses believe it is best for the patient to decide, whenever possible, whether or not to initiate life-support services. To promote patients' self-determination, bureaucratic settings and systems must be revised. In the terms used by Sister Bayley, nursing views dying as having philosophical, not just medical, considerations, and decisionmaking for the terminally ill patient as having moral, not just medical, components.

The taboo against discussion of dying impedes preparation for it. However, death should be planned for as carefully as any other major event in life. If such plans are established, efforts should be made to honor them when the time comes.

Studies by Kübler-Ross and others have shown that dying patients often believe that they have not been given the opportunity to express themselves. These studies have also established that the patient desires assistance with the dying process and does not necessarily want it abruptly terminated. Professor Veatch's article notes an experience of a dying person whose non-verbal clues, intended to show the patient's discomfort with the blazing lights of the ICU, went unrecognized by a nurse and other health care providers. In addition, the hospital's policy did not allow her intimate friends and family to be with her while she died.

The patient should be allowed to choose to have technological methods initiated and continued to prolong life, or to be released from them. The systems established in depersonalized bureaucratic settings must be revised to allow the competent patient to choose death over prolonged pain and suffering, to refuse unreasonable continuance of life-support means, and to be at the center of the decision-making process with health care providers.

For the individual in a coma or a state of irreversible unconsciousness, the principle is well-stated by Sister Bayley: the principal criteria need to be focused upon what is best for the patient. When a patient is not able to state what is best, who best knows the patient's wishes? The individual's wishes are usually known by those closest to him or her, often including the health care team members. Thus, I believe that those closest to the patient should be allowed to decide. The nurse closest to the patient should be involved in assuring that the patient's wishes are communicated.

In altering hospital policies which deter us from providing human support to dying patients, the nurse has a unique contribution to make. The nurse is able to improve and control the milieu in which the patient resides. Florence Nightingale introduced control of the patient's environment; it is a traditional nursing tenet to do so. Many nurses are insisting today that this humanistic goal of meeting the needs of the patient be reached in our highly technological environment. The nurse must have the accountability and authority to accomplish these goals.

Additionally, appropriate multidisciplinary committees must be formed within the hospital wherein ethical issues involving the dying patient, as well as interdisciplinary differences, can be rationally discussed and emotionally defused. The result will clarify concerns in specific situations and enable the health care team members to give support to the patient and family, as well as to the team itself. In these deliberations, cultural and ethnic differences must also be considered by health professionals so that they can be responsive to a variety of situations.

It is important that effort be extended now for the development of hospital ethics committees on a formal basis. Patients' plans for death could be proposed, discussed and considered in these committees. Hemelt and Mackert ask us to consider the possibility of an appropriate advocate.[1] It would seem desirable for a competent person to plan for the possibility of future incompetence and to designate a particular individual to make decisions as advocated. An individual should anticipate the possibility of entering an incompetent state and, thus, not being able to make his or her wishes known. The chosen advocate would know these wishes and would be authorized to act in the patient's interest. Where this works, the courts, health care professionals or anyone else should not interfere. The patient chooses the advocate to speak in her or his best interest. This allows continued decisionmaking by the individual for fulfillment of personal wishes at the moment of death. As a nurse and as a human being, I think these kinds of decisions are too important to leave to anyone else. The question is, will health professionals promote interdisciplinary committees now, and begin to look openly at these situations? Will we utilize a truly patient-centered interdisciplinary approach to allow patients to control their final life moment? In order to accomplish this, life-planning should include plans for death.

A practice plan suggested by Hemelt and Mackert is in congruence with the American Nurses' Association Code of Ethics for Nurses (Code for Professional Nurses). The code identifies the nurse as responsible for affirming and maintaining such consumer rights as the patient's right to privacy and to self-determination. Weber states that the nurse should be encouraged to act as a moral agent, to actively participate in ethical decisionmaking and to assume accountability for professional actions.[2] It is essential that health care institutions devise a formal way to identify legal and ethical concerns. Weber states that moral and other nonmedical values currently affect medical care decisions. He opines that patients can insist that they be treated with dignity, that their personal and emotional needs be attended to and that they have a voice in decisions regarding their own care. The nursing profession advocates these values.

Registered nurses often find themselves caught between what the patient or family says and what the physician says. Nurses need to discuss the ethical questions posed by a specific situation: Am I accountable to the patient, the institution or myself? To whom do I go for help in deciding what action ought to be taken in a conflict—a verbal no code, a walk slow code, etc.? How much risk can I take in the nurse/patient relationship? Will the system punish or support moral behavior? What ought to be done and why?

What is the nurse's obligation to care for the patient when cure is no longer possible? Gadow believes the answer lies in the concept of a human service profession. The professional assists clients to integrate a particular service in their lives according to their own values.[3] Nursing, then, assists patients to achieve their self-determination; a nurse nurtures, counsels, treats and teaches a patient in terms of the patient's freely determined decisions concerning care.[4]

Refusing to answer a dying person's question dehumanizes the patient. On the other hand, disclosure can succeed when trust has been established. Lying exercises dominion over the other person. Yet, nurses often feel obliged to lie out of 1) loyalty to a physician, 2) deference to institutional policy, or 3) concern for their jobs. The decision to inform is a moral question, not a medical one. Yarling suggests that it is imperative for those making such decisions "to understand the nature of the questions before them, observe the limits of their professional prerogative with respect to these questions and allow their decision-making to be informed by a community of moral disclosure which extends beyond the boundaries of the health care professions."[5] The hospital ethics committee can help nurses to put this theory into action.

The hospital ethics committee is a useful forum for health care practitioners to discuss a wide variety of questions:

1) Do we believe a terminal patient's request for no lifesaving measures should be respected?

2) What do we do when a patient requests "no heroics" but the physician refuses to write the order?

3) How do we feel about health professionals giving lethal doses of narcotics to terminally ill patients?

4) How do we feel about not initiating life-saving measures upon the request of the patient and/or family?

5) How do we feel about pulling the plug of a machine which is used on a terminally ill patient who has continual pain and suffering?

6) A patient wants to know the facts regarding his or her state. Does the patient unconditionally have a moral right to have these questions answered?

7) If so, what is the legitimate role of the nurse in answering the questions?

8) Is it ever justifiable to abridge the freedom of self-determination by any competent person in the name of that person's self-interest?

9) Should the individual rather than the professional make the value decision?

Weber observes that nurses are perceived "as competent and professional but also personal and sympathetic."[6] Patients often accept a nurse's moral advice as an expression of concern, not as the word of an authority. However, they seldom regard a physician's advice as anything but "doctor's orders." Thus, nurses are particularly well-suited for the role of the moral agent. We need to assist the patient in making a decision in accordance with his or her values, not in accordance with the values of the health care professionals.

The competent adult patient should have 1) the right to choose death over prolonged pain and suffering, 2) the right to refuse all extraordinary means of life support, and 3) these rights recognized by the health practitioners. Although these rights may be incorporated into law, there may still be some practical problems. For example, when a debilitated elderly person has signed a natural death directive, he or she expects to have it honored. Yet, if he or she is sent from a skilled nursing facility to an acute care emergency room where the physician, who does not know of the directive, determines that something must be done about a bleeding ulcer, the patient's right is not upheld. The conscious, competent, terminally ill adult who may refuse surgical consent, advice, medication, and treatment, and who may determine to what degree to cooperate with a health regimen, should be able to control the decision of how to die.[7]

The California Natural Death Act was effected in 1977, yet I have not seen the Act applied to any significant degree in my area of practice. Generally, the Act is too complicated. The witness choice is especially complicated, and the public seems unaware of it. Nurses in S.N.F.'s critical care units and emergency rooms see few physicians willing to risk being the first cases to test the law. Except for observations of its use in oncology, one wonders what assistance the Act has provided.

For the individual in a coma or in a state of irreversible unconsciousness, the questions become even more difficult. Who shall decide? By what authority? By what criteria? What implications exist for the individual affirming or denying another's right to life?

Decision-making considerations have usually been organized around the frameworks shown in Table 3.1.

Table 3.1. Decision Maker/Functions and
Problems Associated with the Process*

Physician or Group	Special Advisory Committee (Interdisciplinary)	Family	Courts
Advice on medical aspects essential	No legal power to authorize removal of life supporting equipment.	Potential guilt	Authority to decide.
Physician competency not specially developed for awesome task.	Serve to assist the family and physician to arrive at decisions to be made.	Conflict if protracted illness and economic loss.	Can be narrow focus of the situation.
Personal/family inputs may be incompletely explored		Should retain influence and not turn over to the court or to presumed higher knowledge of health professional on a moral issue.	Case by case basis necessary until a body of the law is developed.
Conflicts of interest could occur.			Time consuming
Costly

*Adapted from Hemelt and Mackert, p. 89.

The individual under any of these frameworks may have the opportunity to share his or her final decision with others or may get no opportunity to make the decision.

Conclusion

A pro-active proposal from people could be developed and offered to allow individuals continued direction of their lives. Planning for the final stage of life offers individuals an avenue for making their wishes known, as well as control over the way they die. In Hemelt's and Mackert's proposal for making these decisions and for choosing advocates before the onset of incompetency or terminal illness, the following steps are detailed: the individual chooses a person, tells that person his or her wishes, and authorizes that person to act in his or her best interest. The results could be that the courts would not interfere with planned choice; the health professions would not interfere with planned choice; the family is saved from conflicting emotions in making final decisions; no conflicting benefit accrues to the decision-maker; and if any concern occurred in relation to the decision-making propriety and legality, the court could be called in to review the case.[8]

This process could be part of health care planning. It is an individual's decision during the dying process—what Kübler-Ross calls "the final stage of growth," and it is too important to leave to anyone else. The time has come to develop acceptable ways for patients to make their determinations known and accepted by the health professionals.

NOTES

1. M.D. Hemelt, M.E. Mackert, DYNAMICS OF LAW IN NURSING AND HEALTH CARE (Reston Publishing Co., Reston, Va.)(1978) at 89-90.
2. Weber, L., *Should Physicians and Nurses Give Moral Advice?* HOSPITAL PROGRESS 57(1):68-69, 80 (January 1976).
3. Gadow, S., *The Most Pressing Ethical Problem Faced by Nurses*, ADVANCES IN NURSING SCIENCE 1(3):92-94 (1979).
4. *Id.*
5. Yarling, R., *Ethical Analysis of a Nursing Problem: The Scope of Nursing Practice in Disclosing the Truth to Terminal Patients, Part I*, SUPERVISOR NURSE, pp. 49-50 (May 1978).
6. *Supra* note 2.
7. *Supra* note 1, at 87.
8. *Id.*, at 89-90.

Chapter 4

Deciding for the Legally Incompetent: A View from the Bench

Richard P. Byrne

When the case of *Benjamin C.*[1] was brought into my court, I felt very alone indeed, and before proceeding with this chapter I would like to acknowledge my own limitations in such questions. That case was decided in 1978; I was not an expert then and I do not purport to be an expert in this rather complicated and controversial field at this time.

Basically, I agree with Sister Corrine that the patient should decide, assuming, of course, that the patient is competent to do so. If the patient is not competent, then the family and those closest to the patient, including his or her doctor, should decide according to criteria established by the courts. They may be helped in their decision by a hospital ethics committee. I also agree that while the physician can diagnose the disease or illness and can state the prognosis as "terminal," the question of whether to treat or not to treat is essentially a moral and ethical question—not a medical one. This brings us squarely to what Sister Corrine stated: What are the criteria upon which such decisions must be made? How do we establish the criteria? What happens to us if we do not follow the criteria?

Most people involved in this decision-making process are concerned about the possibility of legal action. Obviously, there are other considerations—moral and ethical considerations—but I became involved with this subject because others were fearful of either civil or criminal liability. In these situations, this fear can be expressed by a doctor, a nurse, a hospital, an ethics committee, or members of the patient's immediate family. In my view, the problem really would not prompt the public concern that it has if it were not for the fear of civil and criminal liability. Civil liability may be taken care of to a great extent by obtaining the informed consent of the people who might sue—members of the family, for example. Waivers and releases from the people and institutions involved will minimize, if not eliminate, the fear of civil liability. But what about the district attorney? What will the district attorney do if life-sustaining medical treatment is removed from an incompetent patient? If someone pulls the plug, will the district attorney prosecute?[2] That, I think, is the heart of the issue. The parties are reluctant to act without a more thoroughly defined set of criteria to follow, criteria that assures them that they will not be held liable, either civilly or criminally.

Even though the patient and his or her family should make the decision to treat or not to treat, criteria are needed. If individuals are concerned about their own family situations, then they would probably be willing to say that they themselves ought to decide. But the public, I believe, is not willing to adopt an approach that allows the family to decide without there being some definite criteria and safeguards.

In order to discuss another important aspect of this problem, I would like to digress for just a moment to discuss the role of legislation in medical matters. In 1967, California adopted the Therapeutic Abortion Act.[3] It was a very controversial law, originally viewed as a conservative measure that would permit abortion only in certain limited cases. Even before the Supreme Court's decision in Roe v. Wade,[4] however, it became clear that the law was not as conservative as originally perceived. The newspapers carried stories about hospitals that specialized in abortions (the so-called abortion mills), babies found in sacks or discarded in rubbish heaps, and things of that nature. The public reacted, and that reaction can be applied to the current controversy as well. Can we really trust the doctors? Can we have faith in those people to whom we entrust the care of our loved ones? There is, I believe, an element of mistrust in the general public and this makes the issue of withholding or withdrawing medical treatment from incompetent patients a very emotional and highly charged one. Similarly, when the California Natural Death Act[5] was passed in 1976, it was the first act of its kind, and its consideration by the legislature was a very emotional experience. There were numerous demonstrations and a lot of public controversy. This is to be expected. When we talk about matters of life and death, do we engender emotionalism when, perhaps, rationally developed criteria are what is required.

How do we establish criteria? How do we get off dead center? The legislature is one place to look for the solution to this problem. However, the experience with the Natural Death Act and the general public reaction, I think, rules out the legislature to a great extent. While some kinds of procedures can be legislated, I believe that attempts to legislate a highly charged subject produces more heat than light. In areas like withdrawing or withholding medical treatment, it is difficult to pass effective legislation without considerable controversy.

It is, I think, much easier to discuss a particular case. In the *Benjamin C.* case, I decided to allow physicians to disconnect a respirator from a comatose minor with irreversible brain damage. The point that interested me the most about the *Benjamin C.* case was that in the course of the entire proceeding, which took about a month and a half, and during the weeks that followed my decision, I received only one letter that disagreed with the proposed and ultimately final action. A lot of letters were received from people who supported the decision. The media in general and the newspapers in particular were in support. Why? Because everyone focused upon a particular situation with which they could identify. And while that case was not appealed, it did establish, at least on a local basis, some kind of precedent which has received public acceptance. Accordingly, it seems to me that the court is the arena in which such cases will be decided. If the players are afraid of being prosecuted, the courts can set up standards that the players can follow in order to avoid prosecution. As each individual case comes before the court, a general body of law will be established which will set limits and guidelines for others to follow.

I do not say this because I want these cases before me or because any other judge wants them. But the nature of society as it is today seems to cause most issues of consequence to gravitate towards the legal system, and I think that is what will happen in this situation as well. Procedures need to be developed so that these cases can be handled as expeditiously as possible for the benefit of everyone concerned. As a result of these cases, precedents will be established which should help eliminate the fear of prosecution or civil liability as well as the mistrust of decisions not subject to public scrutiny.

NOTES

1. In re *Benjamin C.*, Los Angeles Juvenile Court, Case No. J9194419.
2. *See* Oakes, G.A., "A Prosecutor's View of Treatment Decisions" Chapter 19.
3. California Health & Safety Code §§ 25950 *et seq.* (West).
4. *Roe v. Wade*, 410 U.S. 113 (1973).
5. California Health & Safety Code, §§ 7185 *et seq.* (West): *see generally,* Raible, J.A., *The Right to Refuse Treatment and Natural Death Legislation,* MEDICO-LEGAL NEWS 5(4): 6-8, 13 (Fall 1977).

Chapter 5

Reconciling *Quinlan* and *Saikewicz*: Decision Making for the Terminally Ill Incompetent

George J. Annas

I. INTRODUCTION

In one of his *Letters from the Earth*, Mark Twain has Satan observe that, before hell was invented, "death was sweet, death was gentle, death was kind . . . when man could endure life no longer, death came and set him free." Our mortality is also the subject of one of the first syllogisms taught in logic: All men are mortal. Socrates is a man. Therefore, Socrates is mortal. The modern version of this syllogism might run: All people die in hospitals. Hospitals exist to prevent death. Therefore, an attempt will be made to prevent the deaths of all people.

While overstating the case somewhat, this latter syllogism illustrates the quandary of modern man confronted with his own mortality in the hospital setting. All of us will die, most in hospitals. But new technologies and treatments can save lives and sustain bodily functions where previously death was inevitable. Sometimes these technologies only prolong the dying process and create what Twain might have labeled a hell on earth. Choices must be made. Should the ventilator be turned off? Should intensive chemotherapy be used to treat an invariably fatal cancer? Should only palliative treatment be administered? The modern question is not how death can be prevented, but how much effort, if any, should be made to postpone the moment of death. Because such decisions usually take place in hospitals, physicians generally have

Reprinted with permission of the American Society of Law & Medicine from the AMERICAN JOURNAL OF LAW & MEDICINE, Vol. 4, no. 4 (Winter 1979) and of Professor Annas.

assumed that—at least in the case of incompetent patients—such decisions are properly medical ones.[1]

These decisions raise philosophical questions of great importance to persons concerned with "medical ethics." Recently, judges and lawyers have joined the discussion. As of this writing, two state supreme courts have spoken on the problem. In 1976, the Supreme Court of New Jersey decided that the guardian, family, and physicians of Karen Ann Quinlan, a woman in a chronic vegetative state, could disconnect her ventilator and let her die if they agreed that there was "no reasonable possibility" of her ever returning to a "cognitive, sapient state." If a hospital "ethics committee" concurred, all parties involved would be immune from criminal and civil liability.[2] In late 1977, the Supreme Judicial Court of Massachusetts decided that only a probate court could authorize the nontreatment of Joseph Saikewicz, a 67-year-old mentally retarded terminally ill ward of the state who had leukemia, if there was a treatment available that was used as standard medical practice. The court held that in deciding whether to authorize nontreatment, the probate court should determine what Mr. Saikewicz would have decided had he been able to make the decision himself.[3]

The *Quinlan* decision has generally been applauded by the medical profession, while the *Saikewicz* opinion has been widely condemned. For example, Arnold S. Relman, M.D., the Editor of *The New England Journal of Medicine*, wrote approximately four months after the Massachusetts decision: "Above all, we must hope that the New Jersey, rather than the Massachusetts, judicial view of this matter will prevail in the rest of the country."[4] In the Fall 1978 edition of the *American Journal of Law & Medicine*, he continued to lament the *Saikewicz* opinion and to praise the *Quinlan* court as being "generally supportive of long-standing medical tradition."[5] That Article did concede, however, that the judiciary has a legitimate role to play in some "very limited and sharply defined cases."[6]

Understanding the medical reaction to the *Saikewicz* opinion is no easier than understanding the reaction of a patient who is told he or she has a terminal illness. Dr. Elisabeth Kübler-Ross has described the five stages most such patients pass through as denial, anger, despair, bargaining, and acceptance.[7] Physicians in Massachusetts have evidenced all of the first four stages, many moving along the continuum, and some jumping from an earlier stage to a later one and back again. Denial and anger have been the most common medical responses to *Saikewicz*, with some despair and some bargaining—mainly with the legislature.[8]

Without carrying this analogy too far, I hope that this Article will help Massachusetts physicians to enter and remain in the "acceptance" stage, so far as the *Saikewicz* opinion is concerned. It is my thesis that the dichotomy which most doctors and many lawyers perceive between the *Quinlan* decision and the *Saikewicz* decision is a false one. This Article will suggest to the next court that looks at the question of terminating treatment for an incompetent terminally ill patient that the *Quinlan* and *Saikewicz* cases can be reconciled without being procrustean, and that this reconciliation can simultaneously protect the incompetent patient and permit physicians to exercise sound medical judgment.

The first part of this Article is devoted to reconciling *Quinlan* and *Saikewicz*. The second attempts to explain why these two cases have been so thoroughly confused by the medical profession and some of its legal advisors. Post-*Saikewicz* politics and rhetoric have so distorted these cases in the minds of almost all medical professionals, hospital administrators, and many of their legal advisors, that most have made up their minds about the cases on the basis of misinformation. Some have horribly mistreated their patients, not because they wanted to, but because they believed the *Saikewicz* case compelled them to. The perception by these physicians, by the Massachusetts Medical Society, by the Massachusetts Hospital Association, and by the Editor of *The New England Journal of Medicine*, that *Quinlan* and *Saikewicz* are fundamentally contradictory, can only be understood in light of their political and rhetorical context.

II. RECONCILING *QUINLAN* AND *SAIKEWICZ*

The primary task of this Article is to compare the facts and the law of the *Quinlan* and *Saikewicz* opinions to demonstrate that the courts which decided those cases are in fundamental agreement as to both the proper role of the judiciary and the proper role of medical custom in making a decision not to treat a terminally ill incompetent patient. In order to accomplish this goal it is necessary to examine specifically how each court viewed medical custom, the right to privacy, the exercise of this right by an incompetent, and, finally, the role of the judiciary in granting pre-decision immunity.

The main point will be that the *Quinlan* court defined a legally acceptable *medical* standard for decision making which physicians can apply themselves, while the *Saikewicz* court defined a *legal* standard for decision making that only a court can apply. This is the primary difference in the cases, and the one which explains their divergent views on the appropriateness of an "ethics committee."

A. MEDICAL CUSTOM

Both courts viewed customary medical practice (sometimes referred to as "medical ethics") as a critical component in their decision-making process. Their approaches to defining medical custom, however, were somewhat different. The *Quinlan* court had a more arduous task, since at the trial level there was testimony that removing Karen Quinlan from the ventilator would *not* be consistent with medical ethics.[9] The court made two points about this. The first was that while medical custom is persuasive authority, it is never controlling, since ultimately only the courts can determine "human values and rights." In the court's words, "Determinations as to these [human values and rights] must, in the ultimate, be responsive not only to the concepts of medicine but also to the common moral judgment of the community at large. In the latter respect the Court has a nondelegable judicial responsibility."[10]

The second point the court made was that physicians are too often guided by self-interest or self-protection, which makes custom in regard to the terminally ill patient too conservative. To document this conclusion the court specifically pointed to the "modern proliferation of substantial malpractice litigation and the less frequent but even more unnerving possiblity of criminal sanctions. . . ."[11] It concluded that a way must be found to enable physicians to make medical judgments free from "possible contamination by self-interest or self-protection concerns which would inhibit their independent medical judgments for the well-being of their dying patients," and added the hope that its opinion would help in this matter.[12]

The *Saikewicz* court did not, like the *Quinlan* court, label physicians self-protectors. It did, however, agree with the *Quinlan* court that while medical ethics are important, they are not controlling. Specifically the *Saikewicz* court said, "While these [medical ethics] considerations are not controlling, they ought to be considered for the insights they give us,"[13] and later, "Our decision in this case is consistent with the current medical ethos in this area."[14]

B. THE RIGHT TO PRIVACY AND SELF-DETERMINATION

Both courts viewed the right to privacy as a constitutional right broad enough to encompass, at least under some circumstances, the right of a competent patient to refuse life-sustaining treatment.[15] The *Quinlan* court identified two state interests that might outweigh this right: the preservation and sanctity of human life, and the integrity of medical decision making. As to the first, the court argued that the "State's interest *contra* weakens and the individual's right to privacy grows as the degree of bodily invasion increases and the prognosis dims."[16] Further discussion by the court, however, makes it appear that the primary emphasis was on prognosis rather than to the extent of the bodily invasion. Specifically, just six years prior to this opinion, the court had held in another case that it was appropriate to force a 22-year-old Jehovah's

Witness, who had been severely injured in an automobile accident, to have blood transfusions during emergency surgery necessary to save her life.[17] The court distinguished the earlier case, not because a mechanical ventilator is more invasive than blood transfusions during emergency surgery, but primarily because the "patient apparently [was] salvable to long life and vibrant health" as compared to "the instant diametrically opposite case" in which Karen could "only . . . vegetate a few measurable months with no realistic possibility of returning to any semblance of cognitive or sapient life."[18]

The *Saikewicz* court identified four potential state interests which might outweigh the competent patient's right to refuse life-sustaining treatment, but found it necessary to discuss at length only the two dealt with by the *Quinlan* court.[19] Again, it is the emphasis rather than the resolution that is different. The *Saikewicz* court found that no state interest in the continuation of life can overcome the constitutional right "to decline medical treatment in a situation of incurable illness."[20] Since this right is an expression of the sanctity of self-determination, "[t]he value of life as so perceived is lessened not by a decision to refuse treatment, but by the failure to allow a competent human being the right of choice."[21] The "right to refuse necessary treatment in appropriate circumstances is consistent with existing medical mores";[22] and even if it were not, the patient's constitutional rights "are superior to the institutional considerations."[23]

Both courts, then, recognized that the right to refuse treatment, even life-sustaining treatment under certain circumstances, is a constitutional right and that this right can be interfered with only if the state can demonstrate a compelling interest. Further, the state's primary interest is in the preservation of life, but this interest diminishes and becomes noncompelling when the prognosis is hopeless (*Saikewicz*) or when there is no reasonable possibility of the patient's returning to a cognitive, sapient state (*Quinlan*). These are extremely important statements about the rights of competent patients, statements that no state supreme court had made previously. The remainder of both decisions deal with the subsidiary, but more sisyphean, question of how this right can be exercised by an incompetent patient.

C. THE INCOMPETENT'S EXERCISE OF THE RIGHT TO REFUSE TREATMENT

For neither court is the right to refuse treatment forfeited by the incompetent. The *Quinlan* court noted that the right is a valuable one which "should not be discarded solely on the basis that her condition prevents her conscious exercise of the choice."[24] The *Saikewicz* court made the point even more strongly, declaring that the right extends to the incompetent as well as the competent "because the value of human dignity extends to both."[25]

Both courts permitted proxies to make the refusal decision for the incompetent patient on the basis of what the proxy believed the incompetent would decide if able to make the decision—that is, on the basis of "substituted judgment." In the *Quinlan* case, the court gave the power to "the guardian and family of Karen to render their best judgment . . . as to whether she would exercise [her right to refuse treatment] in these circumstances."[26] But the court went further, and seemed to conclude that almost anyone with Karen's prognosis would refuse treatment, when it noted that if the decision is to terminate life-support measures, "this decision should be accepted by a society the overwhelming majority of whose members would, we think, in similar circumstances, exercise such a choice in the same way for themselves or for those closest to them."[27]

The analysis by the *Saikewicz* court was corresponding: the test was to determine what Mr. Saikewicz would do if he could make the decision himself. However, as opposed to *Quinlan*, the *Saikewicz* court had to surmount evidence that "most people elect chemotherapy."[28] Therefore, the court had to find something unique about Mr. Saikewicz that would enable the lower court to find that he would have refused treatment if he had had the chance. One possibility was the fact that Mr. Saikewicz was severely retarded. The court, however, rejected this as the sole rationale on the basis that "quality of life" could not be the determining factor. Nonetheless, the court used Mr. Saikewicz's retardation against him indirectly by finding that, when coupled with the negative factors that competent persons tend to weigh less heavily in the chemotherapy treatment decision (age, probable side effects, low probability of remission, certain suffering), the fact that Mr. Saikewicz would be unable to understand and cooperate with the treatment justified the conclusion that he would have refused it. In the court's words:[29]

> He . . . would experience fear without the understanding from which other patients draw strength. The inability to anticipate and prepare for the severe side effects of the drugs leaves room only for confusion and disorientation. The possibility that such a naturally uncooperative patient would have to be physically restrained to allow the slow intravenous administration of drugs could only compound his pain and fear, as well as possibly jeopardize the ability of his body to withstand the toxic effects of the drugs.

It should be noted that while both courts adopted the subjective "substituted judgment" test in which the guardian or court is asked to determine what the incompetent would do if able to decide, there was almost no basis on which either court could determine the actual desires of the two incompetents involved. Karen had not signed a living will, and had discussed her situation only hypothetically under circumstances that the lower court found insufficient to justify conclusions as to her actual wishes. Mr. Saikewicz, with a mental age of less than three years, never was personally able to formulate any decisions on such questions. Therefore, while the doctrine of "substituted judgment" makes most sense from the viewpoint of protecting the right to privacy and self-determination of the incompetent, in the two cases under discussion, use of the more objective "best interests" test would have been more logical.[30]

D. IMMUNITY: MEDICAL VERSUS SOCIETAL DECISIONS

Thus far, the analysis has described the law of the two cases as identical in most respects. This section will attempt to demonstrate that it was the particular facts of each case and the tests adopted to decide them which prompted the seemingly divergent resolutions, and that the courts agree with each other much more fundamentally than the *Saikewicz* court explicitly acknowledges.

The *Quinlan* court viewed medical prognosis as the key to unfettered exercise of a right to refuse treatment in Karen Quinlan's case, and it viewed its job as finding a way to get physicians to do the "right" thing without worrying about self-protection. Believing that its solution to this self-imposed problem was to create a quasi-administrative agency with the authority to grant civil and criminal immunity in a narrow range of cases decided on the basis of medical prognosis, the court adopted the "ethics committee" approach recommended by pediatrician Karen Teel, as a method of taking the liability burden off physicians by "diffus[ing] the responsibility for making these judgments."[31] It also rejected any requirement of routine court proceedings in cases like that of Karen Quinlan because it viewed such a requirement as a "gratuitous encroachment upon the medical profession's field of competence" and as "impossibly cumbersome."[32]

On the surface, it appears, as it did to the *Saikewicz* court, that the *Quinlan* court was engaged in a wholesale delegation of judicial authority to local, ad hoc administrative agencies called ethics committees. This is certainly one possible interpretation. It is more reasonable, however, to read the decision as one which simply told physicians that when they are making treatment decisions on the basis of *medical* criteria, they should not be worried about immunity. If they are worried, calling in a consultant, here termed an "ethics committee," should relieve them of this fear.

Specifically, the *Quinlan* court permitted the "ethics committee" to grant immunity only after Karen's guardian, family, and attending physicians concluded that there was "no reasonable possibility of Karen's ever emerging from her present comatose condition to a cognitive, sapient state."[33] The ethics committee then, and only then, could be consulted and asked to concur in this narrow prognosis determination.[34] It must be emphasized that while the term "ethics committee" was used by the court, a more accurate description would be "prognosis committee," because that is the *only* issue on which the participants would be asked to consult.[35] Further, since non-medical professionals have no expertise on this issue, the opinion would be more consistent if it simply required the concurrence of one or more medical experts in the prognosis determination.

While no judicial body should abdicate its responsibility to determine ultimately what is legal and illegal, the *Quinlan* decision can be read as simply affirming the general laws of malpractice and negligent homicide; that is, if the physician's decision is challenged in a civil or criminal proceeding, he or she will be judged on whether or not his or her conduct was consistent with custom or "accepted medical practice,"[36] a determination made by a judge or jury only after hearing expert testimony from other physicians on the proper standard of care. Assuming that such experts have been consulted initially, and have agreed in writing that the physician's proposed action is consistent with "accepted medical practice," no liability is likely ever to obtain.[37] Therefore, if one accepts the premise that the *Quinlan* criteria are fundamentally a matter of medical prognosis, then the court's "immunity doctrine" can be viewed simply as a restatement of the law, intended to encourage physicians to fulfill their professional obligations without undue fear of lawsuits.

Interpreted in this way the opinion is sound, and future opinions need only refine the role of the medical consultant or committee by removing the label "ethics committee" and replacing it with a phrase like "qualified medical specialist," or "prognosis committee."

The *Quinlan* court, in summary, viewed the decision concerning continued mechanical ventilation of Karen Quinlan as one that could be based solely on medical prognosis. Since medical prognosis is primarily and most often exclusively determined by physicians, the court found no reason why decisions made on this basis should come to court. To prevent additional cases of this type from coming to court, the court set up an alternative method for physicians to receive "immunity," if they felt they needed it.

It was, of course, the *Quinlan* court's establishment of this alternate, nonjudicial method of gaining immunity that so disturbed the *Saikewicz* court. One must recall, however, that the facts of these two cases differed in critical respects. The *Quinlan* court had to decide whether to overrule a lower court decision in order to permit attending physicians to discontinue mechanical ventilation of a woman who was still alive at the time the opinion was written; the *Saikewicz* court was faced with writing an opinion rationalizing a prior decision it had made against treatment of a mentally retarded cancer victim who, by the time the opinion actually was written, had been dead for more than a year.[38] In addition, Mr. Saikewicz did not meet the *Quinlan* criterion in that he was both cognitive and sapient. Accordingly, a decision in *Saikewicz* could not be based on the *Quinlan* prognosis criterion. As the court stressed in *Saikewicz*, the decision had to be based on a determination involving "substituted judgment," a legal rather than a medical standard.

It was this difference in decision criteria that led the *Saikewicz* court to resoundingly reject the *Quinlan* "ethics committee" approach. Its rejection was based on the premise (which I believe was mistaken) that the *Quinlan* court had permitted the "ethics committee" to make legal or judicial decisions rather than simply to act as a medical consultant on the issue of prognosis. Viewed in the former light, the delegation of judicial authority can be seen as both unprecedented and dangerous to the rights of the incompetent. Since this is how the *Saikewicz* court did view the matter, it condemned such a mechanism, noting that it took "a dim view of any attempt to shift the ultimate decision-making responsibility away from the duly established courts of proper jurisdiction to any committee, panel or group, ad hoc or permanent."[39] It was after this rejection that the court commented that "judicial resolution" of the question is appropriate and cannot be construed as a "'gratuitous encroachment' on the domain of medical expertise."[40] Then followed the sentences many physicians have interpreted as a slap in the face:[41]

> [S]uch questions of life and death seem to us to require the process of detached but passionate investigation and decision that forms the ideal on which the judicial branch of government was created. Achieving this ideal is our responsibility and that of the lower court, and is not to be entrusted to any other group purporting to represent the "morality and conscience of our society," no matter how highly motivated or impressively constituted.

The court takes this view, it seems to me, because the issue in *Saikewicz* was not one of medical prognosis—the court accepted the probate court's finding that the proposed treatment offered a reasonable chance of a remission of from 2 to 13 months or more[42]—but a legal question of "substituted judgment." This latter question has always been a matter for the courts, and is an issue on which physicians have no expertise at all.[43] As to the "ultimate" question of immunity, the

Saikewicz court believed that only a court should make such decisions and that to permit any other agency to make them would be an improper delegation of judicial authority.

E. SUMMARY

In short, as previously suggested, the decisions can be reconciled. *Quinlan* based its final conclusion on the use of a prognosis criterion that is medical. While the court approved the "substituted judgment" test, it found it unnecessary, because it thought almost everyone with Karen's prognosis would refuse treatment if they could. Since the court believed physicians were refusing to exercise their best medical judgment for fear of civil and criminal liability, it set up an informal mechanism by which physicians can be guaranteed immunity before the fact without having to resort to the courts. This mechanism was seen as appropriate both because it is relatively speedy and because the only thing that would happen in court in any event is that medical experts would be asked to testify about the accuracy of the prognosis. The court believed that such determinations were best left in the hospitals, and that its decision would accomplish this end.

The issue in the *Saikewicz* case, on the other hand, was much more complex. It was not a question of medical prognosis, but of whether to use an accepted medical treatment on a mentally retarded individual whose life could be sustained for an indefinite period of time. The court determined that such a question can only be answered on the basis of "substituted judgment," and since this is a legal standard, a court hearing is required. Further, since the issues are complex and the decision irrevocable, the court suggested that such a hearing should be adversary in nature, with arguments presented to the court on both sides of the issue.[44] Only after such a hearing can the ultimate legal question of immunity be answered.

Stated another way, when a patient's condition is "hopeless," or when he or she has "no reasonable possibility of returning to a cognitive, sapient state," the state can *never* demonstrate an interest compelling enough to outweigh the patient's constitutional right to refuse treatment as exercised by a legal guardian. Therefore, there is no reason to require that the legal guardian seek court approval before exercising the incompetent's right to refuse treatment, especially if the courts believe all or almost all persons so situated would refuse treatment if they could. Likewise, if there is a reasonable chance that the patient will return to normalcy, and the case is an emergency, treatment should always be started, because of the state's compelling interest in the preservation of life, without any resort to the courts. It is the cases between these extremes for which neither court offers much guidance.

To conclude that the opinions can be reconciled is not to say that one always can predict how courts will rule in individual cases. For example, should someone bring a case like that of *Quinlan* to court in Massachusetts, a probate court could require continued treatment on the basis that her condition is not "hopeless," she is not suffering, and therefore she would want treatment continued. Also, had the *Saikewicz* case been brought in New Jersey, that Supreme Court might well have decided that treatment should be required in order to promote the state's interest in life, because Saikewicz could be maintained in a cognitive, sapient state. Thus, the focus is not (and should not be) on whether the *Quinlan* and *Saikewicz* courts made the "right" decision concerning treatment, but on whether the procedures and criteria applied in reaching the decisions are likely to be equitable, fair, and prudent when applied to future cases.

Both courts support physicians in their independent exercise of medical judgment. Both courts support patients in their exercise of self-determination in refusing treatment and concur that incompetents have this right as well. Under the facts in *Quinlan*, the decision whether to terminate treatment could appropriately be based on medical criteria alone, so the court devised a mechanism to keep such decisions out of the courts. Under the facts in *Saikewicz*, the medical criteria were not controlling, so a legal determination had to be made. Both courts would agree, I submit, that medical decisions should be made by physicians following accepted medical practices, and that legal or social decisions should be made by courts.

This conclusion is necessary not because judges and lawyers are more intelligent than physicians, but because judges have the social mandate to distill the values and morals of society on which most of these cases must ultimately be decided. In the words of Justice Benjamin N. Cardozo:[45]

> You may say that there is no assurance that judges will interpret the mores of their day more wisely and truly than other men. I am not disposed to deny this, but in my view it is quite beside the point. The point is rather that this power of interpretation must be lodged somewhere, and the custom of the constitution has lodged it in the judges. If they are to fulfill their function as judges, it could hardly be lodged elsewhere. Their conclusions must, indeed, be subject to constant testing and retesting, revision and readjustment; but if they act with conscience and intelligence, they ought to attain in their conclusions a fair average of truth and wisdom.

III. WHY QUINLAN AND SAIKEWICZ ARE VIEWED AS CONFLICTING
DECISIONS

If the arguments presented above are accepted, one must ask why the
medical community has viewed *Quinlan* and *Saikewicz* as conflicting,
and why so much energy has gone into attempting to get the *Saikewicz*
decision legislatively or judicially changed in favor of a so-called *Quinlan* approach. The initial answer, implicit in the preceding discussion,
is that neither the *Quinlan* nor the *Saikewicz* court is completely logical
or clear. The *Quinlan* court, for example, quoting from an article by a
physician, described an "ethics committee" that is far different from
the one needed to answer the narrow question that the court delegates
to it. The court gave no other guidance, such as who appoints the committee, when it meets, who calls the meeting, how and if it votes, what a
quorum or majority is, who the chairman is, whether the incompetent
gets represented, or what the notice requirements are. The resulting
confusion concerning the role of this committee is therefore
understandable.[46]

Likewise, the *Saikewicz* court arguably misunderstood what the
Quinlan court intended as the proper role of such an ethics committee,
and as a result reacted so strongly against it that its opinion has been
read by some as a blanket condemnation of *any* medical decision making in cases involving terminally ill patients. While I do not agree with
such an interpretation of *Saikewicz*, it is certainly one that can be made
by counsel who have not spent a good deal of time studying the cases on
which the court rests its decision, and it is one for which the court must
take some of the blame.

Few judicial decisions are flawless, however, and it is the responsibility of lawyers to interpret decisions in reasonable ways, not in ways that
assume the court does not know what it is doing. A review of some of
the medicolegal advice given in Massachusetts concerning *Saikewicz*
illustrates many of the inherent problems in interpreting these decisions and the limitations of the legal resources currently available to
physicians and hospitals in Massachusetts. It is conceded at the outset
that much of the evidence is anecdotal, but until a formal study is done,
it is the best available.

The medical profession's lack of familiarity with legal reality was
dramatically illustrated nationally during the so-called "malpractice insurance crisis" of 1974 and 1975, which was commonly viewed as a reflection of unfair legal rules rather than substandard medical
practice.[47] The aftermath of the *Saikewicz* case exposes the problem on
a local level. On March 2, 1978, the legal columnist of *The New England
Journal of Medicine* wrote that physicians and news reporters were cor-

rect in concluding that in *Saikewicz*, the Massachusetts Supreme Judicial Court "really did mean that all decisions on either removal of life-support systems or continuation of life-extending therapy in otherwise dying patients who are incompetent . . . must go before a Probate Court for approval."[48] With this encouragement, Dr. Relman wrote an accompanying editorial which concluded that the justices had a "total distrust of physicians' judgments" and that their "astonishing opinion can only be viewed as a resounding vote of 'no confidence' in the ability of physicians and families to act in the best interests of the incapable patient suffering from a terminal illness." As previously noted, Relman urged judges in other jurisdictions to adopt the *Quinlan* approach instead, and suggested additionally that all those who did not agree with him take a "guided visit to a large acute-care hospital."[49]

In the weeks immediately following the publication of these pieces, my colleague Leonard Glantz and I, both of us then with Boston University's Center for Law and Health Sciences, discussed the *Saikewicz* case with a number of physicians. More than once we were told that while we were entitled to our own view of the law, the physician had read *The New England Journal of Medicine* and therefore knew that no action could be taken regarding an incompetent terminally ill patient without an order from the probate court. In one instance, I spoke a number of times with the physician attending a patient who had suffered a massive stroke. I had convinced the physician, who believed his patient's condition was completely hopeless and death was imminent, that he was not legally obligated to resuscitate the patient repeatedly. He called me later and said he had consulted the hospital administrator, who demanded that his patient remain in the intensive care unit until the family took the case to court. I have since learned that the patient was so maintained for an additional four weeks, and finally died the day after a legal aid attorney submitted a petition to the probate court.[50]

Other cases have since been reported, which include a Tay-Sachs baby being repeatedly resuscitated; a Werdnig-Hoffmann's syndrome child being heroically maintained; a dying woman being defibrillated 70 times in a 24-hour period; and a brain-dead individual for whom the implantation of a cardiac pacemaker was being planned—all at the urging of hospital counsel.[51] At medicolegal conferences on the *Saikewicz* case, nurses told of family members barring the patient's door to prevent resuscitation of dying loved ones in hospitals whose counsel had advised them that *Saikewicz* had outlawed "no-code" orders.[52] It appears that many lawyers advising Massachusetts hospitals on the law of the *Saikewicz* case lack experience and training in health law and have little familiarity with either medical practice or hospital procedures.[53] This has resulted in the types of cases described above, primarily because hospital administrators have asked their legal counsel how the hospital could be protected from *any* possible liability.[54] The quest for "100 percent immunity" is both unrealistic and unprofessional, and evidences a desire to put one's self-interest above the interest of individual patients. So pervasive is the desire for self-protection that in a number of instances even brain-dead corpses have been brought to court for judicial permission to cease "treatment."[55] While one need not be surprised that lawyers and hospital administrators would involve themselves in such proceedings, it comes as somewhat of a surprise that the physicians of these brain-dead patients did not effectively oppose such action. Physicians should know at least enough law to be able to tell when the advice their lawyers are giving them is so incredible that it is most likely wrong.[56] They also should recognize that like physicians, different lawyers may have different opinions about the law, and it sometimes pays to get a second or third opinion when your lawyer tells you that you must do something you think is wrong. Finally, physicians should realize that there are no 100 percent guarantees in law any more than in life, and that part of being a professional is taking responsibility for decisions within one's professional competence.[57]

Legal advice once given is not easily withdrawn. For example, an attorney from a large Boston law firm advised a major suburban hospital to go to court to determine if it was proper to put a "do not resuscitate" order on Shirley Dinnerstein, a 67-year-old woman with Alzheimer's disease—a progressive and unremitting degenerative brain disease for which there is no cure—who, at the time of the petition, was completely paralyzed on her left side, in an essentially vegetative state, immobile, speechless, unable to swallow without choking, and barely able to cough. Her condition was "hopeless." It apparently came as a surprise to some that the Massachusetts Appeals Court had no difficulty finding that this was *not* the type of case that the *Saikewicz* court held belonged in court, since there was nothing medical science had to offer this patient.[58]

This same attorney then co-authored a legal advice column on this case in *The New England Journal of Medicine*. The column stands as a classic, illustrating Professor Sylvia Law's observation that "professional medical pulications frequently offer statements about legal standards which are casual, offhand, misleading, or just plain wrong."[59] It is arguably all of these. It incorrectly asserts, for example, that the appeals court decision in *Dinnerstein* is "final authority" in Massachusetts since "it was not appealed." The article is also an attempt to justify the previous legal advice of the writers to their clients,[60] by arguing that the *Dinnerstein* court supports their view that *Saikewicz* "appeared to establish a rule of law that unless such a court determination has been obtained, it is the duty of a doctor attending an incompetent patient to employ whatever lifesaving or life-prolonging treatments the current state of the art has put into his hands."[61] This is, of course, dicta. The holding of the case—that one does not have to get prior court approval for an order not to resuscitate a hopeless patient— is just the opposite.

Nevertheless, this column is likely to be taken as "the law" by many Massachusetts physicians, thus compounding current confusion. For example, Dr. Charles A. Sanders, General Director of the Massachusetts General Hospital, recently wrote in *Hospitals* that the opinion in *Dinnerstein* "effectively removed from the courts the medical decision-making process in virtually all circumstances in which heroic measures might ultimately be used to sustain life,"[62] apparently because he thought *Dinnerstein* overruled *Saikewicz*.

The distortions of *Dinnerstein* continue a story begun with misinterpretations of the scope of both *Quinlan* and *Saikewicz*. Hospital administrators are worried about legal liability. Physicians are worried about both legal liability and professional autonomy. Hospital counsel are generally untrained and inexperienced in health law. Neither physicians nor hospital administrators know how lawyers think, how to ask them for advice, or what to do with legal advice that doesn't seem to make sense. Consequently, we have a growing number of physicians and hospital administrators arguing about the merits of judicial opinions they do not understand. They castigate the *Saikewicz* court for doing something it did not do, and commend the *Quinlan* court for something it did not do.

IV. CONCLUSION

The next state supreme court that speaks on the issue of withholding treatment from the terminally ill incompetent will have the opportunity to synthesize and reconcile the *Saikewicz* and *Quinlan* decisions clearly and with a full discussion of the proper role of both professional medical judgment and judicial decision making. No one wants a system in which all treatment decisions for incompetents are made by judges, or one in which they are all made by physicians. Nor does anyone want a system where the rights of the weakest members of society—the incompetent terminally ill—are not fully protected. It is critical that the rights of these patients be viewed as worthy of the full protection of the law.[63] On the other hand, it is equally critical that physicians not practice medicine solely with a view toward avoiding liability. As Alexander

Solzhenitsyn warned in his much maligned commencement address at Harvard University, while a society without any objective legal scale is "terrible," "a society with no other scale but the legal one is not quite worthy of man either":[64]

> A society that is based on the letter of the law and never reaches any higher is taking small advantage of the high level of human possibilities. The letter of the law is too cold and formal to have a beneficial influence on society. Whenever the tissue of life is woven of legalistic relations, there is an atmosphere of mediocrity, paralysing man's noblest impulses.

Many have argued that such mediocrity and paralysis already have set in, as evidenced by the increase in medical malpractice litigation and its resulting practice of both negative and positive defensive medicine. Certainly the post-*Saikewicz* experience tends to confirm the *Quinlan* court's conclusion that "self-protection" has a strong influence on medical practice. My argument is that such a negative reaction to the law on the part of medicine is primarily motivated by ignorance, perpetuated in part by some leading medical journals. Insofar as this argument is correct, it is optimistic. It postulates that increased understanding by the medical community of the law and the legal process will lead to more personalized medical treatment decisions for competent and incompetent patients alike.[65]

We will all die. And we need not view death as "sweet," "kind," or "gentle" to favor the development of a system likely to assure us of the primary voice in determining how we will be treated when we are near death. In this regard, promoting the rights of the terminally ill incompetent is likely to benefit everyone.

NOTES

1. There is a large and growing literature on the problems confronting dying patients in hospitals. Some of the best volumes include THE DYING PATIENT (O. Brim ed. 1970); ETHICAL ISSUES IN DEATH AND DYING (R. Weir ed. 1977); H. FEIFEL, NEW MEANINGS OF DEATH (1977); E. KÜBLER-ROSS, ON DEATH AND DYING (1969); D. SUDNOW, PASSING ON (1967); R. VEATCH, DEATH, DYING AND THE BIOLOGICAL REVOLUTION (1976); G. WILLIAMS, THE SANCTITY OF LIFE AND THE CRIMINAL LAW (1957). *See also* Annas, *Death and Dying*, CIV. LIB. REV., July 1978, at 71 ("Round-up Book Review").

    There is also a growing consensus that the wishes of a previously competent patient, expressed in a document often termed a "living will," should be honored. *See, e.g.,* Bok, *Personal Directions for Care at the End of Life,* 295 NEW ENGLAND J. MED. 367 (1976); Raible, *The Right to Refuse Treatment and Natural Death Legislation,* MEDICOLEGAL NEWS, Fall 1977, at 6; Note, *In-*

formed Consent and the Dying Patient, 83 YALE L.J. 1632 (1974). Most of the law review articles written on the *Quinlan* case to date have suggested that many of the problems posed by that case could be alleviated by "living will" legislation. *See, e.g.,* Note, *The Legal Aspects of the Right to Die: Before and After the Quinlan Decision,* 65 KY L.J. 823, 872-79 (1976-77) Note, *In Re Quinlan: Defining the Basis for Terminating Life Support Under the Right of Privacy,* 12 TULSA L.J. 150, 164-66 (1976).

2. *In re* Quinlan, 70 N.J. 10,355 A.2d 647 (1976). This case involved a young woman who, following an episode of unresolved etiology, was in a "chronic persistent vegetative state." While not brain-dead, she had neither cognition nor sapience, and experts believed she could not survive without the aid of a mechanical ventilator. Although the ventilator was removed following the decision of the New Jersey Supreme Court, as of this writing Karen Quinlan continues to live and is being cared for in a New Jersey nursing home.

3. Superintendent of Belchertown State School v. Saikewicz, 1977 Mass. Adv. Sh. 2461, 370 N.E.2d 417 (1977). Joseph Saikewicz was a 67-year-old man with an I.Q. of 10 and a mental age of about three years when, on April 19, 1976, he was diagnosed as having acute myeloblastic monocytic leukemia. Chemotherapy is the treatment of choice, and while it causes many unpleasant side effects, there was evidence that it would have afforded him a 30 to 50 percent chance of remission for 2 to 13 months or more. After a hearing, a probate court judge decided on May 13, 1976, that Mr. Saikewicz would be better off without the treatment, and the Massachusetts Supreme Judicial Court affirmed this decision on July 9, 1976. On September 4, 1976, Mr. Saikewicz died of bronchial pneumonia, a complication of leukemia, apparently without pain or discomfort. The court's opinion, explaining its July 9, 1976 action, was handed down on November 28, 1977. Mr. Saikewicz's retardation was the crucial issue in the case which was complicated by the fact that "there has been no consensus within the [medical profession] on what constitutes appropriate medical intervention in mentally retarded patients with major medical needs." Nelson & Crocker, *The Medical Care of Mentally Retarded Persons in Public Residential Facilities,* 299 NEW ENGLAND J. MED. 1039, 1041 (1978). *See* Glantz & Swazey, *Decisions Not to Treat: The Saikewicz Case and its Aftermath,* FORUM ON MEDICINE, Jan. 1979, at 22.

4. Relman, *The Saikewicz Decision: Judges as Physicians,* 298 NEW ENGLAND J. MED. 508, 509 (1978).

5. Relman, *The Saikewicz Decision: A Medical Viewpoint,* 4 AM. J. L. & MED. 233, 234 (1978).

6. *Id.* at 241.

7. *See* E. KÜBLER-ROSS, ON DEATH AND DYING (1969).
    Responding to those who think such issues are exclusively medical, Professor Norman Cantor of Rutgers Law School has noted:

    Many physicians and lawyers have asserted that handling of the terminally ill should be left to the medical profession—that the courts have no role in this context. This is a naive position. . . . [Q]uestions of the legality of withholding or withdrawing life-preserving care are constantly lurking in hospitals and would inevitably surface in the courts, whether through homicide, malpractice, or life insurance litigation. The law must eventually fix decision making responsibility and criteria. Courts and/or legislatures cannot duck these issues indefinitely.

Cantor, *Quinlan, Privacy, and the Handling of Incompetent Dying Patients*, 30 RUTGERS L. REV. 243 n.2 (1977).

8. In the spring of 1978, the Massachusetts Medical Society and the Massachusetts Hospital Association asked the state legislature to enact a statute that would define death, "legalize" and provide immunity for physicians from possible criminal or civil sanctions for making any decisions concerning the dying under the statutory mechanisms suggested. *See* Carroll, *Who Speaks for Incompetent Patients? The Case of Joseph Saikewicz*, TRUSTEE Dec. 1978, at 19, 24. The proposed statute was hastily and poorly drafted, suffering from defects that are almost inevitable in such a grab-bag approach to a complex social issue. While pieces of the proposal like the "living will," deserve support, the thrust of the proposal was to provide immunity to physicians in an area where it is both inappropriate and unnecessary. The bill was referred to study committee, and is likely to reappear in some form during the 1979 legislative session. As of this writing, the proposed legislation continues to be supported by the Massachusetts Hospital Association, although at a legislative forum on December 15, 1978, the President of the Massachusetts Medical Society, Dr. Russell Rowell, indicated that because of the *Dinnerstein* case, *In re* Dinnerstein, 1978 Mass. App. Adv. Sh. 736, 380 N.E.2d 134 (1978), his organization no longer believed such legislation was necessary.

9. *See In re* Quinlan, 137 N.J. Super, 227, 348 A.2d 801 (Ch. Div. 1975). For example, Dr. Sidney Diamond testified that "no physician would interrupt the use of the respirator and that the continued use of the respirator does not deviate from standard medical practice." *Id.* at 247, 348 A.2d at 812. "Dr. Morse [Karen Quinlan's attending physician] . . . refused to concur in the removal of Karen from the respirator. It is his considered position that medical tradition does not justify that act." *Id.* at 259, 348 A.2d at 819.

10. 70 N.J. at 44, 355 A.2d at 665.
11. *Id.* at 46, 355 A.2d at 666.
12. *Id.* at 49, 355 A.2d at 668.
13. 1977 Mass. Adv. Sh. at 2471, 370 N.E.2d at 423.
14. *Id.* at 2473, 370 N.E.2d at 424.

The current state of medical ethics in this area is expressed by one commentator who states that: "[W]e should not use *extraordinary* means of prolonging life or its semblance when, after careful consideration, consultation and the application of the most well conceived therapy it becomes apparent that there is *no hope* for the recovery of the patient. Recovery should not be defined simply as the ability to remain alive; it should mean *life without intolerable suffering.*"

Id. (quoting Lewis, *Machine Medicine and Its Relation to the Fatally Ill,* 200 J.A.M.A. 387 (1968) latter emphases added)).

15. 1977 Mass Adv. Sh. at 2474-75, 370 N.E.2d at 424; 70 N.J. at 39, 355 A.2d at 663.

16. *Id.* at 41, 355 A.2d at 664.

17. John F. Kennedy Memorial Hosp. v. Heston, 58 N.J. 576, 279 A.2d 670 (1971). While one could argue that since Heston's family did want the surgery the only added invasion was the blood transfusions, the language of the *Heston* court makes it clear that the court also would have approved of the surgery had consent been withheld. The post-*Roe v. Wade* justification would be the state's interest in preserving life under these circumstances. The pre-*Roe v. Wade* justification that should *not* survive *Quinlan* was the *Heston* court's finding that "[w]hen the hospital and staff are . . . involuntary hosts and their interests are pitted against the belief of the patient, we think it reasonable to resolve the problem by permitting the hospital and its staff to pursue their functions according to their professional standards." *Id.* at 583, 279 A.2d at 673. *See also* Note, *The Tragic Choice: Termination of Care for Patients in a Permanent Vegetative State,* 51 N.Y.U.L. REV. 285 (1976).

18. 70 N.J. at 39, 355 A.2d at 663.

19. The other two interests identified are the protection of innocent third parties, and the prevention of suicide. The first was not an issue in the case since Mr. Saikewicz had no dependent relatives. Even if he had, one can question whether the interests of third parties should be permitted to overcome an individual's interest in self-determination. The second interest, prevention of suicide, was dismissed in a footnote that ended with the following sentences:

> Furthermore, the underlying State interest in this area lies in the prevention of irrational self-destruction. What we consider here is a competent, rational decision to refuse treatment when death is inevitable and the treatment offers no hope of cure or preservation of life. There is no connection between the conduct here in issue and any State concern to prevent suicide.

1977 Mass. Adv. Sh. at 2480, 370 N.E.2d at 426 n.11.

An almost identical view of this question was enunciated by the *Quinlan* court: "We would see . . . a real distinction between the self-infliction of deadly harm and a self-determination against artificial life support or radical surgery, for instance, in the face of irreversible, painful and certain imminent death." 70 N.J. at 43, 355 A.2d at 665.

Neither court, however, discussed the societal implications of decreeing suicide an acceptable behavior. *See, e.g.,* Hook, *The Ethics of Suicide,* in BENEFICENT EUTHANASIA 57 (M. Kohl ed. 1975). Hook notes that the advocacy of suicide led a French physician, Dr. Binet-Sangle, to suggest, in his *L'Art de Mourir* (1919), the establishment of *un institut d'euthanasie.* More recently, Kurt Vonnegut has suggested that population pressures may make suicide an accepted social behavior, which a government might encourage by establishing "suicide parlors" in which people could voluntarily commit suicide with the aid of an attendent. *See* K. VONNEGUT, *Welcome to the Monkey House*, in WELCOME TO THE MONKEY HOUSE 28 (1970). *See also* Cantor, *A Patient's Decision to Decline Life-saving Medical Treatment: Bodily Integrity Versus the Preservation of Life*, 26 RUTGERS L. REV. 228 (1973); Delgado, *Euthanasia Reconsidered—The Choice of Death as an Aspect of the Right of Privacy*, 17 ARIZONA L. REV. 474 (1975); Note, *Suicide and the Compulsion of Lifesaving Medical Procedures: An Analysis of the Refusal of Treatment Cases*, 44 BROOKLYN L. REV. 285 (1978).

20. 1977 Mass. Adv. Sh. at 2478, 370 N.E.2d at 426.
21. *Id. Cf.:*

> Although the Constitution recognizes that human life is, to most persons, of inestimable value and protects its taking without due process of law, nothing in that document compels a person to continue living who does not desire to do so. Such an interpretation effectively converts a right into an obligation. . . .

Delgado, *supra* note 19, at 483.

22. *Id.* at 2480, 370 N.E.2d at 426.
23. *Id.* at 2481, 370 N.E.2d at 427 (footnote omitted).
24. 70 N.J. at 41, 355 A.2d at 664.
25. 1977 Mass. Adv. Sh. at 2483, 370 N.E.2d at 427.
26. 70 N.J. at 41, 355 A.2d at 664.
27. *Id.* at 41-42, 355 A.2d at 664. This approach has been strongly criticized by the court-appointed guardian of Karen Quinlan who, while agreeing with the outcome of the case, argued that the court had no evidence at all on which to reach this conclusion concerning what the rest of society would do in similar circumstances. Coburn, *In re Quinlan: A Practical View*, 31 ARK. L. REV. 59, 67-69 (1977). *See also* Corbett & Raciti, *Withholding Life-Prolonging Medical Treatment from the Institutionalized Person—Who Decides?* 3 NEW ENGLAND J. PRISON L. 47, 72-73 (1976).
28. 1977 Mass. Adv. Sh. at 2492, 370 N.E.2d at 431.
29. *Id.* at 2494, 370 N.E.2d at 432. All this, of course, is just another way of saying that chemotherapy should not be used on retarded individuals where the probability of success is limited. The court could have avoided this result by adopting the test of judicial review used by Justice Quirico in Nathan V. Farinelli, Mass. Suffolk Eq. 74-87 (1974), who found the only logical test in a similar circumstance of proxy consent was whether the decision was "fair and reasonable" under the circumstances.
30. While an argument can be made that Karen's parents were in a position to determine what decision she would make, Paul Ramsey argues persuasively that the *Saikewicz* court projected "the unknowable into the unknown" and must be viewed as substituting its subjectivity for Mr. Saikewicz's. Ramsey, *The Saikewicz Precedent: What's Good for an Incompetent Patient?* HASTINGS CENTER REP., Dec. 1978, at 36, 39.

That the Massachusetts Supreme Judicial Court has made no final determination on the proper standard is clear from its post-*Saikewicz* decision ordering (against the wishes of the parents) chemotherapy for a two-year-old boy with a reasonable chance of cure. *In re* Custody of a Minor, 1978 Mass. Adv. Sh. 2002, 2031-34, 379 N.E.2d 1053, 1065-66 (1978). *See also* Baron, Botsford, & Cole, *Live Organ and Tissue Transplants from Minor Donors in Massachusetts,* 55 B.U.L. REV. 159 (1975). Probably the primary reason for adopting the "substituted judgment" over the "best interests" test in both cases was that very good arguments can be mustered to demonstrate that continued treatment was actually in the best interests of both Karen Quinlan and Joseph Saikewicz. To the extent that this is true, it is another example of the old adage that "hard cases make bad law." For a discussion of the doctrine of "substituted judgment," see Robertson, *Organ Donations by Incompetents and the Substituted Judgment Doctrine,* 76 COLUM. L. REV. 48 (1976).

31. 70 N.J. at 49, 355 A.2d at 669 (quoting Teel, *The Physician's Dilemma: A Doctor's View: What the Law Should Be,* 27 BAYLOR L. REV. 6, 8-9 (1975)). Note that the court made no independent determination of who should sit on such a committee, how they should be appointed, or how they should proceed. Instead it relied entirely on a quotation from Dr. Teel's article, which said in relevant part: "Many hospitals have established an Ethics Committee composed of physicians, social workers, attorneys, and theologians, . . . which serves to review the individual circumstances of ethical dilemma and which has provided much in the way of assistance and safeguards for patients and their medical caretakers." 70 N.J. at 49, 355 A.2d at 668 (quoting Teel, *supra,* at 8-9). It should also be pointed out that Dr. Teel's "article" is actually a four-page speech and her suggestions were not the result of any elaborate comparison of alternatives. The court reveals its knowledge of this by its use of ellipses in the above quotation to replace the words "(known irreverently in some circles as the 'God Squad')." None of my remarks are meant to reflect on Dr. Teel, who acknowledges at the beginning of her speech that she has no credentials in "medical ethics, forensic medicine, [or] theology," but is speaking from "the perspecitve of a single practicing pediatrician who cares for infants and children and their families."*Id.* at 6.

32. 70 N.J. at 50, 355 A.2d at 9.

33. *Id.* at 54, 355 A.2d at 671.

34. *Id.* It cannot be overemphasized that the issue for the New Jersey court was one of prognosis: "The evidence in this case convinces us that the focal point of decision should be the prognosis as to the reasonable possibility of return to cognitive and sapient life, as distinguished from the forced continuance of that biological vegetative existence to which Karen seems to be doomed." *Id.* at 51, 355 A.2d at 669. The holding is precise:

> Upon the concurrence of the guardian and family of Karen, should the responsible attending physicians conclude that there is *no reasonable possiblity* of Karen's ever emerging from her present comatose condition to a *cognitive, sapient state* and that the life-support apparatus now being administered to Karen should be discontinued, *they*

shall consult with the hospital "Ethics Committee" or like body of the in-stitution in which Karen is the hospitalized. If that consultative body agrees that there is no reasonable possibility of Karen's ever emerging from her present comatose condition to a cognitive, sapient state, the present life-support system may be withdrawn and *said action shall be without any civil or criminal liability therefor on the part of any par-ticipant,* whether guardian, physician, hospital or others.

Id. at 54, 355 A.2d at 671 (emphasis added; footnote omitted). In other words, the *only* benefit received from going to an "ethics committee" is what the physicians wanted: legal immunity. Since the only relevant legal issue is prognosis, one obtains no ethical insights, only legal comfort. It is the Massachusetts Supreme Judicial Court's refusal to permit such "rub-ber stamp," nonjudicial granting of legal immunity that has so upset the Massachusetts hospital and medical community. In almost every other re-spect, the *Quinlan* decision, which Relman endorses, and the *Saikewicz* deci-sion are identical. *See* Annas, *In re Quinlan: Legal Comfort for Doctors,* HAST-INGS CENTER REPORT, June 1976, at 29.

New Jersey, however, understandably remains confused over the prop-er role of such a committee. At the Morris View Nursing Home, for exam-ple, where Karen Quinlan is currently a patient, an ethics committee was formed when the nursing home knew she would be coming there. It con-sists of a physician, an attorney, two clergymen, a social worker, and the chairman, who is also Chairman of the Morris County Welfare Board, which manages the nursing home. This committee apparently sees itself not as a "prognosis committee" but as a committee to deal with "ethical issues." This view may account for the fact that to date the committee, while it has met, has never decided anything and has not yet even devised a method for reaching a decision. Esqueda, *Hospital Ethics Committee: Four Case Studies,* THE HOSPITAL MEDICAL STAFF, Nov. 1978, at 26, 26-27. Nevertheless, the ethics committee approach has not been without de-fenders. *See, e.g.,* Note, *In re Quinlan: One Court's Answer to the Problem of Death with Dignity,* 34 WASH. & LEE L. REV. 285, 305-07 (1977).

35. Apparently in recognition of this, the New Jersey attorney general's guide-lines for setting up such committees describe them as "prognosis commit-tees." *See* Hirsch & Donovan, *The Right to Die: Medico-Legal Implications of In re Quinlan,* 30 RUTGERS L. REV. 267, 286 (1977).

36. *See* HARPER & JAMES, THE LAW OF TORTS, § 17.3 at 977 (1956); WALTZ & INBAU, MEDICAL JURISPRUDENCE, Ch. 4, at 38 (1971); Morris, *Custom and Negligence,* 42 COLUM. L. REV. 1147, 1163-68 (1942). There are a handful of exceptions to this general rule, most based on The T. J. Hooper, 60 F.2d 737 (2d Cir. 1932), but these cases only tend to prove the general rule, and also demonstrate that ultimately courts must decide what the proper standard should be if innocent third parties are to be protected. *See, e.g.,* Helling v. Carey, 83 Wash. 2d 514, 519 P.2d 981 (1974) (physicians liable for not performing glaucoma test on young woman who subsequently went blind, even though such testing was not standard medical treatment,

because the test was accurate, simple, inexpensive, safe, and detected a serious, arrestable condition). On this case see Note, *Comparative Approaches to Liability for Medical Maloccurrences*, 84 YALE L.J. 1141 (1975).

37. *See, e.g.*, Robertson, *Involuntary Euthanasia of Defective Newborns: A Legal Analysis*, 27 STAN. L. REV. 213 (1975); Commonwealth v. Edelin, 1976 Mass. Adv. Sh. 2795, 359 N.E.2d 4 (1976); and the following language in the *Quinlan* opinion:

> Under the statutes of this State, the unlawful killing of another human being is criminal homicide. . . . [But we] believe, first, that the ensuing death would not be homicide but rather expiration from existing natural causes. Secondly, even if it were to be regarded as homicide, it would not be unlawful.
>
> These conclusions rest upon definitional and constitutional bases. The termination of treatment pursuant to the right of privacy is, within the limitations of this case, *ipso facto* lawful. . . . There is a real, and in this case, determinative distinction between the unlawful taking of the life of another and the ending of artificial life-support systems as a matter of self-determination.

70 N.J. at 51-52, 355 A.2d at 669-70 (1976). *See also* Note, *The Termination of Life-Support Measures and the Law of Murder*, 41 MODERN L. REV. 423 (1978).

38. Mr. Saikewicz died, apparently peacefully, within three months of the original court decision to permit the withholding of chemotherapy, but more than a year before the supreme judicial court issued its opinion justifying this action. There was never a full adjudicatory hearing on the issue of treating Mr. Saikewicz, and all lawyers and physicians who appeared before the lower court argued against treatment. If an attorney had been appointed to argue that treatment was indicated, it seems likely that treatment would have been ordered. On the lower court proceedings, see Kindregan, *The Court as Forum For Life and Death Decisions: Reflections on Procedures for Substituted Consent*, 11 SUFFOLK U. L. REV. 919 (1977).

The testimony supports such a conclusion; it was inexact and was based entirely on the opinions of the physicians involved. The same physician who testified that remissions vary from "two months to thirteen months," for example, also testified that they occur in "forty to fifty percent of treatments," *In re Saikewicz*, No. 45596, Transcript of Proceedings 15 (Mass. Probate Court, Hampshire County May 13, 1976), and that "If we give him the chemotherapy, he will become very sick and if we treat him intensively, then he *might live indefinitely and recover*. Q. You say that he might live indefinitely? A. I am saying for a year or so." *Id.* at 22 (emphasis added). Another physician, who put the probability of a remission at 30 percent, testified, "We gave a great deal of thought to whether he should be treated because it wasn't a straight forward issue. One issue certainly had to be, what was the *quality of his life as we saw it* and how we'd influence this one factor. . . . " *Id.* at 24-25 (emphasis added). Near the close of the testimony, the judge made this observation:

> I had a patient, a patient at the State Hospital who didn't want water, and didn't want food. So the doctors were frightened for without water and without food he would die. They had a hearing such as this and they were asking the Court its permission to allow them to force feed this patient. This must have been about two years ago and the patient is living because they did force feed and gave him water and food by force and he is still alive and happy. In effect, they saved his life or that saved his life. This is a similar type of case, in a way.

Id. at 29. Again, at the close of the testimony, the judge said: "I am inclined to give treatment."
Id at 31. Only unanimous and vigorous objection changed his mind. *Id.* at 33. *See* Baron, *Assuring "Detached but Passionate Investigation and Decision": The Role of Guardians Ad Litem in Saikewicz-type Cases,* 4 AM. J. L. & MED.111, 120-22 (1978).
39. 1977 Mass. Adv. Sh. at 2499, 370 N.E.2d at 434.
40. *Id.* at 2501, 370 N.E.2d at 435.
41. *Id.*
42. *Id.* at 2468, 370 N.E.2d at 421.
43. An alternative way to state the issue from the physician's point of view is: "Can I discontinue treatment without fear of liability for medical malpractice or homicide?" Stated this way, the role of the courts is even clearer, since courts ultimately set and apply the standards for both negligence and criminal liability. No one would think it strange to ask a court whether doing "X" was either a negligent or a criminal act. In essence, it is this question that both courts are being asked. One is able to answer it on the basis of medical prognosis, the other is not.

    An analogous differentiation has been made in the literature concerning the insanity defense. Expert witnesses are generally permitted to testify on what are termed "medical facts" (for example: Did the defendant suffer from a mental disease or disorder? Was he capable of knowing right from wrong?), but not on the ultimate issue of responsibility, which is generally characterized as a "legal standard" to be decided only by the jury. *See, e.g.,* A. GOLDSTEIN, THE INSANITY DEFENSE 97-101 (1967).

    Where, as in *Quinlan,* the "medical facts are determinative and uncontested, there is arguable no need for any judicial review, since the "medical facts" have been formally adopted as a "legal standard" themselves.
44. Professor Charles Baron of Boston College Law School urges the court to insist that a true adversary proceeding take place. Baron, *Assuring "Detached but Passionate Investigation and Decision": The Role of Guardians Ad Litem in Saikewicz-type Cases,* 4 AM. J. L. & MED. 111 (1978).

    The importance of such a judicial hearing is well illustrated by Dr. Relman's assertions about Kerri Ann McNulty. He describes her as a child "born with congenital rubella (German measles) found to be blind, deaf, and seriously mentally defective." Relman, *supra* note 5, at 238. Relman describes this case as "distressing" and an "unhappy example of the *Saike-*

wicz decision." *Id.* at 239.

This case illustrates a type of "eugenic" abuse that may be taking place frequently in the hospitals of Massachusetts. The "medical facts" of the case turned out to be much different than initially characterized. After a full hearing, Judge Henry R. Mayo concluded: "[T]he child has serious medical problems including cataracts on both eyes and perhaps additional eye complications. She appears to be deaf. . . . It is *highly probable* that she has *some degree* of mental retardation, the extent of which cannot yet be determined. . . . [S]he can survive if properly treated. *In re* McNulty, No. 1960, Findings of Fact 3-4 (Mass. Probate Court, Essex County Div. Feb. 15, 1978) (emphasis added). In other words, "blind, deaf, and seriously mentally retarded" are conclusions all of which are at least premature, if not inaccurate. Under such circumstances, how can it ever be in a child's "best interests" to die rather than to live? And the idea of accurately testing the mental ability of an infant who cannot see or hear is ludicrous on its face. Even if such a measurement could be made, however, the decision whether to treat is still a societal rather than a medical one. In this regard the *Saikewicz* decision is clear; it calls for court review anytime one proposes to withhold a standard medical treatment that is potentially life-sustaining from an incompetent under circumstances where a competent patient might choose the treatment. In view of the potential abuses without such review, the remedy does not seem extraordinary. Since there is no crime of not going to court, the remedy is not automatic, and most physicians are likely to continue to make decisions knowing that they may someday face criminal or civil charges as a result (the probability of both being very low), rather than seek a declaratory judgment of the type approved in *Saikewicz*.

Some physicians and lawyers have argued that physicians are worse off if they don't go to court after *Saikewicz*, since the fact that they did not avail themselves of the declaratory judgment route suggested by the court may itself be used as evidence against them in a civil or criminal case. The argument, I take it, is that they must have been acting in "bad faith" or had something to hide since if their actions were ethically sound, they would have gone to court. The answer, I think, is that so long as they fully document the reason for their decision, and call in an appropriate consultant on the medical prognosis issue, the allegation of bad faith can be easily rebutted by demonstrating that all actions were done openly and in accordance with good and accepted medical practice. In this regard, documentation of all orders, both in the patient's progress notes and in the physician's order sheet, signed by the physician and including an explanation for the order given, is recommended. *Cf. Standards for Cardiopulmonary Resuscitation (CPR) and Emergency Cardiac Care (ECC)*, 227 J.A.M.A. (Supp.) 833, 864 (1974).

45. B. CARDOZO, THE NATURE OF THE JUDICIAL PROCESS 135-36 (1921). *See also* Baron. *Medical Paternalism and the Rule of Law: A Response to Dr. Relman*, 4 AM. J. L. & MED. 337 (1979).

46. *See* note 34 *supra*. For a more detailed discussion of the "ethics committee" and the problems it poses, see Collester, *Death, Dying and the Law: A Pro-*

secutorial View of the Quinlan Case, 30 RUTGERS L. REV. 304, 319-20 (1977); Hirsch & Donovan, *The Right to Die: Medico-Legal Implications of In re Quinlan*, 30 RUTGERS L. REV. 267, 273-74, 280-86 (1977).

47. *See* S. LAW & S. POLAN, PAIN AND PROFIT: THE POLITICS OF MALPRACTICE (1978). The authors note that many states have made changes in their laws relating to medical malpractice as a result of heavy lobbying efforts by the medical profession and malpractice insurance companies. *Id.*. at 100. They believe two reasons account for the popularity of such changes: (1) physicians and insurance companies wanted them badly and plaintiffs' lawyers, "who had the most accurate understanding of the practical effects, knew that such changes would not make any significant difference," *id.* at 119; and (2) "reforms which can be accomplished by changing the words of a law . . . are always easier to effect than reforms which require the expenditure of public funds or the creation of an agency to administer them." *Id.* The authors conclude: "[R]evising a legal rule is easy. In this case, it is not likely to help."*Id.*

48. Curran, *Law-Medicine Notes: The Saikewicz Decision*, 298 NEW ENGLAND J. MED. 499 (1978). Professor Curran reaffirmed his views in a reply to letters addressing his initial column:

> The courts have never before been so universally intrusive as to demand that *every decision either to continue or not to continue* life-sustaining medical efforts in mentally incompetent persons must go to court for determination. . . . The issue is clear. The Supreme Judicial Court does not trust any part of the private community except the probate court to decide these matters.

298 NEW ENGLAND J. MED. 1209 (1978) (emphasis added). While the distinction between removal and continuance of treatment is literally true, the decision to continue treatment is trivial insofar as potential liability goes, since the suit would not be for negligence or homicide, but would allege a battery. The physician's defense would be privilege, that is, that he was doing his best to save the patient's life, and the likelihood that he would lose such a suit, so long as he was acting in good faith, approaches zero.

It is, however, possible that some day there will be a successful battery suit by the patient's guardian or the administrator of his or her estate against a physician who continued treatment even though the patient had signed a living will and the patient's guardian had demanded that treatment be halted. A successful suit of this type might be more effective than legislation in encouraging physicians to take "living wills" seriously.

49. *See* Relman, supra note 4, at 508-09.

50. This happened at a major Boston hospital during a time when the patient's care was covered by Medicaid and the intensive care unit was not full. Needless to say, hospital administrators have an economic conflict of interest in such decisions, and should generally have nothing to say about maintaining "hopeless" patients against the wishes of the family and

attending physician. *Cf.* Note, *Euthanasia: The Physician's Liability*, 10 J. MAR. J. PRAC. & PROC. 148 (1976).

51. The Tay-Sachs case was reported to me by a nurse involved in the care of the infant; the Werdnig-Hoffmann's case was written up in the Boston Phoenix, May 23, 1978, at 6-7, and featured on the NBC Today Show on November 16, 1978; the defibrillation case was recounted at a meeting of the alumni of Boston University's Health Care Management Program on May 23, 1978; the pacemaker case was recounted by an attorney who was called in by a medical resident in the hospital for independent legal advice.

52. One such conference was sponsored by the Committee on Disabilities and Health Law of the Personal and Probate Section of the Massachusetts Bar Association at the Harvard School of Public Health on May 13, 1978.

53. While this is a harsh verdict, it is justified by the available evidence. For example, on April 10, 1978, the Newton-Wellesley Hospital adopted as policy the interpretation and suggestions concerning the *Saikewicz* case made by the Boston firm of Ropes & Gray. The hospital's executive director, William C. Christenson, in a cover memorandum addressed to each staff physician, wrote: "We must regretfully advise you that as of April 18, 1978, the Newton-Wellesley Hospital will comply with the law under the so-called 'Saikewicz Decision.' " The memorandum later stated: "We deplore the Court's intrusion into an area which has always been highly private and deeply personal. Historically, the decision has been quietly and compassionately made by the patient and/or family and the physician. Now, the Court has established a cumbersome and expensive procedure which attracts notoriety."

Attached to this memorandum was another directed to the Management Council, Nursing Supervisors, and Head Nurses, and a copy of the hospital legal counsel's interpretation of the *Saikewicz* opinion. Memorandum, Inability or Refusal of Patient to Consent to Life-Saving or Life-Prolonging Treatment. While granting that "the possibility of a doctor or nurse being prosecuted and convicted for withholding life-prolonging treatment, based on prior experience, seems remote," *id.* at 1, the attorney's memo explained how liability could be avoided with certainty. The memorandum first discussed the competent patient: "Perhaps the clearest situation is that a competent patient cannot refuse life-prolonging treatment if she is pregnant and the refusal of treatment will adversely affect the fetus." *Id.* at 2. When asked by Leonard Glantz whether the writers of this memo had considered the implications of *Roe v. Wade* on this issue, a member of the firm replied that they had not.

As to who can be considered a "competent patient," the memo suggested that ability "to comprehend the English language" is a prerequisite, as is the lack of "evidence of prior institutionalization for mental problems." No general definition of competence was suggested. *Id* at 3.

The memorandum summarized the *Saikewicz* case as saying that "Court approval is necessary . . . to withhold treatment when the patient needing medical attention is 'incompetent'." *Id* at 3. The memo then argued that "[i]t is not clear whether the *Saikewicz* procedures apply where a patient is incompetent because he has experienced brain death." *Id.* at 4. This is, of course, the equivalent of saying it is not clear whether physicians have an obligation to treat a corpse, since, months before, the Massachusetts Supreme Judicial Court had accepted an even broader definition of brain death than the Harvard criteria. Commonwealth v. Golston, 1977 Mass. Adv. Sh. 1778, 336 N.E.2d 744 (1977), discussed at note 55 *infra*. (The memorandum quoted from *Golston*, but argued that it is not controlling since it only defined death for the purposes of criminal and not civil liability. *Id.* at 4. The memorandum made the incredible suggestion that if all the Harvard brain death criteria are met, "[t]he next of kin of the patient should be consulted about disconnecting the equipment, and their written consent (including a release from liability) should be obtained." *Id.* at 5. Phrased another way, this policy says that physicians should continue to treat dead people until the family releases them from liability for not treating the corpse.

The hospital's physicians were further urged not to "specify any one event as the date of death" but to note three different times: "the time and date on which the last test establishing brain death was completed, the time and date on which any artificial life support equipment was disconnected and the time and date on which the heartbeat stopped." *Id.* at 5. The attorney did not suggest whether one of these three, or all of them, should be entered on the death certificate.

The memorandum advised not writing an "order not to resuscitate" without a prior court order, and suggested that the *Saikewicz* court requires this. *Id.* at 5. See the discussion of the *Dinnerstein* case, *infra* note 58 and accompanying text, on this point. It is, of course, no accident that Dinnerstein was a patient at the Newton-Wellesley Hospital, and that the hospital was represented by the same firm that wrote this memorandum. The memorandum, which was signed by Ronald B. Schram for Ropes & Gray, concluded by advising that "in some cases" the attending physician and the hospital should be represented by separate legal counsel to "avoid possible conflicts of interest." It finally noted that although legislation is being drafted, "[i]t is unlikely . . . that satisfactory legislation will be approved in the near future." *Id.* at 7.

Similar advice was followed outside of Boston. On June 7, 1978, for example, the medical staff of the Cape Cod Hospital received a memorandum from their chief, William P. Luke, saying: "The hospital attorney has informed us that the recent *Saikowicz [sic]* decision requires that a patient may no longer be 'no coded.'"

54. A similar request in 1957 has led to more than two decades of continuing, and arguably unnecessary, litigation.

In that year the president of Boston's Peter Bent Brigham Hospital asked counsel's opinion "as to the civil and criminal liability of the Hospital and its trustees, officers and employees" if the hospital permitted its physicians to transplant a kidney from a healthy 14-year-old into his dying twin. The lawyers who responded to the letter misunderstood the only case they found on point, Bonner v. Moran, 126 F.2d 121 (D.C. Cir. 1941). While they are in good company in this misunderstanding, a careful reading of the case discloses that it stands for the proposition that if a child *and* his or her parents consent to a procedure that does not provide the minor with any benefits, and, indeed, may cause the child harm, the procedure may be performed. Accordingly, counsel could have answered simply that if the donee understood the nature and consequences of his acts, *and* consented to the donation, *and* the parents consented, the procedure could lawfully be performed. Instead, counsel advised that the parents had no authority to consent to the kidney transplant. Counsel concluded, without case citation, that there was also "a serious danger that the procedure would involve criminal liability." The memorandum is reprinted in KATZ, EXPERIMENTATION WITH HUMAN BEINGS 964-67 (1972). Since *Bonner* was not a Massachusetts case, and was decided before the Nuremberg Code (which set international standards for human experimentation) had been enunciated, it could be argued that counsel correctly decided not to rely on it. But these were not the reasons counsel gave for not relying on the case, nor do they explain his misreading of it. Counsel relied on two Massachusetts cases, Banks v. Conant, 96 Mass. (14 Allen) 497 (1867), and Taylor v. Mechanics' Savings Bank, 97 Mass. 345 (1867), holding that a parent cannot recover money paid to a child upon his voluntary enlistment in the Armed Forces. In dicta, one court said that parents had no authority to force their son to enlist against his wishes, and that the money was paid as an inducement "to undertake a service of an arduous and hazardous nature." 96 Mass. (14 Allen) at 498. None of this contradicts the holding of the *Bonner* case, nor is it inconsistent with the view that the consent of both the minor and the parents is sufficient to avoid liability.

At any rate, the Peter Bent Brigham Hospital had a number of options. It could perform the procedure anyway, relying upon the consent of the minor and his parents; it could refuse to perform the procedure; or it could go to court and seek a declaratory judgment that what it was doing was legal and that the court should so declare and further guarantee that it would be free from civil or criminal liability. The hospital opted for the latter course, and thus began a series of Massachusetts cases which now have covered more than 21 years, in which hospitals and physicians routinely seek immunity for performing surgery on minor donees involved in both kidney transplants and bone marrow transplants.

On children's consent to transplants, see ANNAS, GLANTZ, & KATZ, INFORMED CONSENT TO HUMAN EXPERIMENTATION: THE SUBJECT'S DILEMMA 75-87 (1977); on the bone marrow cases, see Baron, Betsford, & Cole, *Live Organ and Tissue Transplants from Minor Donors in Massachusetts,* 55 B.U.L. REV. 159 (1975).

55. Months before the *Saikewicz* opinion, the supreme judicial court had accepted the following definition of death in a homicide case:

> Brain death occurs when, in the opinion of a licensed physician, based on ordinary and accepted standards of medical practice, there has been a total and irreversible cessation of spontaneous brain func-

tions and further attempts at resuscitation or continued supportive maintenance would not be successful in restoring such functions.

Commonwealth v. Golston, 1977 Mass. Adv. Sh. at 1780-81, 366 N.E.2d 747-48. Thus, when a physician says you're dead under the above criteria, which, as the court noted in *Saikewicz* include the Harvard brain-death criteria, you are dead beyond a reasonable doubt. Therefore, no criminal sanctions can be applied for not treating a brain-dead individual. However, since Golston left open the issue of when death occurs for civil purposes, some lawyers thought that civil immunity required a probate court order. The reason why the court left this issue open, however, is that other considerations, such as a fair distribution of an inheritance, might govern—for example, in a will contest involving simultaneous death, where one spouse had been maintained an additional day on a ventilator and declared brain-dead only thereafter. But *none* of these considerations would affect the physician's duty to treat, since when you're dead beyond a reasonable doubt, you're obviously dead by a preponderance of the evidence. In either event, there is no criminal or civil duty to treat a dead person, and taking such cases to court demonstrates great confusion on the part of the lawyers involved and an incredible fear of potential liability on the part of physicians and hospitals. In my opinion, the courts rightfully refuse to hear these cases. Two such cases are described briefly in Annas, *After Saikewicz: No Fault Death*, HASTINGS CENTER REP., June 1978, at 16, 17.

Nineteen states have adopted new statutory definitions of death, and in August, 1978, the National Conference of Commissioners on Uniform State Laws approved and recommended for enactment in all the states the Uniform Brain Death Act, with the following provision:

> For legal and medical purposes, an individual who has sustained irreversible cessation of all functioning of the brain, including the brain stem, is dead. A determination under this section must be made in accordance with reasonable medical standards.

The comment to the Act notes that it "does not preclude a determination of death under other legal or medical criteria," and that the word "functioning" "expresses the idea of *purposeful* activity." National Conference of Commissioners on Uniform State Laws, Uniform Brain Death Act (July 28-Aug. 4, 1978).

See generally R. VEATCH, DEATH, DYING AND THE BIOLOGICAL REVOLUTION 21-72 (1976); Capron & Kass, *A Statutory Definition of the Standards for Determining Human Death: An Appraisal and a Proposal*, 121 U. PA. L. REV. 87 (1972); Kennedy, *The Kansas Statute on Death—An Appraisal*, 285 NEW ENGLAND J. MED. 946 (1971); Veith, *et al.*, *Brain Death—II. A Status Report of Legal Considerations*, 238 J.A.M.A. 1744 (1977).

56. Most physicians, unfortunately for them and their patients, don't even learn enough law in medical school to do this. The 89th Annual Meeting of the Association of American Medical Colleges included a panel on "legal

medicine" on October 26, 1978, in New Orleans. This was the first time anyone attending this session could recall time being given to this topic at the annual meeting. At the session, Barbara Grumet, of the Albany Medical School's Center for Health Law, reported on the results of her questionnaire survey of 118 medical schools. Of the 99 respondents, 39 claimed at least one such elective. Nevertheless, the coverage and quality of these courses were extremely uneven, with the number of hours ranging from 2 to 80.

At Boston University School of Medicine for the past four years we in the Department of Socio-Medical Sciences and Community Medicine have had a required 16-hour seminar, given near the end of the first year, in "Law and Medicine: The Rights of Patients and Their Providers." The objectives of this seminar are (1) to introduce medical students to basic legal concepts and procedures; (2) to change students' attitudes so that they will view the law as an important tool in their work, rather than as an obstruction; (3) to encourage students to develop patterns of self-education so that they will continue to explore legal issues; and (4) to provide students with enough information so that they will have an idea of how lawyers think and will be able both to spot a legal problem and to determine whom to approach for help in resolving it. *See generally* Annas, *Law and Medicine: Myths and Realities in the Medical School Classroom,* I AM. J. L. & MED. 149 (1975), and articles cited therein.

57. Even though the quest for professional immunity seems almost unending (*but see* Relman, *supra* note 5), it is primarily founded on ignorance and fear rather than knowledge and acceptance of professional responsibility. For example, while no physician has ever been successfully sued for stopping and rendering aid to a person experiencing a medical emergency, nervous medical societies have gotten all 50 states to pass statutes immunizing physicians against suit for negligence if they do stop. Even after some of these statutes were passed, the AMA reported that only half of the physicians surveyed in 1963 said they would stop, and the response rate was unaffected by whether the state had adopted a Good Samaritan statute. RE-PORT OF THE SECRETARY'S COMMISSION ON MEDICAL MALPRACTICE, HEW PUB. NO. (OS)73-88, at 16 (1973). Similarly, in cases of medical staff discipline and reporting incompetent physicians to state licensing boards, physicians have demanded immunity from defamation suits, although almost no lawsuits have been filed in such cases. Further, the passage of these immunity statutes has not had a noticeable effect on physician disciplinary proceedings or on physicians' reporting of their colleagues to licensing authorities, recent AMA assertions to the contrary notwithstanding. *See, e.g.,* AMA IMPAIRED PHYSICIAN NEWSLETTER. Dec. 1978, at 3.

Granting physicians immunity for the performance of their professional duties should almost always be seen as against public policy. Either physicians are acting as physicians—that is, treating and diagnosing patients according to their own professional ethics and "accepted medical practice"—or they are acting as nonphysicians and making decisions on some social policy grounds. If they are acting as physicians, they should be held accountable for their actions as physicians. Granting immunity in such cases is completely inappropriate, since it denies innocent potential victims compensation and encourages negligence. On the other hand, if physicians are engaged in making social policy decisions, it is even more counterproductive to grant them immunity, because with immunity they will be free to act without either knowledge or responsibility. *See* Annas, *After Saikewicz: No Fault Death*, HASTINGS CENTER REP., June 1978, at 16.

Professor Robert Burt argues analogously that courts should not consider granting declaratory judgment in cases involving nontreatment of defective newborns, because only by putting both parents and physicians in some personal jeopardy can we insure that their actions are likely to be fair to the child involved:

> The true enormity of these actions to withhold life from newborns, viewed from our contemporary perspective, will remain in high visibility only if *advance social authorization is withheld*, and only if the parents and physicians who wish to take this action are willing to *accept some significant risk* that they will suffer by such action. Their suffering will come in increasing intensity if criminal prosecution is instituted, if a jury finds them guilty of unconscionable conduct and if a judge imposes sanctions on them accordingly. In deciding whether to withhold treatment from the newborn, the parents and physicians will be led to balance the suffering imposed on them by the continued life of the child against the suffering likely from their decision to end the child's life.

Burt, *Authorizing Death for Anomalous Newborns*, in GENETICS AND THE LAW 435, 444 (A. Milunsky and G. Annas eds. 1976)(emphasis added). *Accord, In re* Nemser, 51 Misc. 2d 616, 273 N.Y.S.2d 624 (Sup. Ct. 1966)(petition for guardian to consent to treatment denied on basis that decision was a medical one for which immunity was inappropriate). *See also* Spencer, *"Code" or "No Code": A Nonlegal Opinion*, 300 NEW ENGLAND J. MED. 138 (1979)("Sounding Board"), which argues, "As physicians we have an obligation to keep our priorities straight: to do always what we consider to be in the best interests of our patients and in keeping with our moral and ethical precepts." *Id.* at 140.

58. *In re* Dinnerstein, 1978 Mass. App. Adv. Sh. 736, 380 N.E.2d 134 (1978). In the court's words:

> The judge's findings make it clear that the case is hopeless. . . . Attempts to apply resuscitation, if successful, will do nothing to cure or relieve the illnesses. . . . The case does not, therefore, present the type of significant treatment choice or election which, in light of sound medical advice, is to be made by the patient, if competent to do so. . . . This case does not offer a life-saving or life-prolonging treatment alternative within the meaning of the *Saikewicz* case.

Id. at 746, 380 N.E.2d at 138-39. The Executive Director of the hospital involved—Newton-Wellesley—described the role of his hospital in the

Dinnerstein case: "We took leadership in resolving the ambiguities surrounding the state Supreme Court's decision in the Saikewicz [*sic*] case and *obtained a ruling that restored the right of patients to die in peace."* Christenson, *1977-78: A Special Year,* NEWTON-WELLESLEY QUARTERLY Dec. 1978, at 18 (emphasis added). *See also* note 53 *supra.*

59. LAW & POLAN, *supra* note 47, at 116.

60. *See* note 53 *supra.*

61. Schram, Kane, & Roble, *"No Code" Orders: Clarification in the Aftermath of Saikewicz,* 299 NEW ENGLAND J. MED. 875, 877 (1978)("Law-Medicine Notes"). One reason the *Dinnerstein* case even merited mention in *The New England Journal of Medicine* is because of the confusion generated by previous articles and letters in the *Journal* itself. As the *Dinnerstein* court noted, citing two such pieces, its opinion was seen to be necessary by the plaintiffs because *Saikewicz*

> has been *interpreted by some in the medical profession* as casting doubt upon the lawfulness of an order not to attempt resuscitation of an incompetent, terminally ill patient except where the entry of such an order has been previously determined by a Probate Court to be in the best interests of the patient.

1978 Mass. App. Adv. Sh. at 740-41, 380 N.E.2d at 136 (emphasis added). At one point Schram, Kane, and Roble argue that the consent of the "immediate family should be sufficient" in "no code" situations, and cite two cases, Belger v. Arnot, 344 Mass 679, 183 N.E.2d 866 (1962), and Reddington v. Clayman, 334 Mass. 244, 134 N.E.2d 920 (1946), for that proposition. Schram, *et al., supra,* at 876. Neither of these cases has *anything* to do with a terminally ill patient; *Reddington* involved the consent of a father to have his daughter's tonsils removed, and *Belger* involved the involuntary commitment of a wife to a mental institution under a procedure that has since been changed by statute. At another point in the article the authors string together three cases, *In re* Custody of a Minor, 1978 Mass. Adv. Sh. 2002, 379 N.E.2d 1053 (1978), Commonwealth v. Golston, 1977 Mass. Adv. Sh. 2002, 379 N.E.2d 1053 (1978), Commonwealth v. Golston, 1977 Mass. Adv. Sh.1778, 336 N.E.2d 744 (1977), and *In re* Dinnerstein, 2978 Mass. App. Adv. Sh. 736, 380 N.E.2d 134 (1978), which they assert stand for the proposition that it might be permissible for "a competent patient who is not irreversibly, terminally ill . . . to refuse resuscitation measures whenever his decision would, in the judgment of a competent and reasonable physician, be consistent with 'good medical practice'." Schram, *et al., supra,* at 876. *None* of the three cases cited involved a competent patient (*Golston* was a murder case, *Custody of a Minor* involved a two-year-old child, and the other case was *Dinnerstein* itself). It is, of course, not competent patients, but competent physicians who are legally required to make decisions consistent with "good medical practice."

62. Sanders, *Medical Technology: Who's to Say When We've Had Enough,* HOSPITALS, Nov. 16, 1978, at 66, 68. It is, of course, *Saikewicz* which continues to be the only "final authority" in Massachusetts, any reading of *Dinnerstein*

to the contrary notwithstanding.

63. *See, e.g.,* R. DWORKIN, TAKING RIGHTS SERIOUSLY 205 (1978):

> The bulk of the law—that part which defines and implements social, economic, and foreign policy—cannot be neutral. It must state, in its greatest part, the majority's view of the common good. The institution of rights is therefore crucial, because it represents the majority's promise to the minorities that their dignity and equality will be respected. When the divisions among the groups are most violent, then this gesture, if law is to work, must be most sincere.
>
> . . . [Taking rights seriously is] the one feature that distinguishes law from ordered brutality.

64. Solzhenitsyn, *The Exhausted West,* HARVARD MAGAZINE, July/Aug. 1978, at 22.

65. This is not to say that society will soon, or ever, agree on a way to make all treatment decisions for the incompetent terminally ill patient. Indeed, since it is often a choice between death and continued suffering, the choice can be characterized as a "tragic choice," and as such one that can be made only by sacrificing or seeming to sacrifice, one or more societal values for others (for example, the universal sanctity of human life versus self-determination). In such situations one often sees a transfer of decision-making authority from one group to another or from one forum to another, as specific societal values are threatened. An "*a*responsible" agency such as a jury or an ethics committee, for example, will be chosen to apply societal standards but not required to articulate them either because such an articulation would destroy their effectiveness (as when a decision not to treat is based on the fact that the patient is mentally retarded), or because the values on which the decision seems to be based do not exist (for example, all persons must be treated equally). The attractiveness of "para-juries" has led to their adoption in such settings as human experimentation (Institutional Review Boards) and kidney dialysis. However, when a para-jury sits on more than one case, a pattern of decision making either develops or it does not. If it does, the pattern can be articulated and applied without using the para-jury. If it does not, the para-jury is open to the challenge of arbitrariness, and a lottery, or first-come-first-served method, may prove a fairer and more efficient method of allocating scarce medical resources.

These problems were illustrated in Furman v. Georgia, 408 U.S. 238 (1972), in which the majority's attack on the discretionary power of juries in capital punishment cases was based both on the perception of the intolerable discrimination on the one hand, and the notion that the almost random manner in which the death sentence was being imposed constituted cruel and unusual punishment on the other. A judge may be a better decision maker than a para-jury concerning whether to treat a terminally ill incompetent patient, because the element of process in a judicial proceeding— for example, representation of the patient, required articulation of the reasons for the decision, and the opportunity to appeal— are superior to those in a para-jury proceeding. Nevertheless, it may be that when treatment is advocated, judges will always require it, and this method might have to be abandoned for another, if society determines that the financial expenditures for these patients cannot be justified. The point is that decisions *must* be made, and each method of making a "tragic choice" will necessarily involve major problems which will bring societal values into conflict. Recognizing this, our task is to develop that method of conflict resolution which reaches fair and just decisions as often as possible without destroying important societal values. *See* G. CALABRESI & P. BOBBIT, TRAG-IC CHOICES (1978). *See also* Havighurst, Blumstein, & Bovbjerg, *Strategies in Underwriting the Costs of Catastrophic Disease*, 40 L. & CONTEMP. PROB., Autumn 1976, at 122, 178-95, in which the authors suggest ways in which structuring financing mechanisms for catastrophic diseases may aid in private decision making. *See also,* on the issue of public policy and decision making for the catastrophically ill. J. KATZ & A. CAPRON, CATASTRO-PHIC DISEASES: WHO DECIDES WHAT? (1975); Annas, *Allocation of Artificial Hearts on the Year 2002: Minerva v. National Health Agency,* 3 AM. J. L. & MED. 59 (1977).

Chapter 6

Brain Death and the Persistent Vegetative State

Ronald E. Cranford

This article addresses some of the major medical and ethical aspects of brain death and the persistent vegetative state. It does not discuss the terminally ill patient, but rather the patient who is brain dead or in a persistent vegetative state, neither of whom is terminally ill according to the traditional meaning of the term. Hopelessly ill would be a more appropriate term for such patients. In my view, the problems of treating a patient with severe brain damage are more complex and more significant than the dilemmas posed by the terminally ill patient.

With recent advances in medical therapy, such as cardiopulmonary resuscitation, intubation, defibrillation, antiarrhythmic drugs and a wide variety of newer technologies, we are saving a large number of lives. Yet this new technology poses dilemmas. On the one hand, many patients now survive and leave the hospital without brain damage; yet, as a necessary and inevitable sequelae of these life-saving technologies, we are producing patients with syndromes of severe, irreversible brain damage. The dilemma in an acute care situation is, of course, that it is often difficult to predict the extent and reversibility of brain damage when a person is first admitted to the stabilization room. When patients have the potential for partial or complete recovery of brain functions, vigorous medical support is indicated. After a few days or weeks of medical support, however, it may become apparent that the patient has indeed suffered irreversible brain damage. It is at this point that the question arises: when is it morally justifiable to consider withholding or withdrawing life-support systems?

MEDICAL DEFINITION OF THE PERSISTENT VEGETATIVE STATE

Turning our attention to the persistent vegetative state, it should be noted that Karen Ann Quinlan is probably the best known example of a patient in such a condition. As I understand the case, Brother Fox of New York was also in a persistent vegetative state. A patient in this state has an irreversible cessation of the cognitive or higher cortical functions of the brain. Autopsy studies in these cases may show scattered brain damage, but the brunt of the destruction is to the cerebral cortex, or what is called the neocortex. The majority of these cases, unlike those involving brain death, are related to a cardiac or respiratory arrest, which leads to systemic hypotension (low blood pressure) and/or hypoxia (lack of oxygen) which, in turn, causes a transient decrease in either blood flow to the brain or in the amount of oxygen in the blood to the brain. The area of the brain most sensitive to a lack of oxygen or blood is the neocortex. If there is a total lack of oxygen or blood to the brain for four to six minutes, then fairly severe destruction of the neocortex results. The brainstem, on the other hand, is relatively resistent to hypoxia and, in general, it takes 15 to 20 minutes of total hypotension to cause destruction of the entire brain. So, in Quinlan-type situations, the higher centers are essentially destroyed, but the lower centers, which are relatively resistent to the lack of blood or oxygen, usually recover.

There is no great mystery concerning what happened to Karen Ann Quinlan. She had taken excessive amounts of medication and alcohol and subsequently suffered a respiratory arrest because of brainstem depression. Although she was resuscitated, she suffered brain damage secondary to the respiratory arrest, primarily destruction of the neocortex.

The clinical appearance of patients in a persistent vegetative state is very different from patients who are brain dead. Patients in a persistent vegetative state are awake but unaware. Thus, it is inaccurate to describe them as being in a comatose state. This distinction in medical terminology has significant ethical implications. For example, Ms. Quinlan's state more closely resembles dementia, and, in fact, her condition is probably the most profound dementia known to man, where the destruction of the neocortex occurs within four to six minutes. Yet, patients like Ms. Quinlan are awake. Their eyes are open, and they may have visual tracking movements. They go through sleep/wake cycles, albeit they may not be normal sleep/wake cycles. There may be facial grimacing and yawning. There may be spontaneous but involuntary movements, and brainstem reflexes are usually intact. Thus, it is more medically accurate to say that a patient in a persistent vegetative state resembles a patient who is demented rather than one who is comatose.

Patients in the persistent vegetative state are usually respirator-dependent for anywhere from a few days to a few weeks. The majority of such patients are no longer respirator-dependent after that point, and the question arises as to the management of medical complications, such as pulmonary or infectious problems. After the initial few days or few weeks, most patients do not require intensive medical management. Survival may be prolonged. Ms. Quinlan has been in this condition since April 15, 1975. The longest case of a patient in a persistent vegetative state is from Florida, where a woman existed for 37 years, 3 months and 30 days, and died at the age of 43, after she had suffered complications of an appendectomy at the age of six years. There are now reports of survivors in a persistent vegetative state for two, five, and ten years. Not only will there be more patients in a condition like Ms. Quinlan's, but there will also be more patients with prolonged survival.

Diagnosis of the persistent vegetative state can usually be made within three to six months, often sooner. The physician may have an idea at the beginning that a patient will end up with severe brain damage, but he or she cannot be certain of this for at least a few weeks or longer. Often these patients will have to be periodically reexamined to see if they have any conscious interaction whatsoever with the environment.

There are medical syndromes of severe brain damage that fall between the persistent vegetative state and brain death. The *Benjamin C.* case provides an example of this.[2] As I understand the case, Benjamin C. was not truly in the persistent vegetative state because he was still in a coma and respirator-dependent, a condition resulting from a primary brainstem injury.

MEDICAL ASPECTS OF BRAIN DEATH

There are several important medical differences between brain death and the persistent vegetative state. Brain death is defined as the irreversible cessation of all functions of the entire brain.[3] Autopsies of brain dead persons confirm that there is destruction of the entire brain, both the cerebral hemispheres and the brainstem. It is important to understand the sequence of events that occurs in most cases of brain death in order to distinguish it from the persistent vegetative state. Whatever the primary insult to the brain—head trauma, gunshot wound, or severe hemorrhage—the sequence of pathophysiologic events is the same. The primary insult leads to the development of cerebral edema or brain swelling, and then to a massive increase in intracranial pressure. The brain is encased in a closed cavity, the skull, and thus the cerebral edema markedly builds up intracranial pressure. In the overwhelming majority of brain death cases, the intracranial pressure exceeds the systolic blood pressure within a period of 12 to 24 hours. Thus as a secondary phenomenon, within the first day or two after the primary insult, there is a cessation of blood flow to the entire brain, including the brainstem.

Clinical examination of these patients shows that they are in a coma, the deepest possible coma, and that there are no movements, either voluntary or involuntary, at the cerebral hemisphere or brainstem level. Spinal segmental reflexes may still occur because the spinal cord has a separate circulation. Even though the increased intracranial pressure causes a loss of blood flow to the entire brain, there may still be normal blood circulation to the spinal cord, so that some braindead patients have active spinal segmental reflexes. There are, however, no brainstem reflexes, and patients have fixed, dilated pupils.

The medical treatment of these patients is total respiratory support and intensive medical management to support the heart and lungs. Survival, in terms of continued cardiac functioning, is limited, even with maximal treatment. At my hospital, the Hennepin County Medical Center, twenty-five percent of the patients diagnosed as braindead will experience a cardiac arrest from which they are not resuscitated during the period of evaluation used to confirm that they are brain dead and before the final pronouncement of death. While prolonged survival in these cases is rare, there are instances where the brain dead person has survived for six to eight weeks, especially if the person is a child.

Because of the sequence of events described above, with a permanent loss of blood flow to the entire brain, an accurate brain death determination can be made within a reasonably short period of time. Today, a neurologist, a neurosurgeon or someone competent in neurologic diagnosis can reach a diagnosis of total cessation of brain functions within a period of hours to days with an extraordinarily high degree of certainty.

HISTORY OF BRAIN DEATH LEGISLATION

Ten to fifteen years ago, physicians and others began to advocate that, when a person has suffered from whole brain death, the person was in effect dead. It is becoming increasingly recognized in society that the death of the brain does signify the death of the person. This position has now been recognized in 26 states through statutory recognition, and three states through state supreme court decisions (Colorado, Arizona and Massachusetts).[4]

I have listed below three model acts which have been adopted in some states: the American Bar Association model from February 1975; the Uniform Brain Death Act sponsored by the National Conference of Commissioners on Uniform State Laws from August 1978; and the American Medical Association model of December 1979. The models illustrate how relatively simple a brain death statute can be and the similarities among these various models.

AMERICAN BAR ASSOCIATION (ABA)

For all legal purposes, a human body with irreversible cessation of total brain function, according to the usual and customary standards of medical practice, shall be considered dead.

NATIONAL CONFERENCE OF COMMISSIONERS ON UNIFORM STATE LAWS (NCCUSL)

Section I. For legal and medical purposes, an individual who has sustained irreversible cessation of all functioning of the brain, including the brain stem, is dead. A determination under this section must be made in accordance with reasonable medical standards.

AMERICAN MEDICAL ASSOCIATION (AMA)

Section I. An individual who has sustained (1) irreversible cessation of circulatory and respiratory functions, or (2) irreversible cessation of functions of the entire brain, shall be considered dead. A determination of death shall be made in accordance with accepted medical standards.

On May 23, 1980, one month after the Los Angeles conference, representatives of the ABA, AMA, and NCCUSL met in Chicago and drafted the Uniform Determination of Death Act (UDDA), a composite of the model acts endorsed by each of the organizations. Since that meeting, the UDDA has been formally endorsed by all three organizations as well as by the President's Commission for the Study of Ethical Problems in Medicine and Biomedical and Behavioral Research, the American Academy of Neurology, and the American Encephalographers Society. The UDDA reads as follows:

An individual who has sustained either (1) irreversible cessation of circulatory and respiratory functions or (2) irreversible cessation of all functions of the entire brain, including the brain stem, is dead. A determination of death must be made in accordance with accepted medical standards.

The drafting and acceptance of the UDDA signifies an important landmark in the ten-year history of brain death legislation, indicating an emerging consensus that there is a definite need for uniform legislation in this area and that it is possible to draft a model act acceptable to lawyers, physicians, and legislators.

I will not discuss all the errors, major or minor, made in legislation on brain death, but two of the more prominent errors require comment. First, if we accept brain death, using a whole brain death standard, it should apply for all purposes. In other words, persons should not be considered dead on the basis of brain death for some reasons and not for others. Two states, Georgia and Oregon, have passed brain death statutes which are permissive in nature. In other words, they say that a person *may* be pronounced dead when his or her brain is dead.

The other mistake restricts the applicability of the brain death standard. At least three other states have enacted the brain death definition as part of the Uniform Anatomical Gift Act (Illinois, Virginia, and Connecticut). As a result, people who are brain dead in these states are only legally dead if they are candidates for organ donation. This incongruity was recognized by commentators on a situation in Illinois involving the removal of life-support measures from a tragically injured youth who was brain dead.[5] Since the parents agreed to donate the boy's organs, the respirator was allowed to be disconnected. If the parents had refused to donate the organs, the legality of the withdrawal of treatment would have been unclear. In West Virginia, the brain death definition was originally amended to the Uniform Anatomical Gift Act, but it has now been placed into a separate, independent section.

CRITERIA FOR DETERMINING BRAIN DEATH

Under existing legislation, the term brain death refers only to whole brain death, not partial brain death or cerebral death. Unfortunately, many neurologists and neurosurgeons equate cerebral death with whole brain death. However whole brain death is significantly different from cerebral death, the persistent vegetative state, and neocortical death. I use the term neocortical death as a subcategory of the persistent vegetative state. A patient in the persistent vegetative state may be awake but totally unaware. There is no conscious interaction with the environment and no awareness of self or environment. I use the term neocortical death, however, to denote a patient who is in a persistent vegetative state clinically and who also has a flat EEG. I have seen two patients who are in a persistent vegetative state, who were awake and looking around, who went through sleep/wake cycles, and who also had flat EEGs that satisfied the requirements for electrocerebral silence. The first case in which a patient was allowed to die in Minnesota involved a case of neocortical death.[6]

The current debate centers on whether the death of the neocortex is sufficient to signify the death of the person. In my opinion, this argument will not prevail, now or in the forseeable future. Thus far, no state has passed any law legitimizing the view that the death of the neocortex signifies the death of the person. The major problem for the next five to ten years will, in my opinion, be an ethical debate on the appropriate management of patients who are neocortically dead or in a persistent vegetative state.

The established medical criteria for brain death around the country reflect the whole brain death concept. Probably the most familiar are the Harvard criteria published in 1968.[7] In 1976, the Minnesota Medical Association formulated and sponsored legislation to legalize the concept of brain death, which was defined as the irreversible cessation of the functions of the entire brain.[8] At the same time, an attempt was made to distinguish between what should be legalized through statutory recognition and what should be adopted by the medical profession as a standard of practice. Specific medical criteria were developed for the determination of brain death and were adopted by the Minnesota Medical Association in 1976 as the accepted medical standards for that state. In developing these standards, some minor shortcomings were recognized in the Harvard criteria, and the Minnesota criteria sought to correct these errors. One of the shortcomings involves the ambiguity of the importance of spinal segmental reflexes in determining brain death. The original Harvard criteria can be interpreted as saying that all reflexes, including spinal segmental reflexes, should be gone; however, as explained earlier, spinal reflexes can be observed in patients who are whole brain dead.

In the second brain death case presented to the Minnesota courts, a four-year-old child did not fit the Harvard criteria, but did fit the Minnesota criteria.[9] This child had spinal cord reflexes which became increasingly active as she was maintained on a respirator. The court, in addition to recognizing the validity of the concept of brain death, recognized the standards of the Minnesota Medical Association for the determination of brain death.

Distinguishing between essential criteria and confirmatory criteria in determining brain death is another area which has created a tremendous amount of confusion. In my view, the essential criteria are:

1) cessation of cerebral hemisphere functions;
2) cessation of brainstem functions (pupils mid-position and unreactive to light, absent oculo-cephalic and oculo-vestibular responses; loss of spontaneous respiration); and

3) establishment of irreversibility.

To make a diagnosis of brain death, the physician not only needs to establish the cessation of functions of the cerebral hemispheres and brain stem but also needs to establish irreversibility with an extraordinarily high degree of certainty. It takes five to ten minutes for a neurologist or neurosurgeon to examine a patient and to say that there are no brain functions present. That is relatively simple. However, it may take anywhere from a few hours to several days for the physician to be able to say that the cessation of brain functions is irreversible.

Any patient who is pronounced dead on the basis of brain death must meet the essential criteria. Confirmatory criteria, such as an EEG or a cerebral blood flow study, may be useful in many cases, but are not essential. The Minnesota standards clearly state that the essential criteria are clinical, and that the use and application of the confirmatory tests are the responsibility and judgment of the attending physician and are not mandatory in all cases. The basic diagnosis of brain death is similar to the basic diagnosis of cardiorespiratory death—a clinical diagnosis based upon the bedside examination. If the clinician is uncertain of the clinical criteria for whatever reasons, then confirmatory criteria should be employed.

Nevertheless, some courts and legislatures are confused about the role of confirmatory criteria, and especially the electroencephalogram (EEG) in establishing brain death. In fact, some neurologists and neurosurgeons advocate that the EEG should be essential in many cases. While the EEG is an objective documentation of what is going on, there are a number of technical difficulties that arise when trying to obtain one for electrocerebral silence. At the Hennepin County Medical Center, the EEG is rarely used. When the need arises for confirmatory studies, a cerebral blood flow study is requested since the blood flow ceases in the majority of brain death cases. To do a cerebral blood flow study, we use a portable gamma camera at the bedside of the patient. Within ten or fifteen minutes after an intravenous injection of radioactive material, it can be determined whether there is cessation of blood flow to the brain, thereby establishing and documenting irreversibility. This is particularly helpful in drug intoxication cases. Prior to our use of the gamma camera, in some cases we would have to wait several days (while drugs are metabolized by the body) before establishing irreversibility. Now, even with therapeutic drug levels, we can diagnose brain death by establishing the cessation of brain functions and by establishing irreversibility through the use of the gamma camera.

As to the period of observation or evaluation, there is no magic number of hours. It is variable: the Harvard criteria suggest 24 hours; the

Minnesota criteria state 12 hours. During the period of evaluation, one determines whether there has been an irreversible cessation of brain functions. Therefore, the duration of the period of observation is not nearly as important as what is done during this period.

PHYSICIANS' ROLE

Where brain death statutes exist, the pronouncement of brain death is mandatory, not permissive. If society accepts the view that the death of the brain signifies the death of the person, then the physician is morally, medically, and legally obligated to pronounce a person dead once he or she has experienced brain death. Therefore, the principles of self-determination, informed consent, and consent of the family are not medically or legally relevant to the pronouncement of death. In theory, I agree with this view. In practice, however, I will not pronounce a person brain dead until I have discussed the situation with the family to determine if they have any objections, concerns, or reservations. If the family has any reservations, I will make every reasonable attempt to satisfy them before I pronounce the person brain dead. This presents a dilemma. On the one hand, I am obligated to pronounce a person dead; on the other hand, I am reluctant to do so, for humanitarian reasons, until I make every effort to discuss the case with the family and am certain that they can accept the concept.

DETERMINATION OF TIME OF DEATH

The question as to what should be written on the death certificate concerning the time of death is frequently encountered. The exact time of death may seem minor and unimportant, but in certain situations it may have great legal significance, be it brain death or cardiorespiratory death. For example the moment of death determines such questions as:

When may an estate be probated?

When does a life estate in property end?

When does property pass to a surviving joint tenant?

When do life insurance benefits become payable or health insurance benefits cease?

When are estate taxes due?

In the event that persons having interests in each other's estates perish in a common disaster, who died first?

Recently there has been a tendency toward recognizing the first observation of brain function cessation as the official time of death, no matter when death is actually pronounced. While death may be pronounced after the second, confirmatory examination, the time of death is at the first examination. For example, under the New Mexico statute, death has occurred "when the absence of spontaneous brain function first occurred." This occurs when the first observation of all the criteria is made and not at any reevaluation. Likewise, under the Minnesota criteria, the time of death is the time "when the absence of brain functions was first noted."

But under the Kansas statute, the time of death occurs when the two statutory conditions "first coincide," *i.e.*, when we have brain death and a determination that further attempts at resuscitation or supportive maintenance will not succeed. This would seem to occur upon retesting after some period of time has elapsed.

Thus far, the exact time of death has not been at issue in a legal proceeding; for example in *Golston*,[10] the court simply ignored the exact time of death, finding it necessary to determine only that death occurred prior to the withdrawal of the respirator, even though there was conflicting testimony concerning the exact time of death.

WITHDRAWING TREATMENT AND PVS

In persistent vegetative state cases, the basic medical diagnosis, prognosis, and degree of certainty are primarily clinical. Ethicists, lawyers, and judges, to a certain extent, want objective documentation, which, unfortunately, is not available. People have unduly focused on the EEG because it provides objective documentation—you can *see* the flat line. But as stated earlier, the majority of patients in the persistent vegetative state do not have flat EEGs. At the present time, there is no single laboratory test which confirms the basic diagnosis of PVS with any degree of certainty. The diagnosis is essentially a clinical one based on the history, the underlying etiology, and the clinical examination of the patient. At the point that one is faced with the decision to terminate support, the degree of certainty becomes a moral and legal issue. In the cases that have reached the courts, this degree of certainty has become crucial.

What do we mean by prognosis? Prognosis for what? In cases of the persistent vegetative state, the prognosis is for awareness and conscious interaction with the environment—that is, personal human life at the cerebral cortical level, not biological human life at the cardiorespiratory level.

The continuum of medical treatment that is involved in the care of such a patient can be placed into four major categories. The first could be labelled technology. Treatment modalities in this category are expensive, invasive, and involve an allocation of scarce resources—for example, respirators, pacemakers, heart–lung machines, dialysis. The second major category is medication—for example, antibiotics, vasopressors, digitalis, and insulin. The third major category is fluids and nutrition; and the fourth would be the treatment of hygiene, pain, suffering, discomfort, warmth, dignity, and respect for the person and the body.

The critical question in the decision to discontinue medical treatment of a patient in the persistent vegetative state is where the line is drawn. Some courts have incorrectly focused on the respirator. The courts and others have focused upon the distinction between ordinary and extraordinary treatment, but I agree with Professor Veatch that these terms may not be the most appropriate. Some of the other terms that can be used include beneficial and nonbeneficial, reasonable and unreasonable, useful and useless, appropriate and inappropriate.[11] Since people generally use the terms ordinary and extraordinary and they have an extensive history of use, I will use them in this presentation to apply to cases of PVS.

It seems to me that the primary distinction between ordinary and extraordinary is not a medical determination, nor a question of how much something is used, nor of how common it is. It seems to me that in *Quinlan*-type situations, the distinction between ordinary and extraordinary primarily turns on the potential of benefit to the patient as a whole. This is the caring concept, not the curing concept. It is the condition of the patient that is extraordinary, not the specific type of medical treatment. It is not the respirator nor the antibiotics that are extraordinary, rather it is the condition of Karen Ann Quinlan that is extraordinary. This distinction between ordinary and extraordinary, patient-oriented, rather than treatment-oriented, revolves around whether the treatment will be beneficial to the patient as a whole. If one assumes the primacy of benefit to the patient, then it seems to me that there is no significant moral distinction between withholding antibiotics when pneumonia develops and deciding to withdraw the respirator. They are morally equivalent because neither antibiotics nor the respirator will benefit the individual if she or he is in the persistent vegetative state.

Additionally, in my opinion, there is no significant moral distinction between withholding or withdrawing support. This is an extremely common misconception among medical practitioners, and one which physicians face daily. If all other circumstances are the same, the decision to withdraw and the decision to withhold in the first place are morally equivalent. I am speaking in particular about patients with severe brain damage whom we resuscitate only because we do not know the extent of brain damage. A terminally ill patient with cancer is a different story because one can more readily predict what is going to happen.

One consideration relative to the distinction between withholding and withdrawing is that the withdrawal is more apparent— that is, more culpable. This distinction is false, however, because it is based on a rather shaky premise: it's only wrong if you get caught. The action to withdraw a respirator is no more morally justifiable or unjustifiable than a decision to withdraw antibiotics. Both the law and ethicists recognize that an action is not right or wrong per se. One must examine the intentions and motivations of all concerned, the nature of the act itself, and the consequences, both short-and long-term.

Clinically, however, we must also consider that families and many medical professionals draw a psychological or emotional distinction between withdrawing and withholding treatment. As long as the distinction is recognized as a psychological or an emotional one, then it becomes, in a way, morally relevant.

Another objection to the moral equivalence of withholding and withdrawing treatment is that once treatment is initiated, there is an obligation to continue. This is morally and legally fallacious. No special duty attaches once care of a patient has been initiated. Rather, the same duties arise in both situations: the duty to meet the appropriate medical standards of medical care and the duty to do what is in the best interest of the patient.

CONCLUSION

Concepts such as the sanctity and the quality of life are often mentioned in discussions of these issues. On this point, I believe that there are two types of quality of life—intrapersonal and interpersonal. Intrapersonal quality of life refers to the meaning of life to that individual. People make quality of life decisions all the time which are presumably intrapersonal. Interpersonal quality of life, however, refers to the value of that individual to society—a social worth criterion. The distinction must be understood before the concept of quality of life can be properly applied.

Progress has been made in reaching a consensus concerning the definition of whole brain death, and in addressing the issue of the appropriate management of patients in the persistent vegetative state. But where do we draw the line in terms of the spectrum of brain damage? What will we do, or should we do, with patients who are quadriplegic? Hemiplegic? Quadriplegic and respirator dependent? Aphasic? We will not be able to avoid these questions in the next few years, especially as society's resources become limited and the application of those resources receives closer scrutiny.

Finally, it seems to me that the development of case law, whether one likes it or not, is inevitable, and ultimately there will be legislation in this area. These situations will become more prevalent and very difficult. The issues of withholding or withdrawing treatment will be even more complex than determining brain death, and especially complex will be the issues surrounding the defective newborn.

I will finish with one of the key statements from *Quinlan* which discusses the limits of self-determination and compelling state interests. In this quotation, the court is drawing lines along the continuum discussed throughout this book.

> The claimed interests of the State in this case are essentially the preservation and sanctity of human life and defense to the right of the physician to administer medical treatment according to his best judgment. . . . We think that the State's interest *contra* weakens and the individual's right to privacy grows as the degree of bodily invasion increases and the prognosis dims. Ultimately, there comes a point at which the individual's right overcomes the State interest.[12]

NOTES

1. Cranford, R.E., Smith, H.L., *Some Critical Distinctions Between Brain Death and the Persistent Vegetative State*, ETHICS IN SCIENCE & MEDICINE 6:199-209 (1979).

2. *In re Benjamin C.*, No. J914419 (Super. Ct. of Cal., Los Angeles County, February 15, 1979).

3. For a general discussion, *see* Black, P. McL, *Brain Death*, NEW ENGLAND JOURNAL OF MEDICINE (part one) 299(7):338-44, (part two) 299(8): 393-401 (August 1978); and Veith, F.J., *et al.*, *Brain Death*, JOURNAL OF THE AMERICAN MEDICAL ASSOCIATION (part one) 238(15):1651-55, (part two) 238(16):1744-48 (October 1977).

4. *Commonwealth v. Golston*, 366 N.E.2d 744 (Mass. 1977); *Lovato v. District Court*, 601 P.2d 1072 (Colo. 1979); *Arizona v. Fierro*, 603 P.2d 74 (Ariz. 1979). Brain death statutes have been adopted by the following states: Alabama, Alaska, Arkansas, California, Connecticut, Florida, Georgia, Hawaii, Idaho, Illinois, Iowa, Kansas, Louisiana, Maryland, Michigan, Montana, Nevada, New Mexico, North Carolina, Oklahoma, Oregon, Tennessee, Texas, Virginia, West Virginia, and Wyoming.

5. *Hurt Boy Taken Off Device, Dies; Is His Attacker Now a Murderer?* The Minneapolis Star (March 15, 1978); and *Editorial*, Chicago Tribune (March 18, 1978).

6. *County of Hennepin v. Soderquist*, No. 747901 (Minnesota Dist. Ct., Hennepin County, July 18, 1978).

7. *A Definition of Irreversible Coma: Report of the Ad Hoc Committee of the Harvard*

Medical School to Examine the Definition of Brain Death, JOURNAL OF THE AMERICAN MEDICAL ASSOCIATION 205:337-40 (1968).

8. Cranford, R.E., *Brain Death: Concept and Criteria,* MINNESOTA MEDICINE (part one) 61(9):561-63 (September 1978), (part two) 61(10):600-03 (October 1978).

9. *In re Petition of the Children's Hosp., Inc., in Special Proceedings, for an Order Concerning the Medical Treatment of Stacey Jaton Ellison,* No. 428461 (Minnesota Dist. Ct., Ramsey County, July 11, 1978).

10. *Commonwealth v. Golston,* 366 N.E.2d 744 (Mass. 1977).

11. R.M. VEATCH, DYING, AND THE BIOLOGICAL REVOLUTION (Yale University Press, New Haven) (1976) at 77-115.

12. *In re Quinlan,* 355 A.2d 647, 663-64 (N.J. 1976).

Chapter 7

When Should the Patient Know?

Robert M. Veatch

In surveys during the past 20-30 years, patients consistently have expressed an overwhelming desire to be told about terminal illness. Somewhere between 82 and 98 percent say they would like to be told. Simultaneously, an overwhelming proportion of physicians (up to 88 percent) say they tend not to tell. The data are provocative and controversial; the reasons for the conflict are at once ethical, legal and clinical.

Mrs. Anna Domingues found herself facing the problem in a painfully real way. The 54-year-old woman was born in the Dominican Republic, but lived most of her adult life in New York City. She came to the hospital with a complaint of severe abdominal pain and went to surgery on a Wednesday morning.

The medical student assigned to her case was unsure about what she should be told. He spoke to the resident responsible for the patient, telling him that Mrs. Domingues had stage-four cancer of the cervix, the most advanced stage. They had cleaned out all of the tumor they could see, but since the tumor had spread to the pelvic wall, all they now could do was to try chemotherapy and radiation. The five-year survival rate of stage-four cancer is 0-20 percent—bleak news for the woman.

The medical student was tempted to keep the information to himself, at least for the time being. He thought that it could produce a severe depression and maybe Mrs. Domingues wouldn't cooperate as well in chemotherapy and radiation. On the other hand, he felt that it would not be fair to her to withhold the potent prognosis: somehow, she had a right to know her fate.

Reprinted with permission of the American Bar Association from BARRISTER MAGAZINE, Vol. 8, no. 1 (Winter 1981).

The student discussed the problem in turn with the resident, the attending physician, the staff psychiatrist, the hospital chaplain and a social worker. An enormous dispute emerged. The attending physician was adamant that such bad news should not be disclosed, at least not with the full force of its meaning. The hospital chaplain was equally adamant in the other direction. The resident was confused himself, but reflected the consensus of the majority of his profession; he reluctantly concluded that it would be inhuman to let the woman know the poor prognosis.

Why are there disagreements about telling patients like Mrs. Domingues about their medical conditions? When is it appropriate not to tell patients, and what are the ethical, legal and clinical bases for making such decisions?

HAVING DIFFERING VIEWS OF THE SAME PATIENT

To begin with, different ethical positions support the various stances taken by the student's advisors. First, his mentors were examining different data. The attending physician was afraid that there would be a bad medical outcome if the patient knew; he was afraid that she would become uncooperative in the treatment regimen. The psychiatrist emphasized the psychological impact on the woman; to him the enemy was anxiety, fear and depression for which withholding the negative information was a powerful preventive.

The chaplain looked at very different facts. He knew that the woman was a devout Catholic and had an obligation to prepare spiritually for a period of travail. For him, the religious or spiritual consequences dominated. The social worker, on the other hand, emphasized the social, economic and familial consequences. She was concerned about the impact on the woman's family—the three children who would need care, and the enormous economic consequences for this family of modest means.

Each of the consulting professionals, then, brought to bear very different information. Moreover, they seemed to be weighing the facts differently. The psychiatrist saw the psychological impact as very harmful. The chaplain was not at all convinced that disclosures need be so devastating. Physicians have a uniquely high fear of death, at least according to one study of the problem, and that fear may cause them systematically to overemphasize the bad psychological impact of disclosures about terminal illness. Yet even if all the consultants had agreed upon what kind of facts are relevant, they might have assessed the benefits and harms quite differently.

There may well have been another even more fundamental reason for the disagreement. The people involved in the dispute may have disagreed about the underlying moral principles that would influence the decision.

If we could construct the moral principle that led to the physician's recommendation, it probably would be something like this: physicians should decide whether or not to disclose a diagnosis to someone who is terminally ill by examining all the consequences and then trying to do what they judge would lead to the most good or least harm for the patient. The physician applies the classical Hippocratic ethic in this way and thinks it is his duty to use his personal judgment to benefit his patient. But the legal dimensions of the case may be quite separate from the ethical arguments.

The law calls the physician's argument "the therapeutic privilege." The idea has been with us since at least 1946, when Dr. Hubert Smith published an article entitled *Therapeutic Privilege to Withhold Specific Diagnosis from Patient Sick with Serious or Fatal Illness.*[1] In spite of the fact that Smith recognized that there was no legal authority for such a privilege, there have been hints of its legitimacy in court cases ever since. According to this concept, the doctor is privileged to use his judgment to determine whether the patient would be hurt by disclosure and, if so, withhold the information.

The therapeutic privilege argument has arisen in both research and therapy settings. Research is the easier case to defend. For example, that argument was used by Dr. Chester M. Southam of the Sloan-Kettering Cancer Research Institute in defense of his now infamous study at the Brooklyn Jewish Chronic Disease Hospital in July 1963.[2] He injected cancer cells into terminally ill patients for experimental purposes. He admitted readily that no consent was obtained, arguing that the physician has the right or even the obligation to withhold information that could be distressing to the patient and pointing out that such information might indeed have been distressing to his research subjects.

He was charged by the New York State Board of Regents with a violation of his professional obligation to obtain consent from research subjects. The Board of Regents concluded "it is not uncommon for a doctor to refrain from telling his patient that he has cancer when the physician concludes in his professional judgment that such a disclosure would be harmful to the patient . . . The respondent . . . overlooked the key fact that so far as this particular experiment was concerned, there was not the usual doctor-patient relationship and therefore, no basis for the exercise of their usual professional judgment applicable to patient care."

ARGUMENT PUT IN CONTEXT

The implication was clear: the therapeutic privilege argument is legitimate, but only in a therapeutic setting; it is not acceptable in pure research situations like Dr. Southam's experiment. One cannot argue that withholding the information would have been the most beneficial course to those research subjects because they simply could have been left out of the research entirely, thus avoiding the problem.

In 1977, the same Board of Regents incorporated a limited therapeutic privilege argument in its policy on patient access to medical records. While acknowledging the general existence of such a right, it permits physicians to withhold access in cases where they think the information would be seriously harmful to patients. While that policy has never been tested in the courts, it does represent the current thinking of an important state regulatory body, and apparently acknowledges the legitimacy of therapeutic privilege in cases where the physician believes disclosure to the patient would be harmful.

A case in Hawaii seems to accept the same idea. In *Nishi v. Hartwell*, the court concluded "the doctrine [of informed consent] recognizes that the primary duty of a physician is to do what is best for his patient. . . . [The] physician may withhold disclosure of information regarding any untoward consequences of a treatment where full disclosure will be detrimental to the patient's total care and best interest."[3]

If the law is what is stated in the *Nishi* opinion, then the law accepts the moral principle that the physician should use his judgment to do what he thinks will benefit the patient. I think that is a mistake. The model is one where therapy becomes the ultimate goal. The physician Bernard Meyer conveys this therapeutic metaphor when he argues, "what is imparted to the patient about his illness should be planned with the same care and executed with the same skill that are demanded by any potentially therapeutic measure. Like the transfusion of blood, the dispensing of certain information must be distinctly indicated, the amount given consonant with the needs of the recipient, and the type chosen with the view of avoiding untoward reactions."[4]

A careful reading of some of the earlier court cases reveals that even then there were limits placed on professional judgment. The important 1960 case of *Natanson v. Kline*,[5] for example, often is cited as a justification for the use of professional judgment in placing limits on disclosure. (Mrs. Natanson suffered injury from cobalt therapy and successfully claimed lack of informed consent.) The court said that "the physician's choice of plausible courses should not be called into question if it appears, all circumstances considered, that the physician was motivated only by the patient's best therapeutic interests and he proceeded as competent medical men would have done in a similar situation."[6] That seems to be a blunt justification of therapeutic privilege based on professional consensus. However, the opinion says that the physician's judgment is justifiable and "consistent with the full disclosure of facts necessary to assure an informed consent by the patient."[7] Thus even in earlier decisions, the information had to be full enough for the patient to exercise an informed judgment.

NEW CHALLENGES ARISE

The therapeutic privilege argument recently has come upon hard times. Even if some earlier tendencies were to accept the therapeutic privilege argument, opinion in the last decade has moved in the other direction. Challenges have increased among lawyers, philosophers and even physicians.

There are two objections to therapeutic privilege. First, there is often a high error rate in assessing benefits and harm of disclosure. Physicians may give undue emphasis to medical or psychological consequences. They may incorporate their own uniquely high fear of death. They may overlook values dear to the patient. Predicting the psychological impact of bad news on someone whom the physician normally does not know very well, is an enormously complicated task. The impact may be very subtle. It is simply a difficult prediction to make.

The result is sometimes a rule or guideline that says that in order to do the most good in the long run, one should disclose everything to the patient, even if it appears the patient might be upset. Man, after all, is a fallible animal. If patients say they want information, then the physician who decides that it would do more harm than good to disclose often may be mistaken.

A second objection to the therapeutic privilege argument is far more fundamental. This view holds that all the arguments about benefit and harm miss the point: what is at stake is a basic right of the patient or a basic obligation on the part of the health care provider.

Disclosure of a diagnosis is at the very least a necessary part of any informed consent. Consent might be omitted only if the goal were merely maximum benefit to the patient. A physician may conclude that a prognosis should be withheld on this basis, but those who criticize the therapeutic privilege argument reject this logic in principle. They say that maximizing benefit is not the goal at all; rather, the objective is protecting the patient's right of self-determination. In the case that set the trend to root informed consent in the principle of self-determination, Justice Schroeder concluded that this right is inherent in the Anglo-American legal tradition. He articulated the foundation of the informed consent doctrine saying, "each man is considered to be master of his own body, and he may, if he be of sound mind, expressly prohibit the performance of life-saving surgery, or other medical treatment."[8]

This forcefully restates the right to self-determination articulated decades earlier by Justice Cardozo in *Schloendorff v. Society of New York Hospital*,[9] when he said that "Every human being of adult years and sound mind has a right to determine what shall be done with his own body. . . ."[10] No exception is offered for withholding information necessary for an informed consent on the grounds that the information would be disturbing to the patient. This mainstream of the law, therefore, seems to exclude the therapeutic privilege argument as it often is put forward by physicians.

Consent requires knowledge of the diagnosis or prognosis or it just simply cannot be informed. The real basis for the disagreement between those who believed that Mrs. Domingues should be told and those who believed she should not, may be the difference between those committed to the principle of the fundamental right of self-determination and those who insist on the older, more paternalistic ethic charging the physician with the duty to use his judgment to do what he thinks will make the patient feel good.

If each individual has the right of self-determination and the right of access to information so he can participate in decisions about his care, then the doctrine of therapeutic privilege is dead. This seems to be the conclusion one must reach from the law on informed consent and the principle of self-determination. It is even more clearly the ethical conclusion one must reach.

Even so, sometimes the therapeutic privilege argument gets in through the back door; other rationalizations that are really therapeutic privilege arguments in disguise are offered for withholding information.

SELF-DECEIVING THEORIES

One such kind of self-deception might be called the "you can't tell them everything" argument. Like the attending physician in Mrs. Domingues' case, some people justifiably point out that it really is impossible to tell the patient everything about his or her condition, and thus "fully informed" consent is impossible—adding, no one would be foolish enough to want full information about his condition even if it were somehow possible to define it. But that still leaves open the question of whether the patient should be told reasonably significant or meaningful information regardless of a possibly negative psychological impact. While we can't tell patients everything, we might still tell them the information that a reasonable person would find significant, meaningful or interesting.

A second kind of self-deception is expressed in what might be called "truthful jargon." The patient had leiomyo-sarcoma with disseminated metastatic tissue growth. Dr. Charles C. Lund, who then was in Harvard Medical School's Department of Surgery, captured the technique's usefulness when he advised fellow physicians to proceed cautiously with blunt disclosure. He said "certainly at the start of the interview [the physician] should avoid the words carcinoma or cancer. He should use cyst, nodule, tumor, lesion, or some loosely descriptive word that has not so many frightening connotations." In other words, jargon may be truthful and still not communicate. It may be that the patient should not be told the truth, but a physician using jargon like this should not kid himself into thinking he has been truthful in a meaningful sense.

Another type of self-deception might be called the "we'll never know for sure" argument. It begins with the profound clinical insight that medical prognosis is extremely subtle and complicated. At best, the physician is able to estimate with some degree of probability what the likely outcome will be. But he can say truthfully "we'll never know for sure." The deception comes when he uses this as a rationalization for failure to disclose what he does know—that the prognosis is bleak and the likelihood of long-term survival is small.

Still another kind of self-deception occurs when the physician attempts to make a sharp separation between lying and withholding information. There well may be a moral difference between some omissions and commissions. For instance, in the related area of euthanasia, many believe that there is an enormous moral difference between actively killing a patient and simply letting him or her die.[11] The law seems to make a clear separation.[12]

The critical factor in omission, however, is whether the physician had an obligation to act. It seems clear that a physician has no obligation to act in cases where the patient has withdrawn or withheld consent; in fact, continuing treatment on a terminally ill patient in such a case might be a battery. But withdrawal of consent for continued treatment is radically different from an instruction to actively kill a patient. Even the giving of consent does not necessarily justify any intervention that actively would hasten a patient's death.

With information disclosure, however, the physician is in a very different situation than with omission. He has not been instructed by the patient to refrain from acting; in fact, the patient has not given a signal one way or another. In disclosure, the physician can be seen as in the process of negotiating consent for possible further treatment. Withholding information in such a way that it deceives the patient into thinking that he or she is going to recover is morally very close to lying, perhaps morally identical.

A final kind of self-deception is what might be called the "indirect communication" argument. Sometimes physicians and other health professionals convince themselves that they are able to read signals from the patient about his or her desire for further information or lack thereof. The patient in the midst of a cancer diagnosis workup may talk about long-term plans for building an addition to his home. Physicians have been known to take that signal from the patient that he does not want to discuss imminent death. It is conceivable that some communication between patient and physician may take place using such indirect signals or even body language, but there is great danger that the signals may be misread. It probably is safer to avoid the use of indirect communication arguments whenever possible.

In summary, all of these arguments are really self-deceptions. They don't justify withholding information or deceiving the patient. If that is justifiable at all, it will have to be established on some other grounds.

THOSE "SPECIAL CASES"

There are a number of special cases requiring additional comment. These tend to be the ones brought out in defense of therapeutic privilege. The most obvious case is the emergency situation; if the patient is unconscious, obviously the clinician cannot wait for consent. This is indeed an exception to the general rule that requires a patient's consent based on accurate information about diagnosis and prognosis, but it is a carefully circumscribed, explicit legal exception, one that is not really very controversial except at the margins of its application.

A second special case occurs when the family requests that the patient not be told of the diagnosis. But how does the family know about the situation in the first place? Physicians have a well-recognized obligation to maintain confidentiality. In many jurisdictions, this is elevated to the level of law. If confidentiality is to be broken, it is the patient's right to authorize breaking it and not the family's. Whenever a physician approaches a family member first, without the patient's permission, he has violated confidence. Except in cases where the patient has specifically authorized a family member to advise the physician about the nature of the disclosure, the family seems to have no legitimate or justifiable role in deciding to withhold bad news.

That suggests a third special case in which the patient himself waives his right to information. Normally, patients should not make such requests. They have not only the right but the responsibility to be actively involved in decisions about their own care; but from the point of view of the law as well as of the medical professional, it really is not our business to force patients to have information against their wishes. If a request comes from a patient that such information be withheld, I see no problem ethically with honoring it.

Another special situation also commands attention. Often it is argued that there is a special case in which professional judgment requires that information not be disclosed, in which the consensus of the profession would be decisively against telling. According to this view, disclosure is a matter of professional judgment and it is acceptable to withhold if other practitioners would have made a similar judgment. In one of the most significant legal cases of the 1970s, *Canterbury v. Spence* (the case of a 19-year-old, left paraplegic after a laminectomy, that helped establish the reasonable person standard) the court concluded that therapeutic privilege would justify non-disclosure "when the risk [of] disclosure poses such a threat of detriment to the patient as to become unfeasible or contraindicated from a medical point of view."[13]

DOCTORS SEEM MORE WILLING TO TELL

This sounds like the kind of question about which physicians would have relevant expertise. Critics of the therapeutic privilege argument have pointed out, however, that there are two problems with this argument for professional consensus. First, recent surveys have shown a remarkable shift of physician attitude. In a study at the University of Iowa College of Medicine, researchers asked medical students, recent graduates and college faculty how often they tell their patients their prognoses. Sixty percent of the medical students, 54 percent of the recent graduates and 44 percent of the faculty said they "frequently told."

The researchers repeated the study in 1976 and found the percent willing to disclose had increased in all three groups: 80 percent of the students, 78 percent of the recent graduates, and 61 percent of the faculty said they frequently disclosed prognoses to terminally ill patients.

It appears that at any given point younger members of the profession tend to be more open, but during the 1970s each group drifted toward disclosure. A 1979 study by Dennis Novack and his colleagues found a remarkable tendency favoring disclosure; 98 percent of the participating physicians reported that their usual policy was to tell the cancer patient. If it is true that the consensus of the profession is shifting in the direction of disclosure, it will be harder to prove that professional colleagues would not not have disclosed in any given case.

There is a second, more fundamental problem with the professional consensus approach, however. That standard itself is increasingly suspect. We are beginning to realize that the question of how much information to disclose, of what data are important, of what moral principles should govern decisions about disclosure is really a question that a reasonable person should be able to evaluate.

In the 1970s and 1980s, just as the consensus of the profession seems to be shifting, there is an unmistakable trend challenging the notion that the professional consensus should be decisive in making such judgment in the first place. Judge Robinson, in *Canterbury v. Spence*, says "respect for the patient's right of self-determination on particular therapy demands a standard set by law for physicians rather than one which physicians may or may not impose upon themselves."[14]

Abandonment of a professional consensus in favor of what is often called the reasonable person standard is summarized in *Cobbs v. Grant*, a California case in which the plaintiff suffered a series of complications from gastric surgery leading eventually to splenectomy and gastrectomy. Here the court concluded that:

> the patient's right of self-decision is the measure of the physician's duty to reveal. That right can be effectively exercised only if the patient possesses adequate information to enable an intelligent choice. The scope of the physician's communications to the patient, then, must be measured by the patient's need, and that need is whatever information is material to the decision. Thus the test for determining whether a potential peril must be divulged is its materiality to the patient's decision.[15]

The court cases that sometimes are cited to defend therapeutic privilege do in fact raise a special set of cases where disclosure may not be required. Judge Robinson, in *Canterbury v. Spence*, points out that "patients occasionally become so ill or emotionally distraught on disclosure as to foreclose a rational decision, or complicate or hinder the treatment, or perhaps even pose psychological damage to the patient." The case suggests that when the disclosure would so upset the patient that he would be unable to respond in a rational way or at all, then information may be withheld.[16] Similarly, in *Cobbs v. Grant* information is held to be expendable if it would make the patient unable to "dispassionately weigh the risks of refusing to undergo the recommended treatment."[17] In these cases the patient simply cannot give an informed consent because he or she is incompetent in a subtle way.

The courts in essence are saying that the physician need not get an informed consent from the patient when it is literally impossible to do so. It seems, however, that in such cases the patient should be adjudicated as incompetent for purposes of giving consent; that is, some due process is needed and then the physician should proceed as he would with any other incompetent patient, by getting a consent from a legally authorized guardian. Thus, the apparent opening to therapeutic privilege is really not an opening at all. It is more like an incompetency privilege or even an incompetency duty. When the patient is incompetent to give a consent, then some alternative must be pursued.

WHEN NO NEWS MAY BE ENOUGH

There is one final special case that may ease the burden on health professionals faced with the enormous task of telling patients about their medical conditions and futures. If patients have a right to all information that they would find meaningful in making a decision about the future of their care, might it still be possible that in some situations there is nothing a reasonable person would want to know?

In research medicine, this question arises when researchers want to make use of the waste products of routine clinical care, when a physician wants to use remaindered blood, body waste or the materials removed during surgery. Do such researchers have to get an explicit consent from the patients who would be unwittingly contributing to the research if they were not told, or would it suffice to obtain, upon hospital admission, a general consent statement that such waste may be used for research?

It seems that the proper test would be to ask whether reasonable patients would want to have information about a specific study. Normally, they probably would not, although if there were risks of confidentiality violation, or if the purpose of the study were unusually controversial, they may want more detail. Barring special circumstances, many have concluded that there is simply nothing the reasonable person would want to know. In that case, a general blanket consent statement might prove adequate.

Likewise, in therapeutic settings there may be some procedures so trivial and so commonplace that patients really wouldn't want to know anything about them. Normally, there is not a long explanation before routine blood samples are drawn in a laboratory. This is true in spite of the fact that there is a very small but real risk of infection and blood clots every time blood is drawn. If reasonable people would not want to be bothered by such details and would not find them meaningful in deciding to participate, then the current practice is reasonable and justified.

It seems unlikely, however, that people faced with serious illness—with a lump that looks suspiciously like a malignant tumor, for example—would be as indifferent to the information relevant to their case.

The burden of proof is going to be on the medical professional to demonstrate that reasonable people would not want the information, unless a patient has explicitly waived his right to know. And the burden of proof ought to be very high.

It thus appears that the cases that seem to provide a foundation for the therapeutic privilege may not make an exception to the general rule of telling patients what they would find meaningful. In some cases reasonable people would not want to know anything; in others the patient is literally incapable of giving consent because of his or her condition or the traumatic nature of the information, and in still other cases the patient explicitly waives his right to the information.

CONSENT NOT POSSIBLE WITHOUT INFORMATION

Our public policy is and should remain that competent individuals have the right to self-determination regarding participation in medical treatment and that information necessary to make a decision about participation must be presented for a consent to be adequately informed.

In cases where the patient is not competent to make such decisions, the legal agent for the patient must give permission for the medical treatment. The apparent exceptions to the requirement are really not therapeutic privilege arguments at all. Ethics and law both require that if a patient is capable of understanding his condition, he should be told about it. Many physicians have come to agree, but a consensus of professional opinion cannot be decisive. The ethical and legal mandate remains independent of professional medical opinion.

There is only one situation in which many people might still feel justified in withholding information about a patient's condition: if the consequences of the disclosure were devastatingly and overwhelmingly negative, nondisclosure may be justified. If, for instance, a patient were intermittently suicidal and presently in an acute crisis of depression, his terminal diagnosis might justifiably be withheld until such time as he has passed through the acute crisis. But only a temporary postponement would be called for.

The dangers of permitting an exception, even in cases of overwhelmingly devastating consequences, are so great that many have reached the conclusion that the exception shouldn't be incorporated into our public policy. Then withholding information from a patient becomes something like draft evasion. It is conceivable that there is a moral justification for doing it, but it should require a rigorous defense. It should require a thorough reading of Gandhi and Thoreau. It should require an appeal to some higher law. With one exception, the therapeutic privilege is dead.

When, then, shouldn't the patient know? Never, if he is capable of knowing—as a matter of public policy.

NOTES

1. Smith, H.W., *Therapeutic Privilege to Withhold Specific Prognosis from Patient Sick with Serious or Fatal Illness*, TENNESSEE LAW REVIEW 19(3):349-57 (April 1946).
2. *See generally*, J. KATZ, EXPERIMENTATION WITH HUMAN BEINGS (Russell Sage Foundation, New York)(1972), *The Jewish Chronic Disease Hospital Case*, at 7-65.
3. *Nishi v. Hartwell*, 473 P.2d 116, 119 (Haw. 1970).
4. Meyer, B.C., *Truth and the Physician*, in ETHICAL ISSUES IN MEDICINE, E. F. TORREY, Ed. (Little, Brown, Boston)(1968) at 172.
5. *Natanson v. Kline*, 350 P.2d 1093 (Kans.), *rehearing denied*, 354 P.2d 670 (Kans. 1960).
6. 350 P.2d at 1106.
7. *Id.* at 1107.
8. *Id.* at 1104.
9. *Schloendorff v. Society of New York Hosp.*, 105 N.E. 92 (N.Y. 1914).
10. *Id.* at 93.
11. *See* R.M. VEATCH, DEATH, DYING, AND THE BIOLOGICAL REVOLUTION (Yale Univ. Press, New Haven)(1976) at 80-105.
12. *See* Fletcher, G.P., *Prolonging Life*, WASHINGTON LAW REVIEW 42:999-1016 (1967).
13. *Canterbury v. Spence*, 464 F.2d 772, 789 (D.C. Cir. 1972).
14. *Id.* at 784.
15. *Cobbs v. Grant*, 502 P.2d 1, 11 (Cal. 1972).
16. *Canterbury v. Spence, supra* note 13, at 789.
17. *Cobbs v. Grant, supra* note 15, at 12.

Chapter 8

Code and No-Code: A Psychological Analysis and the Viewpoint of Jewish Law

Rabbi Levi Meier

The decision to write or not to write a no-code or DNR order for a patient is a complex issue. It involves the physician-patient relationship, the physician-family relationship, the rights of the patient and the moral choices of the physician. This paper will address the problem in terms of psychology and *halakha* (Jewish law).

Within the general context of the physician-patient relationship, it is understood that the patient's values, cultural background, and family orientation may differ from those of the physician. In areas where the patient's and physician's values differ dramatically, there is a range of possible modes of behavior. The physician can withdraw from the case, explaining that his or her value system cannot accommodate the patient's desires. The physician can attempt to impose his or her value system on the patient, overtly or subtly; or the physician can differentiate between personal values and professional behavior. Lawrence Kohlberg's analysis of moral development sheds light on the physician's dilemma in such cases.[1]

Kohlberg's theory distinguishes between the pre-conventional, conventional and post-conventional stages of moral development. The pre-conventional stage is characterized by avoiding punishment and satisfying one's own needs. The conventional stage involves the acceptance of the values of the group. Frequently, one follows peer group standards, although group values also include those of the broader community, the state, or the nation. An act is right because it conforms with accepted laws. This is the law-and-order stage, which often leads to the position that national policy should be supported whether it is right or wrong. The post-conventional stage goes beyond specific rules and extends to man's conscience. It is based on abstract ethical principles that are believed to have universal applicability.

Kohlberg's theory recognizes that individuals differ in their values and that a physician's behavior in treating a patient with values different from his or her own may involve:

1) withdrawing from the case because of a value conflict; this reflects the post-conventional stage of moral development where a person's conscience dictates the choice;

2) imposing his or her view on the patient. This is not even an option, according to Kohlberg;

3) differentiating between his or her personal ethic and that of the patient, and accepting whatever the patient requests. This course of action reflects Kohlberg's conventional stage, whereby a physician accepts the values of the group. In this case, the group is represented by every individual patient. This option would allow for a physician treating two patients with identical medical situations to write diametrically opposite orders, depending upon which patient requests a code and which patient requests a no-code. In informal and formal discussions, physicians, nurses and other health professionals frequently justify this position by stating that medical care must be individualized. However, as significant as individualized medical care is, it appears that the moral reasoning in accepting the patient's different significant choices reflects the physician's acquiescence and delegation of this responsibility. Although this course of action is seemingly in accordance with Kohlberg's theory, it appears that in this situation, acquiescence to a patient's desire is not an ethical option.

What is the patient's right in determining his or her own status? Is every individual totally free, or not?

THE PATIENT'S RIGHT

The California Natural Death Act states,

> "The Legislature finds that adult persons have the fundamental right to control the decisions relating to the rendering of their own medical care, including the decision to have life-sustaining procedures withheld or withdrawn in instances of terminal condition."[2]

Prima facie, it would appear that there should be no restraint imposed upon this right. In forensic psychiatry, however, there is precedent for the infringement of patients' rights. The Lanterman-Petris-Short Act of 1969 states that within a therapeutic relationship, confidentiality is necessary.[3] However, confidentiality may be violated in a variety of circumstances, such as when the therapist views the patient as suicidal, homicidal, and/or unable to take care of self (unable to provide shelter, food, clothing, etc.). In these cases, a therapist may inform the authorities of the mental state of the patient in order to commence commitment proceedings. The principle is that patients' rights are circumscribed when patients, because of their mental state, are not responsible for their decisions.

As chaplain of Cedars-Sinai Medical Center, I am currently seeing a terminal patient who has been diagnosed as having cancer of the colon and liver. She has requested a no-code and, for that matter, prefers no treatment at all to treatment that involves secondary pain and suffering. According to the Zung depression scale[4] and the Beck depression scale,[5] she appears to be severely depressed. Clinical interviews have substantiated these test results. She states that her life no longer has purpose and that she would like to die immediately. Should we ignore her psychological condition and accede to her wishes, or should we treat her?

I believe that the therapist-client relationship and the physician-patient relationship share many identical elements. Just as the therapist recognizes that a suicidal desire results from severe depression, a physician can understand that requests for no treatment may be highly motivated by depression. An otherwise healthy person can feel as depressed as a patient who has terminal cancer. We need to devise a method of decision making that takes this sort of problem into account. The principle behind the Lanterman-Petris-Short Act should be operative in other areas of medicine.

In theological terms, too, man's liberty is circumscribed. Life is a gift which has been bestowed and only the One who bestowed it may take it back. It is true that life may involve a tremendous amount of pain and suffering, yet Gabriel Marcel, a French existentialist, said that life is not a problem to be solved but rather a challenge to be lived.[6] Victor Frankl, the founder of Logotherapy, claims that man must find meaning in his tragedy.[7]

PHYSICIAN-PATIENT RELATIONSHIP

Sometimes a physician may say, "If this were my father, I would. . . ." Obviously, this statement comes from a very caring position, but it involves numerous problems. The most important of these is that the patient is not the physician's father. Also, there is frequently a discrepancy between what people say they will do and what they in fact do. Intentions are often modified when it is actually time to make decisions.

In a regular therapeutic situation, no therapist would tell a couple, "Yes, a divorce would be appropriate," or "No, you should stay together." No therapist would ever want such enormous power over a patient. Yet in a physician-patient relationship, which takes the form of a therapeutic alliance, the physician is at times very directive in issues that involve ethics.

PHYSICIAN-FAMILY RELATIONSHIP

A physician deals not only with a patient, but also with the family of the patient and the relationship of the patient to his or her family. When a major decision needs to be made and the patient is unable to communicate, the family's contribution is especially significant. Sometimes a family member of a terminally ill patient may respond in these ways:

1) "There is too much suffering and pain going on. Knowing the patient for the past 70 years, I can tell you that he has faced too much agony."

2) "The family is having a nervous breakdown. Not only is the patient going to die, but her relatives are in mental anguish."

3) "The patient is not functioning. This is not the Dad I knew. He is a different person. There will be no meaning for him in life in any case."

My response to these and similar situations is to differentiate between the patient's expressed need and the family's need. The family, quite understandably, feels completely helpless, which can lead to bitter frustration, anger and resentment. This family is in need of mental health assistance, but their pressing need should not lead to a no-code order. My clinical experience has shown me that a few years after the patient has died, the family begins to ponder the sequence of events again in its entirety. Conflicts that frequently arise are expressed by such statements as:

1) "I should have gone to a different physician or at least had a second consultation."

2) "Perhaps with a different hospital and a better nursing staff, the situation would have been altered."

3) "Why didn't I have them take more medically aggressive action?"[8]

It is human nature to have some guilt feelings about past relationships. Perhaps these feelings can be modified if the physician concentrates primarily upon the patient's needs and provides mental health assistance for the patient's family.

THE JUDAIC TRADITION

Within Judaic tradition, life has infinite value—even a diminished life. The value of a human life is not based upon its potential usefulness to others or upon one's own well-being. It is an absolute value, even when life is accompanied by pain, suffering and mental anguish.

Humans do not possess absolute titles to life. Each is responsible for preserving his/her own life and is obliged to seek food and sustenance to that end. When one is sick, he/she is similarly obliged to seek medical attention. People are never called upon to determine whether their lives are worth living. This Judaic tradition is in direct contrast to the 1979 *Report of the Committee on Policy for Do Not Resuscitate Decisions*, of Yale University School of Medicine, which classifies three approaches to the management of the terminally ill:

1) patients are to receive all curative and functional maintenance therapies as indicated and the primary goal is to achieve arrest, remission or cure of the basic disease process;

2) if any curative therapy is in progress, it will be continued until its outcome has been determined, and further, no new therapy will be implemented. A DNR order is optional;

3) the goals of therapy are to comfort the patient as he is dying, and so a DNR order is appropriate.[9]

In Jewish thought, the quality of the life to be preserved is never a factor to be taken into consideration. Neither is the survivor's life expectancy a controlling factor, nor is the patient's age. A 93-year-old patient with terminal cancer receives the same management as a 39-year-old patient with terminal cancer. Thus, classifications 2 and 3 of the Yale Report are antithetical to Jewish law.

EXPERIMENTAL THERAPY AND HAZARDOUS PROCEDURES

There is no basis in Judaism for a distinction between ordinary and extraordinary forms of therapy.[10] However, a distinction must be made between therapeutic procedures of proven efficacy and those of unproven therapeutic value. If a therapeutic procedure is of proven efficacy, then it is a moral and *halakhic* imperative. Man may no more abstain from the use of drugs to cure illness than he may abstain from food or drink. However, if the proposed therapy is of unproven value, then the patient may legitimately refuse treatment. This is true not only when the treatment itself is potentially hazardous, but also if there is reason to suspect that the proposed treatment may be harmful in any way. In such instances, treatment is discretionary.

Physicians may withhold otherwise mandatory treatment only when the patient has reached the state of *gesisah*, i.e., the patient has become moribund and death is imminent. Even at this stage, the patient (or *goses*) is regarded as a living person in every respect. One must not pry his jaws, anoint him, wash him, plug his orifices, remove the pillow from underneath him or place him on the ground.[11]

THE MORIBUND PATIENT

Although euthanasia in any form is forbidden and the hastening of death, even by a matter of moments, is regarded as tantamount to murder, there is one situation in which treatment may be withheld from the moribund patient in order to provide for an unimpeded death. While the death of a *goses* may not be speeded, there is no obligation to perform any action which will lengthen the life of the patient in this state. This distinction between an active and passive act applies only to a *goses*. When a patient is in the death process, there is no obligation to heal. Therefore, Rabbi Moses Isserles permits the removal of anything which constitutes a hindrance to the departure of the soul (such as a clattering noise or salt upon his tongue), since such acts involve no active hastening of death, but only the removal of an impediment.[12]

It cannot be overemphasized that even acts of omission are permitted only when the patient is in a state of *gesisah*. This leads one to ask how the *gesisah* can be differentiated from other states?

1) If the condition is reversible, there is an obligation to heal. When the moribund condition is irreversible, there is no obligation to continue treatment.

2) Any patient who may reasonably be deemed capable of potential survival for a period of 72 hours cannot be considered a *goses*.[13]

It appears that this state is not determined by a patient's ability to survive solely by natural means for this period, unaided by drugs or mechanical equipment. The implication is that a *goses* is one who cannot, by any means, be maintained alive for a period of 72 hours. The conclusion is that, if it is medically possible to prolong life, the patient is indeed not a *goses*.

THE JUDAIC TRADITION AND CONTEMPORARY SOCIETY

This paper argues for aggressive treatment of terminally ill patients, regardless of the extent of the impairment or the quality of life which may be preserved by such treatment. The Judaic tradition is well aware that the motivation of contemporary society, in seeking not to prolong life in some cases, is brotherly compassion and feelings of love and concern. Nevertheless, euthanasia, even if designed to put an end to unbearable suffering, is classified as murder. Despite the noble intent which prompts such an action, mercy killing is considered an unwarranted intervention in an area which must be governed only by God.

NOTES

1. Kohlberg, L., The Development of Modes of Moral Thinking and Choice in Years Ten to Sixteen (unpublished doctoral dissertation)(University of Chicago)(1958).
2. CAL. HEALTH AND SAFETY CODE § 7186 (West).
3. CAL.WELFARE AND INSTITUTIONS CODE § 5328 (West).
4. Zung, W.W.K., *The Measurements of Affects: Depression and Anxiety*, in PSYCHOLOGICAL MEASUREMENT IN PSYCHOPHARMACOLOGY, P. PICHOT, Ed. (Karger, New York)(1974).
5. Beck, A., Beamesdorfer, A., *Assessment of Depression: The Depression Inventory*, in PSYCHOLOGICAL MEASUREMENT IN PSYCHOPHARMACOLOGY, *supra* note 4.
6. G. MARCEL, THE MYSTERY OF BEING (Regnery, Chicago)(1950).
7. V. FRANKL, MAN'S SEARCH FOR MEANING: AN INTRODUCTION TO LOGOTHERAPY (Beacon Press, Boston)(1962).
8. *See* Lo, B., Jonsen, A.R., *Ethical Decisions in the Care of a Patient Terminally Ill with Metastic Cancer*, ANNUALS OF INTERNAL MEDICINE 92(1):107-11 (January 1980)(wife of diseased man asked several months after his death whether she should have requested more aggressive treatment).
9. Report of the Committee on Policy for Do Not Resuscitate Decisions, R. J. Levine, M.D., Chairman (Yale University School of Medicine, New Haven) (March 1979).
10. Bleich, J.D., *The Obligation to Heal in the Judaic Tradition: A Comparative Analysis*, in JEWISH BIOETHICS, F. ROSNER, J.D. BLEICH, Eds. (Sanhedrin Press, New York)(1979).
11. Shulhan Arukh, Yoreh De'ah 339:1.
12. Shulhan Arukh, Yoreh De'ah 339:1.
13. Shulhan Arukh, Yoreh De'ah 339:5.

SELECTED BIBLIOGRAPHY

BLEICH, J.D., CONTEMPORARY HALAKHIC PROBLEMS (Ktav, New York)(1977).
JAKOBOVITS, I., JEWISH MEDICAL ETHICS: A COMPARATIVE AND HISTORICAL STUDY OF THE JEWISH RELIGION ATTITUDE TO MEDICINE AND ITS PRACTICE (Philosophical Library, New York)(1975 and rev. ed. 1975).

PREUSS, J., BIBLICAL AND TALMUDIC MEDICINE (Sanhedrin Press, New York)(1978).

ROSNER, F., MODERN MEDICINE AND JEWISH LAW (Yeshiva University Dept. of Special Publications,) (1972).

————, MEDICINE IN THE BIBLE AND THE TALMUD (Ktav, New York)(1977).

ROSNER F., BLEICH, J.D., Eds. JEWISH BIOETHICS (Sanhedrin Press, New York)(1979).

TENDLER, M., Ed. MEDICAL ETHICS, 5th Ed. (Federation of Jewish Philanthropies of New York)(1975).

Chapter 9

Whose Life Is It Anyway?

Walter A. Markowicz

An ethical analysis of the questions of whether or not to treat a terminally ill patient will not provide foolproof answers. The ethicist, who deals with ethics, morality or human values, wants to make sure that ambiguity is recognized as ambiguity. Life is full of ambiguities and people need to learn how to live with them.[1] When I first decided to deal with human values or ethics in the context of a medical school, members of the school feared that I would represent a monolithic view and dictate answers to medical problems. After some time and experience in reflection, the fear was replaced by disappointment, e.g., "Well, if you don't give us answers, what good are you?" While I can offer no firm solutions to the problem of appropriate treatment, I do think that the law's attempt to codify responses only adds to the confusion, and that is the problem I wish to highlight.

In general, society has almost always defined caring for the sick and staving off death as noble pursuits. Difficulties and differences arise when living becomes so painful that some patients desire to die, perhaps even ask to be killed. What limits do we then set for what human beings can do for one another—apart from the limit the law itself exercises?[2] As a scriptural passage puts it, "law is the result of transgression." It is after human rights are trampled upon that laws must be developed to protect us. Laws are not generally anticipatory of the problems that humans have with one another in their interpersonal relations but, rather, retrospective in their concern. When we use values or ethics we try to deal with the situation as well as the culture that exists today. Ethics attempt to express the mores that we share, or to discover whether we do share mores on a given point. Eventually, because of discussion and reflection, our mores become reflected in law.

Does one have the right to seek one's own death? If so, under what conditions? Should others be allowed to assist a person in dying? I do not think that our society as a whole, and certainly our law, are clear about any of these questions at the moment. The law does not really guarantee a "right to die"; rather it speaks more to a right not to pursue the continuation of life. The law seems to recognize that it is not necessary to preserve life under every condition.

Another question which naturally follows is whether death is actively brought about or whether it comes because support is withheld.[3] Let us reflect on the distinction. Should every conceivable effort be made to ward off death? How real is the distinction between commission and omission? Legal, moral, and religious traditions have all recognized that it is often more appropriate to specify the acts that people must not do to one another than it is to specify the helpful acts they ought to do. However, there are circumstances when it is no defense to say that we did not *do* anything. A parent who does not feed an infant has not done nothing. A doctor who fails to provide standard treatment to a patient where he had a clear duty to do so has not simply omitted something. There are circumstances where the distinction between omission and commission evaporates,[4] and these differing circumstances are the heart of the problem. Does "omit" simply mean not to begin a procedure, or does it also encompass the discontinuation of a procedure? Where the respirator merely prolongs the process of dying for a patient and there is absolutely no hope of recovery, then the moral warrant for turning off the machine is the same for not instituting such care in the first place. I would propose that in these critical areas of decision making, it is important that health care should be provided by a team whose reflection and dialogue upon these questions go on continuously and do not surface only at moments of crisis.

Dr. Cranford's paper refers to the difficulty in distinguishing between "ordinary" and "extraordinary" medical procedures. There are a hundred and one definitions for ordinary/extraordinary, yet the problem of definition is important. For example, a living will may specify that its author does not want extraordinary care used for the prolongation of his or her life. Without definitions or criteria to decide, we do not know whether the patient would want a specific therapy applied. We are not merely talking about medically extraordinary actions; rather, from an ethical or moral point of view, we must take into consideration all the circumstances of the actual situation. We cannot, therefore, label an I.V. as being either ordinary or extraordinary: the label depends upon the situation. We cannot label the respirator as being either ordinary or extraordinary: that depends upon the situation.

It is a widely accepted ethical position that extraordinary means need not be used to prolong life. Procedures or equipment that make it possible for a patient's life to continue in a meaningful way are ordinary even though it may seem medically to be an extraordinary procedure. Procedures, no matter how simple, that postpone death for no specific reason, no proportionate reason, are extraordinary means.[5] A procedure which may be very simple and routine may be called extraordinary if there are overwhelming reasons why it ought not be undertaken on a specific patient. I am not speaking about usual or unusual treatment with experimental or recognized drugs but, rather, to the patient's circumstances.

The distinctions between ordinary and extraordinary, and omission and commission, are much simpler if they are applied by the patient to his or her own care. Clearly, patients have the right to make the decision. It becomes a different matter and considerably more difficult, however, when one must apply such rationales to the care of another. The existence of a guardian does not automatically abrogate the rights of a patient. The fact that a patient is mentally incompetent or comatose, or that the patient is a minor, does not militate against the maintenance of that patient's rights. If there is a right, the right remains no matter what the condition of the patient. No one can justly take it away nor ignore it. Sometimes it is difficult to judge, however, whether that right is maintained.[6]

In the arena of ethics, an individual's attitude and intention are of the utmost importance. The intention that guides the act which results in death is what determines whether the act itself was a commission or omission. For example, suppose you are treating a patient who is experiencing severe pain, who is diagnosed as terminal, and for whom there is little or no hope of recovery. You provide medications but in your knowledge of the impossibility of a cure you use agents which hasten death as well as relieve pain. What is your motive? A third party may think you are giving this drug only to relieve pain, but in your own mind you question: "Am I giving this drug to hasten the moment of death?" This is an ambiguity that health care professionals must live with.

A few points in regard to do not resuscitate [DNR] orders are appropriate. I think that there are four critical ethical moments in the DNR situation. The first critical moment is the *decision to initiate life-supporting care* in the first place. Should one or should one not? Is this appropriate or inappropriate care?

The second critical moment is the *decision to wean*. When and how do you decide when you should wean the person from the life-support systems? The third and fourth moments involve *decisions to continue* treatment or *decisions to terminate it*. Often, the continuation of treatment only postpones the inevitable. Once one has begun resuscitative procedures that maintain rather than improve life, one may have established an obligatory relationship.

One example of this problem is the situation of a young child who has lost all of his immunity and for whom a special disease-free unit is built. Once the decision to treat the child is made, it must be followed. Whether it was the right decision or not is beside the point. While the continuation of treatment may not do this person any good, since the child must be brought into some sort of contact with real life and, since he cannot survive that contact, we might decide to bring on the crisis now. Such a decision, however, could not be ethically implemented because the providers have established a hope, an expectation, and a procedure.

Occasionally, care is begun to maintain the symbolism of life. For example, we often see a company or governmental agency spend a million dollars to rescue a miner who is trapped in a mine, even though the rescue does little to pass or enforce rules that could have prevented the disaster in the first place. But the rescue still needs to be done, because at the moment of crisis, people recognize the value of a life and the tendency is to use every available means to save it.

Some ambiguities will exist forever; however, we should continue to weigh and evaluate them. Although discussion at the moment of crisis is important, it is also important for us as a society to reflect upon these questions in more peaceful moments and in a prospective way. The answers are not always easy, but asking the questions and continuing a dialogue offer the best hope for reasoned ethical decisions.

NOTES

1. McCormick, Richard A., *Ambiguity in Moral Choice*, Pere Marquette Theology Lectures (Marquette University Press, Milwaukee) (1977).
2. D. MAGUIRE, DEATH BY CHOICE (Doubleday, New York)(1974).
3. *See Death and Dying: Euthanasia and Sustaining Life*, at 261-86, ENCYCLOPEDIA OF BIOETHICS, T. REICH, Ed. (Free Press, New York)(1978).
4. Moore, H.F., *Acting and Refraining*, at 32-38, ENCYCLOPEDIA OF BIOETHICS, *supra* note 3.
5. Jonsen, A.R., Lister, G., *Life Support Systems*, at 840-48, ENCYCLOPEDIA OF BIOETHICS, *supra* note 3.
6. R. VEATCH, DEATH, DYING, AND THE BIOLOGICAL REVOLUTION (Yale University Press, New Haven)(1976).

Part Two

Legal Implications and Responses

Chapter 10

Withholding Treatment and Orders Not to Resuscitate

Teresa A. Brooks

What constitutes a matter of life or death varies with one's historical perspective. For example, infectious diseases which were once considered life-threatening events have become technologically reversible illnesses. Plague, famine, pestilence and death, once known as the four horsemen of the apocalypse, can now be viewed as three deductible expenses and a capital loss. Recent advances in medical technology have effected profound changes, not only in our attitudes toward death, but also in our attitudes toward the specific diseases from which we are likely to die. The place of death has moved from the home to the institution: the hospital, medical center or nursing home. The "life-saving" techniques that were developed to serve human interests have begun to override and displace those human interests. Modern resuscitative methods not only bring to life the difficulty of determining the moment of death, but also create moral and legal dilemmas as to when these methods should or should not be used.

Death is viewed by many as a failure of modern technology. Society's faith in the power of technical solutions to medical problems gives rise to expectations of omnipotence, which are shared to some degree by patients and doctors. Many physicians tend to view death as an accident or a personal failure which they find difficult to reconcile with their social and personal image as healers or "fixers." The patient relies upon the physician, the nurse and the institution for help—to care, to treat, to cure. When those expectations are frustrated, the patient may turn to attorneys and the judicial process for recourse. This response to frustrated expectations demonstrates the need to address the problems of terminally ill patients within the institution. Further, these problems should be addressed as they relate to the needs of a specific patient, of the institution and its staff, as well as to the laws of the particular state. These laws increasingly recognize the right of the patient to decide what treatment he or she will receive. Yet, the patient is not the ideal decisionmaker in every situation. This ambiguity, however, does not obviate the need for rules and models for arriving at decisions.

PATIENT'S RIGHT TO DECIDE

In enunciating the doctrinal basis for the patient's right to determine his or her medical destiny, American courts have stated at least five pertinent rules. First, every adult, competent patient is usually free to reject medical treatment, even if potentially life-saving. This rule has been supported by a number of legal rationales: the right to determine what shall be done with one's body,[1] the right of free exercise of religion,[2] or the constitutionally-based right of privacy.[3] However, whether the constitutionally protected zone of privacy includes refusal of medical treatment where death is likely to result has never been decided by the United States Supreme Court.

Second, the state generally may not interfere with a patient's right to refuse treatment by claiming that it seeks to prevent suicide.[4] Of course, situations and facts vary, but courts tend not to construe the rejection of life-saving measures as an attempt to commit suicide.[5] Indeed, it is misleading to characterize a patient's right to reject treatment as a "right to die." Rather, it is more accurate to say it is the right of self-determination.

Third, the state has a *parens patriae* interest in protecting the incompetent,[6] however, the mere allegation of a patient's incompetence ought not to be used as an excuse to reject a patient's objection to, or rejection of, medical treatment.[7] Incompetence is not established by determining whether or not a patient has the competence to execute a will.[8] Nor is incompetence established when a psychiatrist says a patient is incompetent.[9] Similarly, incompetence may not be assumed by family members or physicians because they consider the patient's refusal irrational.[10] Although incompetence seems elusive, some courts have used the finding of incompetence to severely limit an individual's right to refuse treatment.[11]

Fourth, the interests of the medical profession alone do not constitute a state interest sufficient to justify coercive medical treatment,[12] regardless of whether these interests are characterized as the exercise of professional judgment, upholding the ethics of the profession, or protecting the practitioner from liability. The latter interest may be served by allowing doctors and hospitals access to the courts, with clear directions as to how to proceed whenever a patient in a precarious condition refuses life-saving treatment. Medical personnel, of course, may not be compelled to engage in procedures that are contraindicated by their reasonable judgment. But, conversely, there are few circumstances where individuals should be required to submit to medical treatment.

Finally courts may compel treatment to further such legitimate state interests as preventing the spread of communicable diseases[13] and protecting the well-being of minor children.[14] As the *Osborne*[15] case shows, even this interest can become attenuated when one parent will survive and the child's needs have been provided for. Thus, although the reported cases of compulsory treatment are relatively rare,[16] they tend to demonstrate the complexity of the problems involved. In many of these cases, the courts engage in a discussion of the value of preserving life.[17] Today, however, because medical technology may preserve lives that are not "saveable" many courts are calling attention to the quality of the life that the state is called upon to sustain.[18] Upon examination, courts have found the state interests insubstantial when compared with the suffering that victims of terminal or incurable disease may undergo, and have allowed that a natural death may be a permissible choice.[19]

Thus, in some situations the courts have recognized the patient's right to refuse treatment even when that decision means certain death. These situations include: where the patient was dying and chose a peaceful death over a prolonged life of physical pain and mental anguish;[20] where the patient had no minor children,[21] or had made arrangements for them in the event of his death, and had knowingly refused treatment;[22] or where patient's prognosis for recovery was very poor and medical treatment would do nothing to cure the underlying condition.[23]

THE RIGHT TO REFUSE TREATMENT

The issue of the right to refuse treatment should be viewed in its place on a continuum of treatment rights. At one end, there is the potentially curable patient confronted with the risks and alternatives of selecting treatment. There is the seriously ill patient deciding whether to initiate life-sustaining therapy. And, finally, there is the dying patient, who may be requesting the discontinuation of life-sustaining treatment. This patient asks the medical system not to prolong a condition that it cannot cure, and to allow nature to take its course.

An issue related to withdrawing extraordinary treatment from the terminal patient is the use of do-not-resuscitate (DNR) or no-code orders. There is no precise definition of the phrase "no-code order," but it generally is a direction to the nursing staff from a physician that standard cardio-pulmonary resuscitative procedures should not be used if a patient suffers cardiac arrest. Other expressions, such as "no code blue" send the same message. It should be noted, however, that DNR orders do not include the withdrawal of life-sustaining procedures. Although case law on the subject is scant, there would seem to be a legal distinction between withholding and withdrawing life-sustaining procedures.[24] The distinction would seem to depend on whether the resuscitation effort will "cure or relieve the illnesses" which have precipitated cardio-pulmonary failure.[25]

MODELS FOR DECISION MAKING

There are some basic models that hospitals might consider adopting when grappling with the issue of withholding or withdrawing life-supporting mechanisms from terminally ill patients. The first can be found in the *Saikewicz* decision, which recognizes "a general right in all persons to refuse medical treatment in appropriate circumstances."[26] The practical result of *Saikewicz* is that when a patient is legally incompetent to make such a refusal, a court-appointed guardian or temporary guardian may be sought to make the decision whether to withhold or withdraw treatment.[27] "The guardian must represent the interests of the patient at the probate court hearing on the ultimate issue of treatment."[28] At this hearing, the court will apply a "substituted judgment" test, which requires that it determine the question according to the "values and desires" of the patient.[29]

The decision-making rights of a competent patient were challenged before the Massachusetts Court of Appeals for the first time in *Lane v. Candura*.[30] That court, relying on *Saikewicz*, affirmed that competent patients could refuse life-saving as well as life-prolonging treatment.[31] Thus, the *Saikewicz* model does not require that a court order be obtained in order to validate the refusal of treatment in all cases. The *Saikewicz* requirement of a probate court hearing would seem to apply only to incompetent patients who are wards of the state. *Saikewicz* certainly does not require hearings for competent patients. It leaves unanswered, however, questions concerning the legal role of family members, the status of incompetent persons who are not wards of the state, and what constitutes competency for purposes of making a decision concerning medical treatment.

The second model is suggested by the well-publicized *Quinlan* case,[32] which was decided the year before *Saikewicz*. At this point, it should be noted that *Saikewicz* reflects only the law of Massachusetts, while the *Quinlan* decision, and the procedures it mandated, are the law in New Jersey. These decisions are not authoritative as to the law in other states, unless the courts of those states decide to adopt their analyses.

Karen Quinlan was suffering from irreversible brain injury. Although she was not "brain dead," she had no realistic hope of recovery. In response to her father's petition to be appointed guardian for purposes of declining further consent to her maintenance on a respirator, the Supreme Court of New Jersey held that guardian consent was not enough. The court held that the hospital ethics committee (the existence of which was assumed), the patient's physician, her guardian, and her family must be consulted as to the reasonable possibility of her recovery. Should they all agree, care could be withdrawn. Moreover, no court order would be necessary to justify that decision, and no civil or criminal liability would attach to it.

Although a hospital ethics committee could be very helpful in dealing with this complex issue, it leaves unanswered a number of questions. For example, what persons should compose the hospital ethics committee? The *Quinlan* court did not define such a committee. Nor is guidance provided as to the number of committee members, their professional backgrounds, or the voting methods to be employed. Is a majority vote required, or must the decision be unanimous? Also, the *Quinlan* court required the concurrence of family without defining "family." So, although the *Quinlan* model helped achieve the result that the court wanted to reach, it is not always a workable model.

A third model, developed by the Massachusetts General Hospital, classifies critically ill patients into four treatment categories, each requiring a different level of care and supervision. It creates an "optimum care committee," charged with determining the level of care each patient should receive. Although the personal physician makes the final determination, the committee is considered to be most effective when it convenes with all members of the health care team involved in treating the patient, and when its consultation and concurrence are required before committing a definite act (e.g., turning off a respirator). A major drawback of this model is that it does not work well in crisis situations; it is too time-consuming. Further, the model does not specify whether the decision of the committee is to be majority vote or unanimous.

The fourth model, one developed by Beth Israel Hospital in Boston, provides a structured decision-making process which would be initiated before the issuance of "no-code orders" or the withholding of extraordinary care.[33] Before a DNR order is written, the attending physician must discuss the decision with an ad hoc committee consisting not only of other physicians and nurses attending the patient, but also of at least one other senior staff physician. Once made, the decision can be effectuated only with the informed choice of a competent patient or, if the patient is incompetent, only with the agreement of all appropriate family members. Although this model is less cumbersome than Massachusetts General's, there is one major flaw—the requirement that the consent of all appropriate family members be obtained. Because the model fails to define "family," and because it extends a legal right to family members that does not exist under law, its legal status is problematic.[34]

A fifth model, used by Northwestern Memorial Hospital in Chicago,[35] requires that all DNR orders be written in the patient's medical records by the attending physician. If the physician desires, these orders may include the opinion of the consulting physician, the diagnosis and prognosis of the patient, notes on discussions with the family, and other bases for the order. The policy does not seek to modify the physician's obligations to render ordinary and reasonable care, nor compromise the privilege not to render extraordinary care. Existing legal obligations in relationships are virtually left alone. In other words, when the patient is incompetent or unable to participate in the decision-making process, or both, the physician alone makes the decision and is only required to write it on the chart.

This policy was developed jointly by the hospital's medical and nursing staffs, and was approved by its medical executive committee. The objectives of this model are to free the attending physician to treat the patient without imposing a cumbersome decision-making process that offers no additional legal protection, and to provide specific instructions to the hospital staff as to the wishes of the attending physician. In the event of litigation, the physician, house staff, and nurses are in the position of having acted according to an express treatment plan, and do not have to defend a chart from which a treatment order was purposely excluded.

The sixth model is basically no model at all, i.e., ad hoc decision making. If a hospital has no policy for dealing with these issues, the results are likely to be inconsistent and unresponsive. I believe that these situations can be handled more expeditiously and less traumatically if there are settled procedures that reflect concern for the legal rights and the medical needs of the patient. The psychological needs of the patient's family, the human and professional needs of the hospital staff, the law, and the duties of the hospital to the community are also better served by planning for these inevitable eventualities.

CONCLUSION

It is my belief that seeking judicial intervention in every case involving withdrawal of care is not only not mandated by cases like *Saikewicz* and

Quinlan, but also places a tremendous burden on the patient, family, physicians, and hospital personnel. Although the family should be consulted and advised of the patient's condition and proposed treatment, and their views considered, hospitals should be very careful that their considerations do not suggest or assume the existence of a legal right that families do not have. Except when a family member has been appointed guardian of a patient, or when a parent exercises authority over the treatment of his or her child, no family member should be allowed to dictate the patient's care.

As to the creation and mandatory use of committees, such as in the models described above, I am not convinced that they can provide the answer in every situation. Committees cannot alter the basic legal relationships between the attending physician and the patient. In some cases, the committee by its very existence tends to compromise the physician's ability to execute his or her legal duty or professional judgment. Further, unless the membership, the voting rights, and the procedural rules of such a committee are strictly defined, it can become a cumbersome impediment to the patient's welfare. Finally, the committee structure is not designed to and cannot deal effectively with decisions that need to be made quickly.

One alternative would be to require or suggest that the attending physician consult with another physician who is on the staff of the hospital but not treating the patient. This procedure has been adopted in some hospitals as an attempt to minimize the risks of liability for a physician's alleged failure to treat. Regardless of the procedure adopted, the DNR order should be written in the patient's chart, along with a record of consultations and the reasons for the order. The circumstances surrounding the order should also be set forth in detail, and should include the medical situation, consultation with the patient, his or her consent, and consultation with the family or, if applicable, the patient's guardian. Once a physician has determined that a no-code order is appropriate, it should be written in the patient's chart to provide evidence that the hospital and staff have rendered care as ordered. It should be noted that the Joint Commission on the Accreditation of Hospitals, as well as the Michigan Department of Public Health requires that all diagnostic and therapeutic orders be written in patient charts. Some suggest that a no-code order is not a therapeutic order and, therefore, need not be written. I think that the distinction is artificial—that such an order is a treatment order and should be written. Sound medical practice dictates that no-code orders be of short duration because there are, on occasion, recoveries or changes in a patient's condition. For these reasons, it is appropriate that each patient be re-evaluated periodically to determine whether his or her condition has changed.

Finally, I recommend that before a hospital adopts procedures, such as those described, it should conduct an educational program. Physicians and other hospital personnel need to know the proper procedures to follow and the rationales behind them. Planning and consensus are the key ingredients to any such procedure's success.

NOTES

1. *Erikson v. Dilgard*, 252 N.Y.S.2d 705 (Sup. Ct. 1962).
2. *In re Osborne*, 294 A.2d 372 (D.C. App. 1972); *In re Brooks' Estate*, 205 N.E.2d 435 (Ill. 1965).
3. *Superintendent of Belchertown State School v. Saikewicz*, 370 N.E.2d 417 (Mass. 1977) [hereinafter cited as *Saikewicz*]; *In re Quinlan*, 355 A. 2d 647 (N.J. 1976), *cert. denied sub nom. Garger v. New Jersey*, 429 U.S. 922 (1976).
4. *In re Quackenbush*, 383 A.2d 785 (N.J. P. Ct. 1978).
5. *Satz v. Perlmutter*, 362 So.2d 160, 163 (Fla. App. 1978), *aff'd*, 379 So.2d 359, 360 (Fla. 1980); *Erikson v. Dilgard, supra* note 1, at 106. *But see Application of President and Directors of Georgetown College*, 331 F.2d 1000, 1008–09 (D.C. Cir.), *cert. denied*, 377 U.S. 978 (1964) [hereinafter cited as *Georgetown*].
6. *In re Schiller*, 372 A.2d 360 (Super. Ct. N.J. 1977).
7. *Lane v. Candura*, 376 N.E.2d 1232 (Mass. App. 1978); *In re Quackenbush, supra* note 4; *In re Raasch*, No. 455–996 (Milwaukee County Ct., P. Div., Jan. 25, 1972). *But see In re Storar*, 420 N.E.2d 64 (N.Y. 1981).
8. *The Dying Person: His Plight and His Right*, NEW ENGLAND LAW REVIEW 8(2):197 (1973).
9. *Lane v. Candura, supra* note 7; *In re Raasch, supra* note 7; *In re Nemser*, 273 N.Y.S.2d 624 (Sup. Ct. 1966).
10. *Lane v. Candura, supra* note 7; *In re Quackenbush, supra* note 4.
11. *In re Schiller, supra* note 6; *Georgetown, supra* note 5.
12. *Saikewicz, supra* note 3, at 427; *In re Nemser, supra* note 9, at 629.
13. *Kleid v. Board of Education of Fulton, Kentucky, Independent School District*, 406 F. Supp. 902 (W.D.Ky. 1976).
14. *Georgetown, supra* note 5; *Powell v. Columbia Presbyterian Medical Center*, 267 N.Y.S.2d 450 (Sup. Ct. 1965).
15. *In re Osborne, supra* note 2 (father of young children, a Jehovah's Witness, permitted to decline life-saving blood transfusion).
16. Cantor, N.L., *A Patient's Decision to Decline Life-Saving Medical Treatment: Bodily Integrity Versus the Preservation of Life*, RUTGERS LAW REVIEW 26(2):228–64 (Winter 1973).
17. *Powell v. Columbia Presbyterian Medical Center, supra* note 14; *Georgetown, supra* note 5.
18. *Severns v. Wilmington Medical Center*, 421 A.2d 1334, 1344 (Del. 1980); *In re Quinlan, supra* note 3, at 654–57.
19. *Satz v. Perlmutter, supra* note 5; *Saikewicz, supra* note 3.
20. *Palm Springs General Hospital v. Martinez*, No. 71–12678 (Fla. Cir. Ct., July 2, 1971).

21. *In re Brooks' Estate, supra* note 2.

22. *In re Osborne, supra* note 2.

23. *Severns v. Wilmington Medical Center, supra* note 18; *In re Spring,* 405 N.E.2d 115 (Mass. 1980); *Eichner v. Dillon,* 426 N.Y.S.2d 517 (Sup. Ct. 1980); *Satz v. Perlmutter, supra* note 5; *Saikewicz, supra* note 3; *In re Quinlan, supra* note 3; *Leach v. Akron General Medical Center,* No.C80–10–20 (Ohio Ct. C.P., Summit County, Dec. 18, 1980).

24. *In re Dinnerstein,* 380 N.E.2d 134 (Mass. App. 1978).

25. "Attempts to apply resuscitation, if successful, will do nothing to cure or relieve the illnesses which will have brought the patient to the threshold of death. . . . This case does not offer a life-saving or life-prolonging treatment alternative within the meaning of the *Saikewicz* case." *Id.* at 139.

26. *Saikewicz, supra* note 3, at 427.

27. *Id.* at 433.

28. *Id.* at 434.

29. *Id.* at 431, 434.

30. *Lane v. Candura, supra* note 7.

31. *Id.* at 1233.

32. *In re Quinlan, supra* note 3.

33. *See* Appendix D.

34. *See, e.g., In re Spring, supra* note 23, where the Massachusetts Supreme Judicial Court concluded that it was reversible error of the Probate Court "to delegate the decision [to end treatment of incompetent patient] to the attending physician and the ward's wife and son." 405 N.E.2d at 117.

35. *See* Appendix E.

Chapter 11

Assuring "Detached but Passionate Investigation and Decision": The Role of Guardians Ad Litem in *Saikewicz*-type Cases

Charles H. Baron

I. INTRODUCTION

> We do not view the judicial resolution of this most difficult and awesome question—whether potentially life-prolonging treatment should be withheld from a person incapable of making his own decision—as constituting a "gratuitous encroachment" on the domain of medical expertise. Rather, such questions of life and death seem to us to require the process of detached but passionate investigation and decision that forms the ideal on which the judicial branch of government was created. Achieving this ideal is our responsibility and that of the lower court, and is not to be entrusted to any other group purporting to represent the "morality and conscience of our society," no matter how highly motivated or impressively constituted.[1]

With this language in its recent[2] opinion in *Superintendent of Belchertown State School v. Saikewicz*, the Supreme Judicial Court of Massachusetts unanimously recognizes the proposition that our Society has never conferred upon its medical community the power to decide which of society's members shall live and which shall die.[3] Earlier in the opinion, the court recognizes that this power over each individual life resides primarily in the individual involved and holds, for the first time in Massachusetts,[4] that, where certain specified state interests[5] do not outweigh the individual's right to privacy and right to be free from

Reprinted with permission of the American Society of Law & Medicine from the AMERICAN JOURNAL OF LAW & MEDICINE, Vol. 4, no. 2 (Summer 1978).

nonconsensual invasions of his bodily integrity,[6] the individual possesses a legally recognized right to choose death over life-prolonging medical treatment. However, Joseph Saikewicz clearly was not competent to make that decision[7] for himself since, although he was 67 years of age, he had an I.Q. of 10 and a mental age of approximately 2 years and 8 months. Under those circumstances, the court holds, first, that the right to choose death "must extend to the case of an incompetent, as well as a competent, patient because the value of human dignity extends to both";[8] second, that in making that choice for an incompetent, a proxy decision maker must take into consideration only factors that go to the question of what the individual would have decided for himself[9] and may not consider, for example, such factors as the value of the particular life to society;[10] and, third, in the most widely noted part of its opinion, that the Probate Court of Massachusetts is "the proper tribunal to determine the best interests of "[11] a person incompetent to make such a decision for himself.

Were it not for the history of the development and growth in number of such life and death questions in a medical context in recent years, one might think the court's conclusion to be relatively uncontroversial. After all, doctors and hospital ethics committees[12] are not elected representatives of the people and hold no appointive commission to decide such weighty societal questions. Although doctors are licensed by the state to practice medicine, such practice is defined in Massachusetts as conduct "the purpose or reasonably foreseeable effect of which is to encourage the reliance of another person upon an individual's knowledge or skill in the *maintenance of human health* by the prevention, alleviation, or cure of disease. . . ."[13] There is, of course, no mandate here to decide whether patients will live or die. But, because of the development in recent years of a sophisticated medical technology that provides possibilities for prolonging a merely vegetative existence indefinitely, doctors have found themselves forced by default to decide when life prolongation becomes, by their own individual standards of the moment,[14] senseless from a practical point of view. Although one would expect that many doctors would be happy to have this awesome responsibility taken from them, the more general, and understandable, reaction from the medical community to the *Saikewicz* decision has been resentment of what is seen as the Supreme Judicial Court's "total distrust of physicians' judgment in such matters,"[15] and fear that court involvement in this area will disrupt the work of doctors in ways that will affect deleteriously the treatment that can be given to patients generally. A recent editorial in *The New England Journal of Medicine* describes the position of the medical community:[16]

Traditionally, doctors responsible for the care of "incompetent" patients have abided by the wishes of the next of kin, who are, of course, greatly influenced by the doctor's professional opinion. In the absence of relatives, physicians have customarily used their own best judgment, aided by the advice of colleagues and frequently the opinions of other health professionals, ministers and lawyers; sometimes, they are also advised by special hospital committees organized for this purpose. In the famous *Quinlan* case, the New Jersey Supreme Court acknowledged the appropriateness of such arrangements by delegating to the patient's father, her doctors and the hospital ethics committee the responsibility for deciding whether to withdraw the mechanical respiratory assistance that was believed to be sustaining her hopelessly comatose existence. . . .

In Massachusetts the immediate disruptive consequences of the *Saikewicz* ruling have already appeared. In some cases physicians and next of kin will probably defer urgent medical decisions, both positive and negative, pending court approval. In other cases decisions that had formerly been made expeditiously, but only after full and explicit consultation, will now be made hastily and even furtively, thus returning "to the closet" questions that need open and thoughtful discussion. It will take time and many court decisions to sort out the problem, but in the meantime confusion reigns and much harm may be done. Attorneys I have spoken with do not believe the probate courts can possibly handle the number of cases that will be generated by the *Saikewicz* decision, nor do they believe that court action will be prompt enough in many cases to be helpful.

In the same edition of *The New England Journal of Medicine* cited above, a lawyer who is that journal's regular commentator on medicolegal problems also takes issue with the *Saikewicz* decision, expressing the wish that the Massachusetts Supreme Judicial Court had been more taken with the position of the New Jersey Supreme Court in *Quinlan*, and deploring the fact that under *Saikewicz* each case is to be an adversary proceeding."[17]

It is ironic, given the latter statement, that under the procedures laid out in the *Saikewicz* opinion there is no guarantee that each case will be a true adversary proceeding. That fact, for which some doctors might be grateful, is nevertheless, in the present writer's opinion, the principal *defect* in the *Saikewicz* decision since it undermines the court's own goal of assuring for these life and death questions "the process of detached but passionate investigation and decision that forms the ideal on which the judicial branch of government was created."[18] The present Article describes this flaw in *Saikewicz* more fully, and makes recommendations for correcting the flaw.

II. THE LACK OF ADVERSARY PROCESS IN THE *SAIKEWICZ* PRESCRIPTION

The *Saikewicz* case itself was not an adversary proceeding. On April 19, 1976, when Joseph Saikewicz was diagnosed as suffering from acute myeloblastic monocytic leukemia, he was a resident of the Belchertown State School, where he had lived for many years. Although the school regularly administers simple medical treatment to its residents under its general powers of guardianship, it will not administer elective medical treatment without court approval.[19] As a result, on April 26, it filed a petition in the Hampshire County Probate Court for the purpose of having the court appoint a guardian who would consent to a course of chemotherapy treatment for Mr. Saikewicz. Because the matter was thought urgent and existing law did not seem to provide for the appointment of a temporary guardian for mentally retarded persons,[20] the petitioners also requested that the court forthwith appoint a guardian ad litem in the hope that he would have the power to provide interim consent.[21]

By May 5, when the guardian ad litem was appointed, the doctors attending Mr. Saikewicz had changed their minds about whether it was in their patient's best interests to begin chemotherapy. They had come to the conclusion that he was probably better off being allowed to die from the leukemia. As a result, when the guardian ad litem filed a report with his recommendations on May 6, he concluded, on the basis of consultations with the attending physicians, "that not treating Mr. Saikewicz would be in his best interests."[22] Hence, although the probate court held a hearing on the report of the guardian ad litem on May 13, it would be hard to argue that the hearing constituted an adversary proceeding. On one side were the petitioners, who had originally come to court seeking permission to begin chemotherapy but whose doctors gradually had come around to a position generally opposed to it. On the other side was an incompetent defendant, represented by a guardian ad litem who was also opposed.

The transcript of the May 13 probate court hearing makes the lack of adversary process patent. Although the petition in the case called for the appointment of a guardian who would consent to treatment, counsel for the petitioner put on evidence that essentially proved the case against treatment. Three doctors were put on the stand by the petitioner for the purpose of testifying to some of the surrounding facts and, in the case of two of them, of expressing opinions that Mr. Saikewicz should not be given chemotherapy.[23] When one of the doctors was unclear about that opinion, counsel for the petitioner led the witness with this question: "You feel that the treatment should be withheld since his condition is stable ?"[24] When the same doctor seemed to be muddying the evidence for denying chemotherapy by saying, "If we give him chemotherapy, he will become very sick and if we treat him intensively, then he might live indefinitely and recover," counsel for the petitioner provoked the following clarifying exchange:[25]

Q.   You say that he might live indefinitely?
A.   I am saying for a year or so.
[Q.]   You can be seated. Thank you Dr. Ross.

Through all of this there were no objections by the guardian ad litem, although there was one question asked by way of cross-examination.[26] At the conclusion of the case, the guardian ad litem expressed a relatively equivocal opinion that was taken to be the same as that expressed in his earlier report.[27] The only person in the room who seemed interested in considering arguments in favor of chemotherapy was Judge Jekanowski. At one point, he said: "I feel that if I had a serious disease and with treatment I could live another five or eight years or ten years, whatever, I'd rather take the treatment than just take the chance of dying tomorrow or next week."[28] At another point he recalled:[29]

> I had a patient, a patient at the State Hospital who didn't want water, and didn't want food. So the doctors were frightened for without water and without food he would die. They had a hearing such as this and they were asking the Court his permission to allow them to force feed this patient. This must have been two years ago and the patient is living because they did force feed and gave him water and food by force and he is still alive and happy. In effect, they saved his life or that saved his life. This is a similar type of case, in a way.

But the judge found no support for his position from anyone else in the courtroom, and, although he at one point said, "I am inclined to give treatment,"[30] he ultimately was argued around to the opposite position, after which counsel for petitioner offered to draft the written order authorizing the withholding of chemotherapy.[31]

In an effort to avoid this sort of procedural confusion in the future, the Supreme Judicial Court in *Saikewicz* devotes an unusual amount of attention to the matter of laying down guidelines for future handling of such cases. "The first step," reads the opinion, "is to petition the court for the appointment of a guardian or a temporary guardian."[32] At the hearing that is to be provided upon such petitions, the questions to be addressed are (1) whether the person involved is incompetent,[33] and (2) if the person is incompetent, who shall be appointed guardian.

The court goes on to recognize important functions for the guardian ad litem:[34]

> As an aid to the judge in reaching these two decisions, it will often be desirable to appoint a guardian ad litem, sua sponte or on motion, to represent the interests of the person. Moreover, we think it appropriate, and highly desirable, in cases such as the one before us to charge the guardian ad litem with an additional responsibility to be discharged if there is a finding of incompetency. This will be the responsibility of presenting to the judge, after as thorough an investigation as time will permit, all reasonable arguments in favor of administering treatment to prolong the life of the individual involved. This will ensure that all viewpoints and alternatives will be aggressively pursued and examined at the subsequent hearing where it will be determined whether treatment should or should not be allowed.

The role the court suggests for the guardian ad litem in the quoted passage is much like that proposed by the present writer in a 1975 article that explored problems of nonadversariness in organ and tissue transplant proceedings brought in the state courts for the purpose of securing proxy consent from minor donors.[35] That article, which is discussed in two of the supplementary briefs filed in *Saikewicz* for the purpose of proposing procedures for future handling of *Saikewicz*-type cases,[36] deplored the lack of procedural fairness afforded minor donors that had resulted from confusion regarding the role of the guardian ad litem. Such confusion was natural. The traditional role of a guardian ad litem is to represent in any proceedings the best interests of his ward.[37] However, in those minor donor proceedings, where the parents and hospital were seeking to have the donor child consent to a transplant that might save the life of his sibling, the very question that was to be decided by the court was which result was in harmony with the best interests of the *donor* child: saving the life of his sibling, or refusing to submit to the risks of donation. As a result, a practice had arisen under which the guardians ad litem forsook their traditional advocacy role.[38] They would determine for themselves and report to the court their conclusions regarding the question that was to be decided by the court: whether donation was in fact in the best interests of their wards. This nonadvocacy function, the article argued, undermined what the *Saikewicz* opinion has since then felicitously called "the process of detached but passionate investigation and decision. . . ." The essence of that process comprises a division of role between, on the one hand, advocates who have the primary responsibility for passionate investigation and argument on behalf of their opposed positions and, on the other hand, judges who have the primary responsibility for detached and objective decision making rendered upon a record made full by the advocacy of counsel. "Failure generally attends the attempt to dispense with the distinct roles traditionally implied in adjudication," warns a 1958 report of a committee of distinguished legal scholars and practitioners. "What generally occurs in practice [where those roles break down] is that at some early point a familiar pattern will seem to emerge from the evidence; an accustomed label is waiting for the case and, without awaiting further proofs, this label is promptly assigned to it."[39]

Such was the result in most of the minor donor cases. The guardian ad litem would reach his own conclusion (concerning the best interests of his ward) as a detached decision maker without the benefit of any advocate's passionate investigation and development of the record upon which to make his decision. He would then go into court with his mind virtually made up, thus denying to the court in turn the value of passionate investigation and advocacy in developing a record upon which the court could base its detached decision. Furthermore, the 1975 article observed, "[t]he hospital and the parents assuredly are not engaged in a dispassionate search for truth. They want the transplant to occur, and they go into court with the intention of proving that the participation of the prospective donor is consistent with whatever standard the court decides to apply."[40] Because, in almost every such case, the guardian had already determined that donation was in the best interests of his ward, there was no advocate present to argue the case against donation, and it became[41]

> too easy for the judge to gloss over the evidence and issues in an effort to reach quickly and efficiently what seems to be the right result. Of course, such action need not reach the level of a conscious effort to take the path of least resistance. It may operate merely through the unconscious development of a mental set as to the merits of the case, blinding the judge to the lines of opposing argument and evidence that could have been developed.

In order to obviate this problem, the article proposed:[42]

> Courts should be required to appoint guardians ad litem to represent prospective minor donors in all transplant proceedings. The guardian's role should be defined as that of an advocate of the child's interest in not acting as a donor; the guardian should be instructed to present all the evidence and arguments against his ward's donation and to oppose the positions taken by the hospital and family, regardless of the guardian's personal perception of the child's actual interests.

The system proposed in the 1975 article is now being employed by some of the courts and guardians ad litem handling cases involving organ and tissue transplants from minor donors.[43] On the one hand, such advocacy has not produced thus far any case in Massachusetts in which a court has refused to authorize proxy consent for donation of bone marrow or a kidney to a sibling.[44] This is not, of course, surprising, in light of the fact that these cases normally involve offering great benefit to the recipient at the price of what seems relatively slight risk to the donor.[45] On the other hand, there have been benefits to the donors and to the system. The earliest cases in which guardians played full advocacy roles[46] produced a court-developed scheme for insurance devised to compensate a donor who might be disabled by the donation. One attorney who has handled a number of such appointments on a pro bono basis believes that his strong advocate's position[47] has been responsible for reducing the extent and number of operative procedures upon his wards in some cases and has assured concern for the special risks of anesthesia for one ward who had asthma. He has also found that his commitment to his role as an advocate stimulates a continuing desire to learn more about the details of the transplant procedures so that he can more effectively cross-examine witnesses and develop the evidence for his side. These efforts at education have been assisted by doctors in the field and have included observing a two-and-one-half-hour bone marrow transplant operation on one of his wards.

This attitude of "passionate investigation" is even more important in cases of the *Saikewicz* type, where it is more likely to make a difference in the ultimate outcome. In *Saikewicz*, the Supreme Judicial Court states very clearly that the only substantive standard which the courts are to employ (assuming there are no pro-life state interests to the contrary) is that of taking that action for the ward that he would have taken for himself if he were competent. But without adequate safeguards, other criteria are likely to intrude. Indeed, as the Supreme Judicial Court points out, the probate court in *Saikewicz* could be read to have improperly considered, in reaching its decision against chemotherapy, the fact that Mr. Saikewicz was profoundly retarded and the effect that this had upon "the quality of life possible for him even if the treatment does bring about remission."[48] As a result of the disapproval voiced by the Supreme Judicial Court, this criterion is unlikely to surface explicitly in the future. But without aggressive advocacy, including assiduous cross-examination of witnesses, it still may function as a factor implicitly biasing the testimony of witnesses—as may other forbidden factors such as the potential costs to family, medical facilities, and society of prolonging the life in question.[49]

In light of the crucial importance of the role of the guardian ad litem in assuring objectivity and fairness in the judicial administration of these cases, the fault in the *Saikewicz* opinion is that it does not go far enough in laying guidelines for the development of a full and fair record through zealous representation of all positions.

First, the court neither requires that a guardian ad litem be appointed in every case, nor lays down specific guidelines for when such appointment is necessary or desirable. The opinion says only that "it will often be desirable to appoint a guardian ad litem, sua sponte or on motion, to represent the interest of the person,"[50] that "the Probate Court may appoint a guardian ad litem whenever the court believes it necessary to protect the interests of a person in a proceeding before it,"[51] and that "[t]his power is inherent in the court even apart from statutory authorization, and its exercise at times becomes necessary for the proper function of the court."[52] The cases cited by the court for this last proposition[53] approve it at best only in passing and without themselves giving any criteria for deciding when such appointment might be necessary. That a clear mandate from the court on this subject is needed is evidenced by the fact that many of the kidney transplant decisions in the Commonwealth have authorized the taking of a kidney from a child on the basis of proceedings in which no guardian ad litem was ever appointed to represent the interests of the child.[54]

Second, the court imposes a responsibility upon the guardian ad litem to make "all reasonable arguments in favor of administering treatment to prolong the life of the individual involved,"[55] but it does not say whether this is to be in addition to making arguments as well against treatment. At least one attorney who has served as a guardian ad litem in a post-*Saikewicz* case has interpreted this language as a mandate to the guardian ad litem to remember to raise all such arguments as part of an effort to present relatively evenhandedly arguments both for and against prolongation of life.[56] However, others have interpreted the language to mean that the guardian ad litem is to devote himself primarily to the case for prolongation, leaving to opposing counsel the job of developing the case against.[57] Experience with the latter, more traditional, advocacy role indicates that it is much more conducive to the sort of "passionate investigation" that the court seems interested in promoting.[58]

Third, there is no guarantee that in the *Saikewicz*-type cases even requiring that a guardian ad litem be appointed and that he argue the case in favor of treatment "will ensure that all viewpoints and alternatives will be aggressively pursued and examined at the . . . hearing where it will be determined whether treatment should or should not be allowed."[59] In a case where the only other party is a petitioner who is also arguing for treatment, having the guardian ad litem argue for treatment will mean that the viewpoint against treatment will not be "aggressively pursued and examined." Technically this was the situation in *Saikewicz*. The Belchertown State School had petitioned, as it frequently does, for permission to begin treatment. In that case, as we have seen, it did not really press that position. But there may be other cases where a state institution will come to court prepared to vigorously assert that position. Under those circumstances, the need is to have someone, presumably the guardian ad litem, aggressively pursue the case against treatment. After all, the Supreme Judicial Court has recognized that the right to choose death with dignity "must extend to the case of an incompetent, as well as a competent, patient because the value of human dignity extends to both."[60] It would seem, then, important to make sure that in every case the position against treatment is as adequately represented as the position for treatment.

Furthermore, even in many cases where the petitioner takes the position against treatment, there may be no meaningful representation of that position. Typically, the real moving party in these cases is the medical care facility that wants to be insulated from liability by a court order before it terminates supportive care or services—even though it may have the consent of the patient's family. Even if the principals of the facility and the doctors involved truly believe that care should be terminated, they do not want to be placed in the position of pressing the case for death. Moreover, in many cases, the principals and doctors are not sure what position they should take and are really seeking the court's guidance. As a result, the medical personnel will suggest to the relatives that they petition for an order authorizing termination of care. But the relatives are frequently no more ready than the medical personnel to aggressively press the court for termination of care. They are likely to be very embarrassed about aggressively urging such a position, less able than the medical personnel to find and afford able counsel to represent them in such a specialized proceeding, and just as likely to be really interested in seeking the court's detached and wise guidance.[61] As a result, the position in favor of the patient's right to die with dignity is in danger of lacking adequate representation.

Hence, there may well be as much need for a court-appointed advocate for death with dignity as there is for a guardian ad litem who will make "all reasonable arguments in favor of administering treatment to prolong the life of the individual involved."[62]

III. RECOMMENDATIONS FOR PROCEDURES
FOSTERING AN ADVERSARY PROCESS

For the purpose of attempting to assure an adversary process in *Saikewicz*-type cases, the present writer recommends the following procedural guidelines:

(1) In every *Saikewicz*-type case, a guardian ad litem is to be appointed to represent the positions opposed to those taken in the petition.

(2) That guardian ad litem is to see his role solely as that of an advocate for the positions opposed to the petition. He is to investigate, develop, and present evidence for his side, cross-examine opposing witnesses, and make arguments just as he would if he had a competent client who had retained him to oppose the position.

(3) At any point in the proceedings, the guardian ad litem, any other party, or the judge, may suggest the appointment of a second guardian ad litem whose role will be to represent the position in favor of granting the petition in the same way that the first guardian ad litem is representing the position opposed to it.

At first blush, this proposal might seem to complicate further a system that already has drawn criticism from the medical discretion. In fact, if properly structured, it may make the system more workable from the point of view of both the legal and the medical communities. The Massachusetts Probate Court already has begun discussion of the possibility of establishing a corps of guardians ad litem who have volunteered for pro bono service in the cases that will follow in the wake of *Saikewicz*.[63] With such a corps of experienced guardians ad litem intact, a given probate court could, upon the filing of a petition, immediately appoint one of its members to each side of the case with the expectation that they could prepare the case and argue it in a very short period of time. Preparation for the first *Saikewicz*-type case tends to be preparation in many respects for those that follow. Moreover, the Massachusetts Probate Court plan calls for constant communication between the volunteer guardians ad litem involved, and for efforts at interdisciplinary communication and cooperation with the health professionals in the fields affected. Among the many benefits that might come from such a system, therefore, are continuing proposals for improved procedures, suggestions that certain patterns of cases need no longer be brought to court in order to insulate the medical community from liability,[64] and improved understanding between the legal and medical communities.

These benefits are, of course, laudable but quite speculative. What seems certain is that, without a system, such as that proposed, that assures appropriate advocacy in each case of the interests of the patient both for and against treatment, the ideal of "passionate but detached investigation and decision" is likely to be served no better in the courtroom than it is in the intensive care unit.

NOTES

1. Superintendent of Belchertown State School v. Saikewicz, 1977 Mass. Adv. Sh. 2461, 2501, 370 N.E.2d 417, 435 (1977).
2. Although the case was argued July 2, 1976, and the Supreme Judicial Court issued its order affirming the decision of the Hampshire County Probate Court seven days later, the former court's opinion on the order and on related matters was not issued until November 28, 1977. The July 9 order merely answered in the affirmative the following questions that originally had been reported to the Appeals Court of Massachusetts:

    1) Does the Probate Court under its general or any special jurisdiction have the authority to order, in circumstances it deems appropriate, the withholding of medical treatment from a person even though such withholding of treatment might contribute to a shortening of the life of such person?

    2) On the facts reported in this case, is the Court correct in ordering that no treatment be administered to said JOSEPH SAIKEWICZ nor or at any time for his condition of acute myeloblastic monocetic [sic] leukemia except by further order of the Court?

    Order of the Honorable Harry Jekanowski, Judge of the Hampshire County, Mass., Probate Court, May 13, 1976.
    On the same day that the July 9 order was issued, the Department of the Attorney General of Massachusetts requested permission to file a supplemental brief that would discuss procedural guidelines for the handling of such cases in the future. The Supreme Judicial Court granted such permission on July 15, and supplementary briefs dealing with procedural guidelines were filed by the Department of the Attorney General, the Civil Rights and Liberties Division of the Department of the Attorney General, the Legal Counsel to the Department of Mental Health, the Massachusetts Association for Retarded Citizens, Inc. and the Mental Health Legal Advisors Committee of Massachusetts. Suggested procedural guidelines were also the subject of several law review articles that appeared before the court's opinion was rendered. *See Brant, The Right to Die in Peace: Substituted Consent and the Mentally Incompetent*, II SUFFOLK U.L. REV. 959 (1977); Kindregan, *The Court as Forum for Life and Death Decisions: Reflections on Procedures for Substituted Consent, id.* at 919 (1977); Schultz, Swartz, & Appelbaum, *Deciding Right-to-Die Cases Involving Incompetent Patients: Jones v. Saikewicz, id.* at 936 (1977).
    While the controversy surrounding his case was beginning to build, Joseph Saikewicz died at 7:25 p.m. on Saturday, September 4, 1976, of bronchial pneumonia brought on by his leukemic condition.
3. In this respect, the decision is, as the court recognizes, directly contrary to the decision of the Supreme Court of New Jersey in *In re* Quinlan, 70 N.J. 10, 355 A.2d 647 (1976), where the latter court stated:

> The nature, extent and duration of care by social standards is the responsibility of a physician. The morality and conscience of our society places this responsibility in the hands of the physician. What justification is there to remove it from the control of the medical profession and place it in the hands of the courts?

Id. at 44, 355 A.2d at 665.

> [U]pon the concurrence of the guardian and family of Karen, should the responsible attending physicians conclude that there is no reasonable possibility of Karen's ever emerging from her present comatose condition to a cognitive, sapient state and that the life-support apparatus now being administered to Karen should be discontinued, they shall consult with the hospital "Ethics Committee" or like body of the institution in which Karen is then hospitalized. If that consultative body agrees that there is no reasonable possibility of Karen's ever emerging from her present comatose condition to a cognitive, sapient state, the present life-support system may be withdrawn and said action shall be without any civil or criminal liability therefor on the part of any participant, whether guardian, physician, hospital or others.

Id. at 55, 355 A.2d at 671 (footnote omitted).

The last-quoted sentence from the *Quinlan* opinion highlights what is desired from these cases by the medical community: legal insulation from civil and criminal liability for acts which will cause—indeed may be intended to cause—the death of a patient. What the *Quinlan* court has done is to grant such protection to all persons participating in such acts where there has been the sort of concurrence of opinion laid out by that court. (Note that the protection is granted only for certain acts, e.g., turning off the "life-support apparatus." It is *not* granted for certain *other* acts, e.g., injecting a dose of a painless but lethal drug. As a result of this distinction, Karen Quinlan continues to exist in a comatose state.) In contrast, it is clear that the *Saikewicz* court has refused to make such a blanket grant of protection. Such protection, the court is saying, can come only through a judgment rendered by a court of law on the basis of the fully developed facts of each case.

Beyond that, however, the *Saikewicz* opinion raises more questions than it answers. It is possible to read the court as saying nothing more than that only the courts have the power to grant what is in essence declaratory relief. What the participants in these cases want is assurance that the acts that they wish to perform will not subject them to liability. A traditional method for gaining such assurance is for the persons who are fearful of liability to bring a declaratory judgment action against the persons whom they fear as potential plaintiffs. If they obtain a declaratory judgment of nonliability, they may then perform the desired acts confident that they can raise an effective defense of res judicata in any later action brought by any of the parties to the action for declaratory relief. Under this reading, the court is not saying that failure to seek advance permission from a court makes the participants ipso facto liable for their acts of termination of care. It is not saying that advance court authorization is a *necessary* condition for avoiding liability, only that is is a *sufficient* condition.

However, another interpretation is possible. The *Saikewicz* court could be saying that, at least in some cases, terminating care for an incompetent without first getting court authorization in the form of "proxy consent" (the court or court-appointed guardian's "substituted judgment"), renders the participants liable ipso facto. Here the court would be saying that court authorization is a *necessary* condition for avoiding liability. Much of the case law regarding liability for decisions to *treat* incompetents rests on the theory that treatment without "proxy consent" is ipso facto a battery. *See* W. PROSSER, THE LAW OF TORTS 101–08 (4th ed. 1971). The *Saikewicz* case itself began as a routine request for "proxy consent" to treatment in order to avoid liability for batteries. *See* notes 19–21 *infra* and accompanying text. And there are policy considerations that would favor this approach by the court in the area of decisions *not* to treat. Among them is the fact that there may be little motivation on the part of participants to go to court to obtain a declaratory judgment in a vast range of cases where there is no likely candidate to bring a subsequent suit for damages against the participants and where there is little likelihood of criminal prosecution. Hence, there would be no court supervision of the decision to terminate the life of the incompetent patient in some cases where that supervision might be thought crucial to proper protection of the interests of the patient.

It should be noted in passing that *Saikewicz* also does not deal with the question of whether there are classes of situations in which the courts should not allow participants to immunize themselves from liability in advance of action. Policies against allowing broad immunity to result from decisions that would have to be made without a full development of the facts, because of the emergency nature of the proceeding or for some other reason, might dictate against granting jurisdiction in some classes of cases. One author has suggested another reason for not allowing such jurisdiction in at least those cases that involve consent to causing the death of defective newborns:

> The true enormity of these actions to withhold life from newborns, viewed from our contemporary perspective, will remain in high visibility only if advance social authorization is withheld, and only if the parents and physicians who wish to take this action are willing to accept some significant risk that they will suffer by such action. Their suffering will come in increasing intensity if criminal prosecution is instituted, if a jury finds them guilty of unconscionable conduct and if a judge imposes sanctions on them accordingly. In deciding whether to withhold treatment from the newborn, the parents and physicians will be led to balance the suffering imposed on them by the continued life of the child against the suffering likely from their decision to end the child's life.

This gives no guarantee that every newborn will be kept alive, no matter what. But choosing this social mechanism for regulating the decision to withhold treatment does guarantee that the decision-makers will have powerful incentive to favor the child's continuing life, to uphold what one court has called our felt intuition . . . [that even a blind, deaf and dumb infant] would almost surely choose life with defects as against no life at all. Some current proposals for law change call for child advocacy by an attorney, for example, appointed to present the newborn's perspective to a judge empowered to authorize withholding treatment. But no imaginable formal mechanism for child advocacy could so starkly press home directly on the decision-maker, as possible criminal liability, the proposition that ending the child's life may inflict unjustifiable suffering on him.

Burt, *Authorizing Death for Anomalous Newborns*, in G. ANNAS & A. MILUN-SKY, GENETICS & THE LAW 435, 444 (1975) (footnote omitted).

Because of uncertainty as to the scope of the *Saikewicz* holding, counsel representing medical facilities in Massachusetts have advised their clients that the *Saikewicz* decision should be assumed to require judicial review in order to avoid *liability* in a wide range of cases involving patients who are not competent to consent to termination of medical assistance of a variety of types. As a result, new kinds of cases are being brought to the courts, including actions for "proxy consent" to termination of life support services not only for defective newborns and terminally ill comatose adults, but also for persons who meet most, but not quite all, of the Harvard brain death criteria. *See* Annas, *After Saikewicz: No-Fault Death*, HASTINGS CEN-TER REP., June 1978, at 16. Moreover, the spirit of *Saikewicz* stalks more entrenched sorts of actions such as those brought to obtain "proxy consent" to chemotherapy where the parents of the patient refuse consent, or to removal of a gangrenous foot where an arguably incompetent patient refuses consent, or to use of an experimental drug to treat a cancer where the mentally retarded patient cannot give an effective consent. In every such case, the potential relevance of *Saikewicz* now becomes an issue raised by counsel or the court. Most recently, the *Saikewicz* opinion has brought to the courts the question of whether court authorization is in any sense required before a "no-code" order can be placed on the chart of a comatose patient.

Against this fluid background, it is impossible to give a generally accepted definition to the term "*Saikewicz*-type cases" that is used in this Article. However, for purposes of this Article, it will be used very broadly to refer to any case in which a court is asked to provide "proxy consent" for an alleged incompetent to some act, or omission to act, on the ground that the act, or omission to act, is in the "best interest" of the incompetent.

4. Decisions from other jurisdictions recognizing a right to refuse life-prolonging or life-saving treatment include Montgomery v. Board of Retirement, 33 Cal. 3d447, 109 Cal. Rptr. 181 (Ct. App. 1973) (dictum); *In re*

Osborne, 294 A.2d 372 (D.C. 1972); *In re* Estate of Brooks, 32 Ill. 2d 361, 205 N.E.2d 435 (1965); *In re* Quinlan, 70 N.J. 10, 355 A.2d 647 (1976); Erickson v. Dilgard, 44 Misc. 2d 27, 252 N.Y.S.2d 705 (Sup. Ct. 1962); *In re* Raasch, No. 455–996 (Prob. Div., Milwaukee County Ct. Jan 21, 1972).

5. These were recognized by the court to be "(1) the preservation of life; (2) the protection of the interests of innocent third parties; (3) the prevention of suicide; and (4) the maintenance of the ethical integrity of the medical profession." 1977 Mass. Adv. Sh. at 2477, 370 N.E.2d at 425. The court stated that the first of these interests was the most important, but that it was lessened in significance in a case, such as *Saikewicz*, where the most that could be hoped for through treatment was mere "prolongation" of life. "There is a substantial distinction," the court held, "in the State's insistence that human life be saved where the affliction is curable, as opposed to the State interest where, as here, the issue is not whether, but when, for how long, and at what cost to the individual that life may be briefly extended." *Id.* at 2478, 370 N.E.2d at 425–26. As to the second interest, the court found that, on the facts of the case, it was not an issue, since Mr. Saikewicz had no dependents. The fourth state interest was also found to be no bar since

> the prevailing ethical practice [in the medical profession] seems to be to recognize that the dying are more often in need of comfort than treatment. Recognition of the right to refuse necessary treatment in appropriate circumstances is consistent with existing medical mores; such a doctrine does not threaten either the integrity of the medical profession, the proper role of hospitals in caring for such patients or the State's interest in protecting the same.

Id. at 2480, 370 N.E.2d at 426–27. The third, and perhaps the most intriguing state interest, is consigned to a footnote:

> The interest in protecting against suicide seems to require little if any discussion. In the case of the competent adult's refusing medical treatment such an act does not necessarily constitute suicide since (1) in refusing treatment the patient may not have the specific intent to die, and (2) even if he did, to the extent that the cause of death was from natural causes the patient did not set the death producing agent in motion with the intent of causing his own death. Furthermore, the underlying State interest in this area lies in the prevention of irrational self-destruction. What we consider here is a competent, rational decision to refuse treatment when death is inevitable and the treatment offers no hope of cure or preservation of life. There is no connection between the conduct here in issue and any State concern to prevent suicide.

Id. at 2480, n.11, 370 N.E.2d at 426, n.11 (references omitted).

6. The court bases its opinion in this regard upon "the unwritten constitutional right of privacy found in the penumbra of specific guarantees of

the Bill of Rights," *id.* at 2474–75, 370 N.E.2d at 424, and upon "implicit recognition in the law of the Commonwealth, as elsewhere, that a person has a strong interest in being free from nonconsensual invasion of his bodily integrity." *Id.* at 2473, 370 N.E.2d at 424.

7. Here the choice, as the Supreme Judical Court found it to be on the basis of the record, was between refusing treatment for leukemia, which would mean a relatively comfortable death within a period that might range from a few weeks to several months, and consenting to chemotherapy, which might prolong life for as much as 13 months or longer, but might shorten it and would have side effects including anemia, bleeding, infections, "severe nausea, bladder irritation, numbness and tingling of the extremities, and loss of hair." *Id.* at 2466, 370 N.E.2d at 421. Despite the horrors thus painted of chemotherapy, however, "[i]t was the opinion of the guardian ad litem, as well as the doctors who testified before the probate judge, that most people elect to suffer the side effects of chemotherapy rather than allow their leukemia to run its natural course." *Id.* at 2466–67, 370 N.E.2d at 421.

8. *Id.* at 2482–83, 370 N.E.2d at 427.

9. "[T]he primary test is subjective in nature—that is, the goal is to determine with as much accuracy as possible the wants and needs of the individual involved." *Id.* at 2489–90, 370 N.E.2d at 430 (footnote omitted). For a thoughtful discussion of this standard, see Robertson, *Organ Donations by Incompetents and the Substituted Judgment Doctrine*, 76 COLUM. L. REV. 48, 57–68 (1976).

It was in the subjective nature of the standard that the court found a basis for affirming the lower court's decision despite the lower court's fact finding that most people would elect chemotherapy in an objectively similar situation:

Evidence that most people choose to accept the rigors of chemotherapy has no bearing on the likely choice that Joseph Saikewicz would have made. Unlike most people, Saikewicz had no capacity to understand his present situation or his prognosis. The guardian ad litem gave expression to this important distinction in coming to grips with this "most troubling aspect" of withholding treatment from Saikewicz: "If he is treated with toxic drugs he will be involuntarily immersed in a state of painful suffering, the reason for which he will never understand. Patients who request treatment know the risk involved and can appreciate the painful side-effects when they arrive. They know the reason for the pain and their hope makes it tolerable." To make a worthwhile comparison, one would have to ask whether a majority of people would choose chemotherapy if they were told merely that something outside their previous experience was going to be done to them, that this something would cause them pain and discomfort, that they would be removed to strange surroundings and possibly restrained for extended periods of time, and that the advantages of this course of action were measured by concepts of time and mortality beyond their ability to comprehend. *Id.* at 2488–89, 370 N.E.2d at 430.

10. "The two factors considered by the probate judge to weigh in favor of administering chemotherapy were: (1) the fact that most people elect chemotherapy and (2) the chance of longer life. . . . With regard to the second factor, the chance of a longer life carries the same weight for Saikewicz as for any other person, the value of life under the law having no relation to intelligence or social position." *Id.* at 2492–93, 370 N.E.2d at 431.

> The sixth factor identified by the probate judge as weighing against chemotherapy was "the quality of life possible for him even if the treatment does bring about remission." To the extent that this formulation equates the value of life with any measure of the quality of life, we firmly reject it. A reading of the entire record clearly reveals, however, the judge's concern that special care be taken to respect the dignity and worth of Saikewicz's life precisely because of his vulnerable position. The judge, as well as all the parties, were keenly aware that the supposed ability of Saikewicz, by virtue of his mental retardation, to appreciate or experience life had no place in the decision before them. Rather than reading the judge's formulation in a manner that demeans the value of the life of one who is mentally retarded, the vague, and perhaps ill-chosen, term "quality of life" should be understood as a reference to the continuing state of pain and disorientation precipitated by the chemotherapy treatment. Viewing the term in this manner, together with the other factors properly considered by the judge, we are satisfied that the decision to withhold treatment from Saikewicz was based on a regard for his actual interests and preferences and that the facts supported this decision.

Id. at 2494-95, 370 N.E.2d at 432.

11. *Id.* at 2496, 370 N.E. 2d at 433.

12. These are also referred to as "optimum care committees," "ad hoc committees," and by other designations. (They also have been called "God-squads" due to the awesome nature of the issues with which they deal.) *See generally* Clinical Care Committee of the Massachusetts General Hospital, *Optimum Care for Hopelessly Ill Patients*, 295 NEW ENGLAND J. MED. 362 (1976); Rabkin, Gillerman, & Rice, *Orders Not To Resuscitate*, *id.* at 364 (1976); Teel, *The Physician's Dilemma, A Doctor's View: What the Law Should Be*, 27 BAYLOR L. REV. 6 (1975).

Such committees frequently comprise not only physicians but also social workers, attorneys, and theologians, among others. While the ethics committee concept is not new, such committees have been developed recently by an increasing number of hospitals as forums for principled consideration of moral, legal, and ethical problems of medical practice, which are now being discussed more openly than previously. *See generally* Annas, *In re Quinlan: Legal Comfort for Doctors*, HASTINGS CENTER REP., June 1976, at

29; Cantor, *Quinlan, Privacy, and the Handling of Incompetent Dying Patients,* 30 RUTGERS L. REV. 243, 255 (1977); Collester, *Death, Dying and the Law: A Prosecutorial View of the Quinlan Case, id.* at 304, 319 (1977); Fried, *Terminating Life Support: Out of the Closet!* 295 NEW ENGLAND J. MED. 390 (1976); Hirsch & Donovan. *The Right to Die; Medico-Legal Implications of In re Quinlan,* 30 RUTGERS L. REV. 267, 273–86 (1977); Veatch, *Human Experimentation Committees: Professional or Representative?* HASTINGS CENTER REP., October 1975, at 31.

While the *Saikewicz* decision refuses to confer upon such committees the power to insulate the medical community from liability that was granted in *In re Quinlan, see* note 3, *supra,* the court does recognize that they might play a helpful role in the decision-making process.

> We note here that many health care institutions have developed medical ethics committees or panels to consider many of the issues touched on here. Consideration of the findings and advice of such groups as well as the testimony of the attending physicians and other medical experts ordinarily would be of great assistance to a probate judge faced with such a difficult decision. We believe it desirable for a judge to consider such views wherever available and useful to the court. We do not believe, however, that this option should be transformed by us into a required procedure. We take a dim view of any attempt to shift the ultimate decision-making responsibility away from the duly established courts of proper jurisdiction to any committee, panel or group, ad hoc or permanent.

Id. at 2499, 370 N.E.2d at 434.
13. Mass. Regs. Governing Practice of Medicine, Section 1.4p (1977) (emphasis added).
14. The present writer's experience in working with medical personnel in various medical facilities over the past few years (which includes a two-week stint as a volunteer "medical-ethical consultant" at a chronic care hospital), confirms the fact that, until recently, such decisions were made by participants on the basis of standards that frequently: (1) were not explicitly delineated or consistently worked out at any given time, (2) were not consistently applied over time, (3) differed from participant to participant, and (4) took into consideration factors which the Supreme Judicial Court rejects as criteria in *Saikewicz.* Many of the doctors, nurses, and other medical personnel were well aware of these deficiencies in the decision-making system and have served as a motivating force in bringing the decision making "out of the closet" so that more consistent and just systems could be developed.
15. Relman, *The Saikewicz Decision: Judges as Physicians,* 298 NEW ENGLAND J. MED. 508 (1978).
16. *Id.*
17. Curran, *Law-Medicine Notes: The Saikewicz Decision,* 298 NEW ENGLAND J. MED. 499 (1978).
18. 1977 Mass. Adv. Sh. at 2501, 370 N.E.2d at 435.

19. Conversation with Paul R. Rogers, Esq., Staff Attorney, Belchertown State School, March 7, 1978.
20. At the time of filing, the statute authorizing the appointment of temporary guardians, MASS. GEN. LAWS ANN. ch 201, § 14 (1958), seemed to omit authorization of the appointment of a temporary guardian for a mentally retarded person. The statute was amended to remedy that deficiency on August 9, 1976, when Chapter 277 of the Acts of 1976 was signed into law. MASS. GEN. LAWS ANN. ch. 201, § 14 (Supp. 1978).
21. 1977 Mass. Adv. Sh. at 2461–62, 370 N.E.2d at 419.
22. 1977 Mass. Adv. Sh. at 2462, 370 N.E.2d at 419.
23. *In re* Joseph Saikewicz, No. 45596, transcript of proceedings of May 13, 1976 (Mass. Probate Court, Hampshire County, May 13, 1976).
24. *Id.* at 20.
25. *Id.* at 22.
26. *Id.* at 21.
27. *Id.* at 28–29, 32–33.
28. *Id.* at 28
29. *Id.* at 29.
30. *Id.* at 31.
31. *Id.* at 33. Apparently on the basis of concern that court action would not give full immunity to the petitioners until the appeal period had expired unless quick appellate review were obtained within that period, counsel for petitioner requested that the case be reported to the appropriate appellate court. *Id.* at 29. Immediately upon issuing its order, the probate court did, in fact, report to the Massachusetts Appeals Court the two questions that appear in note 2, *supra*. Shortly thereafter, counsel for petitioner filed an application for direct appellate review by the Supreme Judicial Court, which was granted on June 14, 1976. At that point, the case took on an adversarial quality for the first time. The Department of the Attorney General filed with counsel for petitioner a brief that aggressively pressed the case for reversing the lower court and for giving chemotherapy to Mr. Saikewicz. Among other things, the brief attempted to introduce published reports of empirical studies that cast doubt on the probate court's finding that patients over 60 are less successfully treated by chemotherapy. The court rejected the invitation to consider the studies. "None of these authorities was brought to the consideration of the probate judge. We accept the judge's conclusion, based on the expert testimony before him and in accordance with substantial medical evidence, that the patient's age weighed against the successful administration of chemotherapy." 1977 Mass. Adv. Sh. at 2466 n.4, 370 N.E.2d at 421 n.4. On behalf of appellee, a brief was filed by the guardian ad litem and an amicus curiae brief was filed by the Civil Rights and Liberties Division of the Department of the Attorney General. Other amicus curiae briefs were filed by the Mental Health Legal Advisors Committee, the Massachusetts Association for Retarded Citizens, Inc., and the Developmental Disabilities Law Project of the University of Maryland Law School.
32. *Id.* at 2497, 370 N.E.2d at 433 (statutory references omitted).

33. *Id.* The opinion actually uses the term "mentally retarded" rather than "incompetent." However, read in the context of the paragraph in which it appears and the full opinion, the court cannot reasonably be taken to be suggesting that the question is merely one of mental retardation.

34. *Id.* at 2497–98, 370 N.E.2d at 433–34.

35. Baron, Botsford, & Cole, *Live Organ and Tissue Transplants from Minor Donors in Massachusetts,* 55 B.U.L. REV. 159 (1975) [hereinafter cited as Baron, Botsford, & Cole]. See also Baron, *Voluntary Sterilization of the Mentally Retarded,* in G. ANNAS & A. MILUNSKY, GENETICS & THE LAW 267 (1975).

36. The briefs filed by the Department of the Attorney General and by the Civil Rights and Liberties Division of the Department of the Attorney General cite the article on the role of the guardian ad litem in assuring a true adversary process. However, the article is cited in the *Saikewicz* opinion for a different purpose only. 1977 Mass. Adv. Sh. at 2492, 370 N.E.2d at 431.

37. *See* Kingsbury v. Buckner, 134 U.S. 650 (1889); Rankin v. Schofield, 71 Ark. 168, 66 S.W. 197 (1902); Tyson v. Richardson, 103 Wis. 397, 79 N.W.439 (1899).

38. Baron, Botsford, & Cole, *supra* note 35, at 182–86.

39. *Report of the Joint Conference On Professional Responsibility of the Joint Conference of the American Bar Association and the Association of American Law Schools,* 44 A.B.A.J. 1159, 1160 (1958).

For a later empirical study that supports the Joint Conference Report, *see* J. THIBAUT & L. WALKER, PROCEDURAL JUSTICE: A PSYCHOLOGICAL ANALYSIS (1975). The authors' conclusion is remarkably unequivocal:

> It is perhaps the main finding of the body of our research, therefore, that for litigation the class of procedures commonly called "adversary" is clearly superior.
>
> Our suggestion that the adversary procedure is superior to other classes of procedure rests both on its operating capabilities and on subjective and normative appraisals of its performance. In Chapter 5 [*of Procedural Justice*] the adversary procedure exhibits a capacity to protect against erroneous decisions based on chance distributions of the immediately discovered facts. Advocates who encounter facts unfavorable to their side of the case are instigated to search diligently and persistently for more favorable evidence. In Chapter 6 the procedure has been shown effective in moderating preexisting bias among decision makers. The results reported there do indeed appear to support Fuller's (1961) claim that the adversary mode serves to combat a "tendency to judge too swiftly in terms of the familiar that which is not yet fully known." In Chapter 7 the procedure is found able to correct potential distortions of judgment deriving from the temporal presentation of evidence. We conclude from this research that the adversary trial is remarkably well arranged to neutralize the ultimate effects of order and to insulate the decision-

making process from this source of irrelevant influence. Indeed, paradoxical as it may seem, the very contentiousness of the adversary proceeding may exert a beneficial moderating influence on litigation.

With respect to appraisals of justice, the adversary procedure again appears to be superior. In the research reported in Chapter 8 the procedure has been judged fairest and most trustworthy both by persons subject to litigation and by those observing the proceedings. Moreover, the adversary procedure produces greater satisfaction with the judgment, regardless of the outcome of the case and regardless of the parties' beliefs in their own guilt or innocence. In Chapter 9 a further assessment of some elements of adversary procedure has shown that each of the elements—separation of presentations, alignment of attorneys, and free choice of attorneys—contributes significantly and about equally to heightened satisfaction and judged fairness of the procedure. Chapters 8 and 9 have dealt with the impact of structural variations in procedure on rated satisfaction. In Chapter 10 structure has been held constant and the stylistic performance of roles has varied. The results in Chapter 10 have led us to conclude that as compared to structural variations stylistic differences are less potent determinants of satisfaction with procedures. Likewise, in Chapter 11 the adversary procedure fares well when tested by a normative standard of justice. Participants behind a "veil of ignorance" concerning their advantage or disadvantage in a subsequent trial express a conception of procedural fairness that is recognized uniquely in an adversary system.

Id. at 118.

40. Baron, Botsford, & Cole, *supra* note 35, at 183.
41. *Id.*
42. *Id.* at 186.
43. One judge of the Suffolk County Probate Court regularly appoints two guardians ad litem in cases where the donee, as well as the donor, is a minor.
44. For a case outside Massachusetts in which advocacy by a guardian ad litem developed a record upon which a court felt compelled to refuse to sanction donation of a kidney by a mentally retarded sibling, see *In re* Pescinski, 67 Wis. 2d 4, 226 N.W.2d 180 (1975).
45. Baron, Botsford, & Cole, *supra* note 35, at 163 nn.19 & 20.
46. Nathan v. Farinelli, Suffolk Eq. 74–87 and Nathan v. Flanagan, Suffolk Civil No. J 74–109.
47. Interview with James R. Deciacomo, Jr., Esq., in Boston, March 17, 1978.
48. 1977 Mass. Adv. Sh. 2494, 370 N.E.2d 432 *See* note 10 *supra.*
49. That none of these factors are to be permitted as criteria is a necessary implication of the court's commitment to the "substituted judgment" test. Such factors clearly would not justify termination of life-prolonging treatment for a patient who was competent and refused to consent to termina-

tion. They cannot, therefore, justify termination where an incompetent's "substituted judgment" comes out opposed to termination.

50. 1977 Mass. Adv. Sh. 2497–09, 370 N.E.2d 433 (case reference omitted).
51. *Id.* at 2495–96, 370 N.E.2d 433 (statutory reference omitted).
52. *Id.* at 2496, 370 N.E.2d 433.
53. Lynde v. Vose, 326 Mass. 621, 96 N.E.2d 172 (1951); Buckingham v. Alden, 315 Mass. 383, 53 N.E.2d 101 (1944).
54. Baron, Botsford, & Cole, *supra* note 35, at 181.
55. 1977 Mass. Adv. Sh. 2498, 370 N.E.2d at 433.
56. Interview with Paul Resnick, Esq., March 10, 1978.
57. Interview with James R. DeGiacomo, Jr., Esq., March 2, 1978.
58. *Id.* and Interview with Beverly W. Boorstein, Esq., May 2, 1978.
59. 1977 Mass. Adv. Sh. 2498, 370 N.E.2d at 433–34.
60. *Id.* at 2482–83, 370 N.E.2d at 427.
61. Interview with Ronald Schramm, Esq., and Daniel Roble, Esq., March 24, 1978.
62. 1977 Mass. Adv. Sh. 2498, 370 N.E.2d at 433.
63. The establishment of such a corps of guardians ad litem was discussed at a statewide Judicial Conference of Massachusetts Probate Court Judges held at Framingham, Massachusetts, on March 31, 1978. The principal topic of the Conference was the *Saikewicz* decision and the challenges it presented to the probate court. The idea of establishing a specialized panel of guardians ad litem to assist the court in handling *Saikewicz*-type cases was well received by the judges present. It was well received also by members of the medical community who attended the Conference.

Since the Conference, Chief Judge Podolski has encouraged the development of a list of attorneys who are willing and able to serve in such a capacity, which he will distribute to the probate judges.
64. In those cases where suit need not be brought to avoid liability but only to obtain declaratory relief, *see* note 3 *supra*, it may become clear that certain fact patterns no longer raise the risk of a successful suit on the merits, thus eliminating the motive for bringing those cases to court for what is essentially a declaratory judgment. The "brain death" cases provide a good example of candidates for this sort of treatment. On August 26, 1977, the Supreme Judicial Court adopted a version of the Harvard "brain death" criteria for purposes of establishing the death of a victim in a criminal case. Commonwealth v. Golston, 1977 Mass. Adv. Sh. 1778, 366 N.E.2d 744, Because *Golston* was a criminal case, some medical personnel and their counsel have been concerned about potential civil liability in situations where they terminate life support treatment for patients who are dead by the Harvard criteria but not by more traditional criteria. There is even more widespread concern about terminating such support where most, but not all, of the technical "brain death" criteria have been met. As a result of these uncertainties, medical personnel and relatives who would be participants in terminating supportive services for "brain dead" patients have brought petitions to probate court seeking court authorization for ter-

mination. Since these suits result from uncertainty regarding the precise limits of the law, there is likely to be no need to bring them as it becomes clear that certain fact patterns fall within or without them. Where it is clear in advance that certain acts do not give rise to liability, it would be a waste of court time and taxpayers' money to go through the ritual of obtaining a court declaration of nonliability.

Chapter 12

The *Saikewicz* Decision: A Medical Viewpoint

Arnold S. Relman

The *Saikewicz* decision of the Massachusetts Supreme Judicial Court[1] and the earlier *Quinlan* decision of the New Jersey Supreme Court[2] present two opposing judicial views of a basic question about the practice of medicine which had not been expressly considered in the courts until recent years. Put in simplest terms, the question is this: When patients are physically unable, or legally incompetent, to express their own views, and there is no legally sufficient document to indicate clearly their prior wishes, who should have the authority to decide whether a particular treatment is to be instituted, withheld, or terminated, particularly when that decision may have a decisive influence on the survival of the patient?

In the *Quinlan* case, involving the question of withdrawing respiratory support from a comatose young woman who was believed to have suffered irreversible brain damage, but who did not meet the widely accepted "Harvard" criteria for brain death,[3] the court said that the decision properly belonged with the patient's parents and physicians, provided a hospital-appointed ethics committee concurred with their decision. The *Quinlan* decision was widely viewed with satisfaction by the medical profession, for it seemed to be generally supportive of long-standing medical tradition. Except perhaps for the implication that ethics committees ought to be routinely involved in difficult decisions of this kind, the court's ruling did not appear to call for any major change in medical practice.

Reprinted with permission of the American Society of Law & Medicine from the AMERICAN JOURNAL OF LAW & MEDICINE, Vol. 4, no. 3 (Fall 1978).

But in the *Saikewicz* case—which concerned the decision whether to institute chemotherapy in a profoundly mentally retarded man of 67 who had developed acute leukemia—the court emphatically rejected the *Quinlan* solution, asserting instead that only the courts were qualified to decide life or death issues for incompetent patients. *Saikewicz* stunned and dismayed the medical profession in Massachusetts as had few other legal rulings within memory. Not only did it reject the authority of parents and physicians to make life or death decisions for incompetent patients, but it declared that henceforth all such decisions, after the appointment of a guardian ad litem, would have to be brought before a probate court for an adversarial type of courtroom proceeding and judicial resolution. As interpreted by most lawyers, the *Saikewicz* decision seemed to establish new law which mandated a probate judicial hearing before *any* life or death decisions could be made for incompetent patients, excepting only emergency cases. Even in the latter situation, the justices seemed to be making their preference abundantly clear by suggesting that legislative guidelines for emergencies be drawn up in order to avoid leaving such life or death decisions in the hands of physicians and next of kin.

There was much in the *Saikewicz* opinion to be applauded. There was the forthright statement that incompetent patients have the same rights as those who are competent, and the assertion that these rights include the privilege of declining medical treatment under certain circumstances. The court also indicated its concurrence with the widely held medical view that "extraordinary means" need not be used to prolong a patient's life after it has become apparent that he has an irreversible, fatal illness.

Few would quarrel with these principles. The more difficult question is, of course, who should exercise the right of deciding whether to accept life-prolonging (but not curative) treatment on behalf of the incompetent patient, by what means, when, and in what manner? In a much-quoted passage, the court said very clearly that the exercise of such responsibility belonged solely to the judiciary and was not to be entrusted to any other group. This sweeping declaration has been the main cause of the confusion that has followed in the wake of the *Saikewicz* decision. Difficulties were also created by some less definitive language which seemed to suggest that in deciding whether to institute or withhold life-prolonging treatment, the quality of the life to be preserved was not to be considered. All the constructive aspects of the *Saikewicz* decision were forgotten in the consternation that followed the realization that the court had instituted fundamental changes in the way medicine was to be practiced and that these changes would engender endless problems.[4]

I recognize that not all observers agree with the above interpretation of the *Saikewicz* decision. George Annas,[5] for example, has argued that the court never intended to require a probate hearing in every case but merely wished to suggest that such hearings were necessary if physicians wished to be granted immunity from legal liability for the consequences of their decisions. Charles Baron[6] also has suggested the "immunity" theory as one possible interpretation of the court's meaning, although not necessarily the correct one. I hesitate to offer a legal interpretation, yet I must say that on repeated readings of the *Saikewicz* opinion I fail to find any basis for the "immunity" theory. Neither, apparently, did the great majority of attorneys representing hospitals and medical organizations in the Commonwealth of Massachusetts. What is more important, the Massachusetts Court of Appeals, in the *Dinnerstein* case,[7] recently has found that *Saikewicz* appears to have established a rule of law requiring prior judicial approval for certain types of medical acts involving incompetent patients. In the opinion of the *Dinnerstein* court, however, orders not to resuscitate *terminally ill* patients were not meant to be encompassed by the *Saikewicz* ruling, nor were any medical decisions to institute rather than withhold or terminate treatment.

The *Dinnerstein* decision has been rightly hailed as a useful clarification of *Saikewicz*, which unties the hands of the medical profession in at least one very common kind of clinical situation involving incompetent patients.[8] It allows physicians to write "do not resuscitate" orders, with the approval of next of kin, when it is clear that the patient is suffering from an irreversible terminal illness and that resuscitation would merely prolong the act of dying. However, no clear definition of "terminal illness" is given, and many other kinds of clinical situations not involving resuscitation remain untouched by the *Dinnerstein* decision. Hence, the frustration and confusion of the medical profession in the aftermath of *Saikewicz* have been only slightly dissipated. Furthermore, since the *Dinnerstein* decision was not appealed, it is not yet known how the Massachusetts Supreme Judicial Court will view this interpretation of the *Saikewicz* ruling.

To understand why *Saikewicz* runs counter to the sound traditions of medical practice and to appreciate the problems that will still arise even after *Dinnerstein*, we need to consider briefly certain characteristics of medical practice.

The practice of medicine has always involved decisions affecting the life or death of the patient. The age-old charge of the physician is to cure, prevent, or ameliorate disease whenever possible, but always to comfort. This does not mean that he must prolong life at all costs. There never has been a categorical imperative to treat aggressively, or to attempt to prolong life, no matter what the circumstances. Every physician knows that there are times when to comfort rather than to treat is clearly the best course, because to do otherwise would inflict unjustifiable suffering or would merely prolong the agony of a terminal illness. There are also many situations, as every doctor understands, in which the benefits of treatment are outweighed by their disadvantages to the patient, and still other circumstances in which risky choices between treatment and no-treatment must be made, even though the calculus of risk, discomfort, and benefit is not clear. In all of these situations the traditional responsibilities of the physician demand that he make judgments to treat, or not to treat, which in effect will determine whether, and for how long, and in what condition, the patient is likely to live or die.

At all times, of course, the physician is expected to keep his patients' interests paramount. He is obligated to confer with his patients or their next of kin, to keep them fully informed, and to be guided by their wishes. However, patients and families rely heavily on the professional judgment and experience of the physician, and his advice is usually the decisive factor in most medical decisions. That advice, the *Saikewicz* court's opinion notwithstanding, has always taken into account the quality, as well as the length, of life that might result from each of the courses of action possible in a given case. There are also emergencies and many other occasions (for example, during a surgical operation) in which life or death decisions must be made by the doctor without advance consultation with the patient or his family. Under such circumstances, there is an implicit understanding that the physician, as the advocate of the patient, will do whatever he can to prolong life while still preserving its quality.

The essence of the relation between doctor and patient is *trust*. The patient *trusts* that his physician will do the best thing possible for him under the circumstances, using a reasonable degree of professional skill, and following the ethical traditions of the medical profession.

Contrast my description of medical practice with the recent assertion made by Charles Baron, in support of the *Saikewicz* decision, that "our society has never conferred upon its medical community the power to decide which of society's members shall live and which shall die."[9] Now, if by that statement he means that physicians do not have the authority arbitrarily to terminate a patient's life, he is of course correct. But if he means to convey that doctors have no business deciding whether to institute or to withhold treatment, when such decisions may have life or death implications, then he is simply ignorant of the facts of medical practice. As I have tried to show, those kinds of decisions— always with the informed consent of patients or their families, when such consent is reasonably available—are being made all the time. There is nothing more crucial to a physician's professional role than the making of such decisions. His responsibility for the welfare of his patients often requires that he deal with technical medical issues which are of vital importance to his patients but which they are unable to comprehend fully, if at all, and which they must therefore delegate to him. Unless he is willing to assume this decision-making role on the patients' behalf he is not really doing his job.

I would therefore suggest that the views expressed by the *Saikewicz* court, and defended so eloquently by Professor Baron, represent a challenge to the traditional professional role of the physician, and a new intrusion of the judiciary into an area of medical practice previously considered the private domain of physicians, patients, and their families. By requiring prior judicial approval for certain types of medical decisions in incompetent patients, even when physicians and next of kin are in agreement and no complaint of wrongdoing has been made, the court seems to be taking over responsibilities never before assumed by the judiciary and which the judicial system is ill-prepared to exercise. I understand that there may be legitimate concern for the protection of the rights of incompetent patients, but I do not believe that the routine judicialization of medical decisions is the appropriate response to those concerns. As I hope to make clear, such inappropriate use of judicial authority cannot serve its intended purpose and will in the long run be counterproductive.

Let me explain my concerns by citing some specific clinical examples.

One place where life-or-death decisions frequently are made for incompetent patients is in the newborn intensive care unit. There, infants born with various kinds of congenital defects or injuries acquired during birth are cared for by doctors and nurses who often must make difficult decisions affecting the survival of these babies.[10] How much effort should be exerted to maintain the life of infants born with major birth injuries to their brains, or with their brains irreversibly damaged by hydrocephalus, anencephaly, or other developmental defects? Many such infants are doomed to a purely vegetative existence if they survive, yet with modern intensive care they may be able to live for months or even many years. The overwhelming majority of physicians concerned with the care of newborn infants believes that the decision should be made by the parents;[11] presumably most physicians would advise against efforts to maintain life in many of the examples cited. Sometimes, of course, the decision is easy because the brain has been so damaged that nothing resembling human conscious life can be anticipated. But in other instances, brain damage may be less severe—the baby may simply be seriously defective mentally, as in Down's syndrome—and the other irreversible defects, although major, may be confined to functions such as sight, hearing, or locomotion, thus dooming the patient to a limited existence, but not necessarily a purely vegetative one. In such cases medical advice may be divided, but most physicians still would hold that decisions about how far to go in the maintenance of such infants ought to be made privately and not by the courts. Duff and Campbell[12] have suggested that parents and physicians should have absolute discretion in such matters, but Robertson and Fost[13] argue persuasively that some sort of institutional or professional review would be preferable. I will return to this idea later in the discussion.

In Massachusetts, as I understand the *Saikewicz* ruling, any decision to withhold life-prolonging treatment from a defective newborn child must be approved in advance by a probate court. A case of this sort which was in the headlines earlier this year provoked considerable controversy. A baby girl born with congenital rubella (German measles) was found to be blind, deaf, and seriously mentally defective. She also had a severe obstruction (coarctation) of the main artery leading from her heart, which posed an immediate threat to her life. Without surgery,which carried a 50–50 chance of success, the child would surely die; if she survived the operation she could be expected to live for many years, but would have to be institutionalized because of mental retardation and loss of vision and hearing. After consultation with their physicians and minister, the parents decided that they did not want the baby operated on. However, the probate judge who heard the case held that since an operation had a fair chance of saving the child's life, and since the *quality* of that life could not legally be considered, the physicians were required to go ahead with the operation. According to newspaper accounts, the judge made it clear that, while he was bound by law to order the operation, he personally believed it would be better if the child did not survive. The operation was successfully carried out, and the infant remains alive at this writing.

Another unhappy example of the *Saikewicz* decision in action received much attention in the Boston press recently. A previously healthy 12-year-old boy was accidentally shot through the heart and was brought to a community hospital emergency room in an apparently lifeless state. After intensive resuscitative efforts, his heart action was restored but his respiration had to be maintained by a breathing machine. He never regained consciousness, and subsequent tests indicated beyond any reasonable doubt that his cerebral cortex (the part of the brain responsible for all conscious behavior) had been irreversibly damaged. However, some of the functions of the lower part of his brain evidently were still preserved, as indicated by the persistence of some primitive reflex movements. He had no brainwave activity on the electro-encephalogram and had complete loss of circulation to his cerebrum, but because of his reflex movements he did not meet the "Harvard" criteria for brain death and thus, under Massachusetts law, could not be declared legally dead. Therefore, the petition of the hospital authorities for permission to withdraw life support was denied.

Although medical witnesses testified that there was no possibility of the boy's ever regaining consciousness, he conceivably could have been kept alive indefinitely and so, regardless of the quality of the life being preserved, the probate judge felt constrained by law to order that the intensive care be continued. This decision was rendered *after* the *Dinnerstein* case, so it can only be assumed that the judge either thought the boy was not "terminal" in the sense intended by the *Dinnerstein* court, or that the *Dinnerstein* ruling was not relevant to the removal of life-support systems in this case. In any event, the unfortunate boy was continued on the respirator in his comatose state for a total of about two months, at enormous economic and emotional costs to his family, before finally succumbing.

The two cases cited above are actual examples of the consequences of *Saikewicz*, but other equally distressing scenarios can easily be imagined. Consider, for example, the hypothetical case of a blind and deaf senile man of 80 or 90 years, confined to a nursing home bed with advanced arteriosclerotic degenerative changes of the brain which have rendered him helpless. Unable to move, speak, or otherwise communicate, and totally dependent upon nursing care, his existence is little more than vegetative. Yet he has lived in this dismal state for many months and it is entirely possible that with continuing good care he could survive for many more. He then contracts pneumonia due to a bacterial organism, which could be treated successfully with antibiotics but which, if untreated, probably would end his life quickly and painlessly. Should the physician in charge of the case withhold specific treatment and allow the old man to die? Almost all physicians would think so and, if allowed to follow their own best judgment, would recommend that decision to the family. Pneumonia, in such circumstances, as all physicians know, is "the old man's friend." The next of kin are in full agreement, for they are sure that he would not have wanted to go on living in this way. Yet the *Saikewicz* decision would appear to apply in this case, and it requires that a probate court be petitioned if the family wishes life-preserving treatment to be withheld.

And what, under existing legal guidelines, would the judge probably decide? If the patient could be considered "terminal," and if the *Dinnerstein* decision applied, the petition could be granted. On the other hand, if the judge were to decide that the patient is not "terminal," and if there were no direct evidence that the patient would have wished otherwise, the judge might deny the petition and order that the antibiotic be given, thus indefinitely prolonging the patient's wretched state.

Similar situations involving incompetent patients, but with endless variations of detail, can easily be imagined. The medical issues might be clear-cut, as in the case cited above, or they could be obscure. Diagnosis, prognosis, and the benefits and risks of alternative treatments are often matters of medical judgment. Clinical situations often change from minute to minute or from day to day and what may seem like a reasonable course of action at one time may be quite inappropriate at another. Furthermore, decisions to institute or to withhold certain kinds of treatment in many clinical situations must often be made at once and cannot wait for a judicial hearing, and a decision once made may have profound consequences for the patient that cannot be undone. Yet, under *Saikewicz*, all of these kinds of questions are supposed to be debated in court, in an adversarial proceeding, before a probate judge who is supposed to decide what the patient himself would have wanted under the circumstances! I submit that this is a totally impractical and unworkable way to achieve a laudable objective.

The goal to be achieved here is the exercise of the patient's constitutional right to decide about his own medical treatment, in a manner that protects him from exploitation and assures that humane and medically sound decisions in accordance with his wishes will be made when and as they are needed. The requirements for achieving that objective are simply not within the resources of the judiciary. The courts cannot be expected to exercise sound judgment when the moral issues are so intertwined with complex medical considerations, nor can they act promptly and flexibly enough to meet the rapidly changing needs of clinical situations.

Judges must depend on expert opinion given in testimony in an adversarial type of proceeding—a ponderous method hardly suited to the shifting and subtle complexities of real-life clinical situations. Judicial evaluation of conflicting expert testimony may or may not be a reliable way to settle medical questions in retrospect, as for example in a malpractice trial, but it is certainly not a sensible method of resolving the urgent and complicated problems of medical management that so often are involved in the decisions probate judges would be called upon to make. Moreover, the courts simply cannot respond as rapidly or as frequently as the clinical circumstances often require.

The number of potential *Saikewicz* cases is huge. That so few have reached the courts thus far simply indicates the widespread confusion following in the wake of the original decision, which has led to the avoidance of difficult decisions or, more likely, to "closet" decisions, without discussion or legal approval. "No-treatment" or "withdrawal of treatment" decisions for incompetent patients are being made all the time throughout the hospitals of Massachusetts, but very few are being brought to judicial attention. The reasons are obvious enough, and are implicit in what has already been said. Neither relatives nor physicians want to go to the trouble and expense of obtaining a court judgment, particularly when they have no confidence that the judgment will be medically or ethically sound. If there is real doubt that the court will consider the quality of the life involved, and if the medical recommendations of the physicians in charge of the case, as well as the wishes of the family, are to be examined in an adversarial courtroom proceeding, then most families and most physicians would prefer to stay away from the courts. At present, it commonly is believed that they take very little risk in doing so, but that view could of course be changed by future developments.

In my view, the judiciary has a very limited and sharply defined role to play in cases involving the medical care of incompetent patients. First, when there are no next of kin, the courts must appoint a guardian. Second, when there are differences of opinion, among the family or between physicians and family, as to what should be done, the courts should be consulted. And finally, when there is any complaint of injury or of wrongdoing or malpractice, that is a matter for judicial resolution. But where there is unanimity of opinion between family and physician, where the physician's recommendations have been made under circumstances that assure soundness of judgment and conformity with professional standards, and where there is no complaint of wrongdoing, then I see no justification for involvement of the judiciary.

Such involvement, it seems to me, constitutes an unnecessary, unwarranted, and counterproductive intrusion into a medical tradition that has until now enjoyed wide recognition and general approval. Under this tradition, the responsibility and trust given to the physician must be discharged faithfully to the best of his ability and in accordance with accepted professional standards of ethics and technical competence. As a condition for the trust given him, society holds him responsible for his professional behavior. No legal immunity is needed or should be claimed in the practice of medicine. Physicians should always be liable for their professional actions and should not ask for legislative protection except when necessary to defend against judicial intrusions like *Saikewicz*.

One final point. I think physicians must recognize the possibilities for abuse that exist when decisions are made privately between the patient's family and the attending physician. There is no denying the possibility, however remote, that one or more of the parties to the decision may not always be acting with the purest motives, or with the patient's interest foremost in mind. I have argued that routine prior judicial intervention is an inappropriate and unworkable solution. But I also believe that closed, totally private decisions, unreviewed by any third party, are a cause of legitimate concern. A more reasonable alternative, it seems to me, is to establish some relatively simple and informal, but nonetheless meaningful, consultative process within the profession. When physicians make life or death decisions for incompetent patients (assuming, always, consent of the family or legal guardian), concurrence by several colleagues who have no vested interest in the decision should be documented in the medical record.

The public has a right to be reassured that, when a physician makes a decision to withhold or to terminate life-prolonging therapy in the case of an incompetent patient, the decision has had the approval not only of the family but of an objective group of his professional colleagues. This requirement would guard against willful or inadvertent neglect of the patient's rights, but would certainly not provide an absolute guarantee against abuse or mistakes. No human arrangement I can think of, medical or judicial, will do that. But a "peer review" system would be no less equitable, much sounder medically, more acceptable to families and physicians, and far more practical than the procedure proposed by *Saikewicz*.

NOTES

1. Superintendent of Belchertown State School v. Saikewicz, 1977 Mass. Adv. Sh. 2461, 370 N.E.2d 417 (1977).
2. *In re* Quinlan, 70 N.J. 10, 355 A.2d 647 (1976).
3. Ad Hoc Committee of the Harvard Medical School to Examine the Definition of Brain Death, *A Definition of Irreversible Coma*, 205 J.A.M.A. 337 (1968).
4. Curran, *The Saikewicz Decision*, 298 New England J. Med. 499 (1978); Relman, *The Saikewicz Decision: Judges as Physicians*, 298 New England J. Med. 508 (1978).
5. Annas, *After Saikewicz: No-Fault Death*, Hastings Center Rep., June 1978, at 16.
6. Baron, *Assuring "Detached But Passionate Investigation and Decision": The Role of Guardians Ad Litem in Saikewicz-Type Cases*, 4 Am. J. L. & Med. III (1978).
7. *In re* Dinnerstein, 1978 Mass. App. Adv. Sh. 736.
8. Schram, Kane, Jr., & Roble, *"No code" Orders: Clarification in the Aftermath of Saikewicz*, 299 New England J. Med. 875 (1978).
9. Baron, *supra* note 6, at 112.

10. Duff & Campbell, *Moral and Ethical Dilemmas in the Special-Care Nursery*, 289 New England J. Med. 890 (1973).
11. Shaw, Randolph & Manard, *Ethical Issues in Pediatric Surgery: A National Survey of Pediatricians and Pediatric Surgeons*, 60 Pediatrics 588 (1977).
12. *Supra* note 10.
13. Robertson & Fost, *Passive Euthanasia of Defective Newborn Infants: Legal Considerations*, 88 J. Pediatrics 883 (1976).

Chapter 13

Dilemmas of Dying

Paul J. Liacos

Let me thank you at the outset for the invitation to join with you in exploring the difficult problems that are to be examined within the format of your program over these next two days. I commend the organizers of this program and the various sponsoring organizations for their contribution to the public interest in putting forth a program of this kind. It appears that the representatives of both the legal and the medical professions, as well as the persons in charge of our great hospitals in this Commonwealth, are joined together in an effort to come to grips with one of the great problems of our day as it is reflected in the title of this program, The Dilemmas of Dying.[1]

I would think, if I may respectfully suggest, that the title might well have been, The Dilemmas of Life, because the problems with which you are all concerned deal with the decisions that each of us and the patients involved must make in light of new and rapid developments in the fields of medical science and medical technology.

I confess to feeling a little bit like Daniel who was cast into the den of the lions, except that I have some doubt whether, like him, I shall survive before this morning is over. Nevertheless, as the person chosen to give the keynote address, I believe it to be my responsibility not to discuss with you the details of the problems with which you will be wrestling in the next two days nor even to try to outline to you the case law on the subject. I am sure that those particular aspects of your concern will be well handled in the hours to come. I view my responsibility in a somewhat different light; namely, to try to present to you two or three key thoughts about which I hope your discussions will revolve. It is my hope that as a result of this address, and this program, all of us from the

Reprinted with permission of the American Society of Law & Medicine from LAW, MEDICINE & HEALTH CARE (formerly MEDICOLEGAL NEWS), Vol. 7, no. 3 (Fall 1979).

disciplines of law and of medicine and those of us who are in the courts will come to some greater understanding of our respective responsibilities and a greater understanding, perhaps, of how we interrelate one to the other. I may be overly optimistic but I'm hopeful that we will be successful before this conference is all over.

Basically, there are three thoughts that I would have you think upon in connection with your discussions. First, is that as a result of the *Saikewicz*[2] opinion a good deal of controversy has taken place. That, I think, is healthy. I am bound to tell you, however, that I think that not all of the discussion has been particularly informative. I think that a good deal of it, sadly, has been based on misinformation or misinterpretation of the *Saikewicz* opinion and I think that to be fair about it or to give you all equal protection of the laws, this is not solely due to the doctors, but in large measure to the lawyers who advise doctors on their various problems. I'll come back to them shortly.

What I do not think is necessarily healthy is the fact that there is a good deal of misinformation that has occurred as well, caused not only by those not trained in the law, but by those who ostensibly claim some degree of medical-legal expertise in the field. It is my hope that this conference will help clarify matters in your mind.

The second thought I will seek to address is that one of the fundamental aspects of the *Saikewicz* opinion has been largely overlooked, and that lies in the understanding of the fact that the interest of the state, sometimes defined under the concept of the so-called *parens patriae* power, has been redefined so as to give recognition to the rights of individuals to control their own fate to a much larger extent. Those rights have been guaranteed by *Saikewicz*, not only to the competent, but to incompetent individuals as well.

The third thought I would suggest to you is perhaps the most controversial; namely, that the courts have reasserted, through *Saikewicz*, as has been traditionally the case through all areas of social, ethical and legal significance, their traditional role of safeguarding individual rights by seeing to it that decisions of such great import are made in a principled and public fashion. Before we get into each of these areas in turn, let me just sketch out for you the facts of the *Saikewicz* case.

The probate court was faced with the problem of a 67 year-old man, a ward of the state, suffering from an acute leukemia who was profoundly mentally retarded and, therefore, unable to give informed consent to medical treatment.

A guardian *ad litem* appointed by the probate court reported that the illness was incurable, that the only possible treatment was chemotherapy, that such treatment would cause adverse side effects and discomfort and would be incomprehensible to the patient, and that the treatment was not in the patient's best interests. His attending physicians also recommended against chemotherapy. The probate judge subsequently entered an order withholding medical treatment, which the Massachusetts Supreme Judicial Court affirmed.

You may recall that the case was commenced when the superintendent of the state institution sought appointment as a temporary and permanent guardian so that chemotherapy could be administered to Mr. Saikewicz. When the state initiated this action, it did so under its so-called *parens patriae* duty to protect the incompetent individual's right to have life prolonging medical treatment. This remained the position of the Commonwealth throughout the litigation as it was represented by the Attorney General in his official capacity, acting pursuant to his statutory duty.

One of the less known aspects of the case is that the Attorney General was equally active in presenting the opposite viewpoint. The Civil Rights Division of the Attorney General's office represented, in part, the interests of Mr. Saikewicz and argued that the chemotherapy treatment should not be administered. Both sides of the state proceeded from different theories. The Attorney General stated explicitly, in his brief, that it was the responsibility of the state under its *parens patriae* power to exert every effort to preserve the life of the incompetent individual. The Civil Rights Division, on the other hand, argued that the state's *parens patriae* interest in preserving the life of the incompetent was not sufficient to override or negate the possible exercise of free choice to refuse life prolonging treatment where appropriate. By its very presence and assertion of that view, the Civil Rights Division recognized the duty of the state to insure the unfettered exercise of such choice, even in the face of asserted, but ultimately less substantial, state interests. The Civil Rights Division prevailed not only in result, but also in reasoning.

Now, as to the debate and the controversy. I've read a lot of the articles with great interest and I must tell you that sometimes you get tempted to write or to respond to some of the things that you see. I have not done so and this indeed is the first time since the opinion was released that I have come before any group to discuss the matter. One of the attacks that has been made on the court is an attack that exemplifies a good deal of the misunderstanding.

Let me turn now to the first of my thoughts, and that is the thought that there has been an unfortunate amount of misinterpretation and misinformation from both the medical and legal professionals in the field. I need not recount to all of you the various articles that have been written as part of the ongoing debate as to the meaning of the *Saikewicz* opinion.

Some authors have said that the *Saikewicz* decision cast a pall over the medical profession and indeed one author has said that it was in effect a resounding vote of "no confidence in the medical profession."[3]

I would say to you that anyone who reads the *Saikewicz* case in that light has entirely misconstrued what was involved factually in the case and has also misconstrued not only the intent but also the language of the opinion. I think it is true beyond dispute that the factual pattern upon which this was based is one in which the medical professional persons involved were entirely in accord that in the particular circumstances the treatment commonly called chemotherapy should be withheld, and the court at the trial level and at the appellate level gave every recognition to the value and helpfulness of that medical judgment. Further, the *Saikewicz* opinion emphasized that one of the great interests that the state has is the interest of preserving the integrity of the medical profession. How such an opinion could be viewed as a slap at the medical profession is beyond my comprehension. I would suggest to you, perhaps, that people sometimes panic when something new happens and they have not thought out their positions carefully. I would suggest to you that perhaps it reflects more on those who feel criticized than it does on those who allegedly did the criticizing. I do not intend to get into, as I said, an analysis of the various cases.

You are all aware of some horrible anecdotes and situations that have been attributed to the *Saikewicz* opinion.[4] I will speak only of one of them, and that is the so-called *Dinnerstein* case, decided by the Massachusetts Appeals Court.[5] I need not get into the debate about whether *Dinnerstein* is technically in accord with *Saikewicz* or not. That is not my point in raising this issue at this time. I sit on a court committee that decides whether a case is going to be handled by the Appeals Court or by our court and we decided, and I agreed, that *Dinnerstein* should be handled by the Appeals Court. The reason for that then and now is that the *Dinnerstein* case strikes me as a case that need never have been litigated because it was clearly without the scope of *Saikewicz*. For anyone to advise hospitals that a "DNR" (do not resuscitate order) could not be instituted and that a person who was terminally ill had to be resuscitated time and time again absent legal and judicial determination is an entirely misleading interpretation of the *Saikewicz* opinion. The *Saikewicz* case, after all, upheld the withholding of chemotherapy which might very well have prolonged the life of Joseph Saikewicz for a number of months. It had nothing to do with a person who was "terminal" in the sense of the *Dinnerstein* case; it certainly had nothing to do with cases I've read about with people who are dead under the brain death definition and who have been resuscitated allegedly based on *Saikewicz*.[6]

Thus, I can only say to you, without necessarily accepting the reasoning of the Appeals Court in this matter, that the result there in my view was wholly consistent with what was stated in the *Saikewicz* case. I speak, of course, for myself and not for my colleagues, but I cannot help but say once again that *Dinnerstein* seems to me to have been nothing but an example not only of an abundance of caution but of hysteria on the part of legal counsel who advised hospitals that such extreme measures needed to be taken in order to protect the hospital and the medical staff. This leads to a thought that I would express to you in this fashion, and I am not alone in doing so. If the medical profession seeks to be immunized with certainty from each and every possible claim, civil or criminal, then that is one thing. But let us not confuse that desire as being a motive involving the best interest of the patient. It strikes me rather as a legitimate concern, but one that goes toward the protection of the hospital and the medical staff rather than the interest of the patient. If that be what the medical profession feels it must have, then I would suggest to you that perhaps *Saikewicz* is a boon because, if you want to interpret it that way, you can get a pre-determination of what your rights are rather than suffer the risk of having a hindsight determination in which you might be held to have been acting improperly.

Saikewicz permits, I would think, that kind of procedure. Permits is not to say it requires it. On the other hand, a doctor can act and take the risks that traditionally doctors have always taken, and that is the risk of being judged by hindsight, and *Saikewicz* does not address that possibility. That leaves both courses open to you at this time. I think to be very clear on this I do not criticize the hospital or the doctors in the *Dinnerstein* case. I do criticize, and I will not try to mask it, the rather poor legal advice they got under the circumstances. I only raise this thought to point out to you that there is a difference between acting to preserve the interest of the patient and acting to preserve the interest of the profession. I am sorry to say that it seems to me the lawyers in the *Dinnerstein* case were acting on the latter rather than on the former.

In short, I would say to you this, that the court has recognized and has every confidence in the integrity and in the competence of the medical profession. To say that the court has a role to play in certain of these areas is not a slap at the medical profession but is an indication of its willingness to work with the medical profession in a cooperative way to help resolve some of the most difficult problems of our day.

Let me next turn to the concept of state power that is involved in *Saikewicz*. A clear reading, it seems to me, of this opinion is that for the first time the court in this Commonwealth recognized the right of a person to act reasonably and rationally in regard to whether or not they wished to undertake a course of medical treatment. In so doing, the court rejected *in part or modified* [in effect] the traditional *parens patriae* approach [that the interest of the state, particularly the interest of the state in preservation of life, will always and without qualification prevail against the interest of individuals to make their own choice as to what they want done with their body and their fate].

The state traditionally has claimed an interest in (1) the preservation of life, (2) the protection of interests of third parties, (3) the prevention of suicide, and (4) the maintenance of the ethical integrity of the medical profession. Under existing legal doctrines before *Saikewicz*, these four interests have been arrayed against an individual's informed decision to decline medical treatment. Prior to *Saikewicz*, the state through its public officers was committed to an affirmance of abstract and attenuated state interest in life against the concrete particulars of an individual's decision, actual or imputed, to accept or decline medical treatment. In the *Saikewicz* case we said not necessarily so. There is another right here. That is the right of individual freedom of choice, and we went on as we had to do in the particular factual pattern before us, to say that it is a right of not only a competent person, but of an incompetent person as well. In doing that we effectively engaged in what traditionally has been called in other areas a balancing of the interests.

In recognizing the force of the individual's rights against the state interests asserted, and in imposing on the state the duty to protect the exercise and existence of the individual's rights, *Saikewicz* fundamentally redefined the relationship of state and individual. If, prior to *Saikewicz*, the state interest in preserving life was always deemed to override the individual's actual or imputed decision, that is no longer true. Rather, now the individual's desires may be of equal or greater magnitude. [The protection of the individual's right to accept or reject life prolonging treatment is now a separate and independent state interest to be added to those which traditionally have been used to circumscribe the individual's freedom of choice.]

The question then arises, what in practical terms does this philosophical change mean? If freedom of choice is now a state interest to be protected, it is as much the obligation of the state to enforce the individual's right to have that freedom of choice as it was, in the view of the attorney general, the obligation of the state to enforce its interests in preserving life. If there are efforts being made to infringe the rights of an incompetent individual in its custody to refuse medical treatment, it is the obligation of the state to protect that individual's freedom of choice from such interference. Correlatively, there is an obligation in the state to provide life prolonging treatment, where the individual choice is consistent with such a position. [The state must vigorously protect not only the right to decline but also the right to accept medical treatment. The individual's freedom to decide the fundamental questions involving his privacy and his bodily integrity must be protected.]

That is one reason why the fact that the judiciary now may be involved in these decisions is not only appropriate but indeed necessary. It is traditionally the function of the judiciary to protect individuals against unwarranted exercises of state power. And that is one reason why, I think, the judiciary must be involved in such matters from time to time. It is the only institution that is charged with the responsibility of protecting individual rights; it is the only institution that is charged, and I'm of the view that most of the time it meets this obligation, with the obligation of being impartial; it is the only institution in which these decisions can be made with the protections of due process of law and the procedural safeguards that are necessary to protect the rights of the patient, relatives and family, physicians, hospitals, and the State itself.

The judiciary must insure that the state's actions involving individuals are consistent with the limitations on its power as well as a respect for the integrity of individual rights. If, as I suggest we should, we view *Saikewicz* as redefining the relationship between individual and state, the only forum which has the competence, stature, and authority to protect individual rights from state infringement is the judiciary. The judiciary is the only institution sufficiently disinterested to permit a neutral yet binding resolution to such controversies. Of course, not every medical decision requires a lawsuit. However, some life and death decisions are so fraught with difficulties that the due process and procedural safeguards of the judicial system are necessary to protect the rights of patients, relatives, physicians, and state officers.

Last, let me suggest to you, as an alternative justification for what some of you view as the intrusion of the courts into this area, the fact that many of the questions which you face on the front lines every day cannot any longer be viewed solely as medical questions. At the outset, I suggested to you that perhaps this conference should have been entitled, The Dilemmas of Living, rather than The Dilemmas of Dying. You are all aware, even more so than I, of the fantastic range of new knowledge and technology in the area of medical science. Our society today, and for some recent years, has been struggling to redefine its views on the meaning of life and death; on when life starts and when it ends; on what can be done by the use of implanted organs or transplanted organs; on problems of abortion; on problems of genetic engineering; and on the use of the new technologies that are now available to maintain and perhaps in the not too distant future even to create life. To suggest that these questions are wholly medical questions is to overlook, I think, the concerns, not only of the judiciary, not only of the legal profession, but of the public as well.

I believe it is true that in your own profession the proliferation in recent times of persons who specialize in the study of these issues, not only from the point of view of medicine, but from the point of view of ethics, philosophy, morality, and law, is a reflection of a recognition that many of these questions, albeit not all, are questions that can have the deepest implications for the well being of our society. Those who suggest that *Saikewicz* was a chauvinistic attempt by the judiciary to insert themselves into an area into which they had never ventured before, challenge not just the courts, but the very nature of our society. Questions of life and death, questions of morality and ethics, and questions of individual rights have been traditional concerns of the courts in a wide variety of human endeavors. To say that the medical profession stands alone apart from the scientists, apart from the nuclear engineers, apart from the technicians and experts in every other field, and must be unsupervised and unfettered in its activities, is to deny, I think, the very principles upon which our society has been founded. What we are saying in *Saikewicz* is not that all medical decisions have to be brought to the court. That's one of the messages I want to leave with you today. What we are saying also is that these decisions are not purely medical questions; they are not purely questions of science and technology, but rather they are questions involving ethical considerations, social considerations, moral considerations, as well as medical and legal considerations. This traditionally has been the place where the courts have, and I would suggest most meaningfully, had a role in regulating the development of our society in our democracy.

Now perhaps you think I am being a little bit tough in this approach and I thought about it and thought about trying to mask what I was going to say in much politer language, but I have a training that perhaps many of you share and which I commend to all of you and that is that when it comes to the important issues of our day it is time to discuss vigorously with good faith and in a spirit of cooperation those issues and to bring to bear the insights, the experience, and the knowledge that we all have. I think the courts can make a significant contribution, they can bring to this kind of difficult problem the rule of law that has, I think we might agree, been one of the proudest characteristics of our society, but we cannot do it without the help of the medical profession. We are not viewing the medical profession as an adversary group, we never have, and there is no such intent now. We are willing, we are anxious to work with you toward the goal of principled decision making open to public scrutiny in the areas that are mixed questions as

I've suggested. We are willing to recognize, as the Appeals Court did in *Dinnerstein*, that medical questions are your province alone.

I think if I may leave you with this thought that the controversy, informed and uninformed, is the important thing because it has led to the discussion. We are dealing not always with competent people, but with persons afflicted by some disability or disease as with Joseph Saikewicz. We are dealing with important and sensitive issues to which I think we must all admit that consciously or unconsciously we bring our own set of values. I would like as a judge to be able to write opinions and not be attacked in the newspapers and in medical journals and not to have to come here today (as much as I enjoyed being with you). As a person, I would like that. As a judge and as a professional person, and I hope as a responsible citizen, I welcome the controversy swirling around in my head because if I have as one member of the court caused this kind of debate, caused this kind of a conference in part to come about, then I think no matter what you think of *Saikewicz* as a decision it served a very important public function. I hope that you will walk away after two days well informed by all the experts and by your own discussions. I wish you well and I expect, despite the fact that I hope it doesn't happen, that some of the issues that you focus upon may end up again in the courts.

NOTES

1. The opinion in the case of Joseph Saikewicz, issued by the Massachusetts Supreme Judicial Court in late November of 1977, was certainly the most controversial judicial decision in the health law field during the last two years—if not during the entire decade. The opinion has been the subject of at least one article in four of the last six issues of MEDICOLEGAL NEWS (now LAW, MEDICINE & HEALTH CARE) and in four of the last five issues of the AMERICAN JOURNAL OF LAW AND MEDICINE. In the months following the decision, its author, Justice Paul J. Liacos, was asked to comment on it or to clarify it for members of the bar, the press, and physicians. He steadfastly refused to publicly comment, as is traditional with judges, although he did lead a closed seminar on the subject at the National Conference of Probate Judges in Austin, Texas, in November 1978.

   At the personal urging of the conference organizers, Justice Liacos was persuaded to make a public appearance at a conference entitled "Dilemmas of Dying: Policies and Procedures for Decisions Not to Treat." The conference, held at Boston's Museum of Science on April 28, 1979, was sponsored by Medicine in the Public Interest, Inc. The entire proceedings of the conference were published in 1981 by G. K. Hall & Company of Boston, and MEDICOLEGAL NEWS (now LAW, MEDICINE & HEALTH CARE) wishes to thank them and MIPI's Executive Director, Judith Swazey,

Ph.D., for their help in preparing this manuscript for publication. Justice Liacos' remarks were the keynote address at the conference, which was attended primarily by physicians and lawyers from the New England area.

Finally, it must be emphasized that the statements contained in this article are the views of Justice Liacos alone, and do not represent the views or opinions of any other member of the Massachusetts Supreme Judicial Court or of the court itself.

2. Superintendent of Belchertown State School v. Saikewicz, 370 N.E.2d 417 (Mass. 1977).

3. A. Relman, *The Saikewicz Decision: Judges as Physicians*, NEW ENGLAND JOURNAL OF MEDICINE 298: 508, 509 (1978).

4. *See, e.g.*, G.J. Annas, "Reconciling *Quinlan* and *Saikewicz*: Decision Making for the Terminally Ill Incompetent," Chapter 5.

5. In re Dinnerstein, 380 N.E.2d 134 (Mass. App. 1978).

6. G.J. Annas, *Where are the Health Lawyers When We Need Them?* MEDICO-LEGAL NEWS 6(2): 3 (Summer 1978).

Chapter 14

Legal Criteria for Orders Not to Resuscitate: A Response to Justice Liacos

John A. Robertson

Justice Liacos's comments on the *Saikewicz* decision[1] in the preceding chapter should end much of the debate that has swirled around the scope of this landmark case. However, two aspects of that chapter deserve further comment.

First, it seems unfair to criticize lawyers for not immediately reading the case the way Justice Liacos now says it should have been read. While the opinion in *Saikewicz* is reasonably clear about the substantive rights of incompetent patients, it is imprecise about the procedures to be followed in implementing those rights. For example, in discussing the role of the probate court in such cases, the broad language used in the decision could be read as requiring a judge to review all treatment decisions involving incompetent patients: "We turn now to a consideration of the procedures appropriate for reaching a decision where a person allegedly incompetent is in a position in which a decision as to the giving or withholding of life-prolonging treatment must be made."[2] Further, the opinion states that "the ultimate decision-making responsibility"[3] in such cases rests with the courts and not with any hospital committee or panel as occurred in *Quinlan*.[4] The language of *Saikewicz* contains none of the qualifications or limitations on resort to the courts recognized by Justice Liacos in his speech.

Of course, the opinion can be interpreted to reach the conclusion he now says was intended. However, while some lawyers did suggest that

Reprinted with permission of the American Society of Law & Medicine from LAW, MEDICINE & HEALTH CARE (formerly MEDICOLEGAL NEWS), Vol. 8, no. 1 (February 1980).

the opinion did not go as far as it appeared,[5] lawyers advising persons and institutions dealing with incompetent patients could not ignore language which seemed to suggest that resort to the courts was required for all treatment decisions concerning incompetent patients.[6] After all, it is reasonable to argue, as Baron[7] has done, that courts should review in advance a vast range of treatment decisions regarding incompetent patients. Perhaps a court dealing for the first time with such a complex issue can be forgiven for not realizing how physicians and hospital attorneys might react to such statements. In fairness, however, the justice responsible for the ambiguities should forgive lawyers who found a different meaning in the language than he intended.

A second and much more important reservation about Justice Liacos's speech is his comments about *Dinnerstein*.[8] He seems to suggest that do not resuscitate (DNR) orders present a case for physician discretion, a situation where the principles of *Saikewicz* are inapplicable. In my view, such a position is seriously flawed on two grounds. First, he implies that DNR orders on terminal patients are medical questions for doctors in their discretion to decide.[9] But whether a patient should receive resuscitative measures is no more a pure medical question than is whether a retarded leukemic should be treated. Both involve the ethical or normative question of whether medical care should be given to patients whose prognosis is bleak. Whatever the ultimate role of doctors in these decisions, they remain normative, and not medical, questions. If authority over these decisions is to be properly allocated, it is essential to distinguish between physician decisions that are based on medical science (i.e., diagnosis, treatment, and prognosis) and physician decisions that reflect their own values and normative positions (e.g., which terminally ill patients to treat). While the distinction between technically medical and normative decisions invariably does not hold in clinical practice (for example, value preferences may enter into diagnosis), ignoring the distinction risks erroneous conclusions about the propriety of physician discretion in cases where the decisions are essentially normative.

Second, it is not clear why *Dinnerstein* "was clearly without the scope of *Saikewicz*" as Justice Liacos contends in his article.[10] Here we must be very clear to distinguish between the substantive and procedural aspects of nontreatment decisions.

Substantively, *Dinnerstein* seems to be clearly within the scope of *Saikewicz*. Both cases involve patients with incurable illnesses whose lives could have been prolonged for several months with available medical care. In each case it is unclear whether continued life from the patient's perspective is a benefit worth the cost of the discomforts of treatment. It is by no means obvious that several months of continued existence in a disabled state is not in a patient's interest. Such a judgment will vary with the patient and a variety of contingent circumstances. To assume automatically that "a person who was 'terminal' in the sense of the *Dinnerstein* case"[11] has no interest in further living conflates a number of crucial variables and obscures the basic question: Is it in this patient's interest, given her medical situation, to receive treatment that will prolong her life, or, in light of the burdens of life-extending treatment, is it in her interest to die now? While the Massachusetts Appeals Court and Justice Liacos may be correct in concluding that it was not in Mrs. Dinnerstein's interest to go on living, they appear to reach that conclusion without a careful analysis of whether that decision would be reached under the substituted judgment standards recognized in *Saikewicz*. The legal validity of DNR orders on incompetent patients depends upon their being chosen under that test. Since the *Dinnerstein* court failed to analyze the decision according to this test, physicians may conclude that DNR orders need not be justified under the substituted judgment test—a result which seems contrary to the meaning of *Saikewicz*.

Since *Dinnerstein* seems to me so clearly within the substantive scope of *Saikewicz*, perhaps Justice Liacos meant that it was outside its procedural scope; that is, that *Dinnerstein* was not the kind of case that needed advance judicial approval. But surely he cannot mean that DNR orders should never receive advance judicial approval. Since such orders involve the cessation of life sooner than need occur, it should be an issue in any particular case whether or not it is in the patient's interest, under the substituted judgment test, to be resuscitated. To avoid errors in assessing the patient's interest, it may be desirable to require some procedure of prior review of the decision of physician and family, since the cost of error to the patient is very great and the patient's interest may otherwise not be adequately represented.

Whether or not prior judicial review is required, it is unclear why doctors and families act improperly when they choose to seek advance judicial guidance for DNR orders. Substituted judgment is a doctrine easily misapplied. Interested parties, no matter how well intentioned, may overlook important facts or weigh certain factors arbitrarily. Resort to a process that requires the decision to be publicly justified may reveal aspects of the case that change the decision, a fact that many doctors who have sought advice from lawyers and ethicists have discovered. It would seem that skepticism about one's conclusion to deny life-prolonging treatment and a willingness to have that decision publicly scrutinized would be applauded rather than criticized, especially where the patient will not be harmed by the delay involved in seeking an authoritative decision. (The record in *Dinnerstein*, for example, does not show that the patient was unnecessarily resuscitated while the courts were deciding the question.)

If there are good reasons for utilizing a detached decision-making process for assuring that substituted judgment is properly assessed, Justice Liacos's criticism of the *Dinnerstein* lawyers' decision to seek judicial approval as "poor legal advice" is puzzling. Why is it poor legal advice to counsel a course of action that will minimize errors against the patient, particularly when *Saikewicz* contained language that appeared to require resort to the courts? Such criticism would seem appropriate only if it is clear that prior judicial review is not required, or that it would serve no purpose, other than a hypertrophied sense of caution, since no reasonable person could think that treatment would be in the patient's interests. At the time that *Dinnerstein* was brought, neither was clear. The procedural parameters of *Saikewicz* had not yet been clarified. Moreover, the value of life in a debilitated state to an incompetent patient had, to say the least, not yet been resolved. In retrospect, the fact that the court agreed with the family's and the doctor's view of Mrs. Dinnerstein's interest is no assurance that they were applying the substantive standard correctly, much less that such coincidence would have occurred in other DNR decisions.

With Justice Liacos's remarks supplementing the *Saikewicz* opinion, we are now in a better position to see the important substantive and procedural questions that remain to be resolved after *Saikewicz*. *Saikewicz* took a major step beyond *Quinlan* toward resolving the question of the substantive norm that should be applied to situations involving critically ill incompetent patients. The patient-centered substituted judgment test, if applied as articulated in the decision, should protect patients against decisions that favor the interests of family, doctor, or society over those of the patient. Yet, application of the test in particular cases will often be problematic, simply because of the multitude of variables that must be considered in reaching a decision.[12]

Accordingly, the question of procedures for applying the test in particular cases has great importance. A retrospective judicial review of such decisions is likely to be rare simply because, except in the most egregious cases, there will be no complainant to initiate the review. A prior review system, at least in certain cases, may be necessary to assure the correct application of the substantive test. Prior review to minimize errors, however, need not be judicial review or even highly formal, as long as it is a meaningful review of physician and family decisions. The design of an adequate prior review system depends upon balancing the costs of particular procedures against the benefits the procedures provide to incompetent patients—a policy question beyond the scope of this comment. *Saikewicz*, we now see, only began to address the question of which procedures were appropriate for applying the substantive norms—a question that neither *Dinnerstein* nor Justice Liacos's article has resolved. The dialogue begun in *Saikewicz* must continue if the rights and duties of incompetent patients, their families, and doctors are to be reconciled in a morally acceptable way.

NOTES

1. Liacos, P.J., "Dilemmas of Dying." Chapter 13.
2. Superintendent of Belchertown State School v. Saikewicz, 370 N.E.2d 417 432 (Mass. 1977).
3. *Id.* at 434.
4. *In re Quinlan*, 355 A.2d 647 (N.J. 1976).
5. *See* Annas, G.J., "Reconciling *Quinlan* and *Saikewicz:* Decision Making for the Terminally Ill Incompetent," Chapter 5; Glantz, L., and Swazey, J., *Decisions Not to Treat: The* Saikewicz *Case And Its Aftermath,* FORUM ON MEDICINE 2(1): 22 (January 1979).
6. Of course not all lawyer reactions were reasonable interpretations of ambiguities in the case. See "Reconciling *Quinlan* and *Saikewicz,*" note 5 *supra,* at 387, n.5; Annas, G.J., *Where Are the Health Lawyers When We Need Them?* MEDICOLEGAL NEWS 6(2):3 (Summer 1978).
7. Baron, C.H., *Medical Paternalism and the Rule of the Law: A Reply to Dr. Relman,* AMERICAN JOURNAL OF LAW & MEDICINE 4(4):337 (Winter 1979).
8. *In re Dinnerstein*, 380 N.E.2d 134 (Mass. App. 1978).
9. DILEMMAS OF DYING, note 1 *supra.*
10. DILEMMAS OF DYING, note 1 *supra.* At another point, Justice Liacos states: "For anyone to advise hospitals that a DNR . . . could not be instituted and that a person who was terminally ill had to be resuscitated time and time again absent legal and judicial determination is an entirely misleading interpretation of the *Saikewicz* opinion."
11. DILEMMAS OF DYING, note 1 *supra.*
12. *In the Matter of Earle N. Spring* (Mass. App. Ct. F–79–570, November 1979) shows the errors that doctors, families, and even reviewing courts can make in applying the substituted judgment test.

Chapter 15

Brother Fox and John Storar: An Analysis of the New York Court of Appeals' Decision

C. Dickerman Williams

The case of Brother Fox and its process through the courts of New York attracted almost as much public attention as did the case of Karen Ann Quinlan. The highest court of that state, the Court of Appeals, has now decided Brother Fox's case, and at the same time decided a less publicized case—that of John Storar, a mentally retarded person.[1] In each case, the patient died before the decision was announced but the decision and accompanying opinion will control in subsequent cases and will guide physicians, hospitals, nurses, lawyers, and others concerned with these problems.

The majority opinion of the Court of Appeals differed sharply in many respects from the decision of the Supreme Court of New Jersey in the *Quinlan*[2] case and from those of the Supreme Judicial Court of Massachusetts in *Saikewicz*[3] and *Spring*.[4] It also differed from the decisions of lower courts in the Brother Fox case itself. Briefly summarized, the rulings of the Court of Appeals in these two cases were as follows:

(1) A life-sustaining respirator may lawfully be withdrawn from an incompetent who had, when competent, convincingly demonstrated the wish to die should he or she suffer a terminal illness and require extraordinary treatment.[5]

(2) Neither court nor other procedures are necessary prerequisites to the termination of such life-sustaining therapy.[6]

(3) The evidence that the incompetent patient did, while competent, express such a wish must be "clear and convincing."[7]

(4) No other person, including family or court appointed guardian,

may exercise the right to refuse treatment on behalf of an incompetent patient who has not expressed such a desire, no matter how persuasive the circumstances may be that termination of life is in the best interests of the patient and society.[8]

Judge Wachtler wrote the majority opinion of the seven judges on the Court of Appeals. Judge Jones dissented in the *Storar* case only; he believed that the incompetent's mother should be entitled to exercise his rights. Judge Fuchsberg dissented on the ground that, both patients having died, the cases were moot.

Let us discuss these rulings in order.

1. The Court of Appeals based its first conclusion exclusively on the common law, expressly refusing to find any constitutional basis for the right to refuse treatment as other courts have done, and as the Appellate Division had done in the Brother Fox case.[9] The court relied upon the observation of Judge Cardozo—whose name is still regarded with reverence in New York—who had written in 1914 that every person "of adult years and sound mind has a right to determine what shall be done with his own body; and a surgeon who performs an operation without his patient's consent commits an assault, for which he is liable in damages. This is true, except in cases of emergency where the patient is unconscious, and where it is necessary to operate before consent can be obtained."[10]

Unlike the New Jersey and Massachusetts courts, the Court of Appeals expressly refused to consider whether the so-called right to refuse treatment was based upon the constitutional right of privacy. The court noted that the issue was still disputed and that the United States Supreme Court had refused to act.[11] Although an affirmance of constitutional right would have been helpful, it should be stated in support of the court's position that the proposition of the common law expressed by Judge Cardozo is well settled and has been repeatedly followed.

The difficulty with this aspect of the decision is that the common law right may be swept aside by the legislature in the current "right-to-life" agitation. Despite the fact that the issues relevant to the right to control one's own body are different from those in abortion since no other person is involved, and that the right had existed for decades during which statutes forbidding abortion were regarded as valid and were enforced, activists in the right-to-life movement have attacked euthanasia as well as abortion. Without getting into a profound discussion of the relationship, if any, between euthanasia and abortion, suffice it to say that legislative halls may not be appropriate for a rational discussion of euthanasia at the present time. In the abortion cases, the United States Supreme Court in substance held that a fetus incapable of life outside the mother's womb was not another person, and hence abortion fell within the right of the mother to control her own body; right-to-life activists therefore would deny that right and, constitutional protection absent, they might succeed.

2. One aspect of the Court of Appeals' decision should be welcomed: the court rejected the elaborate procedures imposed by the Appellate Division.[12] There had been some questions as to whether or not these procedures were necessary prerequisites to the withdrawal of life support in all cases, or were merely available to physicians, hospitals or custodial institutions that wished to obtain immunity from malpractice complaints or manslaughter prosecutions before terminating life-sustaining treatment. It was my view that the procedures were intended only as a condition of immunity, but others thought that such procedures were necessary in all cases involving an incompetent.[13] At any rate, in New York, physicians treating a terminally ill patient who has expressed a desire not to have extraordinary treatment, may now proceed to act upon their own best medical judgment. Some hospitals will utilize a "terminal illness policy committee" or similar body to confirm the physicians' judgment, but this is not required. What is required is a consideration of the clear and convincing evidence of the patient's wish, a subject which we shall now discuss.

3. The evidence that the incompetent did, while competent, express a wish not to receive extraordinary care must be clear and convincing. The Court of Appeals expressly rejected the argument put forth by the district attorney that this must be proved "beyond a reasonable doubt," the standard required in criminal cases. It did, however, rule that the evidence of the patient's wish, as expressed while still competent, must be clear and convincing—the "highest standard [of evidence] applicable to civil cases."[14]

The facts were clear that Brother Fox had told Father Eichner, his spiritual superior, of his wishes not to be kept alive by extraordinary remedies, should he become terminally ill and incompetent. This communication occurred in the course of a discussion of the *Quinlan* case. Only a few months before his hospitalization, Brother Fox repeated these views—but the court does not state the circumstances of this second occasion. When operated on for a hernia, Brother Fox, aged 83 years, suffered cardiac arrest and became permanently comatose. Father Eichner then began the process to give effect to Brother Fox's wishes.

Under the accepted facts, the clear and convincing evidence was oral and constituted only a comment upon a current event. The repetition was also oral and made under unstated circumstances. But how many have made similar comments under circumstances which a hearer can persuasively identify? And how many hearers can confidently quote what was said? I am probably not alone in being able to recall discussions of the *Quinlan* case on numerous occasions and with many people, but I would be at a loss to name specific persons and to quote the substance of their remarks.

Obviously, the person who leaves his wishes on this subject to chance remarks made in the course of casual conversation runs a serious risk that there will be no clear and convincing evidence to establish his or her desires. The exception is a spouse. While most married people have probably told their spouses their views on this subject, they may not have considered that their spouses could die, be divorced, become incompetent or even forgetful.

One is forced to conclude that people personally concerned about this subject should put their views in writing and leave copies of the document with their closest relatives, physicians, and perhaps their lawyers. The organization, Concern for Dying, has drafted and distributed over five million copies of a "living will" in which declarants express their wishes.[15] Other groups distribute similar documents.

Another practical question not addressed by the court is how recently the competent had expressed his or her wish to be allowed to die if suffering from a terminal illness. A testamentary will prevails (unless revoked) regardless of when the testator dies, even if many years later. Would a "living will" be accorded such permanent validity? Or must it be periodically reaffirmed as under the California Natural Death Act? Will the circumstances of execution be investigated? What if it is alleged that the declarant signed the paper as a joke or when temporarily depressed?

It is impossible to answer with any confidence all the questions that may arise. It is, however, easy to advise about the execution of a living will. There should be witnesses to the declarant's signature. Copies should be given to more than one person. The will should be kept reasonably up-to-date either by endorsement of the original document or the execution of a new document; in my opinion, every two or three years should suffice.

4. In the absence of evidence as to the patient's wishes, no other person, including family members or guardians, may exercise the right to refuse treatment on behalf of an incompetent patient, no matter how persuasive the circumstances that termination of life would be in the best interests of the patient. The Court of Appeals did not phrase its ruling in precisely these words, but it did, in the *Storar* case, deny permission to withdraw life-saving blood transfusions despite the desires of the incompetent patient's mother, and under conditions that were positively heartrending.

John Storar, aged 52 years, was mentally retarded. His mental age was 18 months. His only relative was his 77-year-old mother, who lived near the institution in which he had resided since the age of 5, and who visited him almost daily. At the time of the hearing in the trial court, Storar was suffering from an incurable and advanced cancer of the bladder and a related loss of blood. The latter could be treated by transfusions, but they were uncomfortable for Storar and he greatly disliked the treatments. His mother applied to the court for authorization to compel the hospital to discontinue the transfusions. The hospital cross-applied for authority to continue them. The Court of Appeals summarized its conclusion as follows:

> Thus, on the record, we have concluded that the application for permission to continue the transfusions should have been granted. Although we understand and respect his mother's despair... a court should not in the circumstances of this case allow an incompetent patient to bleed to death because someone, even someone as close as a parent or sibling, feels that this is best for one with an incurable disease.[16]

While it may seem that a mother's legitimate despair does not count in the Court of Appeals, it should be noted that it became evident during the proceedings that Mrs. Storar, who had been appointed her son's legal guardian, was not well-informed about the specific effects of withholding the blood transfusions. Such uncertainty in the guardian is unfortunate, and may have influenced the Court of Appeals to rule as it did.

The *Storar* decision leaves us with this restatement of the law: while a "parent or guardian has a right to consent to medical treatment on behalf of an infant," a parent "may not deprive a child of life-saving treatment however well intentioned."[17] Further, "[e]ven when the parents' decision to decline necessary treatment is based on constitutional grounds, such as religious beliefs, it must yield to the state's interests, as *parens patriae*, in protecting the health and welfare of the child."[18] It should be recalled that the Court of Appeals refused to acknowledge a constitutional basis for the right to refuse life-sustaining treatment.

In his dissenting opinion, Judge Jones discusses two aspects of the case not addressed by the majority opinion. First, "that the problem is one which the judicial system is unsuited and ill-equipped to solve."[19] The time necessary for appellate review, the adversary system itself, and the fact that courts have "no particular competence to reach the difficult ultimate decision" are all cited as reasons to keep such decisions out of the courts. Moreover, Judge Jones states:

> There is reliable information that for many years physicians and members of patients' families, often in consultation with religious counselors, have in actuality been making decisions to withhold or to withdraw life-

support procedures from incurably ill patients incapable of making the critical decisions for themselves.[20]

Judge Jones therefore suggests that "judicial approval [should] not [be] required for discontinuance of life support procedures . . . and that neither civil nor criminal liability [should] attach simply by reason of the absence of a court order of authorization."[21]

The second aspect is that such cases may nonetheless be properly before the courts for a variety of reasons. Thus, Jones would acknowledge the power of courts "to grant authorization for withholding or withdrawal of extraordinary life support medical procedures, notwithstanding the absence of evidence of an anticipatory expression of the attitude or wishes of the particular patient."[22] Jones states that in its "unreadiness to approve the detailed procedures laid down by the Appellate Division," the majority opinion provides "little if any procedural guidance either to the lower courts . . . or to the medical care providers."[23]

As a practical matter, I think the *Storar* decision need not have an overly restrictive effect. It is difficult to see who can or would bring a private action for damages in such a case. The patient has not endured additional pain and suffering, or expended money for medical assistance, or lost earnings; these are the kinds of damages for which a decedent's estate may recover in an action for wrongful death. Withholding extraordinary medical care would not be manslaughter under usual definitions, and insofar as our research has disclosed, there has never been a prosecution for such action—or nonaction. While there have been a few manslaughter prosecutions for "mercy killings," the juries have, so far as we are aware, acquitted in all cases except one.[24] In that single instance, the offender was soon pardoned. Further, these days district attorneys are only too busy with real crimes; they are not likely to go after fancied ones.

Hence, with regard to an incompetent patient suffering from a terminal illness, the physician would appear safe in withholding or withdrawing life-sustaining treatment despite a lack of evidence as to the patient's wishes, if the family recommended that the patient be allowed to die and there were not circumstances suggesting that the family was not acting in good faith. If the physician is on the staff of a hospital with a terminal illness policy committee, he or she will presumably consult that committee. Health care providers may, however, want to go to court in many cases in order to seek answers to important questions.

The decision of the Court of Appeals will bear most heavily on patients like John Storar— institutionalized incompetents under the complete control of state institutions and financially unable to employ private physicians who might be more inclined to exercise their medical judgment.

To conclude, the decision in *Storar* must be regarded as unfortunate. Under ordinary circumstances, the euthanasia movement would presumably seek legislation authorizing close friends or relatives of incompetents to consult with the physician as to the discontinuance of treatment and decide for incompetents in order that they might be afforded the same rights as competent patients. At present, however, an effort to obtain such legislation might encounter the hostility of the right-to-life forces, and a legislative battle might end in the restriction of legal rights already enjoyed by patients.

One further point should be mentioned: the press and public commentators frequently refer to both the Brother Fox and *Quinlan* cases as affirming a patient's "right to die" or right to discontinue extraordinary medical care. In these cases, what was actually authorized was the disconnection of a respirator which enabled the patient to breathe. As already noted, the *Storar* case concerned the discontinuation of blood transfusions. Although comatose, Karen Quinlan still lives, several years after the prediction of physicians that she would die as a result of disconnecting her respirator. However, she has lost considerable weight and is kept alive by artificial feeding. The order of the trial court in the Brother Fox case also authorized the disconnection of the respirator while allowing continued artificial feeding. It seems to me that in the future, the issue of whether "artificial feeding"— at least for a protracted period— is an "extraordinary remedy" must be dealt with. It is difficult to see what either Miss Quinlan or society has gained from having kept her alive in a coma for several years. It is also difficult to see why it should be permissible to deprive the patient of air but not of food.

NOTES

1. *In re Storar*, 420 N.E.2d 64 (N.Y. 1981), *rev'g In re Storar*, 433 N.Y.S.2d 388 (App. Div. 1980) and *aff'g Eichner v. Dillon*, 426 N.Y.S.2d 517 (App. Div. 1980. For my discussion of the Appellate Division's decision in the latter case, *see* Williams, C.D., *The Case of Brother Fox: Immunity Procedures in the Treatment of Terminally Ill Incompetent Patients*, MEDICOLEGAL NEWS 8(4): 11– 13 (September 1980).

2. *In re Quinlan*, 355 A. 2d 647 (N.J. 1976), *cert. denied sub nom. Garger v. New Jersey*, 429 U.S. 922 (1976).

3. *Superintendent of Belchertown State School v. Saikewicz*, 370 N.E.2d 417 (Mass. 1977).

4. *In re Spring*, 405 N.E.2d 115 (Mass. 1980).

5. *In re Storar, supra* note 1, 410 N.E.2d at 72.

6. *Id. at 71.*
7. *Id.* at 72.
8. *Id.* at 73.
9. *Eichner v. Dillon, supra* note 1, at 537–541.
10. *In re Storar, supra* note 1, 420 N.E.2d at 70, *quoting Schloendorff v. Soc'y of New York Hosp.*, 105 N.E. 92, 93 (N.Y. 1914).
11. *In re Storar, supra* note 1, 420 N.E.2d at 70, *citing* the United States Supreme Court's denial of certiorari in the *Quinlan* case, *supra* note 2.
12. *Eichner v. Dillon, supra* note 1, at 550. The Appellate Division had developed a highly elaborate and complex set of procedures which, if followed, would provide immunity from civil or criminal liability and "ascertain and implement the patient's consent":

　　1)　The attending physicians must certify that the patient "is terminally ill and in an irreversible, permanent or chronic vegetative coma. . . ." Such a certification may be requested by "a member of the patient's family, someone having a close personal relationship with him, or an official of the hospital itself. . . ." Although the court does not expressly say so, presumably, and especially in light of an earlier part of the court's opinion, anyone in these categories is entitled to ask for such a certificate, and so to initiate the proceeding.

　　2)　The recipient of the prognosis shall present it to "an appropriate hospital committee . . . composed of at least three physicians. . . ." If there is no standing committee, "upon the petition of the person seeking relief [presumably the person who asked for the certification], the hospital's chief administrative officer shall appoint such a committee consisting of no fewer than three physicians with specialties relevant to the patient's case."

　　3)　"Upon confirmation of the prognosis, the person who secured it may commence a proceeding pursuant to article 78 of the Mental Hygiene Law for appointment as the Committee of the incompetent, and for permission to have the life-sustaining measures withdrawn. The Attorney General and the appropriate District Attorney shall be given notice of the proceeding and, if they deem it necessary, shall be afforded an opportunity to have examinations conducted by physicians of their own choosing. Additionally, a guardian *ad litem* shall be appointed to assure that the interests of the patient are indeed protected by a neutral and detached party wholly free of self-interest."

　　4)　After a hearing, the court then enters an order either authorizing or not authorizing the discontinuation of life-support measures.

　　5)　If the life-support measures are discontinued on the basis of an order and death ensues, "no participant— either medical or lay— shall be subject to civil or criminal liability. . . ."

13. *See* Williams, C.D., *The Case of Brother Fox, supra* note 1, at 12.

14. *In re Storar, supra* note 1, 420 N.E. 2d at 72.
15. A copy of the Living Will distributed by Concern for Dying is contained in Appendix H.
16. *In re Storar, supra* note 1, 420 N.E. 2d at 73.
17. *Id.* at 73.
18. *Id.*
19. *Id.* at 75.
20. *Id. citing* Kutner, L., *Euthanasia: Due Process for Death with Dignity—The Living Will,* INDIANA LAW JOURNAL 54:201, 223 (1979) and citations to the scientific and lay literature.
21. *In re Storar, supra* note 1, 420 N.E. 2d at 76.
22. *Id.*
23. *Id.*
24. *See, e.g., Commonwealth v. Capute,* (Super. Ct. Mass. 1981) (jury acquitted nurse charged with murder for allegedly giving overdose of morphine to terminally ill cancer patient).

Chapter 16

The Case of Earle Spring: Terminating Treatment on the Senile

Leonard H. Glantz

Since the Massachusetts Supreme Judicial Court's opinion in *Saikewicz*,[1] a great deal of controversy has existed over going to court prior to discontinuing or deciding not to commence medical care for the benefit of an incompetent person; the use of do not resuscitate (DNR) orders; the role of the family in making such decisions; the recognition of "brain death"; and the use of the incompetent's "quality of life" as a basis for making such determinations. Both the legal and medical communities waited expectantly while the Supreme Judicial Court considered the case of Earle N. Spring,[2] with the hope that the court would resolve at least some of these issues. The opinion did clarify a number of important issues, but either did not deal with, or confused, others.

Perhaps the most important question the *Spring* court answered was whether or not *Saikewicz* imposed a requirement that one go to court to obtain permission to terminate or not commence life-sustaining treatment for an incompetent patient. The court states that "our opinions [in *Saikewicz* and *Spring*] should not be taken to establish any requirement of prior judicial approval *that would not* otherwise exist."[3] Thus, the court clearly states that *Saikewicz* did *not* impose such a requirement, although in a given circumstance some law may require such action. In this context it is useful to remember that the *Saikewicz* case arose when the superintendent of the Belchertown State School re-

Reprinted with permission of the American Society of Law & Medicine from LAW, MEDICINE & HEALTH CARE (formerly MEDIOCOLEGAL NEWS), Vol. 8, no. 4 (September 1980).

sorted to the court for approval to commence chemotherapy for an incompetent ward of the state.

In its opinion, the court lists thirteen factors that one might take into account in deciding whether or not to seek court approval. It seems that these considerations are not listed as a guide, but merely as a way of pointing out the complexity of the decision to go to court or not.

In order to allay some fears in the medical community, the court discusses the potential legal liability of those who act without prior court authorization. The court virtually dismisses the possibility of criminal action and states that a physician would be "protected if he acts on a good faith judgment that is not grievously unreasonable by medical standards."[4]

In terms of civil liability, the court concludes that the consent of a parent or of a guardian on behalf of a child or ward constitutes effective consent for purposes of defending a battery action in situations where treatment is rendered. The court is much more equivocal in its short discussion of spousal consent. However, the opinion points out that, in *non-treatment* situations, the issue is not battery, but negligence, and notes that "negligence cannot be based solely on the failure to obtain prior court approval, if the approval would have been given."[5] The court goes on to state the obvious: courts can always make a determination of good faith and due care after the fact if some party initiates litigation. Prior judicial approval, like patient consent, does not absolutely immunize a physician from liability, since the physician may be negligent in carrying out the medical procedure so authorized.

The court clarifies two other issues in a straightforward manner. First, it states that one may cease "treating" a patient after a determination of brain death has been made, since there is "no legal duty to administer medical treatment after death."[6] Second, the court states its approval of the Appeals Court judgment in the *Dinnerstein* case, *i.e.*, that court approval was not necessary before a DNR order could lawfully be ordered for a patient in an irreversible vegetative coma.[7]

UNANSWERED QUESTIONS REMAIN

Problems still exist. First, the court seems to continue to adhere to the dichotomy it set forth in *Saikewicz* between "life-prolonging" versus "life-saving" medical procedures, and emphasizes that the kidney disease which afflicted Mr. Spring was "permanent and irreversible." It would appear that no principled line can be drawn between procedures that are life-saving and those that are life-prolonging, since if you prolong a life long enough, you have saved it. This is especially true where the testimony indicated that kidney dialysis could conceivably keep this 79 year old man alive for five years. Would the court find that dialysis treatment of a 15 year old was life-prolonging but not life-saving? In a case where the disease cannot be cured but can be indefinitely controlled, this seems to be a distinction without substance.

Second, in *Saikewicz* the court was very careful to condemn quality of life considerations when making non-treatment decisions where such a formulation "equates the value of life with any measure of the quality of life."[8] However, if the term "quality of life" was meant to apply to the "continuing state of pain and disorientation precipitated"[9] by the treatment, then a decision based on such criteria was permissible.

In this case, Mr. Spring was senile, a condition the court characterized as an irreversible disease. The court points out that the dialysis treatments will not restore Mr. Spring to a "normal, cognitive, integrated, functioning existence."[10] It is not clear what significance this has in the court's decision, but it is certainly a "quality of life" consideration. This language is especially distressing, since if one were leading a normal, cognitive, integrated, functioning existence, one would not be residing in a nursing home, chronic care institution, or state school. If this is the standard for authorizing the withholding of either "life-saving" or "life-prolonging" treatment, it raises grave legal and ethical questions, even if we could define the distinction.

Finally, the case demonstrates problems with applying the "substituted judgment" test set forth in *Saikewicz*, a test which the court commended itself for adopting because "of its straightforward respect for the integrity and autonomy of the individual."[11] In this case, there was no evidence as to what Mr. Spring would have wanted done if he were capable of expressing his opinion, other than the testimony of his wife and son as to what they felt he would have desired. If court decisions are based upon a family member simply testifying that the incompetent would not want to be treated, then we have a situation in which family members really can make the decision but must have it validated by speaking a few "magic words." This is not to say that families should not have this power. But if they do, it should be given to them directly and not in the guise of protecting the incompetent's integrity and autonomy.

Although this decision will certainly be decried for not answering every question regarding the non-treatment of incompetent patients, it is, on balance, a helpful opinion. Although many will see it as a retreat from the *Saikewicz* opinion, and as providing freedom from what some see as unwarranted judicial intrusion into the practice of medicine, the court's statements shift a certain burden to other arenas. Although the court leaves the door open for individuals to ask its help in making such decisions, there is no obligation to do so. Lawyers, hospital administrators, and physicians will now have to justify their decisions to seek prior court approval to the involved parties, they can no longer say, "we have to do it." And all of us involved in this area will have to start thinking again about how to best protect the interests of all concerned, and especially the patient, and stop focusing on the role of the courts so closely that we cannot see the greater issues.

NOTES

1. *Superintendent of Belchertown State School v. Saikewicz*, 370 N.E.2d 417 (Mass. 1977).
2. *In the Matter of Earle Spring*, 405 N.E.2d 115 (Mass. 1980).
3. *Id.* at 120 (emphasis added).
4. *Id.* at 121.
5. *Id.* at 122.
6. *Id.* at 119.
7. *In the Matter of Shirley Dinnerstein*, 380 N.E.2d 134 (Mass. App. Ct. 1978).
8. *Saikewicz, supra* note 1, at 432.
9. *Id.*
10. *Spring, supra* note 2, at 118.
11. *Saikewicz, supra* note 1, at 431.

Chapter 17

Vox Clamantis in Deserto: Do You *Really* Mean What You Say in *Spring*?

Lee J. Dunn, Jr. and Nancy E. Ator

Probably the most vexing result of the Massachusetts Supreme Judicial Court's [SJC] opinion in the *Spring* case is that judges, lawyers, and others faced with similar problems in other jurisdictions are likely to read the opinion and commend the Supreme Judicial Court for its efforts.[1] Yet, once the background of this case is known, or once one reads the opinions of the Appeals Court[2] or of the Probate Court,[3] or the briefs submitted by the parties and the *amici curiae*, the inadequacies of the opinion become apparent. In our view, the *Spring* decision works a disservice on all those both within and without Massachusetts who seek guidance from the courts as they attempt to resolve similar cases.

The Illinois Association of Hospital Attorneys [IAHA], among others,[4] filed a brief *amicus curiae* in the *Spring* case for three reasons: First, to ask that the SJC reconsider the position it had taken in *Saikewicz*,[5] and thereby to alleviate some of the misunderstanding caused by that decision. Second, to ask the court to reconsider whether the tests it enunciated in *Saikewicz* were truly workable in the contemporary health care delivery system. Third, to suggest to the court some workable criteria and standards for dealing with similar cases in the future. This article will discuss each of these goals in light of the *Spring* decision.

Reprinted with permission of the American Society of Law & Medicine from LAW, MEDICINE & HEALTH CARE (formerly MEDICOLEGAL NEWS), vol. 9, no. 1 (February 1981).

It would be an understatement to say that the *Saikewicz* decision created confusion. The court seemed to say that when a patient has been adjudicated incompetent or is a ward of the state, only a Probate Court can decide whether or not the patient should receive life-prolonging medical treatment. In reaching its decision, the Probate Court was instructed to use the substituted judgment test, which requires the court to determine what the individual would have wanted for himself. The SJC rejected the best interest test, or any standard based on what other similarly situated reasonable individuals would want for themselves. Drawing no distinction between the rights of competent and incompetent patients, the SJC found that the patient's right of privacy in choosing for himself should prevail unless one of four enumerated state interests was deemed by the court as strong enough to override the patient's wishes.[6]

The *Saikewicz* decision also initiated significant discussions in the medical and legal communities concerning its applicability; then opinions of the Appeals Court seemed to narrow the scope of *Saikewicz*.[7] Moreover, in *Commissioner of Corrections v. Myers*,[8] a fifth state interest ("upholding orderly prison administration") was found sufficient to override the rights of the individual patient, whereas the four previously mentioned state interests were not sufficient. When the *Spring* case came before the Appeals Court in 1979, it presented an opportunity for the Massachusetts courts to redefine and clarify their reasoning and their principles. In our view, they failed to do so.

QUESTIONS WITH COMPETENCY

The question of a patient's competence is one of the threshold issues in this area. Under the holdings of the Appeals Court in the *Dinnerstein* and *Candura* cases, court intervention is unnecessary, unless some interested party seeks a judicial declaration of the patient's competence.[9] Prior to the *Spring* case, however, the SJC had not enunciated a test for competency.[10]

If we accept the facts set forth in the Appeals Court opinion,[11] as the SJC did, then markedly insufficient evidence was used to declare Earle Spring incompetent and to order his hemodialysis withdrawn. The facts of the *Spring* case, both prior to and after the SJC's order of January 14, 1980, which approved the Probate Court's factual findings, dramatically demonstrate the need for the courts to establish some standard of determining competency. The evidence before the Probate Court regarding Mr. Spring's competence was sketchy at best. No psychiatric testimony was heard. Two written affidavits from physicians were presented which described Mr. Spring as suffering from chronic organic brain syndrome or senility. The signature on one affidavit was completely illegible; the other affidavit was based upon an examination of Mr. Spring conducted nearly 15 months prior to the appointment of Mr. Spring's wife and son as temporary guardians and their filing of the petition to terminate his hemodialysis treatments. While the report of the guardian *ad litem* indicates that Mr. Spring was confused and disoriented as to time and place when interviewed by the guardian *ad litem*, it is somewhat disturbing that the guardian did not call for periodic psychiatric evaluations. The only medical testimony concerning Mr. Spring's competency, or lack thereof, came from a kidney specialist at the institution where Mr. Spring received his hemodialysis treatments. He testified that, in his opinion, Mr. Spring suffered from irreversible dementia and was incompetent. Based on this evidence, Mr. Spring was found incompetent and his family was authorized to order that his dialysis treatments be withdrawn, despite the absence of any evidence of Mr. Spring's wishes with regard to treatment or his ability to comprehend the nature of his illness and the consequence of discontinuing dialysis. These findings were approved by both the Appeals Court and the SJC.

On January 17, 1980, three days after the SJC's order in the case, the Probate Court entered an order permitting the withdrawal of Mr. Spring's dialysis treatments. Shortly thereafter, evidence surfaced in the news media which suggested, at the very least, that Mr. Spring continued to experience some lucid moments. These reports,[12] which also indicated that Mr. Spring had expressed a desire to live, were presented to the Probate Court along with a motion that its order of January 17, 1980, which allowed the discontinuance of dialysis, be stayed. When the Probate Court refused to stay its order, the guardian *ad litem* appealed to a single justice of the SJC who, on February 4, 1980, stayed the Probate Court's order and ordered that Mr. Spring be examined by three physicians not previously involved in his care. The physicians were to submit separate reports to the Probate Court regarding Mr. Spring's competence to decide the treatment issue, *and*, absent such competence, regarding his capability to express a preference regarding the continuation of dialysis. The Probate Court was also instructed to consider Mr. Spring's preferences, if the medical evidence indicated a capability to express a preference concerning the withdrawal of care. Although these reports were filed promptly with the Probate Court, no hearing was held prior to Mr. Spring's death on April 6, 1980. The discussion of this entire sequence of events is confined to one footnote in the SJC's opinion. It is noted there that the reports filed by these physicians confirmed the Probate Court's earlier findings and concluded that Mr. Spring had been entirely and irreversibly incompetent.[13]

Whatever the state of Mr. Spring's competence, the SJC left un-answered a number of questions that were brought into focus by the *Spring* case and which the parties and several *amici* urged the court to resolve. For example, what standard or test should courts utilize to determine the competence of individuals to make this type of treatment decision?

It is regrettable that the court failed to enunciate a clear test for determining the competency of a patient because the issue will certainly arise again. The court's failure to articulate a test for competency is especially puzzling given the specific proposal, suggested by the IAHA as *amicus curiae*, of a test based on the standard applied in *Candura* and other cases.[14]

Competency and Substituted Judgment

Equally puzzling to those familiar with the entire sequence of events and court orders in the *Spring* case, is the SJC's failure to address the issues delineated in Justice Quirico's order of February 4, 1980. That order, which resulted from new evidence suggesting that Mr. Spring might have been competent, ordered that three physicians be appointed and examine Mr. Spring with regard to his competence, and directed the Probate Court, after receipt of each physician's report, to resolve the following issues:

1) Whether Earle N. Spring is now competent to decide whether his life-prolonging treatment, and in particular his hemodialysis treatment, should be continued or be terminated, and if he is competent to make that decision, what his decision is;

2) If Earle N. Spring is not now competent to make the decision contemplated by subparagraph (1) above, whether he is sufficiently competent to express a preference whether the treatments be continued or be terminated, and if he is competent for the latter purpose, what his preference is;

3) If Earle N. Spring is not now competent to make the decision contemplated by subparagraph (1) above, would he, if competent, choose to continue life-prolonging treatment, including the present hemodialysis treatment, or would he choose to terminate it. In deciding this issue, the judge shall consider, as one of the factors bearing thereon, his findings under subparagraph (2) above.[15]

Mr. Spring died before the Probate Court was able to conduct a hearing on these issues, and the questions posed by Justice Quirico were not fully addressed by the entire SJC. Justice Quirico's order suggested that weight should be accorded to the treatment preference expressed by the patient even though the patient was determined to be incompetent to decide the treatment issue for himself.[16] In its opinion, however, the SJC failed to discuss the results of the examinations performed by the three court-appointed physicians relative to Mr. Spring's ability to state a preference concerning treatment or nontreatment. By not addressing this portion of Justice Quirico's order, the SJC has left open to speculation the mechanism to be used in determining if an incompetent ward has or can express a preference and the weight to be accorded that preference.

Additionally, some commentators have questioned the validity of the substituted judgment test enunciated in *Saikewicz* on the ground that few individuals ever express their wishes on the subject of the provision of extraordinary medical care in the event that they become incompetent.[17] The evidence in the *Spring* case presented precisely this situation. Mr. Spring's wife and son testified that they did not know what the ward would have wanted were he able to express his views on the withdrawal of his medical care, and the report of the guardian failed to produce any evidence of the patient's wishes on this question. The Probate Court, however, having found Mr. Spring to be incompetent, held that Mr. Spring would have refused to submit to the hemodialysis had he been able to make the decision. This finding was sustained by the Appeals Court.

In its brief, IAHA sought to clarify whether the substituted judgment test was practical and appropriate in this setting and/or if the substituted judgment test enunciated in *Saikewicz* was, when applied, actually a "best interest" test. The SJC did not answer these questions either. Rather, it held that the ruling of the Probate Court, that Mr. Spring would not have wished to remain on dialysis, "was not clearly erroneous." The SJC simply disregarded the almost total lack of evidence and turned away from the duties and burdens which it placed upon the Probate Court in *Saikewicz*. Moreover, in holding that "the similarities between the present case and the *Saikewicz* case. . . [were] sufficient to bring into play the substituted judgment standard,"[18] and then applying it in the absence of credible evidence as to what the patient would have wished, the court, as it did in *Saikewicz*, applied a test that was inapplicable to the facts before it. The court then attempted to justify its actions by stating that "an expression of intent by the ward while competent was not essential"[19] to the Probate Court's ruling.

NECESSITY OF SEEKING JUDICIAL INTERVENTION

With so many issues briefed and presented to the court in *Spring*, there was reason to hope that, regardless of the holding in the case at bar, there would be some guidance for future cases. That hope was not realized. In its opinion, the SJC stated that a Massachusetts health care provider need not always seek court authorization prior to the withdrawal of life-supporting care from every patient, but that even if court approval were sought and secured, such approval would not preclude subsequent civil liability or confer immunity from prosecution.[20] Then, in the most troublesome part of the opinion, the court offered "a variety of circumstances to be taken into account in deciding whether there should be an application for a prior court order."[21] Thirteen circumstances and elements were listed, each to be considered by the provider in deciding whether or not to seek judicial authorization for removing or withholding extraordinary medical care from a patient. But the court failed to discuss what combinations or degrees would be determinative; rather, it observed: "we are not called upon to decide what combination of circumstances makes prior court approval necessary or desirable, even on the facts of the case before us."[22]

As a result of *Spring*, there is little that the health care provider can be certain about. Even if all possible combinations of these thirteen elements are employed and a court order is obtained, under no circumstances will the provider be protected from liability for carrying out the order of the court, or secure immunity from liability by virtue of such a court order. Indeed, the potential for civil liability may be expanded as a result of the *Spring* decision. In dictum, the court suggested that liability may be imposed for the negligent execution of a court order authorizing the withdrawal of care,[23] and that an action for negligence may lie for a failure to obtain prior court approval if it can be shown, after the fact, that such a court order would not have been issued had it been sought.[24] For the provider seeking guidance as to the possible exposure to criminal liability, even less guidance was provided. "Little need be said about criminal liability . . . there is precious little precedent and what there is suggests that the doctor will be protected if he acts on a good faith judgment that is not grievously unreasonable by medical standards"[25] was the court's only observation relative to criminal liability. Not only does this off-hand remark reflect an insufficient consideration of the issue, but it also appears to fly in the face of existing criminal law as to the irrelevancy of "good intentions" to criminal liability.[26]

CONCLUSION

The primary reason why the IAHA filed a brief in the *Spring* case was to represent interested parties in other jurisdictions who were looking to Massachusetts for guidance in an area which affects all jurisdictions, and which Massachusetts courts have chosen to address frequently and to litigate profusely. While admittedly concerned about the incorrect reliance upon Illinois law which appeared in *Saikewicz*,[27] the IAHA, whose members represent over one hundred hospitals in the State of Illinois, was attempting to present the critical issues for resolution and to obtain guidance for future cases. Accordingly, the opinion finally rendered was a distinct disappointment. Not only was the opinion inconsistent both with the facts on which it was based and with prior holdings upon which it relied for support, but also it appeared to represent a conscious decision on the part of the court to decline an opportunity to give guidance to health care providers both within and without Massachusetts. Seldom does an appellate court have a case in which the facts lend themselves so well to a clear explanation of the law, a clarification of the relevant legal issues, and an opportunity to provide guidance not only to the parties, but also to others dealing with similar problems. Seldom has an opportunity been so obviously avoided.

There is, however, one saving feature in the *Spring* opinion. The SJC appears to have ruled that a health care provider is not required to seek prior court authorization for the withdrawal of care from all patients, thus effectively neutralizing *Saikewicz*. This gives providers and their counsel the opportunity to judge each individual case on its merits, rather than fearing that each case may only be resolved by litigation. If that is the one clear message from the *Spring* opinion (and even that is uncertain), it is a significant development in the law. Its significance is severely diminished, however, when one considers all that could have been done in this opinion.

It is safe to say that no one's interests were served by the opinion in *Spring*. The law in Massachusetts is more unclear now than it was prior to the opinion. The SJC appears consciously to have turned away from an opportunity to guide lower courts and potential litigants, and in the process has lost an opportunity to take a preeminent position in the resolution of these issues. Apparently, it will fall to the reviewing courts of other jurisdictions to make truly significant contributions to clarifying the law in this area.

NOTES

1. The quotation in the title from the Book of Mark (1:3), literally translated as "the voice of one crying in the wilderness," reflects the concern of attorneys outside Massachusetts with a somewhat baffling series of appellate opinions culminating in *In re Spring*, 405 N.E.2d 115 (1980).
2. *In re Spring*, 399 N.E.2d 493 (Mass. App. 1979).

3. *In re Spring*, No. 49076 (P.Ct., Franklin Co., Mass., May 15, 1979) (temporary guardian, his son, was ordered to refrain from authorizing continued dialysis treatments; on July 2, 1979, a revised order was issued that permitted the ward's wife, son and physician to make any treatment decision.)
4. In addition to the briefs submitted by the petitioners and the guardian *ad litem*, briefs *amicus curiae* were submitted by the American Society of Law & Medicine, the Massachusetts Hospital Association, the Massachusetts Medical Society, and the Mental Health Legal Advisors Committee.
5. *Superintendent of Belchertown State School v. Saikewicz*, 370 N.E.2d 417 (Mass. 1977) [hereinafter cited as *Saikewicz*].
6. The four enumerated "state interests" were: (1) the preservation of life, (2) the protection of third parties, (3) prevention of suicide, and (4) the maintenance of the ethical integrity of the medical profession. *Id.* at 425.
7. *See Lane v. Candura*, 376 N.E.2d 1232 (Mass. App. 1978); *In re Dinnerstein*, 380 N.E.2d 134 (Mass. App. 1978).
8. *Commissioner of Corrections v. Myers*, 399 N.E.2d 452 (Mass. 1979).
9. *Lane v. Candura, supra* note 7, at 1233.
10. A standard of competency similar to that required to execute a will was discussed in *Lane v. Candura, supra* note 7, but no standard was expressly enunciated or adopted.
11. *In re Spring, supra* note 2, at 495–96.
12. *See Boston Globe*, January 23, 1980, at 1, 49 (Spring's guardian *ad litem* responds to affidavits filed by right-to-life advocates and nurses involved in Spring's care by asking for a new hearing).
13. *In re Spring, supra* note 1, at 118, n.l.
14. *See, e.g., In re Quackenbush*, 383 A.2d 785 (Morris Co., Probate Div., N.J. 1978).
15. *In re Spring*, No. 80–37 (Mass. SJC, single justice, interlocutory order dated February 4, 1980).
16. *Id. See also Doe v. Doe*, 385 N.E.2d 995, 1000 (Mass. 1979) (incompetent ward's preference not to be committed to mental institution is "critical factor" to be considered in civil commitment proceeding).
17. One wonders how a test which requires that the Probate Court determine what the patient would have wanted for himself, could arise from or be applicable to a fact pattern in which the patient, Mr. Saikewicz, had an I.Q. of 10, a mental age of 2 years and 8 months, and was functionally inarticulate.
18. *In re Spring, supra* note 1, at 122.
19. *Id.*
20. *Id.*
21. *Id.* at 120–21.
22. *Id.* at 121.
23. *Id.* at 122.
24. *Id.*
25. *Id.* at 121.
26. *See, e.g., People v. Johnson*, 337 N.E.2d 240 (Ill. App. 1975) (intent to cause death not required by statute that defines killing as murder); ILL. ANN. STAT. c. 38,§ 4.5 (Smith-Hurd).

27. *E.g.*, *In re Estate of Brooks*, 205 N.E.2d 435 (Ill. 1965), and *Holmes v. Silver Cross Hospital*, 340 F. Supp. 125 (N.D. Ill. 1972) were cited as authority for the proposition that a patient's right to make treatment decisions is founded upon his right of privacy. In fact, both opinions are based exclusively upon the First Amendment freedom of religious beliefs and do not even discuss a constitutional right of privacy.

Chapter 18

Living Wills and Natural Death Acts

Sidney D. Rosoff

Although this chapter bears the title *Living Wills and Natural Death Acts*, it also encompasses court decisions in this field. Those decisions have been the subject of a great deal of analysis in prior discussions, and it is the intent of this paper to discuss the legal framework of the right to die, insofar as it involves the common law, the statutes, and judicial decisions.

One might ask why so much time is spent discussing judicial decisions relating to death, dying, and terminal care if there are only a handful of cases dealing with the subject. However, these cases are only representative of what is happening in our hospitals. Further, everytime one of these incidents occurs, reported or not, it leaves a scar on the family, on the nurses, and often on the attending physicians.

As physicians learn how to use new medical technologies, they must also learn when not to use them. Many commentators have noted the difficulty of realizing that death is not necessarily an enemy, but in certain cases, death may be a friend. Additionally, it must be recognized that the decision-making process in these cases is not solely medical nor should it be controlled by the courts. There must be a better way of making these treatment decisions and I would like to suggest a method.

But first, it should be noted that families of the dying are now seeking more participation in the course of treatment of their loved ones. Many years ago, patients rarely questioned their physicians about their care; now, they want to know what is being done and why. Questions of treatment are further complicated when a patient is incompetent, has suffered irreversible brain damage, will never regain cognitive function, and can continue to exist only on a respirator. Can the hospital, with consent of the family, terminate "treatment" in that case?

Let me tell you a story which I think focuses on some of these issues. In July of 1978, I was consulted by a brother and sister whose mother was hospitalized in a teaching hospital in New York City. The mother had suffered repeated instances of respiratory arrest with resultant irreversible brain damage and was maintained on a respirator and cared for with 24-hour nursing. I was asked by the adult children if I could have their mother removed from the respirator since her doctors had determined that there was no chance of her regaining cognitive existence. At a conference with the hospital and the hospital's attorney, we formally requested that the life-supporting treatment be removed. The hospital was concerned about liability, but we assured them that the children would waive any such claim. Then they asked what assurance we could give the hospital that the district attorney would not prosecute. We indicated that, in view of the facts of the case, the district attorney would not prosecute, and again asked them to act on our request. The hospital's representative then said: "We'd like to do this. Why don't you bring a lawsuit against the hospital." They indicated that they would cooperate fully and suggested that in this way they would get a judicial determination and immunity. We, however, did not want the adversary proceeding; we could not afford the expense. Further, we felt that it was not fitting to bring this very private matter into the courts, exposing the patient's condition to public view in an adversary climate where, in fact, no controversy existed. We therefore asked that the hospital use its best medical judgment in the circumstances, but the hospital refused and insisted that the children institute a lawsuit.

In cases like this, I believe the hospital should consult the attending physician, the neurologists, the nurses, other specialists deemed advisable, the chaplain, and the institution's administrator to develop a consensus concerning whether the patient had suffered irreversible brain damage and would never regain cognitive existence. On the basis of this full and open determination, the respirator could be removed as a medical decision. In the case I described, the hospital refused to do so and when the woman died five months later the medical bill was $110,000, of which Medicare paid about $80,000. I am convinced that we would take a giant step toward resolving this problem if physicians and hospitals would assume responsibility for their decisions and not thrust the decision upon the courts.

LIVING WILLS

With this story in mind, I will consider some other ways this problem might be resolved. First, there is the "living will." The living will is important because it is a prior declaration of the patient's wishes should the patient ever become incompetent and require extraordinary treatment. Many physicians approve of living wills since they too have difficulty dealing with these situations. The physician who knows his patient's wishes can more easily determine the course of treatment or nontreatment appropriate for that individual.

Additionally, if the decision to withdraw life-sustaining treatment is made by a court, it is important for the courts to know the patient's wishes. It is increasingly apparent that the courts are looking for evidence of the patient's wishes and intent and will give effect to those desires whenever possible.[1] Therefore, the use of the living will should be encouraged. If a patient signs a living will and it is placed in his or her medical record, I think the wishes expressed therein should be observed. In a situation where a living will has been signed and there is a refusal to terminate treatment, there may be recourse through the court to seek obedience to the patient's directive.

JUDICIAL ACTION

I would now like to make a few points about judges, courts, and written decisions. We have spent a great deal of time analyzing court decisions which, as a lawyer, I find interesting. We have discussed, for example, the *Saikewicz*[2] case backwards and forwards, footnotes and headnotes, language and lack of language. This is part of the problem, and one with which we will always be faced if we rely on the courts to make such decisions. Remember that a number of judges were not able to communicate well before they become judges. So, what you're reading in decisions are the words of a lawyer who has become a judge but who may not thereby have gained greater powers of expression to explain the basis for a course of action.

My second point may interest those who have read the book *The Brethren*, which describes the workings of the United States Supreme Court.[3] The authors described in great detail the various factors that go into the preparation and writing of the Court's decisions. As has been shown, Court decisions are often the result of an attempted reconciliation of different philosophies and varying attitudes, combined with personality differences. It is important to realize that most court decisions represent as a starting point, the opinion of one man and then the accretion of his colleagues' comments, thoughts, suggestions and differences. The lay person who has difficulty in understanding the language of decisions has a great deal of company in the legal profession.

Another problem, illustrated by the *Spring*[4] decision, is that the patient may very well be dead by the time the final court decision comes down. The court may hear the case, decide if it has to bring others into the legal proceeding and if so, does so, and appoints a special guardian to make a report. Eventually we get a decision, but the guardian or other parties may appeal an adverse decision. By the time the case is decided by the state's highest court, many months if not years must pass. This is no way to make life or death decisions.

I refer you to an article by George Annas[5] in which he discusses the opinion of the intermediate appellate court in the Brother Fox case.[6] In that case, the court established "simple" procedures to be followed by health providers before terminating treatment: (1) the physician attending the patient must certify that he or she is (a) terminally ill, (b) in an irreversible state of chronic vegetative coma, and (c) the prospects of regaining cognitive brain function are extremely remote; (2) thereafter, a person by whom such certification is made may present this diagnosis to the appropriate hospital prognosis committee of no fewer than three physicians; (3) the committee shall either confirm or reject the prognosis, by a majority vote; (4) upon confirmation of a prognosis, the person who secured it may commence a court action; (5) the attorney general and an appropriate district attorney shall be notified and given an opportunity to intervene; (6) a guardian *ad litem* shall be appointed to represent the interests of the patient; (7) the court shall determine if the prognosis is accurate by clear and convincing evidence; (8) the court shall determine that the patient would decide to terminate extraordinary life support measures if he/she were able to make this decision alone; and (9) an appropriate order for discontinuance of extraordinary measures shall be entered.[7]

By the time we complete this process, it is likely that the patient will have died. It is not wrong for courts to set criteria, to have guardians appointed, and to have the district attorney participate, but this procedure is time-consuming and, at every step along the way, receives wide publicity. This very private problem becomes a public adversary situation. In my view, this is not appropriate.

Finally, even though the parties may agree on what should be done, as in the Brother Fox case and the case I described earlier, the hospital or physicians may refuse to act without first going to court to protect themselves. In this situation, judicial proceedings are far from satisfactory.

What are the alternatives? There was a very interesting case in Florida which went through all three levels of the state courts. All reached the same conclusion: a patient who contracted amyotrophic lateral sclerosis could "pull the plug."[8] This particular patient had tried to do so himself, but when he did, an alarm went off and the nurses put the plug back. His attorney went to court to establish his right to receive no further treatment, but each time they won, the attorney for the state appealed the decision. The case finally worked its way up to the highest court, which upheld the right of the individual to decide about his own treatment.[9]

To support its decision, the court recognized that the right of privacy controlled. But more importantly, the court stated that the question of death with dignity is so complex that it should be left to the legislature. This was also the state's position. The court stated: "Because the issue with all of its ramifications is fraught with complexity and encompasses the interests of the law, both civil and criminal, medical ethics and social morality, it is not one well suited for resolution in adversary judicial proceedings."[10] However, the court stated that a preference for legislative action could not shackle the court in deciding a case properly before it and so it acted.[11]

I believe, just as the judge in that case believed, that this issue is more suitably addressed in a legislative forum, where fact-finding can be less confined and the viewpoint of all interested institutions and disciplines presented and synthesized. Only in this manner can the subject be dealt with comprehensively and the interests of all institutions and individuals properly accommodated. Additionally, by establishing a law to control the providers, there need not be fear to act since the law can be viewed as describing the extent of permissible conduct. For all these reasons, enactment of statutes is most important.

STATE NATURAL DEATH LAWS

The first state law in the United States was the California Natural Death Act,[12] enacted in 1976. In the opinion of many, it is a very unsatisfactory law. It provides that the patient cannot execute the legally effective document until 14 days after the patient has been told that he or she has a terminal condition. Until that time, any document executed by a patient is only an indication of wishes, and the patient's directive need not be observed. Additionally, unlike a regular will, the directive is good for only five years.

Some people counselled Governor Brown against signing the law after it was passed by the legislature on the grounds that its very weaknesses would restrict the physician, and that the law would serve as the basis for enactment of all future legislation. Other people counselled Governor Brown to sign the bill precisely because it was the first bill of its kind and was in direct response to pressures from all sides of the community. I personally disagree with some provisions in the law, and even though the California law is far from perfect, it was a first step and provided the basis for future legislative action.

After the California law, there were laws enacted in Arkansas, Idaho, Nevada, New Mexico, North Carolina, Oregon, Texas and

Washington. At that point, the Society for the Right to Die, in an effort to get as perfect a law as possible, enlisted the assistance of the Yale Law School Legislative Services, which consist of a group of law students who draft bills. The students drafted a model bill which was substantially enacted in the state of Kansas in 1979. The Kansas bill is an improvement over the California bill; it is easier to use and it assures the patient that his or her wishes will be observed. (See Appendix F for a *Comparison of Right to Die Laws* prepared by the Society for the Right to Die.)

Now that there are laws in ten states, one-fifth of the states in the nation, the question is: Where do we go from here? First of all, a law without an awareness campaign is not much better than no law at all, because the laws generally require that individuals sign the documents in advance of the need for which they are intended. The Society for the Right to Die is making an effort to acquaint the citizens of the states that have natural death acts with the provisions of their laws and to encourage organizations within those states to distribute and make available the living will document that must be signed.

To me, the deeper significance of these statutes is that they have opened up lines of communication among physicians, patients, nurses, and other hospital personnel, so that all interested parties have a greater sense of the significance of this problem and input to its resolution. For that reason alone natural death acts have served a very important purpose. Finally, where used properly, the directive provided for by the law can give certainty, avoid delay, and assure that the patient's wishes will be observed.

There are two other issues which I think are important. First, it has become apparent to some interested in this problem that the statutes do not meet one of the most pressing societal needs. That is, what to do in a *Quinlan*-type situation, where the individual has not executed a document and is in a persistent vegetative state. Treatment probably will not be terminated in this type of case because of the fear of legal action. Does one have to go to court with each and every one of these cases? I propose that a statute could be enacted which would set forth guidelines that, if observed by the medical facility, would permit the medical facility to act in the patient's best interest, and consistent with the choice that the patient would have wished, as clearly as that can be determined. Instead of returning to the courts each time, an ethics committee, together with physicians and family, could make a determination, as described by the court in *Quinlan*.[13] Even some judges are reluctant to rely solely on the decision of the patient's family and physician without some clear statutory framework. Therefore, a statutory framework should be enacted which would permit the physician, the family, the prognosis or ethics committee, the hospital clergy, and the administrator to reach a conclusion that would assure protection from possible civil and criminal action. I would hope that from this ongoing dialogue, a draft of such legislation might come.

My final comments concern the question of suicide. Public television has filmed a program of the meetings and discussions held in New York by a woman named Jo Roman before she committed suicide. A number of stations refused to carry the program on the ground that it depicts suicide, as one commentator noted, through rose-colored glasses. Another commentator objected because nothing in the program itself seemed to counsel against suicide. Public television has tried to counter these criticisms by following the program with a discussion of these issues.

Similarly, the British Society for the Right to Die with Dignity has a prepared draft and is considering publication of a pamphlet on suicide. The book advises against suicide generally unless everything is considered. However, the final portion of the book is a how-to-do-it. This book has fermented a great deal of interest and concern in Great Britain and will cause similar concern in the United States if it is published. The television program, *Sixty Minutes*, is going to do a segment on suicide in the Fall. The producer asked and we permitted them to film a meeting of the Board of Directors of the United States Society for the Right to Die, at which there was a discussion of whether the Society should distribute that booklet. At that meeting, it was unanimously agreed that the Society would not distribute the booklet because, in their opinion, it would not be in the best interests of the issue or of the public. The Society's approach in these matters is that even one life needlessly lost is not worth the risk, however good the intent to alleviate suffering might be.

Another reason for the decision is that the Society believes that a great deal of further public consideration must be given to this issue before individuals are simply given "how to" booklets. I bring this matter up because it is, perhaps, an extension of the subject of this discussion. And even if it is not an extension, the professional who is involved with death and dying issues should begin to think about it as an issue, because they may be asked for an opinion by patients. While there is no easy resolution of this problem, it is something which each of us should be able to think about, reaching our own conclusions.

NOTES

1. *See Superintendent of Belchertown State School v. Saikewicz*, 370 N.E.2d 417, 431–32 (Mass. 1977); *In re Quinlan*, 355 A. 2d 647, 664 (N.J. 1976) (court's

concern is what patient would have wanted, not what is deemed in the patient's best interests). *See also Eichner v. Dillon*, note 7 *infra*.

2. *Saikewicz, supra* note 1.

3. B. WOODWARD, S. ARMSTRONG, THE BRETHREN (Simon and Schuster, New York) (1979).

4. *In re Spring*, 405 N.E.2d 115 (Mass. 1980).

5. Annas, G.J., *Quinlan, Saikewicz, and Now Brother Fox*, HASTINGS CENTER REPORT 10 (3): 20–21 (June 1980).

6. *Eichner v. Dillon*, 426 N.Y.S.2d 517 (App. Div. 1980).

7. *Id*, at 550. The procedures outlined by the Appellate Division of State Supreme Court were rejected by the New York Court of Appeals in its decision in the consolidated cases of *Eichner v. Dillon* and *In re Storar*, 420 N.E.2d 64 (N.Y. 1981). In that decision the court held that a guardian could withdraw life-supporting measures from a terminally ill patient who was incompetent to decide for himself or herself only if there is no real chance of recovery and if the patient, prior to becoming incompetent, makes it known that he or she would not want to be kept alive under such circumstances.

8. *Satz v. Perlmutter*, 362 So.2d 160 (Fla. Dist. Ct. App. 1978), *aff'd* 379 So.2d 359 (Fla. 1980).

9. *Satz v. Perlmutter*, 379 So.2d 359, 360 (Fla. 1980).

10. *Id*.

11. *Id*.

12. CALIFORNIA HEALTH AND SAFETY CODE, Part 1 of Division 7, c. 3.9:7187e. *See generally* Raible, J.A., *The Right to Refuse Treatment and Natural Death Legislation*, MEDICOLEGAL NEWS 5(4): 6–8, 13 (Fall 1977).

13. *In re Quinlan, supra* note 1, at 668–69.

Chapter 19

A Prosecutor's View of Treatment Decisions

George A. Oakes

Hypothetically, I would like to take you ahead to 1984, to meet Dr. Robert Smith. Dr. Smith has been practicing medicine for about eight years and has finally gotten everything together. He is having lunch with his wife. It's a beautiful, sunny Friday afternoon, and he feels on top of the world. After lunch they leave the restaurant, he kisses his wife good-bye and she goes off to make some purchases for the family—two lovely daughters who are in their first year of private school (the first time the family could afford that). She drives off in her brand new station wagon. He gets into his Mercedes Benz and goes to his office. As he arrives at his office, he encounters in the lobby two gentlemen who are neat and clean but not too well-dressed. The beautiful receptionist looks a little nervous. He passes into his office. The receptionist enters and informs him that the two men are police officers who wish to speak to him. He invites them in, they sit down and say, "We would like to talk to you about your patient Wilhelmina Jones." "Yes, he replies," I have a patient named Wilhelmina Jones—or I had a patient named Wilhelmina Jones." They say, "Just a moment. Before you say anything else, we would like to advise you of your constitutional rights. You have a right to remain silent. You have a right to an attorney. If you cannot afford an attorney, one will be made available for you at no charge. Anything that you say can and will be used against you in a court of law."

Needless to say, Dr. Smith's beautiful world, at least for the moment, comes to an end. And understandably so; the possibility of criminal proceedings that stretch over a couple of years, lots of adverse publicity, and conviction are real problems. Those of us who enforce the law are aware of these problems. Personally, I would rather not use the power of prosecution in cases involving the withholding or withdrawing of life support systems. Rather, it is important that we work in a cooperative sense with health professionals.

First of all, it should be noted that there are a number of possible crimes that may occur. Murder is the unlawful killing of a human being or of a fetus with malice aforethought.[1] In California, physicians are protected by the Therapeutic Abortion Act from such a charge in cases involving fetuses who are killed during a therapeutic abortion.[2] Relative to this crime and others, it is important to define malice, which may be expressed or implied. Malice is expressed when there is manifested a deliberate, unlawful intention to take away the life of a fellow human being. It is implied when no provocation appears or when the circumstances surrounding the killing show an "abandoned and malignant heart."[3] Murder generally occurs in two types of instances: intentional murders based upon revenge, heat of passion, or financial gain, and those that are done randomly, without any reason, and in a senseless fashion. Based upon this consideration, it is unlikely that the withholding or withdrawing of life support for a terminally ill patient would ever result in a charge of murder against the physician or other involved professionals.

Then we have manslaughter, which is the unlawful killing of a human being without malice.[4] Manslaughter is of three types: voluntary, committed in the heat of passion or quarrel; involuntary, committed negligently or in the commission of some other act which is either legal or short of a felony; and that committed in the operation of a motor vehicle. Obviously, none of the three categories of manslaughter would be applicable to the facts surrounding the intentional withdrawal or withholding by a physician or nurse of life support from a terminally ill patient.

Next there is the crime of conspiracy, which exists whenever two or more persons conspire to break the law, commit any act injurious to the public health or morals, or to obstruct justice or the due administration of the law.[5] Given the very wide parameters of this definition, a charge of conspiracy could conceivably be invoked against physicians and/or nurses, especially where the definition relates to "public health or morals."

The next crime is willful cruelty or unjustifiable punishment of a child, or endangering the life or health of a child. In short, this consists of willfully causing or permitting a child to suffer or to be in danger of unjustifiable physical pain or mental suffering.[6] Under circumstances likely to produce great bodily harm or death, commission of such a crime carries with it a sentence of one year in the county jail or confinement in the state prison. In the absence of such conditions, the crime is deemed only a misdemeanor.

Recently in Los Angeles, we had a case at a prominent hospital that amounted to a willful endangering of the life of a child. Allegedly, the obstetrician decided that he did not wish the defective neonate to go to the neonatal intensive care unit, since he did not want the family to suffer the mental trauma and financial burden of such an action. The physician allegedly decided to pronounce the child dead and to place it in a nearby utility room where it remained alive for approximately 13 hours. The baby was eventually transferred to the neonatal intensive care unit where it was cared for approximately 5 days before it finally died. My office was very interested in this case, and rightly so. A case like this shocks the public and upsets public officials. In the course of our investigation, we found that hospitals, which have invested huge sums of money in advanced equipment and for patient care, have invested no money for dying.

In a similiar case, it was alleged that a major teaching facility in Los Angeles placed a neonate, who had been diagnosed non-viable, in the coffee room to die or to give up whatever vitality it had. That is disturbing, and we made it clear that if such conduct continues, we will prosecute the doctors responsible for it. I believe that a hospital must give basic care to a child or any dying person until he or she has ceased to live, thereby preserving some dignity of life. I would suggest that basic care be given to every neonate, regardless of its viability—basic care being maintenance of body temperature, hydration and nutrition. I do not think that the sensibilities of the citizens of Los Angeles County would be shocked by allowing a non-viable neonate to die in a neonatal intensive care unit so long as he or she is given hydration and nutrition and its temperature is maintained.

Interestingly, in the case of the neonate in the utility room, we discovered some of the law's shortcomings. For example, the doctors testified that the fetus had not been viable. However, during cross-examination, it was brought out that the neonate's life had actually been prolonged by placing it in the utility room. The temperature in the utility room was cool, and as the child's body temperature dropped, its metabolism slowed, and, therefore, the child's life was prolonged. We accepted the doctor's testimony because we did not want to press the issue unless it was absolutely clear that some crime had been committed. We believe that we should exercise the power of prosecution with great restraint and not bring the terrible impact of the criminal process into the lives of people who are trying in total sincerity to save life and service the community. We try hard to support, not tear down.

To assist in understanding the role of the prosecutor and how prosecutorial decisions are made, consider the *Uniform Crime Charging Standards*.[7] These guidelines state:

The prosecutor should charge only if the following four basic requirements are satisfied:

1) The prosecutor, based on a complete investigation and a thor-
    ough consideration of all pertinent data readily available to him, is
    satisfied that the evidence shows that the accused is guilty of the
    crime charged.

2) There is legally sufficient, admissible evidence of a *corpus delicti.*

3) There is legally sufficient, admissible evidence of the accused's
    identity as the perpetrator of the crime charged.

4) The prosecutor has considered the probability of conviction by an
    objective fact-finder hearing the admissible evidence.[8]

Relative to the first requirement, I think it is important to note the
words "data readily available to him." Based upon my discussions with
physicians and other hospital personnel, it seems that the greatest fear
is that a prosecutor acting in ignorance may file a case against someone,
cause them great difficulty, not win the case, but still seriously hurt
both the institution and the individual. It is my opinion that prosecutors have to discuss these things with physicians and others so that we
can better understand what the community practices are and what the
problems are. And it can be a two-way street: prosecutors can describe the limits of prosecutorial discretion and what sorts of acts
are inappropriate.

The second requirement, *corpus delicti*, refers to the substantiated
fact that a crime has been committed. The prosecutor must weigh the
evidence and its admissibility at trial, and determine whether it can be
proved that a crime has been committed. For example, in the first
neonatal case described above, it might be considered that the doctor's
act was not the proximate cause of the child's death, because the doctor's act—placing the baby in the utility room—actually prolonged its
life. Already a disagreement exists with regard to whether there was, in
fact, a crime. Was the child's life endangered or was the child's life
actually benefitted? Of course it seems ludicrous, but the fact of the
matter is that there were professionals in the community who were willing to come forth and testify that the child's life was prolonged by the
doctor's act and that the conduct of the doctor was not the proximate
cause of the child's death. This fact, combined with the fact that the
child weighed just 520 grams, which is very very small, caused my
office to terminate its investigation. If the child had been 720 grams,
there would have been a different reaction by our office and, I am certain, by the obstetrician.

The last requirement, however, is often the most determinative of whether or not a crime is charged. In order to actually charge a person with a crime,

> the admissible evidence should be of such convincing force that it would warrant the conviction of the crime charged by a reasonable and objective fact finder after hearing all the evidence available to the prosecutor at the time of charging and after hearing the most plausible, reasonably foreseeable defense that could be raised under the evidence presented to the prosecutor.[9]

In the example above, the defense would argue that the doctor did not, in fact, act as charged. Furthermore, the defense would show that the parents are very sensitive and that they had indicated prior to the delivery that they did not want a defective child. There would also be testimony that a neonate of 520 grams, if it survived at all, would probably be severely handicapped, and on the tremendous emotional and financial burden placed upon the parents. The point is that the prosecutor must believe he can prove to a jury that a crime occurred. If he cannot, there would be no reason to pursue prosecution of the individuals involved.

One other point about changing standards: public or journalistic pressure should never be a reason, nor should a request to charge by a police agency or public official. I must say, however, that the more things are publicized, the more they become a public matter polarizing people into opposite camps, and greater is the problem of properly resolving the case.

Why Go to Court?

Many health professionals view going to court as a means to immunize themselves from civil or criminal liability for their acts in withdrawing or withholding life-sustaining medical treatment. But courts are not empowered to grant immunity, as the Massachusetts Supreme Judicial Court has held:

> Consent of the patient may not always immunize the physician from a charge of negligence. [citations omitted] Immunity afforded by court authorization would seem to be subject to similiar limitation . . . court approval may serve the useful purpose of resolving a doubtful or disputed question of law or fact but it does eliminate all risk of liability.[10]

There are, however, some good reasons for going to court. First, the court freezes the situation. When the witnesses go into court and are sworn and bear witness, testimony is recorded and the situation is frozen at that point so that everybody can look at it. Also, the facts are presented to an impartial decisionmaker, a professional experienced at weighing testimony and coming to a factual conclusion. Finally, the court has the opportunity of setting forth in a written decision some criteria whereby health professionals can make judgments.

If we are looking for immunity, it might be suggested that the district attorney make some type of statement giving declaratory relief regarding the prospective act. However, this also cannot be done because the district attorney is not empowered to immunize anyone from criminal or civil liability with respect to future acts.

Motive

Consider a charge of murder stemming from an act of active euthanasia. The motives attributable to the defendant could be mercy, finances, emotions, or resource allocation. Mercy is a very poor motive. But, if that is the motive in the United States, the likelihood is that a successful conviction will not be obtained. Financial motives, on the other hand, may very well lead to a conviction. If it's an alleged betting game in Las Vegas, where the nurses are betting on when the person is going to die and somebody wants to collect a few dollars and pulls the plug, the case will be prosecuted because that is a criminal motive for discontinuing life support.

No-Codes

When properly written, no-code or do not resuscitate orders will pose no problem for the prosecutor. As long as the patient was not abandoned, I do not believe that a no-code situation would ever result in any type of prosecution. Withdrawal of life support, on the other hand, is not so clear. The withdrawal of hydration and nutrition may cause physicians to come within the concern of the prosecutor's office. The inevitability of death in those instances is so great that you must attribute an intent to kill to the withdrawal of hydration and nutrition.

Conclusion

If the physician acts prudently and reasonably, considering all of the circumstances, and if other reasonable persons would have acted similarly, and where such acts are within accepted community standards, the possibility of criminal liability being imposed is very remote. The fictitious Dr. Robert Smith need not be concerned with criminal prosecution in his medical practice as long as he is sensitive to the dignities of life and the standards of his community. The value of life, whatever its quality, should be so great that abundant care should be exercised when any decision is made which might hasten death.

NOTES

1. CAL. PENAL CODE § 187 (West). For a further discussion of the meaning of "murder" and the other aspects of the criminal law discussed in this chapter *see* Appendix G *infra*.
2. CAL. HEALTH & SAFETY CODE § 25950 ff. (West).
3. CAL. PENAL CODE § 188 (West).
4. CAL. PENAL CODE§ 192 (West).
5. CAL. PENAL CODE § 182 (West).
6. CAL. PENAL CODE § 273 (a) (West).
7. CALIFORNIA DISTRICT ATTORNEY'S ASSOCIATION, UNIFORM CRIME CHARGING STANDARDS (1980).
8. *Id.* at 13.
9. *Id.*
10. *In The Matter of Earl Spring*, 405 N.E.2d 115, 122 (Mass. 1980).

Chapter 20

The Case of *Phillip B*: A Prosecutor's View

William D. Stein

In discussing the role of the prosecutor in cases of withdrawing or withholding life support from terminally ill patients, it is important to recognize that we are talking about more than mere enforcement through criminal penalties. In California, the Attorney General is the appellate attorney for the prosecution. The district attorneys, such as George A. Oakes, make the tough decisions about which conduct warrants prosecution for what offense. The prosecutor's role goes beyond enforcement of the criminal law, as exemplified by the case of *In re Phillip B.*[1] This case resulted from a non-criminal proceeding, brought by the Juvenile Probation Department of Santa Clara County, alleging that Phillip's parents were denying him the "necessities of life." The specific allegations were that Phillip, who has Down Syndrome and is institutionalized, had a septal defect of the heart which causes the heart to overexert, resulting in increasing damage to the lungs. An operation was recommended by Phillip's doctors, but the parents refused. When the case began, Phillip was twelve years old and the prognosis was that, without an operation, he would die before the age of 30.[2] The prosecutor argued that the operation was, therefore, a necessity of life which the parents refused to provide. The parents argued that the higher-than-average risk involved for Phillip as a Down child precluded any legal requirement for an operation. The case was tried by the local prosecutor before the juvenile court, which found that the operation was not a necessity of life, and agreed with the parents' decision not to consent to the operation for Phillip.[3] The matter came to my attention when an appeal was filed from that order.

As an aside, I would like to state that I agree with the often discussed notion that courts of law are poor procedural devices for resolving the types of questions we are discussing. The legal system has, especially to the untrained, a strange and convoluted logic system. For example, the trier of fact is the heart of the system. Once the trial judge or the jury makes a decision, that decision can be reviewed at several levels of appeal; but with each level the logic system becomes more obtuse. The basic rule is that if the trial judge's decision is supported by sufficient legal evidence, that decision will be accepted by the appellate courts.

Returning to the *Phillip B* case, I argued on appeal that the only evidence presented to the trial court in support of the parents' objections to the operation was their belief that the quality of Phillip's life did not warrant extension. Unfortunately, I was unable to confine the Court of Appeal to such a narrow issue. The court noted that since Phillip suffered from Down Syndrome the risk of open heart surgery was increased. From this, the Court of Appeal concluded that there was a sufficient factual basis to support the trial judge's ruling that the risk of surgery outweighed its possible benefits. The order refusing to authorize surgery was, therefore, affirmed. The *Phillip B* case simply collapsed when the California Court of Appeal found evidence other than "quality of life" to support the trial judge's decision that treatment was not legally required. Although we did attempt to take the case to the United States Supreme Court, their denial of our petition was not unexpected.

I have been asked many times what will happen to Phillip. No one can say. The case was remanded to the trial court and the district attorney may file another petition seeking to have the operation performed if he feels that Phillip's condition has changed significantly. The prognosis is that Phillip will exhibit more and more symptoms because of the septal defect. This presents an example of the conflict between the legal and medical logic systems. From the medical profession's viewpoint, as Phillip's condition worsens and as his lungs become more damaged, he presents a greater surgical risk; in the logic system of the law, the closer Phillip comes to death, the more the benefits of the operation will outweigh its risks. At some time in the future the operation may be ordered.

In Phillip's case, much was made of the quality of life issue. As I mentioned earlier, I felt that the only evidence in the case supporting the trial judge involved considerations of quality of life,—factors that I do not consider relevant. Personally, I can understand when a physician, surrogate, or parent makes a treatment decision based on his or her view of the quality of the patient's life. I am aware that there are finite resources available and that the physician, surrogate, or parent who must make such a decision will probably consider, even if only subconsciously, what the quality of a patient's life will be after the treatment. Yet, while I understand that this issue will be considered in the normal treatment decision-making process, I am offended if quality of life considerations are allowed to enter into the courtroom and affect the court's decision-making process.

Under our system of law we cannot consider quality of life issues in a courtroom. It is contrary to the principles upon which this country was founded: "We hold these truths to be self-evident, that all men are created equal, that they are endowed by their Creator with certain unalienable Rights, that among these are Life, Liberty and the pursuit of Happiness." In reporting the *Phillip B* case, the media picked up and emphasized by quality of life argument. While I seem to have convinced some of my position, I was not successful with the California Court of Appeal.[4]

I am most often asked whether I feel the *Phillip B* case represents the wave of the future. Some commentators have expressed the fear that we may be marching down a trail that leads to abortions on demand and letting Down Syndrome children die. I do not believe that the *Phillip B* case heralds this scenario. I was unable to convince the Court of Appeal that the case turned on the issue of quality of life. The court decided the case on a very narrow legal ground— burden of proof. The decision in the case, therefore, has little impact outside the legal profession. It does leave California attorneys who will litigate such issues or advise their clients in the future somewhat unclear as to what burden of proof they must fulfill and what is sufficient evidence.

When I mention "burden of proof," I am speaking in legal shorthand. Burden of proof is a method by which the law assigns the risk of an erroneous decision. It is similar to an insurance company underwriter assigning a premium on a policy, or the handicapping of horses at a racetrack. I am sure that everyone is familiar with the burden of proof in criminal cases: the prosecution must prove the defendant's guilt beyond a reasonable doubt and to a moral certainty. The law assigns this burden because it believes that it is better for a thousand guilty men to go unpunished than for one innocent man to suffer the loss of his liberty. In criminal cases, the prosecution must fulfill the highest burden of proof recognized in the law so that, if a mistake is made, it will be the state, not the accused, that bears the loss. The law recognizes other degrees of the burden of proof: proof by clear and convincing evidence, proof by a preponderance of evidence, and proof by reasonable cause to believe.

I argued that in life or death medical treatment cases, such as *In re Phillip B*, there is no reason for the incompetent patient to bear the risk of an erroneous decision. If the court errs, the impact of the error should inure to the benefit of the incompetent patient. Before life-sustaining treatment is withdrawn or withheld, I argued that the petitioner should be required to show by the strongest evidence that such a decision is in the best interests of the incompetent patient. Since I did not prevail in the *Phillip B* case, California now requires only proof by clear and convincing evidence in these cases. While California lawyers must work with this burden for now, I do not think it will prevail in future cases; it is an anachronism. The next time this issue is presented to the California courts, I believe that our position will prevail, if not for Phillip, then for the next patient.

In closing, let me endorse the conclusions offered by George Oakes.[5] The law considers the value of life so great that all steps should be taken to preserve it. But, if it is a physician's best medical judgment, consistent with generally accepted medical practice, that a respirator should be removed or a procedure which could extend life should be withheld, and if that decision is detailed and the reasons articulated, the physician should not experience any difficulty when and if the prosecutor reviews his or her decision for possible criminal violations. This is the challenge of the medical profession.

NOTES

1. 156 Cal. Rptr. 48 (Ct. App. 1979), *cert. denied* , 445 U.S. 949 (1980).
2. *Id.* at 50.
3. *Id.*
4. *See, e.g.,* NEWSWEEK, Sept. 3, 1979, at 49; Annas, G.J., *The Case of Phillip Becker: A Legal Travesty,* NURSING LAW & ETHICS 1 (1):4 (Jan. 1980).
5. *See* G.A. Oakes, "A Prosecutor's View of Treatment Decisions," Chapter 19.

Chapter 21

A Prosecutor's View on Criminal Liability for Withholding or Withdrawing Medical Care: The Myth and the Reality

Gregory R. Ginex

Society has entrusted to the prosecutor the function of enforcing the law and bringing to justice those who violate it. The prosecutor must decide, in light of all the facts and circumstances, who to prosecute, when to prosecute, how to prosecute, what charge to file and if the charge(s) can be proved.

One of the more difficult cases to decide is the criminal liability of a physician who makes that fateful decision to withdraw or to withhold medical care. To determine criminal responsibility for a physician's actions or for anyone who is accountable, two factors are reviewed:

1) What action constitutes murder?
2) What is the definition of death?

THE PROSECUTOR'S STANDARD

To determine the definition of murder and its essential elements, prosecutors look first to the common law. Common law defines an essential element of murder as malice,[1] which for this purpose is more than a feeling of ill will. Malice is the intent to kill or knowledge that an act performed will probably cause death.[2] When someone hits a victim, or a physician performs some act which he knows will cause death, the requisite mental state is present to charge the individual with murder.[3] What induced that individual to act is immaterial. Sympathy is of no legal consequence,[4] nor is motive an essential element of the crime of murder.[5] Initially, prosecutors are concerned only with the mental state.[6] When that is present we seek, among other essential elements, the presence of a criminal agency that caused the death.[7] The question here is, was death caused by the physician's act or by the natural consequences of the patient's affliction?

The definition of death is of paramount importance in determining whether the criminal agency was the cause of death. Obviously, one cannot cause the death of a person who is already dead.[8] Accordingly, if death is defined as brain death, then regardless of what a doctor or technician does, he cannot be held legally responsible for the manner in which he treats or fails to treat a patient that has experienced brain death.

The legal definition of death and when it occurs will greatly affect the prosecutor's actions. Historically, legislatures refused to define death.[9] They left it to the courts who in turn passed the burden to the medical community.[10] The common law definition most frequently referred to is the one presented in Black's Law Dictionary: "The cessation of life; the ceasing to exist; defined by physicians as a total stoppage of circulation of the blood, and a cessation of the animal and vital functions consequent thereon, such as the respiration and pulsation . . ."[11] This definition comes from an early series of cases which addressed the legal question of survivorship.

A small number of states have established the definition as "brain death."[12] What is required of a physician in those circumstances? One solution involves an examination of the physician's duty to care for his or her patient. That duty requires a certain standard of care (e.g., what similar physicians in the community would do under similar circumstances) when dealing with a terminally ill patient, but does not exist for one that has experienced brain death.[13] A physician will be exposed to civil or criminal liability for an act of omission only when he or she has a clear duty to act.[14] If that duty does not exist, the physician cannot be charged criminally nor exposed to civil damages.[15]

If the physician accepts an individual as his or her patient the law does impose a duty to continue such treatment, but this duty is limited to the ordinary means necessary to preserve life. There is no corollary duty to employ extraordinary means to preserve life if such employment will not be beneficial.[16] Clearly, there is no duty imposed upon a physician to render extraordinary care to a patient who has experienced brain death. If he or she cannot benefit that patient nor improve the patient's prognosis, the physician has no duty to render extraordinary care. This approach was specifically mentioned in the *Quinlan* case where the court said that a mechanical respirator was an extraordinary means of treatment, and that there was no need to continue such treatment.[17] As a general rule, the extent of the duty applicable in any given situation is defined by the standards of the medical or nursing professions. The criminal law only asks that health care professionals make proper and reasonable medical and nursing judgments concerning decisions to treat, or withhold or withdraw treatment, from terminally ill patients. If they do this they are fulfilling their legal duty to the patient.

THE INVESTIGATION

How does a prosecutor investigate a case of withdrawing or withholding medical care that is brought to his or her attention? Initially, he or she must determine whether accepted medical standards of care were followed by the physician or others in question. What was the intention or the responsibility of the person who authorized the physician, nurse, or other staff? Was someone's act reckless, intentional, an act of gross deviation from medical standards? This review would be accomplished by speaking to physicians and staff familiar with the patient's case, reviewing hospital records, and speaking with the family of the patient to determine whether they were aware of the physician's actions.

Throughout this entire process, the prosecutors and the investigators seek to keep all information confidential. There can be nothing worse than to create innuendo and ruin a professional reputation carelessly. If the physician has proceeded within established medical standards of care, the prosecutor will probably proceed no further. However, if the facts surrounding the case indicate that a gross deviation from the accepted standard of care has occurred, for example, an outright act of euthanasia or any other apparently criminal activity, the investigation will proceed.

Interviews would be conducted with all involved parties, including the potential defendant. Subpoenas would be issued by the grand jury to review records. Scientific tests would be ordered, where required. The autopsy report would become extremely critical, and forensic pathologists would be interviewed. If necessary court orders for exhumation would be sought and subsequent autopsies performed. Statements would be taken by homicide investigators.

Once all pertinent data and evidence have been collected, they would be extensively reviewed by appropriate parties within the prosecutor's office. Once the decision to charge is made, the individual or individuals involved would be either charged by complaint for preliminary examination or indicted directly by the grand jury. Along with the decision to charge come some extremely practical considerations of which prosecutors must remain aware. First, in many cases euthanasia may be accepted as reasonable conduct by the court or jury.[18] Second, some problems may exist as to the causal connection between the physician's act and the actual cause of death.[19] Third, the defendant charged is not the typical criminal. He or she is usually a well respected member of the profession and community with no prior police record. Thus, the problem apparent in the prosecution of any white collar crime case appears in this type of prosecution.

Again, the same difficult question arises: did the physician act in a medically acceptable manner, or was he or she so irresponsible in judgment that the action constituted a crime? These questions, from both the physician's and prosecutor's perspective, are difficult to answer.

THE REALITY

To alleviate some of the concern or alarm the reader may have at this point, I should emphasize that in the eight years that I have been in the prosecutor's office, we have never prosecuted one case of the type discussed above. We have had increasing inquiries in the area but have never had occasion to indict after completing our investigation. Based upon my own observation and experience, there are several reasons this is so:

1) the medical profession is acutely aware of the potential dangers that can arise in this area and consequently acts with extreme care and within generally accepted medical standards of care;

2) before taking definite action, some type of legal advice is generally sought by the physician—either local hospital counsel or private counsel;

3) we are fortunate in Illinois to have adopted the Uniform Anatomical Gifts Act which prescribes a definition of death, at least in cases of organ donation;[20]

4) when an ordinary criminal injures a victim and places him or her in a position where subsequent medical treatment is required, the trend of cases in Illinois is that no civil or criminal liability will be placed upon the physician who follows accepted medical procedures;[21] and

5) as stated earlier, courts are reluctant to impose any duty to treat a patient who has experienced brain death.

For these reasons, health care providers are rarely charged with criminal violations for delivering care to terminally ill patients. Further, even in those rare cases where prosecution is warranted, numerous problems confront the prosecutor. Some of these problems are:

1) the attorney for the defendant physician, even in the most obvious case, will probably be able to find one or more physician experts who will testify that the defendant physician complied with the medical standard of care;

2) the prosecutor must prove beyond a reasonable doubt that the patient's death was caused by the physician's act or omission;

3) the jury, especially where the wrongful act was committed for reasons of sympathy, is often reluctant to find physicians guilty of criminal acts—the white collar crime problem mentioned above; and

4) the accused physician or nurse may have acted according to the wishes of the patient or the immediate family.

CONCLUSION

Health care providers are rarely charged for criminal violations in caring for terminally ill patients. Indeed the fear of such prosecutions greatly exceeds the reality. Physician and nurse compliance with accepted medical/nursing standards of care is the best protection against criminal prosecution. The prosecutor's investigation provides further protection to health care providers, as a charge or indictment should never precede the factfinding that typifies the investigatory process.

As I reflect upon the topic of these remarks—a prosecutor's view—I am compelled to share one of my initial thoughts when I began my research on the subject. The difference between medicine and legal prosecution is that the medical profession is forced to deal with scientific probabilities; prosecutors are forced to deal with facts, only facts. But whatever happens from a prosecutor's standpoint, the issue of death and time of death must of necessity be resolved on an individual case by case basis, supported by testimony of physicians as experts and corroborated by admissible evidentiary facts.

NOTES

1. PERKINS, CRIMINAL LAW 27 (2d. ed., 1969).
2. WHARTON'S CRIMINAL LAW & PROCEDURE § 242 at 522 (Lawyer's Cooperative, Rochester, N.Y.) (1978).
3. WHARTON'S CRIMINAL EVIDENCE § 170 at 314 (Lawyer's Cooperative, Rochester, N.Y.) (1972).
4. *Id.*
5. *People v. Manland*, 30 N.E.2d 428 (Ill. 1940).

6. WHARTON'S CRIMINAL LAW & PROCEDURE, *supra* note 2, at 524.
7. *Id.* at 144.
8. *Id.* at 435.
9. Guthrie, *Brain Death & Criminal Liability*, CRIMINAL LAW BULLETIN 15:40, 41 (January/February 1979).
10. *Commonwealth v. Golston*, 366 N.E.2d 744 (Mass. 1977), *cert. denied*, 434 U.S. 1039; Halley, Harvey, *On an Inter-Disciplinary Solution to the Legal-Medical Definitional Dilemma in Death*, INDIANA LEGAL FORUM 2:219, 234–35 (1968).
11. BLACK'S LAW DICTIONARY at 488 (4th ed., 1968).
12. 16 AM. JUR. *Proof of Facts* at 133, n. 25.
13. 70 C.J.S. *Physicians & Surgeons* § 41.
14. *Euthanasia: The Physician's Liability*, JOHN MARSHALL JOURNAL OF PRACTICE & PROCEDURE 10:148 (Fall 1976).
15. *Id.* at 149.
16. *Id.*
17. *In re Quinlan*, 355 A.2d 647 (N.J. 1976).
18. *See Euthanasia, supra* note 14, at 149; and Collester, D.G., *Death, Dying and the Law: A Prosecutorial View of the* Quinlan *Case*, RUTGERS LAW REVIEW 30:304 (1977).
19. *Id.*
20. ILL. REV. STAT., ch. 110 1/2, § (b) (1979).
21. *People v. Gionvatti*, 387 N.E.2d 1071 (Ill. App. 1979); *People v. Dixon*, 397 N.E.2d 45 (Ill. App. 1979); *People v. Gulliford*, 407 N.E.2d 1094 (Ill. App. 1980).

Part Three

Special Problems with Newborns and Children

Chapter 22

Legal Aspects of Withholding Medical Treatment from Handicapped Children

John A. Robertson

Withholding necessary medical care from defective newborns in order to cause their death is a common practice in many medical centers across the United States. Noted doctors have described their practices of withholding care in the *New England Journal of Medicine*[1] and before Congress.[2] Other physicians have reported that they would not do a surgical procedure to remove a life-threatening intestinal blockage in retarded children, though they would in normal children.[3] Goldstein, Freud and Solnit assert in their influential *Before the Best Interests of the Child* that parents should be able to refuse necessary medical care for a child who has no "opportunity for either a life worth living or a life of relatively normal growth toward adulthood."[4]

An important feature of this practice is its haphazard and often arbitrary occurrence. The frequency of conditions that call forth non-consensual passive euthanasia of defective newborns varies with the hospital and the parents and doctors involved. In most instances there are no written rules or guidelines. Either the parent or doctor will suggest nontreatment, depending on their view of the severity of the case. It is not unknown, however, to have children with relatively mild defects, such as Down Syndrome[5] or low-lesion meningomyelocele[6] selected for nontreatment, as well as those who have very severe brain damage or who will die in a few days or weeks despite very aggressive medical care.

Doctors involved with the care of such newborns have often recommended the widest possible discretion for parents and physicians facing these choices. For example, Dr. Raymond Duff, who publicized his practice at the Yale-New Haven Hospital in an article in the *New England Journal of Medicine*, has recommended that:

[T]he burden of decision making must be borne by families and their professional advisors because they are most familiar with their respective situations. Since families primarily must live with and are most affected by its decisions, it therefore appears that society and the health professions should provide only general guidelines for decision making. Moreover, since variations between situations are so great, and the situations themselves so complex, it follows that much latitude in decision making should be expected and tolerated.[7]

No doubt much of the leeway claimed for parents in these decisions comes from a firm tradition of giving parents freedom in raising their children. Sometimes spoken of as the "natural rights of parents," decisions concerning the child's education, lifestyle, medical care, and well-being are generally thought to be within parental discretion, and not subject to public views of what is good for the child.

Although the commitment to parental authority is a strong one, it is also well-settled that parental rights are not absolute. As one court has stated: "The parental right to control a child's nurture is not grounded in any 'absolute property right' which can be enforced to the detriment of the child, but rather is akin to a trust subject to . . . a correlative duty to care for and protect the child."[8] This "trust" is terminated when the parents fail to discharge their obligations to the child. Thus, when parental conduct threatens a child's well-being in a significant way, the interests of the State and of the individual child may mandate intervention, although the state should have a heavy burden of justification before it is permitted to abridge parental autonomy.[9]

The grounds for state intervention in child rearing are well-established. When the child is abused or neglected, is denied education or necessary medical care, there is little question that parental rights give way to the child's right to a healthy development and well-being, even when the parental wishes are grounded in deeply-held religious views.[10] A classic statement of this position arose in a case in which Jehovah Witness parents had refused to give their permission for blood to be transfused to their seriously-ill child.

The right to practice religion freely does not include the liberty to expose . . . a child . . . to ill health or death. Parents may be free to become martyrs themselves. But it does not follow that they are free, in identical circumstances, to make martyrs of their children before they have reached the age of full and legal discretion when they can make that choice for themselves."[11]

A second factor which leads some people to defer to parental wishes to withhold life-supporting treatment from a defective newborn is the great sympathy they feel for the parents of such a child. The parents were looking forward to a healthy baby and suddenly they are told that the infant is not "normal," is seriously ill or deformed, and may not live or may not develop into a healthy child. We can empathize with the shock, grief, anger, guilt, and resentment that they feel at the birth of such a child, and understand their feeling that they would never be able to cope with the financial costs or with the physical and psychological stresses of caring for such a child at home.

Behind these sympathies, however, may lie a bias against the physically and mentally handicapped. Care of the handicapped child does present substantial burdens to parents, family, and even taxpayers. It draws upon depths of care and concern that many people lack or fear that they lack. In addition, the very existence of such children is a grim reminder of our own dependency, and the way in which our own lives may be twisted irreparably by fate.

The tradition of parental authority, sympathy for the parents, and dislike of the handicapped may explain the practice of passive euthanasia of defective newborns is to ask whether the law should support a criminal prosecution of the parents and doctor. Could a district attorney the caretakers of vulnerable infants intended to cause their death. In this paper I will first describe the possible legal consequences that could arise when parents decide against necessary medical treatment of a handicapped child and doctors and nurses acquiesce, and then describe the circumstances in which passive euthanasia of defective newborns should be legally recognized.

The legal question may be considered from the perspective of the physician and parents faced with the decision to provide or withhold an essential life-sustaining medical procedure to a child with Down Syndrome or a meningomylocele, such as repair of a duodenal atresia or the closing of the lesion on the child's spine. May the parents ever legally refuse treatments for children in such situations? May the doctor legally decide not to treat when the parents request it? What if the doctor wants to treat and the parents say no? What if the parents want to treat and the doctor says no? To answer these questions let us consider two situations in which questions of legality could arise: (1) criminal prosecution for nontreatment, and (2) court authorization to treat when the parents refuse.

LEGALITY OF WITHHOLDING TREATMENT FROM DEFECTIVE NEWBORNS: CRIMINAL LIABILITY

One way to understand the legality of the practice of passive euthanasia of defective newborns is to ask whether the law would support a criminal prosecution of the parents and doctor. Could a district attorney legally bring charges? Could a jury legally convict parents and doctors of a crime for failing to treat? Although the courts have not directly addressed these questions, a reasonably clear answer may be extrapolated from the general criminal law.

Since the law takes a patient-centered approach to treatment decisions involving children, parents and doctors who withhold necessary medical care from a newborn in order to cause its death could be prosecuted for several crimes, ranging from homicide to child abuse and conspiracy.

LIABILITY OF PARENTS

Generally, homicide by omission occurs when a person's failure to discharge a legal duty to another person causes that person's death. If the required action is intentionally withheld, the crime is either first- or second-degree murder, depending on the extent of premeditation and deliberation. When the omission occurs through gross carelessness or disregard of the consequences of failing to act, the crime is involuntary manslaughter.[12]

In the case of a defective infant the withholding of essential care would appear to present a possible case of homicide by omission on the part of parents, physicians, and nurses, with the degree of homicide depending on the intent and extent of premeditation. Following a live birth, the law generally presumes that personhood exists and that there is entitlement to the usual legal protections, whatever the specific physical and mental characteristics of the infant may be.[13] Every state imposes on parents a legal duty to provide necessary medical assistance to a helpless minor child.[14] If they unreasonably withhold such care and the child dies, they may be prosecuted for manslaughter or murder, as has occurred when parents have refused or neglected to obtain necessary medical care for nondefective children.[15] Although I am unaware of any prosecutions of parents for withholding care from defective neonates, the well-recognized rule would appear equally applicable to nontreatment of defective infants. Defenses based on religious grounds or on poverty, if public assistance is available, have been specifically rejected, and other legal defenses, such as the defense of necessity may not apply.[16] While "extraordinary" care may be omitted if there is only a minimal chance of survival, when survival is likely, treatment cannot be withheld simply because of cost or the future social disutility of the infant.[17]

In addition to homicide, parents may also be liable under statutes that make it criminal for a parent to neglect to support or to provide necessities, to furnish medical attention, to maltreat, to be cruel to, or to endanger the child's life or health.[18]

LIABILITY OF ATTENDING PHYSICIAN

The attending physician who counsels the parents to withhold treatment, or who merely acquiesces in their decision and takes no steps to save the child's life, may also incur criminal liability. Since withholding needed medical care by the parents would in many states constitute child abuse or neglect, the physician who knows of the situation and fails to report the case to proper authorities would commit a crime in the 20 or so states where failure to report child abuse is a crime.[19] While failure to report is only a misdemeanor, under the common law "misdemeanor-manslaughter rule" a person whose misdemeanor causes the death of another is guilty of manslaughter.[20] Further, since reporting might have led to the appointment of a guardian and the possibility that the child's life would be saved, the physician who fails to report could be guilty of manslaughter.

The physician may also be guilty of homicide by omission, by the same reasoning discussed above, because he has breached a legal duty to care for the child and thereby caused the child's death. This legal duty of the physician in an emergency to intervene directly by carrying out the necessary procedure, or in other cases to report the case to public or judicial authorities who may then intervene to save the child, is based on several sources. One is the child abuse-reporting statutes, which impose a legal duty to report instances of parental neglect even though the failure to report is not criminal.

The duty may also derive from the physician's initial undertaking of care of the child. Although it may appear that by refusing consent the parents have terminated the physician's legal duty to care for the child, there are at least three possible grounds for arguing that the parents are not able to terminate the physician's obligations to the infant/patient once that relationship has begun, if the patient will be substantially harmed by the physician's withdrawal.

1. The first argument is based on the law of contract. The attending physician has contracted with the parents to provide all necessary medical care for a third party, the infant. When the child is born, this contractual obligation to provide services begins. Under the law of third party beneficiary contracts, the parties contracting for services to another cannot terminate the obligation relative to a minor, if the minor would be substantially harmed.[21] Therefore, the parents are powerless to terminate the physician's legal duty to care for the child, including his or her obligation to take such steps as are necessary to protect the interests of the child. If emergency treatment were required, the physician would be privileged to proceed without parental consent.[22] In most cases, however, the physician's duty would be fulfilled by seeking the appointment of a guardian who could then con-

sent to treatment deemed necessary to save the life of the child.

The attending physician's contractual duty to care for the child over parental objections would not exist if the physician clearly agreed to treat the child only if born normal, or, if the parents made their agreement with the physician subject to modification in case of a defective birth.[23] However, neither parents nor physicians are likely to be so specific in prenatal consultations.

2. Even if the contract theory were rejected, a physician attending a defective newborn would still have a legal duty to care for the child under the traditional tort doctrine that one who assumes the care of another, whether gratuitously or not, cannot terminate such care or assistance if the third person would be hurt thereby.[24] This rule is based on the idea that one who undertakes care prevents others who might have come to the infant's aid from doing so.[25] From this legal duty the physician could withdraw only by notifying public or hospital authorities, which would protect the child by leading to the appointment of a guardian.

3. It could also be argued that the physician would have a legal duty to protect the child on the ground that he has placed the child in peril through his role as a source of information for the parents. A person who puts another in peril, even innocently and without malice, incurs a legal duty to act to protect the imperiled person.[26] By giving the parents adverse prognostic information regarding the handicapped infant—the economic and psychologic burdens they will face, and so on—he may be the immediate cause of nontreatment of the infant, leading the parents to a decision they would not otherwise have made or perhaps even considered. Under this theory even a consultant might be liable if he communicated information which led to a nontreatment decision and death, particularly if the information was incorrect or unfairly presented, and he took no action to save the child.[27]

In addition to liability for homicide by omission or under the misdemeanor-manslaughter rule, the physician may also be subject to homicide liability as an accessory before the fact, *i.e.*, one who "orders, counsels, encourages, or otherwise aids and abets another to commit a felony and who is not present at the commission of the offense."[28] This would be clearest in a case where the physician counseled or encouraged the parents to withhold treatment. If omission of care by the parent is criminal, then the physician's liability as an accessory would follow. If the physician were indifferent to the child's fate, or preferred that it would live, but felt obligated to provide the parents with all the facts, it is less likely he would be culpable, since the requisite intent would be lacking.[29]

Additionally, the attending physician may be guilty of conspiracy to commit homicide or to violate the child abuse or neglect laws. Conspiracy is an agreement between two or more parties to achieve an unlawful objective with (in most jurisdictions) an overt action toward that end.[30] If parents and physician agree that a defective newborn infant should die, and take any action toward that end, conspiracy could be alleged. Similarly, a staff conference on a particular case could amount to conspiracy, if the attending physician and others agreed that medical or surgical procedures should be improperly withheld from the child.[31]

LIABILITY OF NURSES

Nurses who participate or acquiesce in parental decisions to withhold treatment may also be at risk. While a nurse's care is subordinate to the orders of a physician, her legal duty is not fulfilled simply by carrying out physician orders with requisite skill and judgment. Where the patient's protection requires it, a nurse is required to act independently, or even directly counter to the orders of the physician.[32] For example, consider a case where two nurses, the attending physician, and the hospital were held civilly liable when a patient died from postpartum cervical hemorrhage. At trial it was shown that the nurses were aware the mother was in peril but did not contact the attending physician because they thought he would not come. The court found that they had a duty to report the situation to a superior, and failing to do so, they were liable for the injury.[33]

THE POSSIBILITY OF PROSECUTION

The existence of potential criminal liability is no guarantee that parents, physicians, nurses, and hospitals will in fact be prosecuted, nor that a prosecution would be successful. Parents who have actively killed defective children have often been acquitted (though not always),[34] and to my knowledge no parent has been prosecuted for withholding care from a defective newborn infant. Similarly, in the only cases that I know of where physicians were prosecuted for homicide in euthanasia situations involving terminally ill patients, both were acquitted.[35] To my knowledge, no doctor has been prosecuted for passive euthanasia of a defective newborn infant to date.

The infrequency of criminal prosecutions in the past, however, may not be a reliable guide for the future. As the practice becomes more openly acknowledged, public pressure to prosecute may build, and some prosecution (or at least civil litigation) is likely, if only to clarify the law. The *Edelin* case, where a physician was charged with allegedly causing the death of a viable fetus after a lawfully performed abortion,[36] illustrates the dangers of ignoring the legal issues, and the politics of the process by which a prosecution might be initiated. Physicians, parents, and others may decide that they are willing to risk prosecution, or believe that the law should be broken. Such a position entails risks, and one cannot safely predict from past experience that criminal liability will not be imposed.

JUDICIAL AUTHORIZATION TO TREAT OVER PARENTAL OBJECTIONS

The legality of withholding treatment from defective newborns may also be raised in a petition to a court to treat the child over the parents' objections. The attending physicians or the hospital may seek authority to treat for two reasons. First, the doctors might disagree with the parents' decision and think that the child should be treated. Or, they might be fearful of legal liability and want to be sure that withholding treatment is legally justified.

In such a proceeding a court is likely to authorize treatment, for the law generally protects all persons equally, regardless of their physical and mental handicaps. For example, in a 1974 case from Maine, when the parents refused consent to a repair of a tracheal esophageal fistula on a newborn child who had some unknown measure of brain damage, no left eye or ear, and a malformed left thumb, the court had no hesitancy in issuing an order for treatment. It stated:

> [At] the moment of live birth there does exist a human being entitled to the fullest protection of the law. The most basic right enjoyed by every human being is the right to life itself. . . . The issue before the court is not the prospective quality of the life to be preserved, but the medical feasibility of the proposed treatment compared with the almost certain risk of death should treatment be withheld. Being satisfied that corrective surgery is medically necessary and medically feasible, the court finds that the defendants herein have no right to withhold such treatment and that to do so constitutes neglect in the legal sense.[37]

Similarly, in a New York case involving a newborn girl with a meningomyelocele, the court granted the hospital's petition to be appointed guardian for the purpose of consenting to the surgical repair of the meningomyelocele.[38] The parents had refused to consent to surgery to close the lesion on the child's back, and insisted on taking the child home to "let God decide if the child is to live or die."[39] At the time the extent of the child's handicaps from the meningomyelocele were not known. However, since the lesion was very low on the spinal column, it appeared likely that she could be ambulatory with braces and would have normal intellectual development, though she would have no bowel or bladder control and might need a cranial shunt in case of hydrocephalus. The court ordered treatment for the child, noting that she "has a reasonable chance to live a useful, fulfilled life."[40] The court emphasized that it was not confronting a case of "hopeless life," and did not indicate how it would rule in such a case.

Despite the nearly uniform practice to grant petitions to authorize treatment over parental objections,[41] courts may sometimes refuse to order treatment. There is a class of treatment decisions, discussed below, in which refusal of the petition could be justified by the courts as being in the child's own interests. In some cases of Down Syndrome, meningomyelocele, or other congenital anomalies involving mental retardation, such refusals seem unwarranted and hard to reconcile with the basic principle of equal respect for the life of all. An example of such unwarranted refusal is the widely-publicized Phillip Becker case.[42]

When the case arose, Phillip Becker was a 12 year-old boy who was mildly retarded as a result of Down Syndrome. His IQ was about 60; he was educable, could communicate verbally and tend to many of his needs. His parents never took him home after his birth, though they visit him occasionally at the private group residence in which he lives. His living expenses are paid for by the state of California.

A routine medical examination revealed that Phillip was suffering from a ventricular septal defect (v.s.d.), a not uncommon cardiac defect that involves a hole between two chambers of the heart. If the v.s.d. is repaired, which ordinarily occurs early in a child's life when it is first noticed, the child will usually have normal longevity. If it is not repaired, the child will slowly deteriorate as the heart is forced to work harder, eventually pumping unoxygenated blood through the body. During the later course of illness he will be unable to walk, will be gasping for breath, and will eventually die from lack of oxygen.

Although advised of this possibility, the parents refused to consent to the operation needed to repair the defect. The persons caring for him informed the state child welfare authorities, who brought a petition asking that Phillip be considered neglected and that a guardian be appointed to consent to the surgery. After a hearing before a trial judge, the petition was rejected. On appeal to the California intermediate appellate court, the Court of Appeals, this decision was affirmed. Petitions for discretionary further review to the California and United States Supreme Courts were rejected.[43]

In my opinion, the Becker decision does not withstand critical scrutiny, and is unlikely to be followed by other courts that carefully consider the issue. Indeed, it has binding effect only within the fourth appellate district of California—the San Francisco Bay area. The decision cannot be cogently rationalized as serving the child's interest. Although there is a 5 percent risk of mortality from the proposed surgery, and post-operative complications are more likely to occur with a Down Syndrome child than in the case of a normal child,[44] it is very difficult to argue that the operation was not in Phillip's best interest. Without it, he is certain to die a slow, painful death in the next five to ten years, with the last years full of agony and suffering. With it, he has the potential for a long life of ordinary health. Although the surgical risk is significant, it is not so high that reasonable people would reject the operation. Indeed, it is widely recognized that if Phillip were normal, the operation would clearly be seen to be in his best interest.

The parents stated that they opposed the operation because they were concerned that Phillip might continue to be institutionalized after their death. But this concern hardly seems sufficient to justify denying Phillip a procedure without which he is sure to die in the next several years. Unless life in an institution was so horrible that death were preferable, the parents' concern would not justify denying him such a necessary medical procedure. Nor is the risk of the surgery so great relative to the benefits that the decision should be left to parental discretion.

One surmises that neither the parents nor the court gave due regard to the interests of the child, and instead were swayed by uncritical scrutiny of claims of parental autonomy, and perhaps by a bias or prejudice against the retarded. Unless the retarded are to be deemed as having fewer rights to life than others, the *Phillip B* decision is unsupportable and should not be followed by other courts.

WHEN IS WITHHOLDING TREATMENT LEGALLY AUTHORIZED?

Although it is likely that the courts would find a legal duty to treat most children with Down Syndrome or a meningomyelocele, it would be a mistake to think that treatment would be legally required for all defective children. Although life is ordinarily a good for the person, even if the person is severely handicapped and might spend it in an institution, it is not always nor necessarily a good. The situation may be such that viewed solely from the perspective of the patient, further life is not in a patient's interests when it is so full of suffering or so devoid of meaning that the burdens of the medical care necessary to keep him or her alive do not seem worth it. When adults find themselves in this situation and decline further care, we respect their choices. When they are incompetent and cannot speak for themselves, we make such choices for them. There is no reason why the same decision cannot be made with severely deformed newborns, as long as it proceeds truly and authentically from concern for them and not concern for others. Respect for life means that we show equal respect for the lives of all. It does not mean that all human life must be preserved whatever the cost, circumstances, or condition of the patient.

To understand how these principles apply to the situation of passive euthanasia of defective newborns, consider the following situation that confronted pediatricians and neonatalogists at a major academic medical center. A baby boy born 7 weeks premature, with a weight of 900 grams, had severe respiratory problems that led to bronchopulmonary dysplasia. Intracranial bleeding during this period caused irreversible brain damage that made development beyond the most minimal level highly unlikely. He was still respirator-dependent at 5 months after birth, and his prognosis at that point was very poor even with the most aggressive medical care. The parents insisted that further care be stopped, and eventually the doctors acquiesced. The respirator was removed and the child died.

It seems to me that the legality of this action is very different from our analysis of situations involving nontreatment of children with Down Syndrome and meningomyelocele children. Prosecution is even more unlikely here than in those cases, for one might reasonably conclude on the basis of the principles discussed above that the child's right to treatment had not been violated. In this case it is very difficult to argue that further living, from the child's perspective, serves its interest. First, the brain damage may be so severe that it may not be meaningful to speak of the child as having interests. We do not, for example, find it easily comprehensible to talk about people in chronic vegetative states as having interests. At the bottom end of the IQ scale, as with anencephalic or severely brain-damaged children, the same may be true. More importantly, even if this infant has interests, it has an interest in life only if that life holds some good for it. If life will be full of irremediable pain and suffering, then he or she may have no interest in staying alive.

It is important to recognize the source of the judgment being made here. It does not arise out of concern for the interest of others, nor is it based on a view that severe handicaps alone deprive a child of an interest in living. Instead, it is a patient-centered approach that focuses solely on the needs and interests of the child, from the child's perspective as best we can understand or infer it. Indeed, its scrupulous concern with the interests of the child means that very few cases meeting this criteria will be found. There are few conditions so disabling that we can say with reasonable certainty that from the infant's perspective continued living is a fate worse than death.

For example, most cases of Down Syndrome and myelomeningocele, though they involve hydrocephalus, kyphosis, incontinance, nonambulation, and mental retardation, do not fit this category. These infants may suffer from repeated medical interventions, and may not have access to the full range of opportunities available to nondisabled persons. But the perspective of the healthy, normal individual is the wrong perspective to take. The view of ordinary people who know ordinary capacities for experience and interaction, and who may view the infant's existence as a fate worse than death, does not tell us how the infant who has no other life experience views it. For that child life in a severely disabled form would seem better than no life at all, even if it is lived in the custodial wards of a state institution.

Where the child's existence would involve incessant, unrelievable pain, or is devoid of any possibility of realizing even the most minimal experiences or states of being which make life for even the most disabled person good; or with lesser degrees of pain, where death is very imminent and unavoidable, a judgment that treatment is not, from the child's perspective, in his or her interests seems justified. Such judgments can be limited to these extreme cases without spillover into situations where treatment is warranted. Even physicians who are the most thoroughly committed to preservation of life recognize that at some point further treatment hurts, rather than advances, the interest of the patient.[45] Zealous concern for the rights of handicapped children should not blind one to the fact that these are cases where further medical procedures are not, from the patient's perspective, warranted.

In such cases it is very unlikely that prosecution of the parents or the doctors would be successful, or that a petition to authorize treatment would be granted. There is growing legal precedent for withholding care from adult patients in such circumstances. For example, state supreme courts in New Jersey,[46] Massachusetts,[47] and New York[48] have granted petitions seeking authorization to withhold medical procedures from incompetent adult patients on the basis of a patient-centered approach that gives priority to the interests and needs of the patient. Although their reasoning is not consistent it is clear that a legal consensus is developing that would authorize withholding medical procedures from patients when it reasonably appears that it is no longer in their interest to be treated. There is no reason why these precedents should not apply to treatment decisions involving children who are in equally dire circumstances.

CONCLUSION

The law's emphasis on a patient-centered approach to withholding treatment from patients incapable of deciding for themselves protects the interest of most handicapped newborns in receiving medical treatment essential to their survival. Legal analysis of the nontreatment decision shows that many, perhaps most, instances of passive euthanasia of handicapped newborns are illegal. The wishes of parents to allow such children to die can be overridden by judicial authorization of treatment. In egregious cases, parents and the doctors and nurses who acquiesce in their decision could be prosecuted for a variety of crimes connected with the nontreatment decision, though in the current climate prosecutions are unlikely, and, in most instances, may not be the best way to deal with this difficult situation.

The illegality and immorality of many nontreatment decisions should not, however, be interpreted to mean that all such decisions are illegitimate. In some extreme cases omission of further medical treatment may be the best alternative for the child, from the child's own perspective. Although the courts have not yet drawn clear lines defining those situations, the lines now evolving for withholding treatment from incompetent adults should apply to infants as well. Our concern for the well-being of handicapped newborns need not blind us to the situations in which respect for them requires that further medical procedures be stopped.

NOTES

1. Duff, R.S., Campbell, A.G.M., *Moral and Ethical Dilemmas in the Special-Care Nursery*, NEW ENGLAND JOURNAL OF MEDICINE 289 (17):890-94 (Oct. 25, 1973) [hereinafter cited as Duff and Campbell].

2. *See* Robertson, J.A., *Involuntary Euthanasia of Defective Newborns: A Legal Analysis*, STANFORD LAW REVIEW 27:213-69, at 214 (Jan. 1975) [hereinafter cited as Robertson, *Involuntary Euthanasia*].

3. Todres, I.D., *et al.*, *Pediatricians' Attitudes Affecting Decision-Making in Defective Newborns*, PEDIATRICS 60(2):197-201 (Aug. 1977).

4. J. GOLDSTEIN, A.FREUD, A.J.SOLNIT, BEFORE THE BEST INTERESTS OF THE CHILD (The Free Press, New York) (1979) at 91-92.

5. *In re Phillip B.*, 156 Cal. Rptr. 48 (Ct. App. 1979), *cert. denied*, 445 U.S. 949 (1980) (Down Syndrome, or mongolism, is a chromosomal disorder caused by the presence of 47 rather than the normal 46 chromosomes in a person's cells. The disorder produces mental retardation, and is marked by a distinctively shaped head, neck, and torso).

6. *Application of Cicero*, 421 N.Y.S.2d 965 (S.Ct. 1979) (Meningomyelocele is a condition evidenced by a protrusion of the membranes and cord through a defect in the vertebral column. Failure to repair the opening presents a danger of perforation and highly probable infection, usually spinal meningitis, and death).

7. Duff and Campbell, *supra* note 1, at 894.

8. *Custody of a Minor*, 379 N.E.2d 1053, 1063 (Mass. 1978), *quoting Richards v. Forrest*, 180 N.E. 508, 511 (Mass. 1932).

9. *Custody of a Minor*, *supra* note 8.

10. Wald, M., *State Intervention on Behalf of "Neglected" Children: A Search for Realistic Standards*, STANFORD LAW REVIEW 27:985, 1028 (April 1975) (only *serious* neglect of medical care will be sufficient for the state to disregard parent's religious beliefs).

11. *People ex rel. Wallace v. Labrenz,* 104 N.E.2d 769, 774 (Ill. 1952), *quoting Prince v. Massachusetts,* 321 U.S. 155, 166, 170 (1934).

12. For a further discussion *see* Robertson, J.A., *Medical Ethics in the Courtroom,* HASTINGS CENTER REPORT 4(1): 1-3 (Sept. 1974) [hereinafter cited as Robertson, *Medical Ethics*]. See also LAFAVE and SCOTT, note 14 *infra,* at 190, 586-87.

13. *People v. Chavez,* 176 P.2d 92, 95 (Cal. Dist. Ct. App. 1947); *see also* Robertson, *Medical Ethics, supra* note 12, at 2.

14. W. LAFAVE, A. SCOTT, A HANDBOOK OF CRIMINAL LAW (West, Minneapolis) (1972) at 184 [hereinafter cited as LAFAVE and SCOTT]; *see* Robertson, *Involuntary Euthanasia, supra* note 2, at 218.

15. *State v. Crawford,* 196 N.W.2d 915 (Neb. 1972); *State v. Williams,* 484 P.2d 1167 (Wash. Ct. App. 1971). *But see State v. Clark,* 261 A.2d 294 (Conn. Cir. Ct. 1969) (conviction on statutory charge of "cruelty to children" even though one child died due to parental neglect).

16. *State v. Stehr,* 139 N.W. 676 (Neb. 1913) (poverty); *People v. Pierson,* 68 N.E.243 (N.Y. 1913) (religious beliefs); Robertson, *Involuntary Euthanasia, supra* note 2, at 239-43 (necessity).

17. *See* Robertson, *Involuntary Euthanasia, supra* note 2, at 235-37.

18. *Id.* at 232-33.

19. *E.g.,* VT. STAT. ANN., tit. 13 §1304 (1974); CAL. PENAL CODE §273a(1) (West 1970).

20. LAFAVE and SCOTT, *supra* note 14, at 188.

21. *Rhodes v. Rhodes,* 266 S.W.2d 790, 792 (Ky. 1954) (in third-party beneficiary annuity contract, termination invalid unless right of recission reserved in contract); *Plunkett v. Atlins,* 371 P.2d 727, 731-32 (Okla. 1962) (third-party beneficiary contract cannot be modified to decrease benefits of child without child's legal consent). For a further discussion *see* Robertson, *Involuntary Euthanasia, supra* note 2, at 225-27.

22. *Jackovach v. Yocom,* 237 N.W. 444, 449-50 (Iowa 1931) (arm amputation).

23. *See Rhodes v. Rhodes, supra* note 21.

24. LAFAVE and SCOTT, *supra* note 14, at 185-86.

25. *Id.* at 185.

26. *See e.g.,* VT. STAT. ANN., tit. 13 §1304 (1974); CAL. PENAL CODE §273a(1) (West 1970).

27. Robertson, *Involuntary Euthanasia, supra* note 2, at 229-30.

28. LAFAVE and SCOTT, *supra* note 14, at 498.

29. *Nye and Nissen v. United States,* 336 U.S. 613, 619 (1949); *Hicks v. United States,* 395 F.2d 468 (8th Cir. 1968). *Also see* Robertson, *Involuntary Euthanasia, supra* note 2, at 231-32.

30. LAFAVE and SCOTT, *supra* note 14, at 453, 476.

31. *See* Robertson, *Involuntary Euthanasia, supra* note 2, at 234-35.

32. *Id.* at 225, notes 82, 83.

33. *Goff v. Doctors' Hosp. of San Jose,* 333 P.2d 29, 32-33 (Cal. Ct. App. 1958).

34. *Commonwealth v. Noxon,* 66 N.E.2d 814 (Mass. 1946); *Repouille v. United States,* 165 F.2d 152 (2d Cir. 1947).

35. *See* R. VEATCH, DEATH, DYING AND THE BIOLOGICAL REVOLUTION (Yale Univ. Press, New Haven)(1976) at 78-80.
36. *Commonwealth v. Edelin,* 359 N.E.2d 4 (Mass. 1976).
37. *Maine Medical Center v. Howle,* No. 74-145 (S.Ct. Maine, Feb 14, 1974).
38. *Application of Cicero, supra* note 6.
39. *Id.* at 966.
40. *Id.* at 968.
41. *See* Robertson, *Involuntary Euthanasia, supra* note 2.
42. *In re Phillip B., supra* note 5, at 51.
43. For the view of the state's attorney in the Phillip Becker case, *see* Stein, W.D., "THE CASE OF *PHILLIP B.*: A PROSECUTOR'S VIEW," in Chapter 20.
44. *In re Phillip B., supra* note 5, at 50.
45. For example, Dr. Everett Koop, a committed and compassionate defender of the rights of handicapped newborns, has described the circumstances under which he will cease treatment on certain newborns. At Americans United for Life, Conference on Infanticide of Handicapped Children, Chicago, Illinois, Dec. 6, 1980.
46. *In re Quinlan,* 355 A.2d 647 (N.J. 1976).
47. *Superintendent of Belchertown State School v. Saikewicz,* 370 N.E.2d 417 (Mass. 1977); *In re Spring,* 405 N.E.2d 115 (Mass. 1980).
48. *Eichner v. Dillon,* 426 N.Y.S. 2d 517 (S.Ct., App. Div. 1980), *aff'g. as modified,* 423 N.Y.S.2d 580 (S.Ct., Special Term 1979); *In re Storar,* 433 N.Y.S.2d 388 (S. Ct., Monroe County) (1980). These cases were consolidated before the New York Court of Appeals and a decision was rendered on April 1, 1981.

Chapter 23

Ethical and Legal Responsibilities of the Physician Toward the Dying Newborn

Bernard Towers

You may have noticed that the title of this paper reverses the word order in the title of this book. It was not premeditated but simply emerged as "ethical and legal responsibilities" instead of "legal and ethical aspects." I am always interested in word order. For example, I think it is very appropriate for the American Society of Law & Medicine to put law up front, since I assume that the greatest percentage of the Society's members are lawyers. When I started the *Medicine and Society Forum* at UCLA, it was within the medical school, and I was concerned with having clinical input and the need to consider clinical cases. When the series developed into a larger program, I invited another faculty member to work with me as co-director—Dr. Winslade, who is both a trained philosopher and a lawyer. We debated a great deal about what to call the program, but because it originated in the school of medicine, and because clinical problems are pre-eminent in our deliberations, we called it the UCLA Program in Medicine, Law and Human Values. I think we tend to express our own values when we decide which word to use first in a title. So, in this paper I have put ethics first because I think ethics always comes first. I believe that we must put our human values in order before we begin to explore professional aspects of withholding or withdrawing life-sustaining medical treatment from terminally ill patients.

At the outset, I should note that I am a physician, and I describe myself as a developmentalist. As an "antenatal" pediatrician, I study development before birth, both in the laboratory with animal experi-

This article is an edited version of an informal luncheon talk given by Dr. Towers at an April 1980 conference in Los Angeles.

ments and in the clinical field. Of course, development continues after birth, and so I am very interested in the newborn period and in development throughout childhood, adolescence, and adult life. I disagree with the Freudians who say that our psychological development is essentially determined by the age of three or five. I think we continue to undergo psychological development and change throughout adulthood. The concept of development tends to spread both forward and backward in time. I tell my students that I am talking in four dimensions, namely about the development of a three-dimensional organism which is changing in time.

Development of an individual starts with the fertilization of a human ovum, and thus I am very interested in genetics and genetic counseling. This is not a theoretical connection, but a practical one; for example, as many as two thirds of all fertilized human ova are destined, through natural causes, to live out their brief lives in utero and fail to make it through the period of gestation. This figure often astonishes people who have never heard it before. The reasons so many fail are mostly genetic, either from inheritance from parents or from new mutations or translocations which may have occurred at the time of the reduction division of either the egg or the sperm. Such events result in a defective fertilized egg.

However, a good many of the losses that occur in utero occur because the environment is not appropriate or maximal for the developing embryo. While this seems strange, it is just an expression at the human level of a general law that operates throughout nature. Nature is very profligate concerning reproduction since it provides for a selection process for biological organisms. Thus, as a developmentalist, I become interested in the question of evolutionary development—the evolution of the human species. Only in the last 100 years have we become aware that we are products of and are capable of analyzing a history of development which stretches over millions of years. This realization has been described by Julian Huxley as "consciousness squared."

When we look at the developing fetus and the newborn in this way, we see them as expressions of a natural process that has been in continuous development over a very, very long period of time. It is into this process that humanistic concerns and disciplines such as history and philosophy become integrated. Fundamentally, we are a society of creatures which have been developing in this evolutionary process from primate groups, from mammalian groups, and way back through vertebrates and invertebrates. Human society, it seems to me, has always depended on a basic sharing and caring between its members for its success and survival, although that idea might come as a surprise to those who are aware of popular theories about evolution and the nature of man as a product of evolution. Some evolutionists have said that basically man is aggressive and competitive, and that he has always been at war with himself and with the rest of nature. And when we examine our society today, we see many examples that affirm this view.

I often refer to the 1960s as the decade of "the naked ape." It was the decade when Desmond Morris published his book of that title, and I collaborated with an English anthropologist to produce a book which we entitled *Naked Ape or Homo Sapiens?* Morris, a biologist, Robert Ardrey, a dramatist, and Conrad Lorenz, with his book on aggression, swept the market. Their theme about the nature of evolution and the nature of man viewed members of the species homo sapiens as essentially the inheritors of aggressive tendencies from pre-human ancestors. I regarded that view then and regard it now as totally misguided. It is more than 100 years out of date.

We should remember that the man who coined the term "nature red in tooth and claw" was not a scientist. He was a poet: Tennyson's "In Memoriam" was published almost ten years before Darwin's *The Origin of Species.* It is becoming increasingly evident that the concept of "nature red in tooth and claw" is erroneous. Nature, when seen as a total ecological system, is a cooperative venture. There are many groups and subgroups, and when one takes a wrong path, it ends in extinction—not necessarily through the aggression of other groups. They end in extinction in the same way that two-thirds of human eggs do, simply because their biological mechanisms are inadequate.

The idea that nature is red in tooth and claw, when transposed to the human community, led a reviewer of Desmond Morris' book to say in the *British Sunday Observer,* "we now see ourselves as hairy, warring, fascist brutes prepared just to screech at our neighbor and to shout 'mine, all mine.'" She goes on, "I take some comfort in that. These authors have let us off the hook, as it were. We can explain everything by virtue of our animal inheritance."

Within the last ten to fifteen years, a number of works have been published indicating that the evolutionary process is more benign than malign. The older ideas, which have been around since Tennyson, produced the philosophy of Social Darwinism in the nineteenth century. This philosophy formed the basis for a great many social evils and provided the justification for the enormous industrial fortunes that were developed in America. The idea was that by promoting aggressive competitive endeavors, the process of evolution would be advanced.

The result of such thinking would seem to be a completely uncaring society. But human beings continually demonstrate that philosophy is wrong. The majority of people have a natural disposition toward caring and concern for the sick and for those whose rights are abused. In a caring society, doctors and nurses are simply special "caretakers." This kind of helper existed long before lawyers, long before there was any official profession of medicine. But disputes between professionals are bound to arise, given individual freedom and our natural tendency to lean toward the group in which we have a special interest or special knowledge. Accordingly, society needs some rules—rules of law, rules of right conduct—which will express the prevailing ethos.

DECISIONS FOR NEWBORNS

When I first came to UCLA on sabbatical leave from England in 1965, I was housed in the department of pediatrics, particularly in the division of pediatric cardiology. Every week I would attend an interdisciplinary patient conference between cardiologists and thoracic surgeons. We reviewed the data on each patient in order to determine the nature of the heart defect (most were congenital or cardiovascular), and whether it would be appropriate to undertake surgery or a less invasive therapy.

A number of these cases involved Down Syndrome, where there is a higher incidence of congenital heart defects than in virtually any other group of children. I discovered two schools of thought within our team of cardiologists and surgeons. One favored active, interventionist therapy (e.g., if a hole in the heart can be corrected, we are obligated to do the surgery). The other would say: "Are we really helping the Down child by subjecting him or her to open heart surgery? Such surgery is traumatic and, in Down children, there is a higher mortality rate. We are not going to correct or cure the underlying condition. Let us look at the whole child a little more carefully to determine what is appropriate."

I used to try to get the two groups to discuss what led them to their different conclusions, but I discovered it was impossible. They said that those are value questions, and value questions are matters of opinion. Because such questions cannot be answered quantitatively, they are inadmissible in medical science, according to this school of thought.

Both the interventionist group and the more conservative group declared that they were guided by their own personal philosophy, but they did not mean a philosophy in the sense of a thoughtful, logical argument. What they were guided by were their gut feeling. They were really saying: "I will do whatever I can live with comfortably in my conscience." And by extension each group implied, "Don't send me your patients and I won't send you my patients, and we will live happily with this irresolvable conflict of human values." The physician—the cardiologist or the surgeon—knows that by proposing a certain course of action to the patient's parents he or she can influence, if not effect, the ultimate decision. All of this, of course, is very paternalistic, as the phrase usually goes.

When I thought about these Down children, it occurred to me that it would be a matter of chance as to whether the parents consulted a conservative cardiologist or an aggressive one. This did not seem quite right: the needs of the patient ought to come first and life or death decisions ought not be left to luck. So when I returned to UCLA to join the faculty, I tried to sound out colleagues, medical students, and nurses about the basis of their ethical judgments.

BASIS FOR ETHICAL JUDGMENTS

I am not a trained philosopher, but I have read a good deal. In ethics, there is what I call a "science" of normative ethics, which is case-oriented and geared toward resolving problems. There is also a science of meta-ethics, which deals with more rarefied questions such as the nature of good and evil. Normative ethics has to come first.

Aristotle's textbook on physics was an investigation of natural phenomena. His second textbook, which examined the concepts underlying his analysis of physical and biological phenomena, was simply called "after physics," i.e., metaphysics. Metaphysics subsequently came to mean one branch of philosophy. As an Aristotelian, I believe that the experience of the reality must always come first. Only then can the underlying concepts be analyzed.

There are two major groups to be distinguished among philosophers and colleagues who write about normative ethics. Rule-oriented ethics is called deontological ethics, and the deontological ethicists are further divided into those whose rules stem from religion and those whose rules are from a secular analysis of the nature of man or of society. Whether purely philosophical, sociological, or anthropological, the set of rules defines how members of society ought to behave if society is to survive. In other words, the rule-oriented ethicist tends to have pre-set rules and looks to them to decide specific cases.

The other major group of ethicists are the consequentialists. They do not look for a prior rule into which they can fit the case; rather, they look at the situation and work out what will be the consequences of this or that action. Then they determine whether or not there are benefits and if so, what benefits and to whom.

It seems to me that the consequentialist ethicists are subdivided into two major groups. The utilitarians, who are empirical in their analysis, would say that the right action is that which will promote the greatest good for the greatest number of people. And then, there are those like

Joseph Fletcher who have developed a situationist ethic in which they look at the individual situation, try to work out the consequences of various actions, and seek to do what is in the best interests of that particular patient.

However, most people are inconsistent, borrowing from each of these philosophical stances. Generally, they have not thought their own position through. Very few are logical and consistent in their approach to normative ethical problems, but are eclectic. I, too, am eclectic, and I think such a position is not entirely inappropriate. But I subject my eclecticism to what to me is an overriding principle—one of evolutionary development. I look for what will advance the progress of what Teilhard de Chardin referred to as the "noosphere," the thinking layer, which is developed in and out of the biosphere, the living layer of matter. I am interested in promoting the further development of the thinking layer, of conscious awareness and self-reflection in this present phase of psychosocial evolution. Teilhard's thinking (and I do not agree totally with him) leads directly to a spiritual interpretation in which there is a primary concern for justice and love.

MEDICINE

The practice of medicine has developed a powerful deontology ever since Hippocrates first laid down rules for physicians. The three major rules are (1) to save or preserve life at all costs, (2) to relieve suffering, and (3) to do no harm to the patient. These rules were adequate for most of history, but today the rules often conflict. Today, the meaning of "to save a life" is not altogether clear. What is life? What is the definition of death? What about the patient who has suffered brain death but whose heart continues to beat? When is cardiopulmonary resuscitation justified to save life? Are all patients to be subjected to CPR unless there has been a no-code written onto their chart? What about the patient in a persistent vegetative state who suffers a cardiac arrest? It may well be that what is accomplished through resuscitation is not saving a life at all, but simply prolonging the dying process. If this happens, particularly if it involves pain and suffering to the patient, then the patient is actually being harmed. So the primary rule of saving life may be in direct conflict with the other two rules of relieving suffering and doing no harm.

It could be argued that we could justify saving a life even under such ambiguous circumstances, if additional knowledge might be acquired, if there would be a benefit to some other patient down the road. For example, in our pediatrics department we have a monthly mortality conference where we survey all the patients who died on the service during the previous month. On one occasion, one of our residents re-ported on a child who had very severe central nervous system defects from birth and severe cardiopulmonary problems, and who had been on a dying trajectory. The resident, as concluded in his report, stated that at 2:10 a.m. on a certain day the patient died, "despite repeated attempts at resuscitation." I challenged him and said, "How do you jus-tify attempts at resuscitation on a dying infant?" He responded by saying, "Well, I had a new intern on the ward, and I thought it would be good practice for him." An initial reaction to this might be that it is in-humane, that the utilitarian theory underlying this approach would also sanction what the Nazi doctors did in the concentration camps. On the other hand, the resident was not seeking new knowledge but new expertise and was trying to give instruction to some unskilled person who may be able to use those skills in the future to benefit another pa-tient. But is it ethical to use whatever knowledge or skills we acquire through an unethical act? Currently, there is considerable debate as to whether the results of unethical inquiries should ever be published in the professional literature.

It seems to me that physicians are trained to be reactionists—not necessarily reactionary, but reactionists. In other words, physicians tend not to do anything unless a situation presents itself to which they must then react in whatever way seems appropriate. Another major feature of medical school education is that students often develop the impression that they will learn exactly what to do in every situation. However, medicine is full of uncertainties, and our physicians must be trained to realize and analyze the dilemmas they will confront.

The dead or dying newborn is common enough. Even though many fetuses cannot endure the gestation period, and those infants actually born alive are the comparatively strong ones, there is still a death rate of up to two percent during the first few days. If the prognosis is hope-less, if it is clearly recognized that the patient is on a dying trajectory, then are physicians entitled to put a needle into an infant to draw a blood sample? Are they entitled to place an arterial or a venous line? Where the prognosis is clear, may they ethically intubate a dying patient? To me, it is appropriate that we analyze our efforts and the expected results rather than do all kinds of invasive procedures based on a rationalization that maybe something will happen that will allow survival.

I think that many physicians are instinctively reactionists in most or all situations. They react in the way they do partly because they fear the legal consequences of doing nothing. If a physician is called to the wit-ness stand, and has done everything possible, he or she can swear that everything that could have been done was done. But medicine practiced out of fear is defensive and cannot possibly be good.

Another feature of current medical training is hubris—the pride that we instill in physicians, the idea that they do have the right answers, that they know with certainty what they are doing, that they have to command the situation. Still a third characteristic of many doctors is the fear of death itself. The fear of death, and of a sense of failure if a patient dies, has been recognized for a number of years. Herman Feifel of Los Angeles did psychological studies which indicate that physicians and other health professionals are more afraid of death than is the general public. It intrigues me when I interview candidates for admission to medical school and ask about their motivation, how often they relate that at age seven or fourteen a close friend or family member died. They felt so helpless and enraged that somebody they loved had been taken away, that they determined then and there to grow up and learn everything they could to fight the enemy—death. So many physicians are conditioned to respond in what I regard as inappropriate ways. I sometimes say to housestaff, "For God's sake don't do something, just stand there. Watch and learn about the dying process, because this is the one thing that all your patients are going to do sometime and it is well to become familiar with, knowledgeable about, and comfortable with the concept of death." Much of the responsibility for the direct care of patients is left in the hands of relatively young, inexperienced and scared individuals. In order to watch a patient die and not be too upset by it, one must develop experience, maturity, and the clinical understanding that there is no point in intervening at that stage. The natural tendency, however, is to do something.

Physicians are reactivists and are fearful of the law. It might create a very intriguing situation if sometime a case were brought against a physician for inflicting cruel and unusual punishment or for committing assault and battery on a dying infant. We would need only one case for the whole medical profession to go up in steam, of course, and I would relate to that. It may well be, as some of my colleagues would say, that "you're damned if you do and damned if you don't," so physicians had better think pretty carefully about what it is they prepare to do. I believe there is too much unreflective, reactionist medicine being practiced today. Plato said, "The unexamined life is not worth living," and I would say that unexamined medicine is not worth practicing. If we could have good ethics, good medicine, and good law, then there would be no need for anybody to fear an adversarial confrontation. In those happy circumstances of cooperative endeavor all there would be, finally, would be good will. And that constitutes evolutionary progress in my book.

Chapter 24

Ethics, the Law, and the Treatment of Seriously Ill Newborns

Albert R. Jonsen

The law and ethics relative to the care of newborns are unexplored territory. Like Mount Everest before Hillary and the explorers, there are several high peaks but there are also many unknown crevices. The problem with ethics and law in neonatology is that lawyers and philosophers have been looking at the peaks and have very little awareness of the crevices into which one can easily fall.

The reason for this limited view is that the issues which have reached the courts deal with a certain kind of case which is not typical of the nursery's problems. The legal and philosophical discussions about withholding treatment from the defective or seriously ill newborn (the title under which a veritable flood of articles has appeared during the last decade) are almost exclusively devoted to two kinds of cases atypical to the everyday problems of neonatologists.

The first kind is the case of a child who, when born, is immediately recognized to be suffering from Down Syndrome and is then diagnosed as having a minor physical anomaly such as an intestinal obstruction, which could be corrected surgically. The question is whether the child should go to surgery for correction of the anomaly. Such a decision is not problematic in the ordinary child, but the issue becomes clouded when the child has Down Syndrome. A number of these cases have reached the courts in the form of a request for an order to operate, generally because the parents would not consent to the surgery. To my knowledge, the courts have granted such orders in every case.

The second problem which has been discussed in the philosophical and legal literature as a typical case is posed by a child born with myelomeningocele or spina bifida. Here a question is also asked about surgery: should the child's lesion be closed surgically to prevent imminent death from infection, even though the underlying problem will not be corrected? A long and serious debate was carried on between the English pediatric surgeon, John Lorber, and the American pediatric neurologist, John Freeman, about the appropriateness of surgery in such cases.[1]

The legal and philosophical discussions relative to neonatology are almost exclusively devoted to these two kinds of cases. In both, there is the question over a surgical intervention for the immediate saving of the child's life (as in the Down child with duodenal atresia) or to protect the child from a life-threatening infection (as in spina bifida). This problem has captured the attention of commentators. Interestingly, if one turns to the best and most extensive articles in the legal literature,[2] one finds in the footnotes a long list of the problems facing the neonatologist. Spina bifida and Down Syndrome are both mentioned, yet I have never found any mention of the problem which is the most prominent in the nursery. There is an entire area of pediatrics which is not cited in these legal articles, and because there is no mention of the prominent problem, the legal analysis of neonatology misses the point.

The dominant problem in the newborn nursery is prematurity: children born prematurely and of low birthweight, usually defined as less than 38 weeks of gestation and below 2500 grams (about 5½ lbs.). Their primary problem is that their lungs are not yet mature enough to breathe from the ambient air, resulting in severe deprivation of oxygen and subsequent acute and chronic lung disease. While prematurity causes a variety of problems, respiratory problems and their consequences are the most serious. At present, about 200,000 infants pass through neonatal intensive care units each year in the United States. Of these 200,000, about 75,000 suffer from the problems attending prematurity and 25,000 of these will die from respiratory diseases even with the best care. Contrast this with the approximately 5000 babies born each year with spina bifida, and the very small proportion of the 3000 or so Down Syndrome babies who require life-saving surgery. Simply in terms of numbers, the children with respiratory disease are the dominant problem in the nursery, and this sort of child poses the most agonizing and difficult questions.

The peculiar ethical and legal problems facing the neonatologist can be summed up by describing three particular issues. The first is the nature of prematurity and of intensive care for the premature. The premature infant is essentially unfinished. It is not ready to face the challenge of the new environment into which it is untimely thrust. The last two or three weeks in the womb are very important in the development and integration of an organ system ready to meet the world. This is particularly so with the premature lung, but it is true of the fetus' entire organ system. Basically, it suffers from a problem of incomplete integration when it comes into the world. The intensive care brought to bear upon the premature infant allows time for its organ systems to begin to function in an integrated manner. For the premature, the question is how long do we keep trying in order to see whether this unfinished organ system will get going on its own. The question of "how long" is indicative of the particular sort of questions asked about the neonate.

The second issue is directly related to the first. I call it by a horrendous title: endemic iatrogenicity. Iatrogenic problems are those caused by the doctor. Any kind of physical intervention into the body for the sake of healing has side effects which can harm. In some cases, iatrogenic harm is the result of negligence. However, a great deal of iatrogenic harm has nothing to do with negligence, but simply with the very nature of an intervention into the physical body, either with drugs or with a knife. In neonatology, iatrogenicity is epidemic because an organism that is not yet finished has a peculiar vulnerability. Introducing powerful agents like drugs and oxygen into the newborn organism can do severe damage. The most dramatic instance of iatrogenicity occurred some 25 or 30 years ago in the early days of pediatric intensive care, when the first attempts were made to tide over the premature newborn by administration of oxygen. It was slowly recognized that such massive administration of oxygen appeared to cause blindness in many of these newborns. It was a shock to realize that this life-giving element was dangerous. Since oxygen must be used for the premature newborn, it is used now with particular care. However, this discovery illustrates that the help given to the newborn during this period of crisis can be dangerous in itself.

One organ which is particularly vulnerable to the kinds of insults that can arise, both from the intervention and from the general nature of prematurity, is the brain. The brain of the premature infant can be damaged, sometimes severely, while the rest of the immature organs get pulled together fairly well. The lungs can heal, the kidneys begin to function, but often the insult to the brain is irreversible. While the baby may be pulled through this period of nonintegration, a severe gap may be left in the organ we esteem most highly in our culture: the brain. The result of intensive care, therefore, may be a person who becomes mature enough in the lungs and in the heart, but who never develops intellectually. That poses a very serious problem in neonatology.

The third issue follows directly from the nature of the premature infant. I call it prognostic perplexity. It is the very nature of medicine to make a prognosis. A diagnosis is nothing but the first step in prognosis. Prognosis is difficult in all areas of medicine, although much of it has become second nature because certain diseases are familiar to the practitioner and have well-known courses. In neonatology however, prognosis is extraordinarily difficult. The future course of a child may be cloudy because as he or she grows, many new factors must be considered. The immediate prognosis for the next day or the next week is rather difficult, but no more difficult than in intensive care generally. However, long-term prognosis is extremely difficult in neonatology, particularly with the child who has suffered an insult to the brain. For example, although a terrible intercerebral hemorrhage may be diagnosed in the third or fourth day of a child's life, at age five the child may be acting quite normally. But another child with a hemorrage of the same size and in the same place may become severely retarded. While there may be some agreement, there is a great deal of uncertainty and disagreement about the prognosis of future development of premature newborns.

These three issues—the nature of the premature infant and the nature of intensive care for the premature infant, iatrogenicity, and prognostic perplexity—leave us in a strange and unfamiliar place in regard to the law. Articles seeking to represent the state of the law to the neonatologist are, I find, deficient and perhaps unduly threatening. For example, John Robertson's article in the *Journal of Pediatrics* exposes the theoretical liability in great detail.[3] In fact, the article might be subtitled, "57 Ways in Which a Physician Can Become a Felon." Every possibility for the physician to step off the very small ground of legality is detailed. Professor Robertson asserts that the physician must provide extraordinary and ordinary care, but notes that since it has not been tested legally, the distinction is unclear and the final result uncertain. He concludes by saying that the "clearest and most indisputable grounds for withholding care must exist" if liability is to be avoided. However, he fails to recognize that the clearest and most indisputable grounds will never exist in the most difficult cases, which are intrinsically unclear and very disputable.

The questions posed to conscientious neonatologists are: to what extent they should try to treat and how extreme the deficiencies in the neonate are. Since these are questions of contingent facts and guesses, there are no rules to answer them. The experiences of other neonatologists, to whom one might look for answers, are often not well correlated. Further, each year we see improvements in the science of neonatology, but the disagreements still exist. Assessments of children who were treated five years ago cannot be applied to current neonatology because the technology has changed so dramatically. Thus, the neonatologist's judgment is one of contingent fact and depends little on science. It is a "judgment call"—an informed guess based on one's own experience and on what can be learned from one's colleagues. The law review articles, however, ask for clear criteria for withholding care from newborns, failing to realize that such legal standards of care are not clinically realistic. The standard of practice of other physicians in the community has come under a great deal of criticism, and although recent court decisions have modified that standard in other areas, the old standard is still used in neonatology: the physician's best judgment in accordance with the best standards of practice either in the medical community generally or in the subspecialty of neonatology.

A second problem is the parents' role in making treatment decisions for their seriously ill neonate. About 10 years ago, Dr. Raymond Duff started much of the debate about neonatology by publishing a very frank article in the *New England Journal of Medicine,* in which he acknowledged that he lets babies die in his nursery.[4] This caused a great deal of concern to everyone who did not know what went on in nurseries. Dr. Duff continues to assert that the decision must be the parents'. In his view, the physician should inform the parents and then the parents should decide whether or not to continue treatment. This approach, in fact, is advocated by many people when discussing the withdrawing or withholding of life-sustaining treatment from incompetent patients. In neonatology, this still remains a serious ethical problem. If the criterion or standard to be followed is the medical one—the physician's best judgment about whether or not this baby can be fully integrated—then no one but a neonatologist should attempt to use the criterion and make that decision. If society turns the decision over to the parents, saying, "You make up your own mind," we risk the possibility that decisions will be made on irrelevant grounds or inappropriate motives. If we permit families to make these decisions, then we must confront a problem of values which is unsettled in our society: to whom does the infant belong? What are the roles of the family and of society? Can or should parents decide if their seriously ill newborn will live or die? As I said, we do not have answers, only unsettled problems of values that need discussion and debate.

I will conclude by suggesting that as long as neonatologists are told by lawyers that their exposure to both civil and criminal liability is great (which is probably theoretically true), then the decisions in the nursery will be inappropriately made. This threat of liability arises from an unsuitable analysis; that is, the wrong kinds of cases have been used to develop the legal analysis. I think the courts have correctly responded, in both legal and ethical terms, by ordering the surgery and thereby saving the life of the Down child with duodenal atresia. To decide otherwise simply because the child has Down Syndrome is discriminatory and barbaric. But, to apply that thinking to the daily problems of decision making in the nursery is inappropriate. An inappropriate analysis will not only lead to inappropriate conclusions, but will also inhibit the development of a legal and ethical analysis more appropriate to the peculiar problems faced by those who dare to try to finish a job unfinished by nature: to make the premature baby live and live well.

NOTES

1. *See* Freeman, J.M., *To Treat or Not to Treat: Ethical Dilemmas of Treating the Infant with a Myelomeningocele,* CLINICAL NEUROSURGERY 20:134-46 (1973); Lorber, J., *Selective Treatment of Myelomeningocele: To Treat or Not to Treat?* PEDIATRICS 53: 307-08 (1974); Freeman, J.M., *Shortsighted Treatment of Myelomeningocele,* PEDIATRICS 53:311-13 (1974).

2. *E.g.,* Robertson, J.A., *Involuntary Euthanasia of Defective Newborns: A Legal Analysis,* 27 STANFORD LAW REVIEW 213 (1975); Robertson, J.A., Fost, N., *Passive Euthanasia of Defective Newborns,* JOURNAL OF PEDIATRICS 58:883 (1976); MacMillan, E.S., *Birth-Defective Infants: A Standard for Nontreatment Decisions,* 30 STANFORD LAW REVIEW 599-633 (February 1978).

3. *Passive Euthanasia of Defective Newborns, supra* note 2. *Also see* J.A. Robertson, "Legal Aspects of Withholding Medical Treatment from Handicapped Children," Chapter 22.

4. Duff, R.S., Campbell, A.G.M., *Moral and Ethical Dilemmas in the Special-Care Nursery,* NEW ENGLAND JOURNAL OF MEDICINE 289:890-94 (1973).

Chapter 25

Withholding Treatment from Seriously Ill Newborns: A Neonatologist's View

Joan E. Hodgman

Dr. Jonsen has presented an excellent analysis of the major problem facing neonatologists. To continue in that vein, I would like to discuss the problems I face in a busy neonatal intensive care unit and how I deal with them.

First, much is said about the legal responsibility of physicians and their nervousness and fear over the legal response to their actions. Generally, I do not worry about the legal implications of my actions. This may be naive of me, but what I really worry about are the medical decisions and, honestly, my major fear is being wrong. If I give the best care that I believe can be given, then I feel there is little need to worry about the prosecutor or a family member suing me.

Second, I believe that much of the discussion about the family's involvement in the decision making surrounding a dying patient is specious. In the real world, I believe that families do not decide what happens very often; usually, they have little opportunity to express their wishes. This is at least partly because the institutional setting and technology are intimidating. And even if they are given an opportunity to voice an opinion, they often have difficulty expressing it to the physician. I'm afraid that a good deal of the family involvement we are talking about is more theoretical than actual at the present time. In my institution, we have been making an effort to involve the family in decision making, but we have not asked them to make the life or death decision. In our opinion, letting the family decide may lead to eventual feelings of guilt if their baby dies. But as Dr. Jonsen said, there is no real scientific basis for this belief. I do have a nagging feeling that families are frequently stronger than we imagine; perhaps they would indeed prefer a more active role.

It is also important to recognize the danger that physicians will force their own moral judgments on families. I would like to see research in this area to test our opinions and those of society at large. In making the medical decision, as we do numerous times a day, we try to sense the family's feeling and present recommendations. If the family feels strongly that the infant should be supported, we continue intensive care in spite of our reservations. If the family wants support withdrawn and we feel it should be continued, we are in trouble. Our present method of dealing with this situation is messy and frequently results in confrontation when our role should be supportive. It is not, however, a common problem, and arises more frequently in surgical cases.

In my hospital, we use a team approach in making decisions to withdraw life support. We try to involve representatives of all the caretakers which, in our institution, includes house officers and nurses in addition to the medical faculty. We also have a social worker on the team who is very active and helpful—a true professional. If we are in trouble at 2:00 a.m. Saturday, she will come to the hospital to meet with the family and the rest of the health care team. This team approach is, I believe, extremely important in that it allows all members of the involved medical community to feel comfortable (or at least as comfortable as possible) with a specific treatment decision. It also deflects the burden of responsibility from the parents.

Much of the discussion surrounding the termination of life-sustaining procedures seems to center on the differences between omission and commission. My own feeling (and one that is shared by most physicians) is that I'm more nervous about omissions. It is easier for me to live with the consequences of something I've done than it is to worry about something I have not done which might have given better results. This is particularly true in life-and-death situations. As such, it is our policy, with very few exceptions, to resuscitate every live-born infant. I believe that the decision to support or not to support life should not be made in the crisis atmosphere of the delivery room. The response to crisis must be support. Minutes, hours or days later, a more carefully considered decision can be made and appropriate action taken. This means that we start life-support machinery that we might later want to withdraw, and I have no particular problem with that. I'm not committed to a respirator; I'm committed to a baby and his or her family. To administer treatment until we're sure we should back off is an easier and safer decision than trying to decide under crisis conditions whether or not we should treat the child.

The major problem in the newborn nursery, as indicated by Dr. Jonsen, is the premature infant, particularly the infant of very low birth weight. We now have the technology to support very small babies. At the start of my career, infants weighing less than 1250 grams (2.75 lbs.)

were considered too small to be viable. Shortly thereafter, babies down to 1000 grams (2.25 lbs.) birth weight were considered viable and were aggressively treated; infants under this weight were not given intensive care as they were considered not viable. Now, we are saving newborns as little as 650 grams (1.5 lbs.). The problem, however, is larger than how to manage an infant following birth. Intensive care starts with the fetus. If the infant is asphyxiated during delivery, the best chance for intact survival is compromised. To prevent asphyxia in a very immature infant, the mother should probably have a Cesarian section, because a small and fragile infant does not go through labor well. But this option also presents problems. Should I recommend a Cesarian section for the mother of a 26-week gestation infant? If the mother is not delivered by C-section and the baby is live-born but asphyxiated, what should I do, medically and ethically, to support the already damaged infant? Should I go all out or should I back off? These decisions are difficult, but we must make them everyday in my nursery. The problem is further complicated because therapy is not innocuous. There are serious complications associated with treatment, of which blindness is most prominent. No treatment is 100 percent effective and, even when effective, carries its price in morbidity.

Other decisions we must make concern the differences between brain death and the persistent vegetative state that Dr. Cranford has discussed. In the nursery, we see infants in both states, although the distinction may often be blurred. Brain death occurs primarily in small infants on ventilators who have associated massive intracranial hemorrhage. Where brain stem function is gone, thereby requiring both cardiovascular and ventilatory support, the infant will degenerate over time in spite of our best efforts. We are trying to identify these infants in my nursery and are withdrawing support after diagnosis. This is not terribly gutsy because we are identifying babies that will inevitably die. It is not a question of yes or no, but a question of Tuesday or Thursday. We are not making quality of life decisions because we do not know how, but we are doing a lot of talking and agonizing.

I agree with Dr. Jonsen that decisions in this area are difficult because in many instances one can never be sure of the prognosis. One difference between the adult and the newborn is the growing, developing and very plastic brain. One of the things that makes us human is our adaptability. The future of the infants I care for is frequently unclear. This is the main reason we are not making quality of life decisions in my hospital at the present time. The criteria for such are simply not clear enough.

Finally, I would like to mention a consideration that generally gets discussed obliquely if at all. That is the financial cost of intensive care.

No one wants to place monetary value on a patient's life, although the courts are often forced to do so. But if we do not look at the costs, which are high, and if we do not consider the best allocation of our limited resources, we are being irresponsible. There are no guidelines, much less a consensus, on whether it is appropriate to consider the financial cost of saving the life of a seriously ill, defective newborn. Society and the medical community have a long way to go.

Chapter 26

Decision Making for Newborns

Walter R. Trinkaus

During his discussion of the still unresolved ethical questions facing society concerning the withdrawing and withholding of life-sustaining treatment from newborns, Dr. Jonsen asked: "To whom does the child belong?" To that basic issue in this perplexing problem, I would answer that the child belongs to no one.

There was a time not so long ago that the law treated a child like chattel, a piece of property belonging to the parents. When the parents separated or became divorced, they argued over the child in the same way that they argued over the ownership of the car or the furniture. But times have changed and we have begun to recognize that children are people entitled to all of the rights that other persons have. When children cannot decide for themselves, any decisions that are made pertaining to them should be made only by the criterion of what is in their best interests.

Of course, in determining the best interest of the child, we generally defer to the parents because parents generally have the best interests of their children at heart. But when the issue is the withdrawal of life-sustaining medical treatment, health care professionals cannot simply turn to the parents and ask, "What do you want us to do?" The parents are not in a position to make a dispassionate judgment. Emotions are involved, and there is the potential for a conflict of interests. I have seen, firsthand, situations where children who have Down Syndrome are a burden to their families. While they may be happy, they will always be children, and we cannot make determinations concerning their welfare by virtue of what is best for the families. It just cannot be done that way.

It has been my belief for a long time that decisions concerning the termination of life-support services are the responsibility of the physician. I do not mean to suggest that the physician alone should decide, but rather that he or she must guide the decision-making process. I have addressed medical groups on the subject of terminating life-support services for nearly 20 years, and every time I say this, I get frozen looks from my audience, who would like to see such decisions left up to the family. Depending upon the way the question to the parents is worded, the physician will generally be pleased with the result, and this is as it should be. If the physician fully explains the situation, the prognosis, and the decisions that need to be made (in a brain damage case for instance), and then asks what should be done, the family will be prepared to accept the route that the physician suggests. If, however, the physician simply asks, "Shall we pull the plug on Grandma?" of course the family will say no. In both approaches, the physician has influenced the family. These are decisions for physicians, and, I'm afraid, they cannot shirk the responsibility.

This decision-making process is frequently discussed, and one phrase that is often used as a rationale in decision-making is "quality of life." This expression frequently refers to a prognostication about the kind of life that a child will lead. At other times, however, the term refers to the immediate quality of life. These different definitions can lead to distortion and confusion of the issues involved in decisionmaking. For example, Dr. Jonsen has used this term to refer to the immediate quality of life. Jonsen was accused by Paul Ramsey of using language from an article by Richard McCormick which amounted to an undue extension of what McCormick was saying.[1] Quality of life can mean much or little depending on whether one views life as a point, or a range on a continuum.

I do not wish to enter this debate, but would only like to suggest that these arguments can be distorted or used to support something that was not intended by McCormick. Additionally, the term "quality of life" can be distorted by utilitarians, who say that these decisions should be based on projections into the future. Perhaps some utilitarians would consider economic circumstances, family stability, the effect of a continued existence of this child on the family, and whether the child would be a burden to society. Once we start to consider these elements, we venture onto very thin ice. The expression "quality of life" is poorly defined, open to abuse, and should be avoided.

When one makes these decisions, I think that two basic premises must be assumed. First is the recognition of the extreme fallibility of human judgment in the decision-making process. This is a limitation that we all share; we are not omniscient. The second premise is that the newborn child whose fate is at stake is a very special being, unique in all the vastness of the universe. This child is a person. And, as I mentioned before, the word "person" has a technical meaning in law—it means having a capacity for rights.

Simply because of his or her humanity, every human being is a person possessing rights. The right to life is the most basic and paramount of all, because when this right is denied, all others are denied with it. Consequently, when considering our obligations toward the newborn child, and particularly the premature infant, it is imperative to start with the basic premise that this is a person with the same right to life that is possessed by all other persons. In evaluating rights, it is appropriate to conclude that one person's right outweighs another's interest (e.g., the child's right to life versus the parents' right to decide). Because of the limitations on our vision and perspectives, we cannot say that one person is more valuable than another. Nevertheless, we are faced with the dilemma of two opposing rights when we consider ending life-support services for the terminally ill patient. Society, the medical profession, and the law must be acutely sensitive to any threatened encroachment on the right to life. Yet a person also has a right not to have the natural process of dying prolonged artificially if there is no hope of benefit proportionate to the burden imposed. This is the traditional moral distinction between "ordinary" and "extraordinary" means of prolonging life. The distinction turns upon the burdens that the treatment imposes upon the patient. Some commentators have backed away altogether from the use of the distinction between ordinary and extraordinary because this distinction deals with the future of the patient, thus encroaching upon the forbidden value of life criterion.[2]

INTENSIVE CARE OF THE INFANT

The problems which accompany brain damage in adults are similar to the problems which occur in premature infants. A brain-damaged patient may be given the assistance of a respirator, for example, while a determination is made whether the patient's life can be saved. If it is later determined that the effort is futile and that a continuation of the respirator is only a needless prolongation of the natural process of dying with no hope of benefit to the patient, the respirator can properly be removed. What began as an ordinary means of treatment has now become extraordinary.

Similarly, intensive care of a premature infant, which is administered in order to allow time to determine whether the infant can survive, is ordinary care and thus a moral and legal obligation. As Dr. Hodgman notes, the delivery room is an inappropriate place for the decision to withhold treatment. The determination to withhold or terminate intensive care should not be lightly made. It would be extremely hazardous to make that judgment simply on the basis of the infant's weight or because the infant is not responding as rapidly as hoped. As Drs. Jonsen and Hodgman point out, some of this intensive care (such as the administration of oxygen) is itself dangerous and has to be handled carefully. If it is ultimately discovered that the result is going to be disproportionate to the means, then the means can be discontinued.

The physician should not hesitate to begin intensive care simply because there may be difficult legal problems resulting from the initial prolongation of life, nor should the physician fear legal liability if a determination is made not to use extraordinary means. Admittedly, there are uncertainties surrounding the labels of extraordinary and ordinary. And of course, such decisions will never be easy or certain. But there is no escape from these uncertainties nor from the decision to withdraw life-supporting treatment. The family should be consulted; but the real judgment must be made by the physician.

NOTES

1. P. RAMSEY, ETHICS AT THE EDGE OF LIFE (Yale University Press, New Haven, Conn.) (1978) at 238, *citing* Jonsen, A.R., *et al.*, *Critical Issues in Newborn Intensive Care*, PEDIATRICS 55(6) (1975), *discussing* McCormick, R.A., *To Save or Let Die: The Dilemma of Modern Medicine*, JOURNAL OF THE AMERICAN MEDICAL ASSOCIATION 229(2):172-76 (July 8, 1974).
2. P. RAMSEY, ETHICS AT THE EDGE OF LIFE, *supra*, note 1 at 331-32.

Part Four

The Health Care Team

Chapter 27

The Health Care Team: Changing Perceptions of Roles and Responsibilities in Caring for the Critically Ill Patient

Sandra J. Weiss

Within the last two decades, an increasing sophistication in the knowledge of disease processes, diagnostic mechanisms and therapeutic technology has created a health care system of a scientific scope that is truly astounding. Yet health care has never been so openly criticized by both health professionals and the public alike. Much of this criticism reflects a demand for greater attention to the context of health care, specifically the human relationships through which care is given and received.

This major impetus to examine the relational aspects of care stems, in large part, from the ambiguity and strain which currently surround the ethics of existing roles on the health care team. The symptoms of role strain and role conflict take many forms. They appear perhaps most dramatically in the shape of burnout or impaired professional syndromes. These syndromes are evidenced in an increasing incidence of turnover and actual departure from the health professions, in self-destructive behaviors such as excessive drinking, smoking and drug use among professionals, and in rising levels of frustration and anger which are displayed in openly caustic interactions with patients and others with whom the professional works.

Other symptoms of role dissatisfaction lie within the emerging and strengthening consumer activist movement. High levels of energy are expended by consumer groups to demand involvement in health planning efforts as well as in the daily decisions which affect their own health and health care. Many, if not the majority, of these consumer activities are efforts which exclude health professionals and which ultimately reflect a struggle for power in an arena where consumers have previously possessed little influence and minimal control.

Finally and likely the most controversial, a major symptom of perceived need for change is manifested in the growing regulatory actions of the government regarding health care delivery. Since the sixties with Kennedy's Declaration of Rights for Consumers, Johnson's Consumer Advisory Council and the inception of the Department of Consumer Affairs, the federal government has become rapidly involved in monitoring and assuring established roles and a specific context for health care relationships.

And yet, the exact nature of this context, the exact expectations of consumer groups, and the exact reasons for professional burnout have remained unclear. What is clear is that the duties, responsibilities and rights embodied in the roles of health professionals and the patients who employ their services look quite different when viewed through the eyes of various members of the health care team. Previously, the roles of nurse, physician and patient seemed absolute and transparent. The physician was viewed as an expert in the diagnosis and treatment of diseases, and partly because of this expertise, was considered responsible for directing the nurse and patient in the nature of their roles. As one group of authors note, "the patient is expected to follow the orders given him by his doctor; . . . the nurse is expected to carry out all the doctor's orders, to accept his judgment on medical matters."[1] But times change and so do expectations regarding roles and responsibilities. From the sixties until now, disparity in regard to role expectations has dramatically increased.

ASSESSMENT OF TEAM NEEDS

In an attempt to delineate the current, problematic areas within health care relationships and to clarify expected roles of team members a research project called the Collaborative Health Program was conceived.[2] This research, funded by NIH, has been a joint effort of nurses, physicians and members of the general public throughout the San Francisco community. Its ultimate purpose has been to develop a behavioral model and a multidisciplinary curriculum which will identify and teach the principles and strategies necessary for more effective relationships among consumer, nurse and physician.

The first step in bringing about this outcome was to convene a demographically and philosophically representative group of physicians, nurses and consumers who worked with the research project for two years. Meeting every month, four multidisciplinary groups of eighteen persons each participated in structured dialogue sessions in which they

discussed current stressors in health relationships, collaborative strategies to modify these stressors, factors which influenced the ability to
assume more collaborative modes of relationship, and the benefits
and risks of changing existing health care roles. Using a classification
system based on Beckers' Health Belief model,[3] data from eighty separate dialogue sessions were analyzed from verbatim transcripts preserved by court reporters.

In addition to the transcripts, data came from a pre- and post-test
battery of questionnaires as well as videotapes of group sessions. Surveys seeking opinions and approaches of randomly selected individuals within the community have assured a wider representation to
the data base which is being built.

Findings described within this article represent a preliminary and
descriptive translation of specific quantitative results which are yet to
be finalized. Reference will be only to those aspects of the research
which are relevant to the critically ill patient, and only as they relate to
the team members of nurse, physician and patient.

An initial needs assessment with the research groups validated the
diversity in stressors and perceived needs for satisfaction which are experienced by individuals in specified health care roles. Physicians saw
their greatest concern in health care as the economic issues surrounding the health relationship. These issues included discussion and nego-
tiation of finance with the patient and family as well as the difficulties
encountered in choosing between an extensive and expensive treatment regime versus a more limited and cost-effective approach to care.
The second major stressor for physicians centered on the external regulatory and bureaucratic forces affecting their health care practices.
Forces such as hospital policies and governmental controls were seen to
˙severely hamper and frustrate medical judgment and physicians'
rights.

Neither of these problem areas were viewed as exceptionally important by patients or nurses. Instead the primary concern of nurses lay in
the area of consumer decisionmaking, where they faced recurring
moral and interactional dilemmas around informed consent, access to
medical records and patient choice. Next in stress potential for nurses
were two equally rated factors: discrimination in health care relationships and communication patterns between physician,and nurse.
Issues of discrimination focused on existing bias and inequality resulting from agism, sexism, ethnocentrism, and elitism within the patient-
professional and physician-nurse relationship. Similarly, physician-
nurse communication presented an intense degree of pressure for
nurses who saw themselves as continually struggling with physicians in
order to have their contributions heard and accepted as valid additions

to a patient's diagnosis and treatment plan.

For patients, the major stressors were again unique and different from those of nurse and physician. Patients wanted most of all to have clarification regarding their specific responsibilities on the health care team. Basic to this desire was a sense of impotence resulting from instances where (1) they were not even identified as a member of the team, and (2) they were not given the final authority in matters related to their own health care. In addition to these concerns, patients also experienced a lack of attention to their lifestyle as it related to necessary physical care. The stress here stemmed from the absence of cultural, emotional, familial and job-related considerations when plans were being made for treatment of a physical problem. This stress represented the second priority concern of those individuals using health services.

TEAM AGREEMENT IN REGARD TO CHANGING ROLES

The upshot of such diversity in the expectations and needs of physician, nurse and patient is an ever increasing trend toward changing the existing nature of health care roles. Some of the changes being suggested to modify stress have actually achieved a high level of agreement as to their pragmatism and validity in health care relationships.

PATIENT-PROFESSIONAL CONCORDANCE

One of the most firmly acknowledged modifications can be conceptualized as patient-professional concordance. This concept is in direct contrast to the more traditionally accepted and ethically questionable phenomenon of patient compliance. Underlying concordance is a basic assumption that the patient is indeed a member of the team, not merely the focus of the team's efforts. Concordance rejects such constructs as patient defaulting or noncompliance and, instead, places the burden of achieving full patient participation in treatment as much on the professional as on the patient. The skills required in a concordant relationship include the ability to negotiate from the inception of one's relationship with the patient, to identify with the patient feasible ways to follow through on treatment in the context of the patient's own lifestyle and to modify what might be considered the best approach in order to achieve a potentially more realistic, if less dramatic, result. The nurse-physician relationship is seen as key to the effectiveness of this concordant effort. If the physician fails to recognize and use the nurses' expertise in diagnosing the patient's lifestyle needs and if the nurse shirks the responsibility to communicate his/her diagnosis to the physician in a direct and clear manner, then the likelihood of achieving concordance is minimal.

MINIMIZING DISCRIMINATION

Another area of mutual agreement among members of the team lies in the need to minimize discrimination in patient care. Essential changes regarding behavior toward the elderly, toward women and toward ethnic minorities seem well recognized. The fundamental behaviors required are ones which give every individual the same rights and respect, as well as the equal potential for being able to assume responsibility. Three vivid stereotypes which act as barriers to these behaviors were identified by the groups:

1) Older people want to be taken care of and are, more likely than not, incapable of thinking clearly;

2) Women make decisions mostly based on emotion and are not mental or logical enough in their orientation to effectively participate in decisionmaking; they also should be protected from anxiety-producing information; and

3) If a person has difficulty speaking English he/she must not be very bright.

Breaking through the barriers reflected by these stereotypes necessitates that professionals give every person the benefit of the doubt regarding his or her inner strengths and individually assess, in an unbiased fashion, the unique potential and limitations inherent within each individual.

Interestingly, the team views the nurse's role in preventing discrimination as a major one. Specific examples of these expectations are that she arrange interpreters for non-English speaking patients, monitor other nurse and physician interactions in regard to discrimination, and basically be an advocate for the equal rights of all patients. The allocation of this responsibility to nursing seems to reflect the belief by some that the socialization and status of physicians inhibits their ability to empathize with those who differ from them in financial holdings, verbal ability, professional position, and other attributes indicating personal or political power.

COGNITIVE AND EMOTIONAL PRIORITIES IN CARE

Another surprising area of consensus centers on a shift toward more cognitive and emotional priorities in care rather than a strictly technical or biomedical focus. The emphasis on these characteristics of care has been strongly manifested in nursing research, education and practice over the years; however, the movement of medicine toward such priorities is indeed an innovative trend. For the physician, this role modification involves an expanded interviewing style to include more information on the patient's home and work life, family relationships, fears and coping abilities. It also means that a physician will more frequently encourage a patient to talk with the primary nurse about feelings and concerns or to bring together patients with the same diagnosis or proposed treatment for a dialogue.

One motive behind this shift in priorities is a growing realization that underlying a person's illness may be a complex interplay of biological and psychosocial factors, not easily manipulated by a clean sweep of the knife or a sophisticated chemotherapy regime. In addition, professionals are steadily recognizing the important role which illness can play as a healthful experience in a patient's total life picture. More than ever, people are using critical illness as a tool for reassessing meaning in their lives and identifying new values which can bring greater quality and satisfaction to living. The professional's intimate role in this process requires skills in reinforcing the healthy parts of sick people, in helping them look at the meaning of their symptoms, and in encouraging them to examine the positive, growth-producing aspects of their illness. While some of this change has already taken hold in health care relationships, the vast majority of interactions are structured to exclude such possibilities. Such strategies for integrating a patient's cognitive and emotional needs into his or her treatment may be philosophically valued but are often given little weight in actual practice.

CONTROVERSY REGARDING CHANGING ROLES ON THE TEAM

EGALITARIAN DECISIONMAKING

Inasmuch as there is agreement as to needed change in health care roles, there is also significant controversy. Egalitarian versus hierarchical decisionmaking among team members appears to be the primary controversial issue. In the eyes of its proponents, egalitarian relations provide for an allocation of responsibility based on assessment of the unique capabilities of each team member, rather than responsibilities based strictly on credentials or prescribed role. This allocation of responsibility does not mean an absence of levels of authority, but rather that authority would be more flexibly defined to allow for better application of individual skills in specific aspects of care. To critically ill patients, equality means having input to decisions about their care, being included in conferences where they are discussed and having the opportunity to respond to what is said about them in these conferences as well as contribute their own personal insights to their care. Egalitarianism would also indicate that when these discussions are taking place, patients will take the initiative to ask professionals what any of their jargon means so that they can relate to other team members with equal knowledge and equal responsibility.

This structure for health care relationships was encouraged as far back as 1956 when Szasz and Hollander described a more flexible model for patient-physician relations.[4] They pointed to a continuum of relationships beginning at "active physician/passive patient," moving to the "guiding physician/cooperative patient" and evolving into one of "mutual participation." It is this latter aspect of the continuum which many patients are struggling to achieve.

To the nurse, egalitarianism represents the right to fully use the skills that s/he has been educated to use. The ethics of not using all of the resources at their disposal is becoming a dilemma for many nurses. To insure that their skills will be drawn upon effectively, nurses are initiating more direct communication lines with physicians. They are offering suggestions regarding treatment and encouraging modification of treatment plans when they determine that changes are needed. The lack of this type of communication in the past has been documented in both medical and nursing literature.[5] One particular physician, Leonard Stein, has pointed to a process he calls "transactional neurosis." Basically, this pattern of communication between physician and nurse involves the nurse delicately and carefully disguising suggestions to the physician through indirect questioning strategies or projection of the idea onto the physician, as if the physician had initiated the subject. Stein proposes this communication pattern as a mutual endeavor by physician and nurse, to maintain clear hierarchical lines of power in the relationship; but he questions the value of this approach to patient care in that the nurse's suggestions are not often strongle heard nor implemented. This type of approach has emerged as a central example of what both nurses and physicians are beginning to question.

To the physician, egalitarianism represents a contrasting picture to the meaning it may hold for nurses or patients. From the vantage point of the physician, giving more weight to the input of other team members allows for increased data for decisionmaking and thus more likelihood of an effective decision. The attraction of egalitarianism for many physicians stems from the greater humanness and realism it allows in terms of others' expectations for what the physician can actually accomplish. These changing expectations create a context where a physician's personal needs can more readily be met—the essence of these needs being the opportunity to share anxiety and vulnerability with other members of the team, to experience professional and patient relationships which allow support for the physician as well as for nurse, patient and family members, and to work out the best solution in joint dialogue rather than carrying the burden of total responsibility for what is often expected to be an "infallible" judgment.

Clearly, opponents to the egalitarian stance view the team's capabilities and needs in a different light. Those with faith in hierarchical role relations believe that most patients can't really understand the various options for their treatment and don't want to know the risks involved. It is thought that patients would rather trust their physician's judgment. Opponents to egalitarianism also maintain that (1) a nurse's decisions in giving patient care should be based totally on the responsibilities outlined by physicians, since his/her essential role is to carry out treatment programs established by physicians; and that (2) considering their training, physicians are the only ones with sufficient knowledge to make the majority of health care decisions. Hierarchically oriented individuals propose that effective delivery of health care is indeed dependent upon physicians determining and limiting all actions taken by the health care team.

The disparity between value systems which uphold egalitarian and hierarchical standards has already begun to affect ongoing health care interactions. Based on what our research is indicating, the movement toward egalitarianism is increasing in strength as more members of the general public are exposed to this option through the media, and as more professionals are socialized to the egalitarian mode in their education.

INFORMING THE PATIENT

A second controversial issue centers on the operational definition of an informed patient. While everyone seems to agree that patients should be informed, the actual shape which this process takes is the source of much debate. One camp of thought proposes that patients should not only be told their diagnosis, treatment options and potential risks but that a detailed procedure be used which would include the following. The physician would share any uncertainty in regard to the diagnosis and treatment, revealing to the patient if s/he is not fully confident of the suggested approach. The physician would share his or her comparison of the patient's prognosis with various treatments as well as without treatment. The patient would then have a substantial period of time to read a variety of information, to talk with other providers as well as with patients who have chosen various treatment option, and to defer a decision until having digested the impact which different approaches could have. This time period would be encouraged and supported by the health care provider regardless of the critical nature of a patient's health condition. The patient would also be encouraged to bring a family member or other significant person in his or her life to consultations and conferences with physicians and nurses. The function of this significant other would be to help the patient get important information, to provide a recall and feedback mechanism for the patient, and to synthesize with the patient any information which evolved from the conference or consultation.

Expectations for the physician would be to provide outcome statistics, when possible, for each treatment option and to arrange for an unbiased second opinion if desired by patients. The physician would also suggest that patients discuss the information further with the primary nurse before actually signing any consent form. Physicians and nurses alike would be accountable to patients to share what they write in their charts with them to interpret any unclear statements and to discuss the meaning of the charting to their total care.

In addition to facilitating access to medical records, the change in nursing responsibility can best be exemplified in the area of informed consent. Nurses would necessarily be present during a patient's informed consent, so that they can assess the patient's actual comprehension of the information, determine any gaps in what the patient knows, and follow up in the educational process to assure the patient's complete understanding of the treatment plan to which s/he is consenting. The nurse would also be expected to tell the physician if he/she determines that the patient doesn't truly understand, to proffer his or her own professional assessment to the patient regarding the benefits and risks of proposed treatments, and to encourage the patient not to sign a consent if s/he still has unanswered questions regarding what is being proposed. The basic premise underlying these behaviors is that the patient, no matter the critical quality of the illness, does not want to be protected from knowledge but rather to be fully apprised of the severity of the disease and allowed the opportunity to assess its implications.

Opposing perspectives on this premise contend that too much knowledge can be injurious to patients by increasing their anxiety and demeaning the trust in the professional's ability to help them survive their illness. In addition, the patients' capacity to understand and intelligently use information is questioned as well as the cost effectiveness of time put forth in educating them. Those in favor of providing limited information also believe that the nurse has a minimal role in informing patients and should discuss any aspect of treatment with them only after s/he has acquired a physician's permission. The medical record is viewed as the professional's domain and objections to its use as an educational tool reflect the belief that its sole function is as a mechanism for intraprofessional communication and legal accountability. In a similar vein, the consent form is defined not as an educational opportunity but as a legal format grounded in institutional requirement and self protection. These contentions appear to stem not from lack of moral values or insensitivity to patient needs, but rather from the firm conviction that patients have neither the motivation nor the competence to use information specific to their health care.

FINAL AUTHORITY ON THE TEAM

The locus of ultimate authority on the team is a third area of disagreement in regard to changing roles. Traditionally, the final authority in all health care decisions has been the physician's. However, there is a growing segment of both patient and professional populations who want this authority to unquestionably rest with the patient. This philosophical stance has created new demands on the way professionals handle their responsibilities. For example, the physician and nurse would need to begin their relationship with the patient by establishing a mutual agreement concerning the ground rules which will determine how decisions are made. This agreement would also delineate the amount of authority which the patient chooses to give the professionals whose services she/he has employed. The physician's role would entail an acceptance of a patient's wish to have final approval of each step of care and any course of action before it takes place. The patient's right to the final decision requires something often very difficult from the physician. For example, the patient may choose a less orthodox or nontraditional approach to treatment rather than that prescribed by the physician, or he/she may choose to die rather than endure a particular treatment for the illness. Within these parameters of care, the physician must first fully discuss his/her concerns about the decisions but then accept the patient's decisions, continuing to provide supportive interventions.

Patient authority as a concept mandates that the nurses define themselves as working for the patient in making an independent decision regardless of the pressures by other professionals to choose a specific treatment strategy. Nurses also must assure that, if the patient is unconscious or otherwise incapable of making a decision, then the family or other health professionals will be brought in to mutually determine the best treatment for the patient, rather than allowing the decision to be made by one attending physician.

Within this framework, patients are also viewed as having the freedom not to exercise their right of choice. In the event that patients consciously choose not to assume this authority, then the health professionals must just as readily make decisions for them. The increasing trend toward patient authority in care lies mostly in an awakening need to have control over one's life, to resist the more radical, intrusive procedures of a technological wave for more conservative, less extreme approaches, and to live a life of quality rather than mere length.

The rationale for opposing such a trend has many similarities to that proposed for limiting the nature of information to the patient. However, there is an additional underlying assumption that the patients' decisions may very well not be the best ones and that they may regret, at a later date, mistakes in judgment they have made. The burden of responsibility for outcome which hovers over patients if they assume final authority is also defined as a nontherapeutic force in their attempt to combat disease. Although the issue of patients assuming authority is important, it would appear that the core of the controversy is even more central to the validity of physicians limiting their own authority. There are many individuals, both professionals and public, who *do* maintain that the physician is the only person with sufficient expertise to be ultimately responsible for what happens to the patient.

COST AS A DECISION-MAKING CRITERION

The final major area of controversy deals with roles of the team in cost considerations. The public in particular is demanding a new approach to finances in the health care relationship. The fundamental characteristic of this approach is an open discussion of finances as one decision-making criterion for patients when considering various options for treatment regimes. The role behaviors required of a physician in this type of relationship include the following:

1) The physician would have an orientation meeting with a new patient, including an overview of the physician's hourly cost of service;

2) the physician would do minimal diagnostic testing, avoiding additional more costly testing;

3) the physician would not pressure patients to undergo certain diagnostic tests, but would present the limits and benefits of the tests in an unbiased fashion;

4) the physician would compare costs of various tests or treatments for the patients, helping them to weigh the economic impact and the therapeutic gain;

5) the physician would negotiate costs with patients, making any adjustments in fees which are feasible.

The nurse's role assures that the patient has an opportunity to discuss financial concerns in detail and to find out specific costs of daily items and procedures. Nurses are expected to intervene and suggest less expensive alternatives to care if a patient is concerned about cost and the physician is not. If a financial discussion has not been initiated by the physician, the nurse functions as mediator and coordinator in bringing together physician and patient to formulate a plan which considers cost concerns. If the patient is not capable of participating in such discussion due to the circumstances of the illness, his or her family should be involved as spokespersons in the financial dialogue. The emphasis in these controversial strategies again underlines a movement toward clarifying all factors which influence health care, including cost, and away from protecting the patient. This approach does not force the financial issue upon the patient if, in the professional's judgment, the issue is damaging or untimely. But it does mandate that the professional offer the opportunity for discussion in all but the most contraindicated cases and that he/she be responsive to such dialogue if brought up by the patient.

A contrasting viewpoint in regard to these changes asserts that broaching the issue of finances can dramatically influence the patient's ability to make the wisest decisions. He/she may become more concerned with cost than with the quality and comprehensiveness of the care. Quality of care is also seen to be seriously undermined if only minimal diagnostic procedures or treatment approaches are employed. Many physicians feel that they are not fully actualized in their practice if not using the complete complement of technological tools at their disposal. Even more basic, any lack of an "all our effort" to heal the patient appears to tap a deep reservoir of guilt and ethical responsibility within many professionals, whether or not the patient feels that the treatment effort is sufficient.

The Collaborative Health Program research indicates that increasing numbers of professionals and patients not only philosophically uphold the various changes just described, but are actually experimenting with their application in the context of everyday team relationships. Above and beyond the stratified sample of seventy-two research participants, randomly selected respondents from the larger community clearly supported a great majority of these changes. In fact, random surveys have shown a 57% agreement with items on which the stratified sample could not achieve consensus.

CONCLUSION

It remains to be seen whether or not such changes in the team would fulfill the ethical responsibility being felt by team members, or increase the health or satisfaction of patients, or improve the effectiveness and fulfillment of health professionals, or even in the long run decrease costs of care. Until research has answered these questions, it is important for every individual, whether s/he is currently working to change or maintain the existing responsibilities of the team, to carefully weigh the risks and benefits inherent in change. What if sufficient care is not taken to translate and interpret raw information given the patient—could this oversight encourage patient confusion, misunderstanding or anxiety? Or can information in its myriad forms truly help patients to cope more effectively with their illnesses and achieve a greater sense of control over their lives? Would the continual need to negotiate and clarify role parameters bring about a lack of willingness on the part of team members to assume responsibility for care? Or would greater utilization of the nurse's expertise and the patient's internal resources result in more total team commitment to the overall treatment regime, in decreased costs of care, and in more accurate clinical judgments based on a fuller understanding of the patient's need? What if the burden of increased responsibility proved too much for patients or nurses to handle—could this decrease the quality of care and further encumber an already tenuous health delivery network? Or would full use of nurses and patients to their best advantage ensure long overdue support and new potential for satisfaction to physicians who have borne unrealistic expectations for decades?

The responsibility to scrupulously evaluate such outcomes represents an ethical issue for every human being. Resulting assessments will not merely signify idiosyncratic opinions regarding roles in health care, but reflect a society's moral commitment to the human rights of self-determination, autonomy and actualization, for individuals and professions alike.

NOTES

1. D. KRETCH, R. CRUTCHFIELD, E. BALLACHEY, INDIVIDUALS IN SOCIETY (McGraw-Hill, New York) (1962) at 311.
2. Weiss, S., The Collaborative Health Program, A Grant Proposal to the National Institutes of Health, #NU00597 (1977).
3. Becker, M., Maiman, L., *Sociobehavioral Determinants of Compliance with Health and Medical Care Recommendations*, MEDICAL CARE 13 (1):10–24 (January 1975); Becker, M.H., *Selected Psycho-Social Models and Correlates of*

Individual Health Related Behaviors, MEDICAL CARE 15(5):27–46 (May 1977).

4. Szasz, T.S., Hollender, M.H., *A Contribution to the Philosophy of Medicine*, ARCHIVES OF INTERNAL MEDICINE, 97:585 (1956).

5. Kalisch, B., Kalisch, P., *An Analysis of the Source of Physician-Nurse Conflict*, JOURNAL OF NURSING ADMINISTRATION 7(1):51–57; Stein, L., *The Doctor-Nurse Game*, ARCHIVES OF GENERAL PSYCHIATRY 16:699–703 (1967).

Chapter 28

The Health Care Team and the Need for Dialogue

Donna F. Ver Steeg

The ultimate problem of professionals in any field concerns how we deal with the decisions that we make. I was struck by Dr. Weiss' reference to Stein's designation of the doctor-nurse game as "transactional neuroses." Melville Dalton, who is now emeritus on the faculty at UCLA, discovered exactly that kind of relationship between line and staff men working in industrial settings several years before Stein decided that it had some hidden psychological significance. The game has to do with how one deals with responsibility when one has no authority, and the fact that nurses and physicians engage in it has nothing to do with their disciplines or their sexes.

There is a basic principle of scientific research that understanding the question is the first step in arriving at the solution. The essence of a collection such as this is the opportunity for sharing the different ways we establish our question. It is of special concern to nurses because we usually get caught in the middle. We are expected to implement the decisions of physicians, protect the reputation of the hospital, and still practice our own profession in a way that is at least minimally acceptable to ourselves.

In order to understand the questions regarding changing perceptions of roles and responsibilities, we have to look at the structural elements—who can do what? Who tells whom what to do? In the situations discussed in these chapters, the one told is usually the nurse. Who can fire or cause to be fired? In a hospital the one fired has usually been the nurse. Traditionally, the law has been interpreted to mean that physicians can do anything and are, therefore, responsible for everything. Nurses and other health professionals have been seen as a subset of medicine and therefore under the control of physicians. Structurally this does one important thing: it reduces the uncertainty facing all participants because the locus of control is clear. The logic of decisionmaking is unidimensional because decisions rest with the physician only. But in recent years we have seen the credibility of physicians reduced. This is not just symptomatic of the times but has happened cyclically throughout history. There was a period in Jacksonian America when eight states abolished their medical practice acts because they had so little respect for physicians.

When others, not using medical logic, insist on having a role in the decisionmaking, they impose new systems of logic and increase the uncertainty involved. I think one of the things that we have to bear uppermost in our minds, and which we often tend to forget, is that the logic systems and therefore the decisions of law, medicine, religion, economics, and of the behavioral sciences (which provide the logic base for nursing) are not totally compatible. Any efforts at dialogue among these groups must therefore involve considerable patience and a will to persevere. The purpose of collections such as this is to provide a forum for that dialogue.

Another area of difficulty in examining the decisionmaking that goes on around these problems has to do with the differences between the processes expected of nonprofessionals—"technicians"—and those expected of professionals. In the final analysis we are talking about the differences between algorithmic, computerizable, yes-no decisions and heuristic decisions which are based on principles and iterative in nature. Ethical decisions based on moral competence have been thought to rest with the professional and tend to be heuristic in nature. Technical decisions, based on technical competence, are usually algorithmic and have traditionally been shared by technicians and professionals. Unfortunately, with increasingly complex technology requiring increased education come increased instances where the decisions must be heuristic and based not only on an iterative process, but on the need for great immediacy. There is not a time frame allowing for consultation. In other words, the ethical, heuristic decisions have to be made by the persons who are there— not in morning and evening rounds, but at two in the morning and over the weekend. This need upsets the balance of the entire system and results in changes in the potential power bases. Either the physician stays in the facility twenty-four hours a day to make those decisions, or the physician must be willing to share responsibility. As a sociologist, I can tell you that the usual first step in a situation of that kind is to attempt to disguise the sharing by withholding formal recognition of its existence. It is kept invisible.

For a considerable period of time I have been involved in a multiprofessional group which discusses questions involved in the care of patients. How does one go about making visible the decision to code or not to code? As nurses become better educated, their means to deal with flaws in decision-making processes have to change. Traditionally we have taught nurses who have doubts about what is going on to report those doubts to their supervisor. It has always been assumed that the supervisors, with their superior knowledge and their superior ability to engage in game playing, can deal with those problems.

That is not the way things are in 1981. Now nurses may choose to leave nursing, as has been noted; to reduce their practice to algorithmic or cookbook types of decisionmaking, seeking their rewards outside the area of their practice (and this is the most frightening development of all to me); or to insist on knowledgeable participation in the decisionmaking. The barrier usually raised to such participation is a legal one, rather than the real ones which have their roots in the need to reduce uncertainty on the part of the health care team. We find ourselves arguing these issues with the legislature, trying to walk the thin line between expression of social responsibility (which is what I think the law is about), and having lawyers and judges practicing medicine and nursing for which they do not have the education and expertise.

As nurses, our goals are based on certain structural realities. It is the nurse who provides the heat, light, nourishment and social contact for that anacephalic child. It is the nurse who spends the hours with dying or defective patients, resulting in an emotional bond which must ultimately be dealt with. That does not mean that a physician is not devastated by the death of a patient. It does mean that it is a different sort of experience based on different kinds of bonds and requiring different interventions for the relief of the professional who is in pain. It becomes increasingly necessary for us to understand each other's logic because different logics result in decisions which may not only be different, but incompatible. Decisions must be made in concert because only then can the real truth of a situation be considered. Only in concert will there be consistency in care which is based on the best interests of the patient rather than those of the provider.

There is no answer in isolation. Medicine does not have it; law does not have it; religion does not have it; nursing does not have it; administration does not have it; social workers do not have it. Individually, we lack the omnipotence of divinity. Collectively, we can only strive against the Tower of Babel diversity in our logic systems which hinders our mutual decisionmaking. Ultimately, we must look to a new locus of control which must be the patient or the patient's agent.

Chapter 29

Physicians and Nurses: Roles and Responsibilities in Caring for the Critically Ill Patient

Inge B. Corless

Most health professionals today would agree about the necessity of interdisciplinary health care for clients. The optimal division of labor, however, has been a source of concern if not outright disagreement.

Literature on professional status and the interrelationships of health professionals abounds, possibly leading one to the conclusion that everything worth saying has already been said. However, developments in health care and in professional education are of a dynamic rather than static nature. For this reason alone a reconsideration of the roles and relationships of health care team members is justified from time to time.

Determining whether the health care system meets the needs of service recipients is only one important reason for studying role interactions. One question which has been raised all too infrequently is the degree to which the purveyors of care might help one another solve their problems. For example, if the issues facing physicians, such as when to refrain from providing further chemotherapy aimed at cure, were shared with other professionals, patients and families, then the stress of all those involved might be ameliorated.

This paper argues that a revision of health care responsibilities will provide a higher quality of service to patients and that this reformula-

Dr. Corless would like to thank Dr. Michael Murphy, Medical Director of St. Peter's Hospice, Ms. Eileen Herbert, R.N., Head Nurse, and Mrs. Christine Schiponi, R.N., Assistant Head Nurse, Intensive Care Unit of St. Peter's Hospital, for the thoughts they contributed to this paper.

tion will also help improve relations between physicians and nurses as well as other professional groups. A distinction is also made throughout between medical cure (physician) and health care (nurse).

The roles of physician and nurse are the focus here not because other health care providers are less important but because the physician and nurse are the essential locus for reformulation. The acute care setting of an intensive care unit and the terminal care setting of a hospice will be used as models to show how a reformulation of roles can produce benefits.

THE PHYSICIAN

The role of the physician has served as the paradigm of professional practice.[1] The heavy responsibilities which rest with physicians, particularly in life and death situations, the esoteric knowledge possessed, and the lack of medical knowledge among the lay public help to account for the high status accorded them.[2] Traditional formulations of this role do not include the demands on the medical person for long hours nor a consideration of the heavy psychological toll exacted by a medical model which allows for no error.[3]

The public's expectations of physicians are a source of stress for medical practitioners. Compounding this are a number of other factors which intensify stress. In making rounds with a busy oncologist in a hospital, one is struck by the brevity of each physician-patient interchange, and the need to document the contact and observations of the patient in the progress notes. Most oppressive is the pressure to move on to the next patient so as to complete the hospital rounds before office hours. In one such practice, oncologists divide hospital responsibilities on a weekly rotating practice. This practice disrupts the continuity of patient care. While many patients are familiar to the oncologist with rounding responsibilities, clearly some are not. Furthermore, distinguishing the histories and clinical and social developments of so many patients is a herculean task.

These responsibilities make it all the more difficult for the physician to find the time necessary to provide information, let alone to counsel the patient's family. Exchanges with patients and families then take the form of physicians simply providing the diagnosis, treatment and prognosis of patients. The prognosis usually includes some sort of "personal impact assessment"—that is, "If all goes as we expect, you can plan to be out of the hospital in so many days and back to work at such a time." Clearly, the personal impact assessment is what is most salient to the patient and the family. Unfortunately, this is often the most slighted aspect of the interaction between the physician, patient, and family.

The scientific explanation of cause and cure and the intermediate linkages are of interest to the patient and family, but their immediate question is one of meaning: "Will this illness limit the way I live or the length of my life?" All too often physicians give the explanation in a scientific language which stifles discussion with the patient and significant others.[4]

Disease labels and their connotations may also inhibit interaction among patient, family and physician. This is because diseases have both societal and personal meanings. Susan Sontag noted the similarity between tuberculosis and cancer. Both are diseases which serve as metaphors for the disorganization of the times and conjure a military response—"the war on cancer."[5] Add to this the personal meanings which a disease such as cancer evokes, and there is little wonder why patient and family are in shock when given the diagnosis. The term cancer or multiple sclerosis or whatever is heard, and the societal-personal reverberations of these words act as an impediment to the absorption of any additional information. Thus, when the physician asks whether there are any questions, the patient and family literally do not have their wits about them enough to ask the many questions associated with such news. Only later, when the physician is no longer present, do the patient and significant others think of questions which are meaningful to them.

Thus, the physician's typical workload leaves limited time and, therefore, limited opportunity for physician-patient-family interchanges. The conferences which do occur are typified by one-way exchanges in which the physician relays scientific information which the family receives passively. This very model and the expectation that families should "take the news well" further exacerbate the problem of deficient communication.

In these days of super-specialization, several physicians may be involved in a single case, and they may issue orders which are inadvertently contradictory. An attending or primary physician should sort out these difficulties. In some situations, particularly for service patients, there is no attending physician readily available, and the nurse looks to a consultant to take a leadership role in the comprehensive medical management of the patient. Other times, when a subspecialty service is involved, there may be general problems which are overlooked. Additionally, there may be a reluctance within the service to seek consultations. This can result in fractionated and inadequate treatment of patients. Thus, the nurse is the professional caregiver who is most typically bombarded with the patient's queries.

THE NURSE

The nurse is the health care worker primarily involved in the total care of the patient. Structurally, nurses can be in contact with a patient and family 24 hours per day. A primary nurse—that is, the nursing professional responsible for planning the care of the patient—is on the service approximately 40 hours per week. During this time, he or she has the opportunity to form a therapeutic relationship with the patient.

The 24-hour per day monitoring and care of patients is a nursing responsibility. Changes in status, whether due to the primary illness, a reaction to treatment, or a response to the environment, need to be noted and communicated to the primary physician so that the appropriate measures may be initiated. Likewise, lab results, consultation reports and other pertinent data need to be called to the physician's attention so that he or she may incorporate these facts and recommendations in an appraisal of the patient's current needs and in developing a course of action. The physician is the professional best equipped to provide such a plan of care. Other physiological and non-physiological considerations which may affect the results of such planning need to be discussed with the nurse, who is the professional with the educational preparation necessary to provide such a dialogue.

Another difference between the nurse and the physician is the number of clients which each of these professionals serve. In the situation where the nurse works on a discrete unit, the physician sees many more clients than does the nurse. As noted earlier, these physician-patient interactions tend to be brief and in some instances, perfunctory. Part of the problem is the number of patients with whom a physician comes into contact. While the nursing caseload is heavier than the physician's in terms of the work entailed with each patient and family, it is lighter in terms of the number of individuals cared for. The amount of time that the nurse spends with each patient is also greater, due in part to the nature of the work itself.

REFORMULATING THE ROLES OF THE PHYSICIAN AND NURSE

The opportunities for patient-family interaction available to the nurse, the constraints on the physician, and the gaps in service to the health care consumer, suggest that a reformulation of health care responsibilities would enable the relevant professionals to provide the care for which they were educated.

To illustrate the competencies expected of primary care nurses at the Master's level, let us examine the twelve curriculum objectives identified by the University of Michigan's program in Primary Care Nursing:[6]

1) Assess physical, emotional and environmental status of the adult health care consumer in the context of his or her family in order to provide comprehensive nursing care.

2) Assess the consumer's perceptions of, responses to, and methods of coping with illness and stresses of daily living in order to plan for nursing interventions built on family strengths and coping patterns.

3) Analyze health behavior and its relationship to psychosociological and cultural variables.

4) Encourage consumers to be active participants in health care planning.

5) Collaborate with consumers in identifying health needs and in initiating corresponding actions.

6) Provide primary nursing health care to the adult and his or her family for common acute conditions and/or stabilized chronic conditions.

7) Initiate referrals to appropriate health and social agencies and personnel.

8) Form and sustain collaborative relationships with the health care delivery team members to the end that nursing will assume full partnership in the health care delivery system.

9) Analyze issues in primary health care delivery in general and specifically in relation to primary care nursing.

10) Conduct clinical nursing research relevant to primary health care.

11) Examine ethical issues in primary care with attention to health behavior, values and attitudes.

12) Continue professional development in accord with changes in health care need and practices.[7]

Given the assumption that physicians are primarily involved in those diagnostic and treatment modalities which result in care and/or prolongation of life, let us proceed with our reformulation.

The phrase, "reformulation of health care responsibilities," is understood by some as an implied attack on medical prerogatives. Such is not the case. This clarification of role responsibilities is not, as has been termed elsewhere, "delegated physician science," but instead specifies what transpires in the best health care situations and suggests a few additions which will improve the delineation of role responsibilities and role relationships.[8]

Research into joint practice is currently being conducted under the auspices of the National Joint Practice Commission.[9] Units involved in the demonstration projects include the Hillcrest Medical Center, Tulsa, Oklahoma; Eskaton American River Health Care Center, Carmichael, California; York Hospice, York, Maine; and SUNY Downstate Medical Center in New York.[10] The purpose of these projects is "to provide the best possible medical and nursing care through collaborative effort."[11]

The focus of joint practice is on the patient's well-being with conflicts being resolved in terms of the patient's best interests. In joint practice, physicians and nurses talk openly and directly with one another. In doing so, they communicate information based on the direct observation of the patient and family, laboratory findings, consultants' recommendations and share planning activities along the cure-care continuum.

What may be even more vital is that nurses and physicians share expectations of one another. A good example of effective communication which resolved some difficulties is given by Blackwood in her discussion of the effects of joint practice.[12] The difficulty which concerned the nurses was the expectation that they be mind readers: "You see, some doctors will allow a nurse to take certain actions based on her judgment, rather than on explicit orders and even criticize her if she doesn't use her own judgment. Other doctors, however, will raise the roof if a nurse does exactly the same things for their patients."[13] Actions expected by some physicians and not others include "ordering a heating pad, giving Tylenol for a headache or Cepacol for a sore throat, increasing ambulation if it's tolerated well or decreasing it if it's not."[14]

One of the results of clarifying expectations has been a reduction in calls to the physician day and night.[15] And, while the reduction is desirable, the most important outcome is the increased satisfaction of patients with their care. In addition to verbal reports of contentment, Blackwood notes, "Even more concrete evidence that patients are responding well since we initiated joint practice is the reduction in the requests for and use of tranquilizers, sleeping pills and analgesics on our unit."[16] Although researchers will want to examine such a causal linkage more carefully, the relationship does seem plausible. How then might a reformulation of the nurse's role incorporate the advances we have already mentioned and alleviate the gaps which result in less than optimal care?

As a first step, the nurse needs to be legitimized as the coordinator of care. In this role, the nurse could determine whether patients are receiving the medical and nursing care deemed appropriate by the primary physician, the primary nurse and the patient. The nurse could meet with consulting physicians, giving information about particular patients, receiving the consultant's assessment, and sharing it with the primary physician. Conflicting recommendations would be drawn to the primary physician's attention and resolved by him or her.

The needs and changing responses of the patient and the family to the illness should be discussed by the primary nurse and physician. The nurse, as coordinator of care, would be responsible for assuring that there are no gaps in care and that the patient receives the therapies which are required for his or her well-being. If the patient is to have surgery, it would be the nurse's responsibility to verify that all concerned agree as to the objectives and requirements of the patient care plan. The nurse would then transmit this information to his or her counterparts in the operating room or the recovery room. In this role, it would be appropriate for the nurse to visit the recovery room to assess the patient's responses to the surgery and to provide both patient and family with needed support. At this time, as well as at less critical periods, the nurse would serve as the patient/family advocate, doing what the individual would do for himself or herself, were that possible. Primary nurses would use their knowledge of the institution to cut a path through its bureaucracy to secure what is needed by the patient and the family. Just as lawyers attempt to secure legal justice for their clients, so would the nurse-advocate seek to obtain medical care/health care equity for her or his clients.

In addition to being coordinators and advocates, nurses would also serve as behavioral specialists interpreting the meaning of the illness in the broader context of the patient's life. Illness often serves as a solution to an irresolvable dilemma, literally as a way out. When this is appreciated early in the disease process, the patient can be helped to recognize the secondary gain which accrues to him or her from the illness, and other less damaging solutions can be found for these problems. Treatment directed merely to the physical aspects of illness would succeed only for a short time, if at all. Patients with ulcers need more than the standard medical and/or surgical regimen for their disease if a recurrence is to be prevented. It is appropriate for nurses to assume this role because their education emphasizes the psychological aspects of patient care.[17] In another context, Ludden et al. note that nurses are more sensitive than physicians to these issues of the psychological concomitants of illness.[18]

Essentially, I am distinguishing between medical cure and health care, with the physician providing the leadership in the former sphere and the nurses in the latter. If we accept the premise offered by

Dachelet that "medicine and nursing are two separate, distinct, professions each with an equally valuable skill to offer and each sharing a common goal," we begin to explore the opportunities for true collaboration.[19] Smoyak defines these skills further by saying that nurses have expertise in "caring, comforting, counseling and helping patients and families to cope with their health care problems," where the "physician's expertise is acknowledged in diagnosing illness and curing disease."[20] As Dachelet points out, "this is a subtle distinction, a distinction between health care and medical care."[21] Both are important and necessary for the well-being of our patients.

THE INTENSIVE CARE UNIT

How would this abstract reformulation of role relationships work in the technically sophisticated environment of the intensive care unit? The primacy of the physician with regard to certain physiological aspects of the patient is not a matter for dispute. During the time that the doctor diagnoses and provides curative treatment to the patient, the nurse not only supports these efforts but also works with the family and significant others, doing crisis intervention. Using his or her skills as a behavioral specialist, the nurse is able to secure valuable background information about the patient and family as well as to resolve some of the immediate stress of the family and friends, who are in an alien environment with a loved one who is in mortal danger, and who apparently can do nothing to alleviate the situation.

Depending on the specific situation, family and friends can participate in the patient's care. At a minimum, they can provide information. After family members have had the opportunity to verbalize their fears, they are in a better position to focus on tasks which require their attention. For example, family members, friends, and various agencies may need to be called; blood donations may be required; arrangements for younger family members may be necessary.

The nurse also provides care to the patient, interpreting the environment to the patient and interpreting the patient's responses to the physician. The interpretation of the environment is important on general medical/surgical units. It is the sine qua non for the prevention of ICU psychosis or the onset of some of the other deleterious emotional aftereffects of ICU placement.

The imposing array of technology present in modern ICUs is impressive to those initiated in medical folkways. It is overwhelming to the medically unsophisticated, all the more so when added to the trauma of insult to the body. Unless a friendly guide shows the way, most patients are terrified by the ICU environment.

Observation of the patient's response to the illness and to the treatment has long been a function of nursing care. These observations are then conveyed to the physician so that he or she has the information vital to the optimal performance of the medical role. The nurse's role as the continual monitor of the patient's condition has permitted the doctor to attend to the many while the nurse safeguards the few. In so doing, the nurse is the best judge as to changes in the status of the individual patient and becomes a valuable resource and colleague in the planning of the patient's regimen.

Typically, the physician provides information to the family concerning the patient's condition and the plan of care. And, while the doctor may give a brief explanation of the course of action, the more important reason for the meeting with the family is to allow them the opportunity for contact with the person responsible for the medical cure of their loved one. Such contact can be very reassuring.

Because the preparatory work and crisis intervention has already been accomplished by the nurse, the dialogue with the physician can be substantial rather than superficial. Obviously, this introduces a new challenge to the physician for significant interaction rather than for the all too common "inert" action. The nurse needs to know the nature of the communication so that she or he can answer the patient's and family's questions later. This is especially important when the doctor gives a prognosis which involves some uncertainty. In these instances, it behooves the physician and nurse to hold a joint conference with the family. The joint conference would provide two perspectives on the status of the family and their response to the illness, as well as a dual assessment of the coping ability of the individual family members. The joint conference would also be a prelude to further collaboration when difficult issues need to be decided—for example, which or whether heroic measures are to be employed.

It is also a good idea to ask how various professionals can offer collegial support to one another. Caregiving is a wearying and wearing occupation, not to mention an awesome responsibility. Support by the doctor and nurse for each other and for other team members helps us care for professionals as well as for patients. Such collegial concern reduces the isolation of the individual professional in coping with the emotional concomitants of involvement with patients and families. The recent plethora of materials on burnout of nurses as well as the suicide statistics on physicians suggest that if we continue to neglect this area, we do so at our peril. Support systems are relevant not only to the well-being of patients and families, but also are pertinent to health care practitioners who need support—both professional and personal—from their colleagues and families.

THE HOSPICE

A hospice is an innovative program of care for the dying. It differs from an ICU and, on the surface, would not seem to lend itself to a similar apportionment of responsibilities.

In the terminal care setting of the hospice, the nurse also serves as the coordinator of care. Here, as in other areas of the hospital, the primary nurse has an opportunity to get to know the patient and family as well as observe responses to therapy and the total milieu. In this role, the nurse gathers the relevant physical, psychological, social, and spiritual data on the patient and family as an initial assessment of the problems facing them. After the assessment, an interdisciplinary team of professionals can formulate the plan of care, which is monitored by the nurse.

While the nurse is responsible for monitoring the plan of care and for verifying the efficiency of the pain medication, the physician provides the expert knowledge on the management of pain. This demands a high level of proficiency in the relative merits of the various palliative modalities. Developments in the pharmacology of pain in the terminally ill are occurring very rapidly today; they demand more than a casual acquaintance if masterful care is to be provided to the patient. The subtleties of the use of palliative radiation, nerve blocks and other therapies need to be appreciated as well.

The hospice nurse should also play the role of the behavioral specialist. Before the psychological, social and spiritual needs of the patient and family can be met, the patient's most distressing physical needs must be relieved. Although the physician is primarily responsible for this, the nurse can provide support; for example he or she can introduce a relaxation regimen. Such supportive therapies are part of the nurse's comprehensive care of the patient and family. Of course, the provision of comprehensive care is very demanding of nurses, and so it must be a team effort. And, if the interdisciplinary team is to succeed, all its members must agree on the objectives of care and on the domain of their responsibilities.

Not only must the professional staff agree on the plan of care, but also a conference with the patient and family must be held. During this meeting, the staff should present its observations and suggestions to the patient and family for their consideration. Thereafter, meetings should be held periodically to assess the need for new goals and for the updating of the plan of care.

CONCLUSION

Clearly, the collegial concern and teamwork outlined in this paper involve effort. Also required is a sense of humor, the maintenance of which may be one of our most important responsibilities. Without an appreciation for the meaning of the sublime and the ridiculous we can no more contribute to the well-being of our patients than we can to each other.

As we revise and clarify our roles and responsibilities, we must realign authority commensurate with responsibility. Failing this, no real change will occur; rather, nurses who do have de facto responsibility will continue to be frustrated. The implementation of changes in the roles and responsibilities of health care providers will not resolve all patient care problems. The incorporation of these changes will enable the members of the health care team to use their specific skills better and, consequently, to be more effective collectively. As a result, the health care team will be more likely to respond successfully to challenges, both current and future.

NOTES

1. *See, e.g.,* E. FREIDSON, PROFESSION OF MEDICINE (Dodd, Mead, New York) (1970); Rueschemeyer, D., *Doctors and Lawyers: A Comment on the Theory of the Professions,* in MEDICAL MEN AND THEIR WORK, E. FREIDSON AND J. LORBER, Eds. (Aldine) (1972) at 5–19.
2. For further discussion of the characteristic of a profession *see* Goode, W.J., *Community within a Community: The Professions,* AMERICAN SOCIOLOGICAL REVIEW 22: 194–200 (1957); Goode, W.J., *Encroachment, Charlatanism and the Emerging Profession—Psychology, Sociology and Medicine,* AMERICAN SOCIOLOGICAL REVIEW 25:902–17 (1960); Goode, W.J., *The Theoretical Limits of Professionalization,* in THE SEMI-PROFESSIONS AND THEIR ORGANIZATION, A. ETZIONI, Ed. (The Free Press, New York) (1969); Greenwood, E., *Attributes of a Profession,* in MAN, WORK AND SOCIETY, S. NOSOW AND W.F. FORM, Eds., (Basic Books, New York) (1962); Hughes, E.C., *Professions,* in PROFESSIONS IN AMERICA, K.C. LYNN and Editors of Daedalus, Eds. (Beacon Press, Boston) (1962); Parsons, T., *The Professions and Social Structure,* in ESSAYS IN SOCIOLOGICAL THEORY (The Free Press, New York) (1954).
3. *Id.,* Goode and Rueschemeyer discuss the ideal of service as a characteristic of professions. The meaning of "service" is somewhat ambiguous.
4. Goode, W.J., *Community within a Community: The Professions, supra* note 2, at

194 (mentioning the characteristic of a language common to the community which is "understood only partially by outsiders").

5. S. SONTAG, ILLNESS AS METAPHOR (Farrar, Straus & Giroux, New York) (1978).

6. K. KRONE, *et. al.*, GRADUATE CURRICULUM COMMITTEE RESPONSE TO THE NATIONAL LEAGUE FOR NURSING GRADUATE CURRICULUM RECOMMENDATIONS (The University of Michigan, Ann Arbor) (June 7, 1979).

7. *Id.* at 7. *See also* Secretary's Committee to Study Extended Roles for Nurses, *Extending the Scope of Nursing Practice*, NURSING OUTLOOK 20:46–52 (January 1972).

8. Corless, I., *Nursing, Professionalization and Innovations*, at 149 in CURRENT PERSPECTIVES IN NURSING: SOCIAL ISSUES AND TRENDS, FLYNN AND MILLER , Eds. (C.V. Mosby Co., St. Louis) (1980).

9. Blackwood, S.A., *Interview: At This Hospital, "The Captain of the Ship" Is Dead*, RN MAGAZINE 42 (3):77–94 (March 1979).

10. *Id.* at 94.

11. *Id.* at 78.

12. *Id.*

13. *Id.*

14. *Id.*

15. *Id.*

16. *Id.* at 85.

17. Ludden, J.M., Winickoff, R.N., Steinberg, S.M., *Psychological Aspects of Medical Care: A Training Seminar for Primary Care Providers*, JOURNAL OF MEDICAL EDUCATION 54 (9):722 (September 1979).

18. *Id.*

19. Dachelet, C.Z., *Nursing's Bid for Increased Status* , NURSING FORUM 17(1):23 (1978).

20. Smoyak, S., *Co-Equal Status for Nurses and Physicians*, AMERICAN MEDICAL NEWS (February 11, 1972).

21. Dachelet, *supra* note 19, at 24.

BIBLIOGRAPHY

ASHLEY, J.A., HOSPITALS, PATERNALISM AND THE ROLE OF THE NURSE (Teachers College Press, New York) (1976).

BECKER, H.S., GEER, B., HUGHES, E.C., STRAUSS, A.L., BOYS IN WHITE: STUDENT CULTURE IN MEDICAL SCHOOL (Univ. of Chicago Press, Chicago) (1961).

Blackwood, S.A., *At This Hospital, "The Captain of the Ship" Is Dead*, RN 42(3):77-94 (March 1979).

Bonaccorsi, J., *MD: "Nurses Are Subordinates"* RN 42(7):7 (July 1979).

Bucher, R., Strauss, A., *Professions in Process*, in MEDICAL CARE— READINGS IN THE SOCIOLOGY OF MEDICAL INSTITUTIONS (John Wiley & Sons, New York) (1966).

COE, R.M., SOCIOLOGY OF MEDICINE (McGraw Hill, New York) (1970).

Committee to Study Extended Roles for Nurses, *Report: Extending the Scope of Nursing Practice*, NURSING OUTLOOK 20:46–52 (January 1972).

DAVIS, F., THE NURSING PROFESSION: FIVE SOCIOLOGICAL ESSAYS (John Wiley & Sons, New York) (1969).

Devereux, G., Weiner, F.R., *The Occupational Status of Nurses*, AMERICAN SOCIOLOGICAL REVIEW 15:628–635.

Driscoll, V., *Liberating Nursing Practice*, NURSING OUTLOOK 20:24–28 (January 1972).

FREIDSON, E., PROFESSION OF MEDICINE—A STUDY OF THE SOCIOLOGY OF APPLIED KNOWLEDGE, (Dodd, Mead, New York) (1970).

Gage, L.W., *Partners in Primary Care*, in CURRENT PERSPECTIVES IN NURSING (C.V. Mosby, Saint Louis) (1977).

FIELDING, F.H., AN INTRODUCTION TO THE HISTORY OF MEDICINE, 4th Ed. (W.B. Saunders, Philadelphia (1929).

Goode, W., *The Theoretical Limits of Professionalization*, in THE SEMI-PROFESSIONS AND THEIR ORGANIZATION, A. ETZIONI, Ed. (Free Press, New York) (1969) at 266–313.

GRIFFIN, G.J., GRIFFIN, H.J., JENSEN'S HISTORY AND TRENDS OF PROFESSIONAL NURSING, 5th Ed. (C.V. Mosby, St. Louis) (1965).

Grissum, M., *On Becoming a Risk-Taker and a Role Breaker*, in WOMANPOWER AND HEALTH CARE (Little, Brown, Boston) (1976).

Hughes, E.C., *Professions*, in THE PROFESSIONS IN AMERICA, K.S. LYNN, EDITORS OF DAEDALUS, Eds. (Beacon Press, Boston) (1965) at 1–14.

Johnson, M.M., Martin, H.W., *A Sociological Analysis of the Nurse Role*, AMERICAN JOURNAL OF NURSING 58:373–77 (1958).

Jordan, J.D., Shipp, J.C., *The Primary Health Care Professional Was A Nurse*, AMERICAN JOURNAL OF NURSING 71:922–925 (May 1971).

Keller, N.S., *The Nurse's Role: Is It Expanding or Shrinking?* NURSING OUTLOOK 21:236–40 (April 1973).

Kisch, A.I., *Planning for a Sensible Health Care System*, NURSING OUTLOOK 20:640–42 (October 1972).

Lee, A.A., *How Nurses Rate with MDs—Still the Handmaiden*, RN 42(7):21–30 (July 1979).

Lee, A.A., *Nursing's Shopworn Image—How It Hurts You . . . How It Helps*, RN 42(8):43–47 (August 1979).

Ludden, J.M., Winickoff, R.N., Steinberg, S.M., *Psychological Aspects of Medical Care: A Training Seminar for Primary Care Providers*, JOURNAL OF MEDICAL EDUCATION, pp. 720–24 (September 1979).

Mauksch, H.O., *Churning for Change* HANDBOOK OF MEDICAL SOCIOLOGY, H. FREEMAN, *et al.*, Eds. (Prentice-Hall, N.J.) (1972).

Means, J.H., *Homo Medicus Americanus*, in THE PROFESSIONS IN AMERICA, K.S. LYNN, EDITORS OF DAEDALUS, Eds. (Beacon Press, Boston) (1963) at 47–69.

Mereness, D., *Recent Trends in Expanding Roles of the Nurse* , NURSING OUTLOOK 18:30–33 (May 1970).

Merton, R.K., *The Search for Professional Status*, AMERICAN JOURNAL OF NURSING 60:622–64 (1960).

Rogers, M.E., *Nursing: To Be or Not to Be?* NURSING OUTLOOK 20:42–46 (January 1972).

Rueschemeyer, D., *Doctors and Lawyers: A Comment on the Theory of Professions*, CANADIAN REVIEW OF SOCIOLOGY AND ANTHROPOLOGY 1:17–30 (1964).

Saunders, L., *The Changing Role of Nurses*, in MEDICAL CARE—READINGS IN THE SOCIOLOGY OF MEDICAL INSTITUTIONS (John Wiley & Sons, New York) (1966).

Schlotfeldt, R.M., *This I Believe . . . Nursing is Health Care*, NURSING OUTLOOK 20:245–46 (April 1972).

Shoemaker, J., *How Nursing Diagnosis Helps Focus Your Care* RN 42(8):56–61 (August 1979).

Spengler, C., *The Indoctrination of Female Nurses*, in WOMANPOWER AND HEALTH CARE (Little, Brown, Boston) (1976).

Chapter 30

Reflections on the Health Care Team Concept

Walter A. Markowicz

With respect to the health care team, it is my opinion that we must be bolder and broader to include not only the doctor and the nurse, but other professionals involved in the total care of the patient. To the terms "care" and "cure," perhaps we can add "healing," which would add another dimension to health care delivery. People can be cared for and cured without ever being healed, in the sense of being made whole.

This entire care/cure/healing process takes a cooperative effort among multidisciplinary professionals functioning as a team and respecting one another's expertise. This usually works best in a critical care unit, whether for intensive care patients or for the chronically, terminally ill. Within an intensive care unit physicians may be willing to initiate the idea of cooperative team care by discussing a case with the nurse in charge, the social worker, the pharmacologist, the chaplain, the dietitian, or perhaps the therapist. Each can offer advice from his or her standpoint regarding the case. Both the patient's personal and physical needs can be fulfilled by these professionals and this can best be achieved by working cooperatively with a maximum of communication, understanding and support.

What is the value of the multidisciplinary team in providing the patient with holistic care? For one thing, it helps to prevent the staff from identifying the patient as simply a disease entity. The availability of multiple health care provides a broader forum for questions about problems, helps reduce patient/family anxiety, and increases cooperation and compliance with the method of treatment. It provides integrated, total patient/family care and patient/family posthospitalization follow-up by appropriate team members. That cannot happen when a team consists of only the physician and the nurse.[1]

Some of the objectives of multidisciplinary health care, many of which are presented in Dr. Corless' article, are: (1) to provide comprehensive care for each patient and family so as to meet all of their needs; (2) to facilitate communication among all of those involved in the care of the patient; (3) to facilitate appropriate and timely consultation regarding the patient; and, (4) to optimally involve both patient and family in their care and plans.

Another objective, but one which we tend to dismiss too lightly in health care and especially in the healing process, is to provide an atmosphere where grief can appropriately be expressed by the patient, the family, and frequently by the staff. One way this can be accomplished is by scheduling regular multidisciplinary team conferences. I participated in such regular meetings for one and a half years, after which the team dissolved due to the transfer of members. However, during this time, the meetings had strong staff support and resulted in great patient and family satisfaction. This, too, cannot be accomplished by only the doctor and nurse. For example, through such a team conference a social worker can report on family dislocations that had not been revealed earlier. Additionally both the team and the family are better able to reach a decision as to what is best for the patient in the future.

Other advantages of regular meetings are: (1) to increase staff morale; (2) to afford the opportunity for feedback, questions, and affirmations of jobs well-done; (3) to develop, clarify and utilize the skills of all team members; and (4) to build an understanding and appreciation of roles. Effective communication decreases time spent. If there is communication among all team members they don't have to hope that other members have read a report, buttonhole them to find out if they read it, or remind them to read it. All essential information is digested in one meeting by all members.

I believe that the final decision of whether or not to use life-support systems must ultimately be made by the physician. However, other people must also be involved. A physician may decide to discontinue use of the respirator and simply direct someone to do it. However, exchange of information as to why it's being turned off can make the actual task somewhat easier.

Within this team structure, the chaplaincy also makes a specific contribution to total care. It is important to note that one-quarter of all the voluntary, acute hospital beds in the country are under the jurisdiction of churches, where pastoral care is automatically understood, and 325 other institutions are licensed by the Association for Clinical Pastoral Education to provide the training of chaplains, chaplain supervisors and teachers.[2]

Therefore, the pastor's role is linked closely with the care and healing of patients. But what, precisely, is that role? One of the tasks of the pastoral person is to have an understanding of anger and be prepared for its dynamics and the masks it wears. Through understanding the theology of anger and how it is integrated into the spiritual personality, the pastor can ascertain, through gentle inquiry and active listening, the degree to which the patient's anger should be integrated into his or her belief system. By consulting with the nurse and physician, the pastor may discover physician or drug-related causes for anger or depression and, if appropriate, he or she can share the patient's spiritual conflict with them. Other areas in which the pastoral care person needs to be knowledgeable are grief and grief resolution for patient, family and staff. He or she needs to treat "loss of future lives," physical dependency and self identity conflict. The pastoral person can work with the patient on understanding treatment purpose and process, and could be especially beneficial in follow-up with the family directly or by referral to the home community, religious or otherwise. I say "could" because I also realize the time constraints under which a pastor functions.

In designing and implementing a pastoral plan for the patient, it makes little difference to the chaplain that some patients do not have a spiritual approach to life. This is true, but in the foxholes of hospitals there's a very high percentage of spiritual belief. What belief there is should not be dismissed, but harnessed and used.

The pastoral care person, therefore, is an integral part of the health care team. Traditionally, the clergy has served as caregiver during the period of grief, when the reality of loss is realized and can be eased by the pastoral care person.

Frequently, the family of a terminally ill patient has been deeply involved in the caregiving of their loved one and has anticipated bereavement over a period of years perhaps. Consequently, when death occurs, they are emotionally exhausted and may attempt to avoid additional pain, relying solely on the funeral to extinguish all feelings that accompany bereavement. Bereavement may be unanticipated or rejected, and it is necessary at this time to have support from all disciplines, including the chaplaincy. People naturally seek support from the pastoral care person because they expect to receive it from that particular source. One advantage of receiving such support is that the clergy never prescribe pills or put in IVs. They are involved in caregiving rather than curegiving.

The pastor will offer family members support for affirmation and acceptance of the entire life of the dying or deceased, including the palliative and terminal phase. Furthermore, he or she can support the integration of their own religious belief systems and the movement toward new affirmation of their lives.[3]

In any case involving a hospital patient, it is not just the patient who needs to be cared for, but also others who are involved with that patient. This includes people who were deeply involved in the caregiving of the patient as well as family and friends.

I agree wholeheartedly with those who support the team concept, but I would prefer that the concept of total health care be expanded to include the onset of bereavement and the period of grief. This can be done most effectively in smaller units and in the critical care aspects of the terminally ill patient.

NOTES

1. M. Reed, *Multi-disciplinary Team Care and the Oncology Patient*, an unpublished manuscript (1976).
2. *See Pastoral Ministry*, at 1192, ENCYCLOPEDIA FOR BIOETHICS (The Free Press, New York) (1978).
3. From Draft for Pastoral Care Program at Harper Hospital, 1978.

Chapter 31

Do Not Resuscitate Orders: Sources of Conflict

John J. Allman

The individual patient is the most important point of reference in medical decisionmaking. Deciding whether the patient is competent and deciding whether the patient should receive treatment, whether treatment should be withheld, whether it should be stopped once started, or whether the patient should have a Do Not Resuscitate order creates a great amount of conflict among the staff. An adequate decision has not been made if any member of the staff does not feel a part of that decision, or if the doctor knows that he or she will not order resuscitation and only verbalizes this to the staff. If it is not on the patient's chart and if it is not clearly communicated, then others are being asked to make the decision. Communication and documentation are absolute necessities.

Another source of conflict is the professional's personal view of death or dying, of the patient's willingness to live and the patient's right to make decisions. This subject has been dealt with in conferences, in-service education programs, and the literature. It is each individual's responsibility to take a long, hard look at herself or himself and work from there.

It is important to realize that cases in intensive care and cardiac care units, where withholding treatment becomes an issue, are relatively few in number compared to the entire hospital's patient occupancy. But their very presence generates medical, moral, emotional and legal problems out of proportion to their numbers. Some ask whether the system plays God if life-support systems are removed once started. Others counter by asking if it is possible that we have played God in the beginning by simply starting the machine if we were not sure that it would ultimately end in the recovery of that patient. Again, this subject is one that tends to produce more questions than answers. Indeed, the conflicts generated by the DNR problem may stimulate the questions that will ultimately produce the answers. The compatibility of law and medicine, and of lawyers and doctors, is not always evident; on these particular issues, the legal and medical professions must put aside the adversary role and work together. This is not only possible, it is necessary.

Although solutions to the DNR problem will eventually be found, hospital staff members today are still faced with problematic decisions. Staff communication and the documentation of the decision-making process are extremely important. The following Treatment Decision Protocol has been designed to minimize the problems of DNR decision-making.

Model
Treatment Decision Protocol

In the event that a situation should arise where there is conflict, confusion, or indecision regarding the question of whether to treat or not to treat a patient, or circumstances of questionable hospital liability or duty, the following Protocol should be followed:

I. Identification
   A. Should such a problem be identified by the attending or house physician, the physician should contact the Protocol Coordinator directly.
   B. Should such a problem be identified by a party other than a physician or a nurse, that party should contact the Protocol Coordinator directly.
   C. Should such a problem be identified by a nurse, that nurse should contact the Nursing Supervisor/Assistant Director of Nursing immediately. The Nursing Supervisor/A.D.O.N., if unable to resolve the problem, will contact the Director of Nursing. If the Director of Nursing is unable to resolve the problem, she will contact the Protocol Coordinator for further action.

II. The Protocol Coordinator shall be responsible for contacting, informing, and gathering opinions from the following as necessary or appropriate:
   A. Attending or House Physician
   B. Chief of Service
   C. Chief of Staff

  D. Hospital Administration

  E. Hospital Legal Counsel

  F. Medical Staff Liaison

  G. Nursing Director

  H. Nursing Unit

  I. Patient and/or patient's family

  J. Other parties (Chaplain, Minister, etc.)

III. It will be the responsibility of the Protocol Coordinator to maintain a flow of communication, ensure that necessary documentation is available, and maintain a progress record of the events of the case.

IV. Should contact with a court be required, it will be the Hospital Legal Counsel or their designee that will make such contact. The Protocol Coordinator will be responsible for communicating any court order or decision to all interested or involved parties.

V. Decisions will be based on consensus among the interested and involved parties. The Protocol Coordinator will be responsible for ensuring preparation of necessary letters, forms and other paperwork required for the follow-up and implementation of any decision reached; court ordered decisions will prevail if rendered.

VI. The Protocol Coordinator(s) will be designated by the Hospital Administration.

VII. The Protocol Coordinator will, at the resolution of the case, meet with the Director of Nursing, Medical Staff Liaison, and Hospital Administration to evaluate the case and prepare recommendations, if needed, for future action or modification of this Protocol.

Appendix A

Guidelines for Discontinuance of Cardiopulmonary Life-Support Systems Under Specified Circumstances, Los Angeles

A. The general principles which should govern decisionmaking in this area are:

1. It is the right of a person capable of giving informed consent to make his or her own decision regarding medical care after having been fully informed about the benefits, risks and consequences of available treatment, even when such a decision might foreseeably result in shortening the individual's life.

2. Persons who are unable to give informed consent have the same rights as do persons who can give such consent. Decisions made on behalf of persons who cannot give their own informed consent should, to the extent possible, be the decisions which those persons would have made for themselves had they been able to do so. Parents (or the guardian) of a minor child, or the conservator of an adult patient, must consent to the decision. Family members of adult patients should always be consulted, although they have no legal standing under present California law to make such decisions on behalf of the patient.

3. A physician may discontinue use of a cardiopulmonary life-support system (i.e. mechanical respirator or ventilator), and is not required to continue its use indefinitely solely because such support was initiated at an earlier time.

Developed by the Joint Ad Hoc Committee on Biomedical Ethics of the Los Angeles County Medical Association, Los Angeles County Bar Association. Adopted by the Council of the Los Angeles County Medical Association on March 2, 1981, and by the Board of Trustees of the Los Angeles County Bar Association on March 11, 1981.

4. The dignity of the individual must be preserved and necessary measures to assure comfort be maintained at all times.

5. It is the right of individual physicians to decline to participate in the withdrawal of life-support systems. In exercising this right, however, the physician must take appropriate steps to transfer the care of the patient to another qualified physician.

B. Three sets of circumstances in which decisions to discontinue the use of cardiopulmonary life-support systems can be made without the necessity of prior approval by the courts are:

1. Brain Death
Section 7180 of the California Health and Safety Code states: "A person shall be pronounced dead if it is determined by a physician that the person has suffered a total and irreversible cessation of brain function." This statute also requires that a second physician independently confirm the death and that neither physician be involved in decisions regarding transplantation of organs.

a. The physicians should document in the medical record the basis for the diagnosis of brain death.

b. The patient should be pronounced brain dead before disconnecting the respirator or ventilator.

c. It is desirable to explain the brain death law to family members and other interested persons before this procedure is implemented.

2. California Natural Death Act
Sections 7185 through 7195 of the California Health and Safety Code (the California Natural Death Act) provide that cardiopulmonary life-support systems must be withdrawn from patients who have signed a "valid and binding" Directive to Physicians. For further information, physicians should consult the Guidelines on the California Natural Death Act adopted by the California Medical Association and the California Hospital Association (CHA). These guidelines are reproduced in the CHA Consent Manual.

3. Irreversible Coma*
Cardiopulmonary life-support systems may be discontinued if all of the following conditions are present:

---

*While paragraphs B(1) and B(2), dealing with brain death and the California Natural Death Act, are based on provisions of the California Health and Safety Code, this paragraph, dealing with irreversible coma, is not based on any California statute or court decision, but rather reflects our view of good medical practice and the current standard of medical care in Los Angeles County.

a. The medical record contains a written diagnosis of irreversible coma, confirmed by a physician who by training or experience is qualified to assist in making such decisions. The medical record must include adequate medical evidence to support the diagnosis;

b. The medical record indicates that there has been no expressed intention on the part of the patient that life-support systems be initiated or maintained in such circumstances; and

c. The medical record indicates that the patient's family, or guardian or conservator, concurs in the decision to discontinue such support.

The comfort and dignity of the patient shall be maintained if death does not occur on discontinuation of cardiopulmonary life-support systems.

Appendix B

Guidelines for No-Code Orders, Saint Joseph Hospital, Orange

The following statement was adopted at the National Conference on Standards for Cardio-Pulmonary Resuscitation and Emergency Cardiac Care held in May, 1973, and sponsored by the American Heart Association and the National Academy of Sciences:

> The purpose of cardio-pulmonary resuscitation is the prevention of sudden, unexpected death. Cardio-pulmonary resuscitation is not indicated in certain situations, such as in cases of terminal, irreversible illness, where death is not unexpected, or where prolonged cardiac arrest dictates the futility of resuscitation efforts. Resuscitation in these circumstances may represent a positive violation of an individual's right to die with dignity. When CPR is considered to be contra-indicated for hospital patients, it is appropriate to indicate this on the physician's order sheet for the benefit of nurses and other personnel who may be called upon to initiate or participate in cardio-pulmonary resuscitation.

DEFINITION

A no-code order refers to the written order to suspend the otherwise automatic initiation of cardio-pulmonary resuscitation.

PRINCIPLES

1. Competent adults have the right to direct the course of their own medical treatment.

2. Questions of when to withhold or withdraw medical treatment are not only medical questions; they involve personal values as well. Therefore, decisions in these matters are not to be made by the physician alone, but do involve the patient and those closest to the patient.

Accepted by the Saint Joseph Hospital Board of Trustees, Orange, California, January 24, 1980.

3. Biological life need not be preserved at all costs. There are times when it is more in keeping with respect for life to let it go than to cling to it.

4. A decision to withhold or withdraw treatment which is potentially life-saving does not mean the staff has abandoned patients, but rather represents the time for an intensification of efforts to provide physical and emotional comfort.

GUIDELINES FOR NO-CODE ORDERS

1. Competent patients should be involved in the decision and their wishes followed.

2. For incompetent patients, the following steps are suggested:

   a. It should be determined by the attending physician that the patient has an irreversible or terminal illness.

   b. The decision not to resuscitate should be discussed with and concurred in by the guardian of the patient, if there is one. If there is no guardian, those closest to the patient should be consulted, and their concurrence obtained. Documentation that this discussion has taken place should be made in the chart.

   c. The no-code order must be written in the patient's chart.

   d. The order should be re-evaluated periodically to be sure it is in accord with the patient's condition.

3. Slow-codes or half-codes* benefit nobody and are therefore not justified.

---

*This includes defibrillation without other resuscitative measures, or vice versa.

Appendix C

Principles and Guidelines for the Treatment of a Patient for Whom a No-Code Order Has Been Written, St. Joseph Hospital, Orange

PRINCIPLES

When a no-code order has been written, questions arise as to the type of care such a patient receives thereafter. The term euthanasia comes up in discussion. We make a distinction between active and passive euthanasia as follows:

A. ACTIVE EUTHANASIA is a deliberate act, whose intent is to cause death. We are firmly opposed to it under all circumstances.

B. PASSIVE EUTHANASIA is the withholding or withdrawal of life-support measures which offer no hope of recovery, prolong the act of dying, and are burdensome to the patient. This is acceptable, subject to the following guidelines:

GUIDELINES

A. We recognize, at the outset, that no-code orders may be written for two groups of patients: those whose death is expected and imminent and those with a fatal disease in whom death is *not* expected and imminent.

B. Both groups must be assured of the utmost efforts on the part of the medical team to ensure their physical comfort, spiritual and emotional care, with an emphasis on human contact.

C. With specific regard to the patient who has a no-code order written and whose death is expected and imminent, emphasis should be placed on the comfort-care-contact triad, and all procedures not directly related to this may be omitted:

Accepted by the Saint Joseph Hospital Board of Trustees, Orange, Caifornia, May 29, 1980.

1. Examples of what *may be omitted* under the above circumstances are:

   a. laboratory work

   b. diagnostic procedures

   c. vasopressors

   d. dialysis

   e. transfusions

   f. ventilatory support

   g. hyperalimentation by mouth or by vein

   h. antibiotics

   i. transfer to critical care units

2. There are certain items which, by their nature, do not prolong the act of dying, but may contribute importantly to the comfort-care-contact triad. Some examples of what should not be omitted are:

   a. basic nursing care, including body cleanliness, mouth care, positioning

   b. adequate analgesia

   c. suction

   d. intake for comfort, including hydration

   e. oxygen for comfort

D. Patients with a fatal disease and a no-code order, in whom death is *not* imminent, receive all aspects of care and treatment, except for the code itself.

Appendix D

Guidelines for Orders Not to Resuscitate, Beth Israel Hospital, Boston

SUMMARY

The Medical Executive Committee has adopted guidelines for the entry of orders not to resuscitate. If questions arise which are not answered by the Guidelines, the Administrator on call should be consulted. The Committee's recommendations are described in full in the attached Guidelines.

MEDICAL RECORD

Orders not to resuscitate (DNR) should be entered in the patient's record with full documentation by the responsible physician as to the patient's prognosis and the patient's concurrence (competent patients) or family's concurrence (incompetent patients).

CHIEF OF SERVICE

The Chief of Service (or his designee) must concur in the appropriateness of a DNR order on *incompetent* patients. This second opinion should be entered in the patient's record.

The Chief of Service (or his designee) must be notified promptly of DNR orders on *competent* patients.

DAILY REVIEW

All DNR orders should be reviewed daily.

COMPETENT PATIENTS

Competent patients must give their informed consent to a DNR order.

If, however, it is the responsible physician's opinion that a full discussion of whether CPR should be initiated would be harmful to the patient, this conclusion and its rationale should be documented. If the physician and the Chief of Service deem a DNR order appropriate, and the patient's family concurs, the order may be written.

INCOMPETENT PATIENTS

The assessment of incompetence should be documented, together with the documentation of patient's medical condition and prognosis and the concurrence of the Chief of Service or his designee.

If the patient's available family agrees that a DNR order is appropriate, the order may be written.

If there are no available family members, the responsible physician may enter an order with the written concurrence of the Chief of Service.

JUDICIAL APPROVAL REQUIRED

Judicial approval should be obtained before entering a DNR order if:

1) Patient's family does not agree to a DNR order.
2) There is uncertainty or disagreement about a patient's prognosis or mental status.

The Administrator on call must be contacted on any case which warrants judicial review.

For Full Details See Complete Policy Available at all Nursing Stations and Departmental Offices

SUMMARY

In certain circumstances it becomes appropriate to issue a "Do Not Resuscitate" (DNR) order and to enter this order in a patient's medical record. In all cases, the procedures and documentation described below should be carried out. Observe that in certain cases the Hospital Administrator on call must be contacted to assess the necessity of prior judicial approval. In all cases the Chief of Service should be kept informed as specifically listed below.

The following procedural guidelines have been adopted by the Medical Executive Committee of the Beth Israel Hospital to promote thorough decision-making, and to ensure accurate and adequate record keeping and the clear communication of all such decisions. When individual patient decisions present questions which are not answered by these guidelines, or when judicial approval may be required, nursing and medical staff should contact the Hospital administration through the Administrator-on-call who is available 24 hours a day.

A. THE COMPETENT PATIENT

A competent patient, for the purpose of these guidelines, is an adult (18 or over, or an emancipated minor) patient who is conscious, able to understand the nature and severity of his or her illness and the relative risks and alternatives, and able to make informed and deliberate choices about the treatment of the illness.

The competent patient may request the entry of a DNR order at any time without prior judicial approval. The attending physician must then consult with the patient to insure that the patient understands his or her illness and the probable consequences of refusing resuscitation treatment, that is, that the decision represents the informed choice of a competent patient. The patient's mental condition should be documented in the medical record. If there is any question about the patient's competence, a consultation should be obtained from the psychiatry service.

The execution of a "living will," if any, should be considered by the staff, but it is neither essential nor sufficient documentation of a decision to order the entry of a DNR order.

In this circumstance, approval of the next-of-kin is not required, and their refusal of such approval is not sufficient to overrule the informed decision of a competent patient. Nevertheless, the patient's family should be informed of the patient's decision and of the Hospital's intention to abide by that decision.

In all instances where a competent patient requests entry of a DNR order, the Chief of Service or his designate must be informed promptly that such orders have been written, even though the Chief of Service cannot deny such a request from a competent patient.

If in the opinion of the attending physician the competent patient might be harmed by a full discussion of whether resuscitation would be appropriate in the event of an arrest, the competent patient should be spared the discussion; therefore if the physician and the Chief of Service deem a DNR order appropriate and the family members are in agreement that the discussion might harm the patient and that resuscitation is not appropriate, the DNR order may be entered by the physician. In such cases, the physician shall follow the procedures described below for orders on incompetent patients.

B. THE INCOMPETENT PATIENT

An "incompetent" patient, for the purpose of these guidelines, is a patient who is under 18 (unless an emancipated minor) or who is unable to understand the nature and consequences of his or her illness or is unable to make informed choices about the treatment of the illness.

If an incompetent patient is *irreversibly and terminally ill, and death is imminent,* DNR orders may be entered without prior judicial approval, if family members concur in this decision. Before entering such an order the attending physician must consult with the patient's family including, at least, the same family members who would be sought out to consent to post-mortem examination. In addition, the attending physician should consult with, *and have the concurrence of,* the Chief of Service or his designate, before entering such orders. This second opinion as to the irreversible nature of the patient's illness and his or her moribund condition should be entered in the patient's record as well as the opinion of the first physician.

If the patient has no family who can be contacted, the DNR order may be entered by the responsible physician with the written concurrence of the Chief of Service or his designee.

C. REVIEW

DNR orders for all patients should be reviewed at least daily to determine if they remain consonant with the patient's condition and desires. Therefore, it is most appropriate for the physician to discuss his or her opinion and decision with nursing and house staff from the outset and frequently thereafter.

D. DOCUMENTATION

When a DNR order is decided upon, the order should be entered in the patient's chart along with the justification for the order and notes by all consultants involved. Specific reference should be made to:

1) Summary of a staff discussion regarding the patient's condition.

2) A descriptive statement of patient's competence or incompetence. For the incompetent patient, the record should include a notation of signs or conditions which indicate or constitute his or her inability to understand and make medical decisions on his or her own behalf.

3) A statement of the circumstances of the consent by the patient if the patient is competent, including staff discussions with the patient concerning the consequences of the DNR order, and any discussion with the family. For the incompetent patient, note in detail the discussions with the concurrence of all involved family.

E. PRIOR JUDICIAL APPROVAL

In any instance where judical review is sought, the Administrator on call and the Chief of Service or his designate must be consulted in advance. The decision to seek judicial approval of an order not to resuscitate should be made jointly and the hospital counsel should be consulted prior to initiating contact with the court.

Prior judicial approval should be sought if:

1) an incompetent patient is not suffering from a terminal illness or death is not imminent;

2) family members do not concur in the entry of a DNR order.

F. SUPPORT AND COUNSELING FOR PATIENTS, FAMILIES AND STAFF

Nothing in these procedures should indicate to the medical and nursing staff or to the patient and family an intention to diminish appropriate medical and nursing attention for the patient, whatever his or her situation.

When the incompetent patient is sufficiently alert to appreciate at least some aspects of the care he or she is receiving (the benefit of doubt must always assign to the patient the likelihood of at least partial alertness or receptivity to verbal stimuli), every effort must be made to provide the emotional comfort and reassurance appropriate to the patient's state of consciousness and the condition regardless of the designation of incompetence.

In every case in which DNR orders are issued, the Hospital shall make resources available to the greatest extent practicable to provide counseling and other emotional support as appropriate for the patient's family and for all involved Hospital staff, as well as for the patient.

Appendix E

Guidelines for Do Not Resuscitate Orders, Northwestern Memorial Hospital, Chicago

I. Purpose:

It is the purpose of this policy to enunciate clearly the practice which should be followed when a member of the Medical Staff issues an order that "heroic" or extraordinary means should not be employed on behalf of his patient. Such orders are often colloquially referred to as "Do Not Resuscitate" orders, but it should be understood that the use of the words "Do Not Resuscitate" is not determinative of the policy or the issues involved. The writing of any order, irrespective of the language used, which has the effect of precluding the use of extraordinary or "heroic" measures to maintain life is covered by this policy.

II. Definition:

For purposes of this policy, "resuscitation" will be defined as any extraordinary or "heroic" means employed to maintain the life of a patient including any *one* of the following: intubation/ventillation, closed chest cardiac massage, and defibrillation. Resuscitation does *not* mean or refer to ordinary or reasonable methods used to maintain life or health.

III. Written Order:

All orders not to resuscitate a patient *must* be written or signed by the member of the Medical Staff attending the patient on the Physician's Order Sheet in the patient's medical record. The writing of the order in any other document (e.g. Kardex) will be violative of this policy. *Failure to write such an order in the chart will result in the initiation of resuscitative measures.* In addition to the order itself, physicians may wish to write an entry attendant to the order in the progress notes which includes the following information:

1. A short description of the patient's physicial condition corroborating the terminal prognosis.
2. Reference to any consultations which corroborate a DNR order.

3. Reference to any discussions concerning the prognosis or the DNR order with the patient, his family, conservator or guardian.

Such an entry is *not* legally required, for it should only constitute a distillation and/or restatement of information found elsewhere in the patient's record, but it may be made if the member of the Medical Staff desires.

IV. Communication with Patient and Family:

Physicians should realize that members of the patient's family either individually or collectively do not necessarily have a legal right to impose their wishes or decisions either on a physician or his patient as to the care to be rendered to that patient. If the patient is an adult, the decision not to resuscitate need only be discussed with him, or, in the event that the patient has been adjudged to be mentally incompetent by a court of competent jurisdiction, with the patient's guardian or conservator. In the event that the patient is a minor (under the age of 18), the decision need only be discussed with the minor's parent or legally appointed guardian. (In the event the minor's parents are divorced, the physician should discuss the decision with the parent who has been awarded custody of the minor.) Conversations and discussions with family members who do not have the legal authority to act for the patient may be advisable for a variety of reasons, but are not necessarily legally binding upon the physician.

V. Verbal Orders:

Verbal DNR orders can be received only by a licensed physician and must be witnessed by *two* other individuals. These individuals must each individually hear the order and document it with the physician's order in the chart. Verbal or telephone orders must be authenticated and countersigned by the member of the Medical Staff attending the patient within twelve hours.

Authority: Patient Care Committee, January 19, 1978
Medical Executive Committee, February 13, 1978

The following is an addendum to policy 5.53.

1) The DNR order must be written and signed by an attending physician in the physician's order sheet. The order is invalid if written anywhere else.

2) Verbal order must be written only by a licensed physician and must be witnessed by two other individuals who personally hear and document the order. Verbal order must be countersigned by an attending physician within twelve hours of its being given. If it is not countersigned within that time period, it is invalid.

3) Failure to comply with paragraphs one and/or two result in the patient being resuscitated.

4) Explanatory notes may be written in the progress notes by the attending physician.

5) As used in this policy, the term "Medical Staff" means attending physicians *only*. It does not include resident physicians.

Appendix F

Comparison of Right to Die Laws

	Arkansas ACT 879 March, 1977	California A.B. 3060 September, 1976
Title		Natural Death Act
Purpose	Permits an individual to "request or refuse in writing...procedures calculated to prolong his life."	To recognize the right of adult person to make a written directive instructing physician to withhold or withdraw life-sustaining procedures in event of terminal condition.
Who May Elect?	Any adult. Also permits a proxy to execute document on behalf of minor or incompetent.	Any adult person.
How to Elect	Voluntary execution of a document requiring two witnesses and notarization. For minors and incompetents, document can be executed by specified family members.	Voluntary execution of Directive to Physician, legally binding when executed 14 days after diagnosis of terminal condition; otherwise it is advisory.
Is Form Included?	No.	Yes.
Formalities of Execution	As with a will of property, two witnesses and notarization of document.	Directive requires 2 witnesses not related, nor entitled to estate nor in employ of physician. Must be made part of patient's medical record.
How Long is Document Effective?	In force unless revoked.	5 years.
When Does Document Become Controlling?	Law is imprecise except to state person's right to "die with dignity."	1, Certification of terminal condition by 2 physicians; 2) attending physician must determine validity of directive; 3) death must be "imminent" in judgment of physician.
Revocation Procedures Specified?	No.	Yes.

Reprinted with the permission of the Society for the Right to Die, 250 West 57th Street, New York, NY 10019.

Is Document Binding on Physicians?	No penalty for non-compliance.	Yes. Unprofessional conduct for failure to comply unless arrangements made to transfer patients.
Are There Immunity Provisions?	Yes, for "person, hospital or other medical institution."	Yes, for physician, health facility and health professionals.
Penalties for Destruction, Concealment, Falsification Of Directive or Revocation	No.	Yes.

Idaho S.B. 1164 March, 1977	Kansas S.B. 99 April, 1979	Nevada A.B. 8 May, 1977
Natural Death Act		
To recognize right to execute written directive instructing physician to withhold or withdraw life-sustaining procedures when such a person is in a terminal condition.	To recognize an adult's right to make a written declaration instructing the physician to withhold or withdraw life-sustaining procedures in the event of a terminal condition.	To protect the terminal, comatose patient by means of an advance directive which is advisory only to physician.
Adult persons diagnosed as terminal.	Any adult person.	Any adult person.
Voluntary execution of a document which is legally binding if executed after diagnosis of a terminal condition.	Voluntary execution at any time of a written document directing the withholding or withdrawing of life-sustaining procedures in the event of a terminal illness.	Voluntary execution of "Directive to Physicians."
Yes.	Yes, but may include other specific directions.	Yes, but need only be followed "substantially."
Signed, written directive, two witnesses with same exclusions as California. Requires notarization.	Signed, written, witnessed directive, same witness exclusions as California. Permits signing by another on behalf of declarant, incapable of so doing, in his/her presence and under his/her direction.	Directive requires two witnesses, same exclusions as California. Must be made part of patient's record.
5 years.	In effect unless revoked.	In force unless revoked.
After determination by attending physician that death is imminent if patient is unable to communicate instructions.	Upon certification of terminal condition by two physicians.	Advisory only.
Yes.	Yes.	Yes.
No penalty for noncompliance.	Yes. Failure to comply or effect the transfer of a qualified patient constitutes unprofessional conduct.	No. Physician shall give weight to declaration but may consider other factors.
Yes, for physicians and health facilities.	Yes, for physician, health-care professionals, medical care facilities.	Yes, for physician, hospital, health professional.
No.	Yes.	Yes.

	New Mexico S.B. 16 April, 1977	North Carolina S.B. 504 June, 1977 as amended
Title	Right to Die Act	Right to a Natural Death; Brain Death.
Purpose	To allow an adult of sound mind to execute a document directing withholding of maintenance medical treatment when certified as terminal; also has provisions for terminally-ill minor.	To provide a procedure for the individual's right to a peaceful and natural death.
Who May Elect?	1) Adult of sound mind. 2) On behalf of a terminally-ill minor by specified family members with court certification.	Competent individual. No age provisions specified. Also on behalf of terminal, comatose patients by specified family members.
How to Elect	Voluntary execution of a document with same formalities as will. On behalf of minor by family member after certification of terminal condition by two physicians and requiring court certification of document.	Voluntary execution of an advisory document directing the withholding or discontinuance of extraordinary means.
Is Form Included?	No.	Yes, a suggested form to meet requirements of law: "Declaration of a Desire for a Natural Death."
Formalities of Execution	Requires two witnesses and notarization.	Signed declaration with 2 witnesses, same exclusions as California. Must be "Proved" before notary or clerk of court.
How Long is Document Effective?	In effect unless revoked.	Valid until revoked.
When Does Document Become Controlling?	After certification of terminal illness by two physicians.	Upon certification of terminal condition by 2 physicians.
Revocation Procedures Specified?	Yes.	Yes.
Is Document Binding on Physicians?	Yes, but no penalty for noncompliance.	No. Only advisory.
Are There Immunity Provisions?	Yes.	Yes.
Penalties for Destruction, Concealment, Falsification of Directive or Revocation	Yes.	No.

Oregon S.B. 438 June, 1977	Texas S.B. 148 August, 1977	Washington H.B. 264 March, 1979
Act Relating to the Right to Die.	Natural Death Act.	Natural Death Act.
To allow an individual to execute or re-execute a directive directing the withholding or withdrawal of life-sustaining procedures should declarant become a qualified patient.	To establish a procedure for a person to provide in advance for the withdrawal or withholding of life-sustaining procedures in event of a terminal condition.	To allow adults to control decisions relating to their own medical care, including decision to have life-sustaining procedures withheld or withdrawn in event of terminal condition.
Adult of sound mind.	Any adult person.	Any person at least 18 years old, of sound mind.
Directive must be signed 14 days after diagnosis and certification of terminal illness to be legally binding.	Voluntary execution of Directive to Physicians legally binding when executed after the diagnosis of a terminal condition; otherwise it is advisory.	Voluntary execution of advance directive directing the withholding or withdrawal of life-sustaining procedures in a terminal condition.
Yes.	Yes.	Yes, but may include other specific directions.
Directive requires 2 witnesses not related, nor entitled to estate nor in employ of physician. Directive must be placed in patient's medical record.	Directive requires 2 witnesses not related, nor entitled to estate nor in employ of physician. Must be made part of patient's medical record.	Signed declaration, requiring two witnesses with same exclusions as California. To be made part of patient's medical record.
Five years.	In force until revoked.	In force unless revoked.
When attending physician determines "death is imminent" and when life-prolonging procedures would only prolong dying. Physician need not determine validity of directive.	Upon diagnosis and certification of terminal condition by two physicians (one the attending). Physician must determine validity of directive.	Upon written verification of terminal condition by two physicians when life-sustaining procedures would only prolong "moment of death."
Yes.	Yes.	Yes.
No. Shall make "reasonable effort" to transfer patient.	Yes. Unprofessional conduct for failure to comply unless arrangements made to transfer patient.	No. Must make a "good faith effort" to transfer patient.
Yes.	Yes.	Yes. Physician, health personnel and facility.
Yes.	Yes.	Yes.

Appendix G

Crimes Which May Be Committed Against Critically and Terminally Ill Patients

George A. Oakes, J.D.

I. Crimes Defined

   A. § 187. Murder defined; death of fetus

   1. Murder is the unlawful killing of a human being, or a fetus, with malice aforethought.

   2. This section shall not apply to any person who commits an act which results in the death of a fetus if any of the following apply:

   a. The act complied with the Therapeutic Abortion Act, Chapter 11 (commencing with Section 25950) of Division 20 of the Health and Safety Code.

   b. The act was committed by a holder of a physician's and surgeon's certificate, as defined in the Business and Professions Code, in a case where, to a medical certainty, the result of childbirth would be death of the mother of the fetus or where her death from childbirth, although not medically certain, would be substantially certain or more likely than not.

   c. The act was solicited, aided, abetted, or consented to by the mother of the fetus.

   3. Subdivision (b) shall not be construed to prohibit the prosecution of any person under any other provision of law.

   B. § 188. Malice, express malice, and implied malice defined

   Malice defined. Such malice may be express or implied. It is express when there is manifested a deliberate intention unlawfully to take away the life of a fellow creature. It is implied, when no considerable provocation appears, or when the circumstances attending the killing show an abandoned and malignant heart.

   C. § 192. Manslaughter; voluntary, involuntary

Manslaughter is the unlawful killing of a human being, without malice. It is of three kinds:

1. Voluntary—upon a sudden quarrel or heat of passion.
2. Involuntary—in the commission of an unlawful act, not amounting to felony; or in the commission of a lawful act which might produce death, in an unlawful manner, or without due caution and circumspection; provided that this subdivision shall not apply to acts committed in the driving of a vehicle.

D. § 182. Conspiracy, Definition

If two or more persons conspire:

1. To commit any crime . . .
2. To commit any act injurious to the public health, to public morals, or to pervert or obstruct justice, or the due administration of the laws.

E. § 273a. Willful cruelty or unjustifiable punishment of child; endangering life or health

1. Any person who, under circumstances or conditions likely to produce great bodily harm or death, willfully causes or permits any child to suffer, or inflicts thereon unjustifiable physical pain or mental suffering, or having the care or custody of any child, willfully causes or permits the person or health of such child to be injured, or willfully causes or permits such child to be placed in such situation that its person or health is endangered, is punishable by imprisonment in the county jail not exceeding one year, or in the state prison.

2. Any person who, under circumstances or conditions other than those likely to produce great bodily harm or death, willfully causes or permits any child to suffer, or inflicts thereon unjustifiable physical pain or mental suffering, or having the care or custody of any child, willfully causes or permits the person or health of such child to be injured, or willfully causes or permits such child to be placed in such situation that its person or health may be endangered, is guilty of a misdemeanor.

II. The Uniform Crime Charging Standards

The primary responsibility of a prosecutor in charging is to determine whether or not there is sufficient evidence to convict the accused of the particular crime in question and to authorize the filing of appropriate charges.

A. Basic criteria for charging

The prosecutor should charge only if the following four basic requirements are satisfied:

1. The prosecutor, based on a complete investigation and a thor-

ough consideration of all pertinent data readily available to him, is satisfied that the evidence shows the accused is guilty of the crime to be charged.

2. There is legally sufficient admissible evidence of a corpus delicti.

3. There is legally sufficient, admissible evidence of the accused's identity as the perpetrator of the crime charged.

4. The prosecutor has considered the probability of conviction by an objective fact-finder hearing the admissible evidence. The admissible evidence should be of such convincing force that it would warrant conviction of the crime charged by a reasonable and objective fact-finder after hearing all the evidence available to the prosecutor at the time of charging and after hearing the most plausible, reasonably foreseeable defense that could be raised under the evidence presented to the prosecutor.

Commentary

The prosecutor should go through this four-step process in evaluating a case even though these steps are integrally related and the issues often overlap. This four-step process will help prevent the filing of inadequate cases because the failure to consider one or more of these issues separately could cause a prosecutor to overlook an issue or problem in the case.

B. Improper bases for charging

The following factors constitute improper bases for charging:

1. The race, religion, nationality, sex, occupation, economic class, or political association or position of the victim, witnesses, or the accused;

2. The mere fact of a request to charge by a police agency, private citizen, or public official;

3. Public or journalistic pressure to charge;

4. The facilitation of an investigation.

III. Areas of conduct where a crime may be committed

A. Active Euthanasia

1. The crime of murder

2. Motives for the act of euthanasia

a. Mercy

b. Financial

c. Emotional

d. Other (i.e., resource allocation)

B. Passive or Non-treatment

1. Failure to seek medical assistance

a. Child endangering

      b. Motive

      c. Persons

        —Child

        —Incompetent

        —Adult

    2. "No Code"

      a. Murder

      b. Involuntary Manslaughter

      c. Motive

      d. Persons

        —Child

        —Incompetent

        —Adult

    3. Withdrawal of life support

      a. Cardio-pulmonary support

      b. Hydration

      c. Nutrition

      d. Other (drugs, antibiotics, etc.)

      e. Crimes

        —Murder

        —Manslaughter

        —Child endangering

      f. Motive

      g. Persons

        —Child

        —Incompetent

        —Adult

IV. Several cases on point

    A. People v. McKenna

    B. In re Benjamin C.

    C. Baby Boy Damon

    D. People v. Corbin

    E. People v. Emory

    F. Others

V. Discussion and conclusion

In all of the above instances, if the decision maker acted prudently and reasonably considering all of the circumstances, and if other reasonable persons would have acted similarly, and where such acts are within accepted community standards, the possibility of criminal liability being imposed is very remote.

The value of life, whatever its quality, should be so great that abundant care should be exercised when any decision is made which might hasten its demise.

The emphasis should not be shifted to the caretaker, for he, or she, is changeable; it should remain centered on the patient.

Appendix H

A Living Will

To make best use of your Living Will

1. Sign and date before two witnesses. (This is to insure that you signed of your own free will and not under any pressure.)

2. If you have a doctor, give him a copy for your medical file and discuss it with him to make sure he is in agreement.

   Give copies to those most likely to be concerned "if the time comes when you can no longer take part in decisions for your own future." Enter their names on bottom line of the Living Will. Keep the original nearby, easily and readily available.

3. Above all discuss your intentions with those closest to you, NOW.

4. It is a good idea to look over your Living Will once a year and redate it and initial the new date to make it clear that your wishes are unchanged.

. . . .

TO MY FAMILY, MY PHYSICIAN, MY LAWYER AND ALL OTHERS WHOM IT MAY CONCERN

Death is as much as a reality as birth, growth, maturity and old age—it is the one certainty of life. If the time comes when I can no longer take part in decisions for my own future, let this statement stand as an expression of my wishes and directions, while I am still of sound mind.

If at such a time the situation should arise in which there is no reasonable expectation of my recovery from extreme physical or mental disability, I direct that I be allowed to die and not be kept alive by medica-

Prepared by Concern for Dying, an educational council, 250 West 57th Street, New York, NY 10019.

tions, artificial means or "heroic measures". I do, however, ask that medication be mercifully administered to me to alleviate suffering even though this may shorten my remaining life.

This statement is made after careful consideration and is in accordance with my strong convictions and beliefs. I want the wishes and directions here expressed carried out to the extent permitted by law. Insofar as they are not legally enforceable, I hope that those to whom this Will is addressed will regard themselves as morally bound by these provisions.

Signed_____

Date_____

Witness_____

Witness_____

Copies of this request have been given to_____

_____

_____

_____

. . . .

IMPORTANT

Declarants may wish to add specific statements to the Living Will to be inserted in the space provided for that purpose above the signature. Possible additional provisions are suggested below:

1. a) I appoint_____
        to make binding decisions concerning my medical treatment.

                                OR

    b) I have discussed my views as to life sustaining measures with the following who understand my wishes

_____

_____

_____

2. Measures of artificial life support in the face of impending death that are especially abhorrent to me are:

    a) Electrical or mechanical resuscitation of my heart when it has stopped beating.

    b) Nasogastric tube feedings when I am paralyzed and no longer able to swallow.

    c) Mechanical respiration by machine when my brain can no longer sustain my own breathing.

d) —————————————————————————

3. If it does not jeopardize the chance of my recovery to a meaningful and sentient life or impose an undue burden on my family, I would like to live out my last days at home rather than in a hospital.

4. If any of my tissues are sound and would be of value as transplants to help other people, I freely give my permission for such donation.

Appendix I

Directive to Physicians Under the California Natural Death Act

Directive made this_____day of_____(month, year).

I _____ being of sound mind, willfully, and voluntarily make known my desire that my life shall not be artificially prolonged under the circumstances set forth below, do hereby declare:

1. If at any time I should have an incurable injury, disease, or illness certified to be a terminal condition by two physicians, and where the application of life-sustaining procedures would serve only to artificially prolong the moment of my death and where my physician determines that my death is imminent whether or not life-sustaining procedures are utilized, I direct that such procedures be withheld or withdrawn, and that I be permitted to die naturally.

2. In the absence of my ability to give directions regarding the use of such life-sustaining procedures, it is my intention that this directive shall be honored by my family and physician(s) as the final expression of my legal right to refuse medical or surgical treatment and accept the consequences from such refusal.

3. If I have been diagnosed as pregnant and that diagnosis is known to my physician, this directive shall have no force or effect during the course of my pregnancy.

4. I have been diagnosed and notified at least 14 days ago as having a terminal condition by _____, M.D., whose address is_____ and whose telephone number is_____
   I understand that if I have not filled in the physician's name and address, it shall be presumed that I did not have a terminal condition when I made out this directive.

5. This directive shall have no force or effect five years from the date filled in above.

This Directive complies in form with the "Natural Death Act" California Health and Safety Code, Section 7188, Assembly Bill 3060 (Keene).

6. I understand the full import of this directive and I am emotionally and mentally competent to make this directive.

Signed_____

City, County and State of Residence_____

_____

The declarant has been personally known to me and I believe him or her to be
of sound mind.

Witness_____

Witness_____

Appendix J

Administering Medical/Nursing Care to Critically Ill Patients Who Are Incompetent or Who Refuse Treatment

J. Kay Felt

SUMMARY

   I. Individual interest in freedom from nonconsensual invasion of bodily integrity gives rise to right to refuse medical care and treatment.

  II. Individual right to be free from unwanted bodily intrusion may be overcome only by a compelling state interest.

 III. Incompetents do not forfeit the right to decline life-prolonging treatment; rather, the issue becomes how best to give effect to that right.

 IV. Minors have the right to expect ordinary and necessary care and treatment and do not forfeit the right to decline life-prolonging treatment.

  V. Factors to be considered in determining whether the right to be free from unwanted bodily intrusion may be upheld or overcome.

 VI. Procedures to be utilized by hospitals and health care providers in dealing with treatment refusals.

   I. Individual interest in freedom from nonconsensual invasion of bodily integrity gives rise to right to refuse medical care and treatment.

     A. Adult, competent patient has the right to be inviolate in his or her person and need accept medical care and treatment only with in-

Appendix J is an outline of material presented at the conference sponsored by the American Society of Law & Medicine in Detroit, November of 1979.

formed consent (common law right of free choice and self-determination).

Schloendorff v. Society of New York Hosp., 105 N.E. 92 (N.Y. 1914). "Every human being of adult years and sound mind has a right to determine what shall be done with his own body." Cardozo, J., at 93.

Natanson v. Kline, 350 P.2d 1093 (Kan. 1960). A man "is considered to be master of his own body, and he may, if he be of sound mind, expressly prohibit the performance of life-saving surgery or other medical treatment... The law does not permit [a physician] to substitute his own judgment for that of the patient." At 1104.

Canterbury v. Spence, 464 F.2d 772 (D.C. Cir. 1972), *cert. denied*, 409 U.S. 1064 (1972). A touching of another without prior informed consent is a battery; this theory forms the common law basis for the right to refuse treatment. At 783.

Erickson v. Dilgard, 252 N.Y.S.2d 705 (Sup. Ct. 1962). Refusal of blood transfusion upheld.

Winters v. Miller, 446 F.2d 65 (2nd Cir. 1971). Christian Scientist involuntarily committed to a mental hospital given forced medication over religious objections; right to refuse treatment where not adjudged incompetent upheld. At 69-71.

Rennie v. Klein, 462 F. Supp. 1131 (D.N.J. 1978). Involuntarily committed mental patient who is alert and aware of drugs and their side effects is entitled to a due process hearing before forced administration of drugs, except if emergency exists and drugs are required to protect patient from self-harm and harm to others. At 1142-47.

B. Statutory and regulatory rights to self-determination.

Michigan Public Health Code codifies the common law; patient is entitled to receive from the appropriate individual in the health care facility information about his or her medical condition, proposed course of treatment, and prospects for recovery in terms the patient or resident can understand, unless medically contraindicated, as documented by the physician; patient is entitled to refuse treatment to the extent provided by law and to be informed of the consequences of that refusal; when a refusal prevents a health facility or its staff from providing appropriate care according to ethical and professional standards, the relationship with the patient may be terminated upon reasonable notice. (M.C.C. §333.20201).

California Natural Death Act (California Assembly Bill 3060) permits a patient to execute a written directive instructing physicians not to use extraordinary life-sustaining measures to prolong life when recovery is not possible; other states follow this model, including Oregon, Texas, Idaho, North Carolina and Nevada.

Arkansas (Act 79) and New Mexico (Senate Bill 16) permit an agent to sign a directive to a physician outlining care to be given or not to be given and allow a person in good health to sign a directive for future use. The proposed Michigan Medical Treatment Decision Act is based on this model.

C. Constitutional right of privacy against unwanted infringement of bodily integrity.

In Re Quinlan, 355 A.2d 647 (N.J. 1976). Right to privacy "broad enough to encompass a patient's decision to decline medical treatment under certain circumstances." No external interest of state compels patient to endure the unendurable only to vegetate a few months without the possibility of returning to a semblance of cognitive or sapient life. At 663.

Ninth Amendment to the U.S. Constitution recognizes fundamental rights of the people arising from the traditions and collective conscience of the people. *Griswold v. Connecticut, infra,* Goldberg, J., concurring, at 487, 493, *citing Snyder v. Massachusetts,* 291 U.S. 97 (1934), at 105. Right of personal privacy recognized in *Griswold v. Connecticut,* 381 U.S. 479 (1965) (marriage relationship and use of contraceptives), and in *Roe v. Wade,* 410 U.S. 113 (1973) (termination of pregnancy).

Satz v. Perlmutter, 362 So.2d 160 (Fla. Dist. Ct. App. 1978). Right of individual to refuse medical treatment is tempered by state's interest in preservation of life, prevention of suicide, the need to protect innocent third parties, and ethical integrity of the medical profession. At 162, *citing Saikewicz,* 370 N.E.2d 417 (Mass. 1977). But competent, 73-year-old adult with terminal condition and unable to breathe without respirator may discontinue treatment based on right of privacy; normal life expectancy 2 years with respirator, one hour without; not compelled to endure the unendurable. At 162.

Lane v. Candura, 376 N.E.2d 1232 (Mass. App. 1978). A 77-year-old patient refused surgical amputation of leg; would result in death. At 1233. Where patient is legally competent, court will not order guardianship or authorize amputation despite irrationality of decision. At 1235-36.

In Re Quackenbush, 383 A.2d 785 (N.J., Morris County Ct. 1978). A 72-year-old with gangrenous legs requiring amputation; split of medical opinion re competency) court visited and determined competent and capable of exercising informed consent; right of privacy permits patient to decline treatment where extensive bodily invasion involved; here prognosis not dim. "The state's interest in preserving life weakens and the individual's right of privacy grows as the degree of bodily invasion increases and the prognosis dims, until the ultimate point when the individual's rights overcome the state's interest in preserving life." At 789, *quoting Quinlan, supra,* at 664.

D. Constitutional right to freedom of religious expression. First Amendment right to religious beliefs absolute, but conduct in pursuit thereof is not free from restraint.

In Re Estate of Brooks, 205 N.E.2d 435 (Ill. 1965). The appointment of conservator to order transfusion where no notice given to patient is unconstitutional infringement on freedom of religion. At 442. Adult patient was a Jehovah's Witness; not pregnant, no minor children, no danger to society involved. Patient had filed notice of rejection of transfusion with physician and executed documents releasing physician and hospital from civil liability; court found insufficient proof to establish incompetency. At 441-42.

In re Milideo, 390 N.Y.S.2d 523 (Sup. Ct. 1976). Competent 23-year-old without minor children; order for transfusion refused, even where transfusion may be necessary to save life.

Contra, J.F.K. Mem. Hosp. v. Heston, 279 A.2d 670 (N.J. 1971). No constitutional right to die; result is not changed by fact that patient's religious beliefs ordain death; conduct in pursuit of religious beliefs not immune from governmental restraint. At 672. "Compelling state interest" test chosen over "clear and present danger" test. At 674.

Cf. In Re Quackenbush, supra. Quackenbush distinguishes *J.F.K. Hosp.* as involving minimal bodily invasion (blood transfusion) as opposed to significant bodily invasion (amputation), and as involving potential for return to vibrant health and long life. (Note: *Quackenbush* does *not* involve dim prognosis.)

E. Emergency exception to the patient's right to be free from nonconsensual invasion.

In an emergency, where patient cannot by reason of condition consent to procedure for preservation of life, limb, or bodily function, consent to whatever care is reasonably necessary to preserve the same is implied.

In Re Collins, 254 N.Y.S.2d 666 (Sup. Ct. 1964). Patient cannot put hospital in impossible situation of deciding between operating without consent or letting patient die for lack of consent. At 667.

II. Individual right to be free from unwanted bodily intrusion may be overcome only by a compelling state interest.

A. State interest in the preservation of life and the prevention of suicide.

Distinction between prolongation of life and life-saving treatment.

Right to decline treatment in incurable illness.

"The state's interest in preserving life weakens and the individual's right of privacy grows as the degree of bodily invasion increases and the prognosis dims, until the ultimate point when the individual's rights overcome the state's interest." *In Re Quinlan, supra,* at 664.

1. State will interfere.

No constitutional right to choose to die; suicide, formerly a crime, at least against public policy. *J.F.K. Mem. Hosp. v. Heston, supra,* at 672-73.

The result is not changed by adding that one's religious beliefs ordains his death. *J.F.K. Mem. Hosp. v. Heston, supra,* at 673 *citing Reynolds v. U.S.,* 98 U.S. 145 (1978), at 166: "Laws are made for the government of actions, and while they cannot interfere with mere religious belief and opinions, they may with practices." Patient did not wish to die, wanted to live, but faith precluded transfusion; transfusion ordered.

If suicide were a crime, refusal of treatment resulting in death could not be honored; *Application of the President and Directors of Georgetown College, Inc.,* 331 F.2d 1000 (D.C. Cir. 1964); *cert. denied,* 337 U.S. 978 (1964). At 1008-09.

2. State will not interfere.

Erickson v. Dilgard, supra. Adult has right to refuse blood transfusion even if tantamount to suicide and even if suicide is a crime. At 706.

In re Estate of Brooks, 205 N.E.2d 435 (Ill. 1965). Appointment of a conservator without notice to patient is unconstitutional infringement on freedom of religion where no minor children and welfare of society not involved. At 442.

Holmes v. Silver Cross Hosp., 340 F.Supp. 125 (N.D. Ill. 1972). Court order authorizing blood transfusion where hospital, doctor, and court waited until objecting patient lost consciousness to obtain order sufficient to support civil rights claim against physicians and hospital for conspiracy under Civil Rights Act of 1971, 42 U.S.C. §1983, court and conservator immune. At 131.

Satz v. Perlmutter, supra where patient did not induce self-affliction, and wants to live, refusal or discontinuance of treatment is not suicide but is only an act of self-determination in the face of painful and certain imminent death; no specific intent to die. At 162-63.

B. *Parens patriae* interest in protecting innocent third parties.

1. Protection of minor children from abandonment.

Application of the President & Directors of Georgetown College, supra. Court allowed blood transfusion contrary to patient's wishes; patient did express will to live. At 1007. Since patient *in extremis,* and hardly *compos mentis,* is considered as incompetent as a child; and since parent has no right to forbid saving of life of child, husband *a fortiori* had no right to reject treatment for adult wife resulting in death. At 1008.

Holmes v. Silver Cross Hosp., supra. State's interest in preserving life is not sufficient alone to outweigh individual interest, but impact on minor children would be a factor which *might* have critical effect on the balancing process. At 130.

In Re Osborne, 294 A.2d 372 (D.C. Ct. App. 1972). No compelling state interest justified order of transfusion in case of 34-year-old man with two children, where relatives showed adequate resources to support children and undertook to provide care and nurture them if he should die. At 374-75.

2. Protection of unborn children.

Raleigh Fitkin-Paul Morgan Mem. Hosp. v. Anderson, 201 A.2d 537 (N.J. 1963), *cert. denied,* 377 U.S. 985 (1964). Transfusion of Jehovah's Witness mother ordered to save her life and the life of her unborn child.

C. Interest in maintaining the ethical integrity of the medical profession.

1. Traditional obligation of the provider of medical care is to prolong life and to do no harm.

U.S. v. George, 239 F.Supp. 752 (D.Conn. 1965). Adult Jehovah's Witness' refusal of blood transfusion denied on theory that patient cannot seek medical care and simultaneously insist physician undertake a course of treatment amounting to malpractice. At 754.

Collins v. Davis, supra. Spouse of comatose patient cannot refuse surgery required to prevent death of patient, where the patient sought care and looks to the institution to provide it. At 667.

As medical advances give physicians control over the time and nature of death, prolongation of life may only inflict a prolongation of suffering. *Saikewicz, infra,* at 423.

Physicians distinguish between curing the ill and comforting and easing the dying; physicians refuse to treat the curable as if they were dying or ought to die and sometimes refuse to treat the hopeless and dying as if curable. *In Re Quinlan, supra,* at 667.

All ordinary measures should be applied, but extraordinary means of prolonging life or its semblance should not be used when there is no hope for recovery. Recovery should mean life without intolerable suffering. Lewis, *Machine Medicine and Its Relation To The Fatally Ill,* JOURNAL OF THE AMERICAN MEDICAL ASSOCIATION 206: 387 (1968).

Definitional dilemma: What is extraordinary?

a. Substantial interference with bodily privacy yet causing minimal interference.

b. For purpose of prolongation of life vs. saving life or curing illness.

c. All care or treatment which cannot be used without excessive expense, pain, or other inconvenience or which, if used, would not offer a reasonable hope of benefit. *See, generally,* Mueller, R.A. and Phoenix, G.K., *A Dilemma for the Legal and Medical Professions: Euthanasia and the Defective Newborn,* ST. LOUIS U. L. J. 22:501-18 (1978).

d. Care that constitutes such a burden that it cannot in all conscience be imposed on the family. *The Prolongation of Life,* THE POPE SPEAKS 4:395-97 (1958). *Also see* Bishop Lawrence B. Casey, *amicus curiae in In re Quinlan, supra.* Medical science is not expected to prevent inevitable death. At 659.

2. Avoidance of civil liability.

Physician is bound to uphold applicable standards of professional practice; ethics committee approach suggested in *In re Quinlan, supra,* at 668-69, of great assistance.

3. Avoidance of criminal liability.

Termination of life support in case where no reasonable expectation of restoration to cognitive function not homicide; rather, it is expiration from natural causes. *In re Quinlan, supra,* at 669-70.

Exercise of constitutional right is protected from criminal prosecution; *Stanley v. Georgia,* 394 U.S. 557 (1969).

Failure to act where applicable standard of practice would so require, or action contrary to standard, that causes death or shortens life is subject to prosecution unless constitutionally protected right involved. *See People v. Conley,* 411 P.2d 911 (Cal. 1966).

III. Incompetents do not forfeit the right to decline life-prolonging treatment; rather, the issue becomes how best to give effect to that right.

A. Person who is adjudged incompetent must have guardian appointed to exercise right to make medical decisions whenever decision requiring informed consent is at issue. *In re Schiller,* 372 A.2d 360,367 (N.J. Super. 1977).

1. Cannot wait until patient is unconscious and then invoke emergency exception or seek court order where there is knowledge that patient would object. *Holmes V. Silver Cross Hosp., supra.*

2. Family members not appointed guardians are not legal substitute for consent of the patient.

Karp v. Cooley, 349 F.Supp 827 (S.D. Tex. 1972). Any information given to or withheld from wife could not affect informed consent of husband. At 835.

Beck v. Lovell, 361 So.2d 245 (La.App. 1978). Absent emergency, husband-wife relationship does not grant authority to permit surgery. At 250.

Gravis v. Physicians and Surgeons Hosp. of Alice, 427 S.W.2d 310 (Tex. 1968). Marriage relationship does not make one spouse agent of other. At 311.

B. The state must recognize the dignity and worth of an incompetent and afford that person the same panoply of rights and choices it affords the competent individual.

Superintendent of Belchertown State School v. Saikewicz, 370 N.E.2d 417 (Mass. 1977). Institutionalized 67-year-old profoundly mentally retarded man (unable to communicate verbally, not aware of dangers, disoriented outside immediate environment) with incurable acute myeloblastic monocytic leukemia; otherwise in good health; treatment with chemotherapy may cause remission of 2 to 13 months or longer in 30 to 50 percent of cases; age over 60 reduces rate of remission; unpleasant, painful treatment, difficult to tolerate; if untreated, relatively painless death within weeks or months. At 420-21.

Probate judge ordered no treatment "except reasonable and necessary supportive measures to safeguard well-being and reduce suffering." At 422. Factors in favor of treatment: longer life anticipated, most patients elect to be treated despite toxic effects and risk of failure. At 422. Factors against treatment: age, inability to cooperate, adverse side effects, low chance of remission, immediate suffering, low quality of life (continuation of pain and disorientation—no attempt to equate quality with value). At 422.

"Best interests" of an incompetent person does not require submission to noncurative treatment that will increase suffering while not substantially prolonging life. At 428. Application of substituted judgment principle by the court: would a majority of people choose treatment if told they would experience pain, discomfort, and restrain in strange surroundings for advantages measured by concepts of time and morality beyond their ability to comprehend; at 432. Goal to determine insofar as possible the wants and needs of the individual, taking into account the present incompetency as one factor. At 431.

In re Piotrowicz, (no. 1948, Mass. Prob. Ct., Essex County 1977). Guardian authorized to withhold consent for further life-prolonging treatment where no reasonable likelihood of cure of underlying condition existed.

In re Quinlan, supra. A 21-year-old brain damaged patient in chronic persistent vegetative state without reasonable possibility of restoration to cognitive, sapient existence. At 655. Court held that father, as guardian, could exercise daughter's right to privacy by authorizing removal of artificial support system. At 664. Application of substituted judgment principle to permit guardian and family to decide whether she would accept or refuse treatment in these circumstances after receiving advice of hospital ethics committee as to possibility of emergence from comatose state. At 664.

C. Procedures,

    1. Guardianship proceedings.

        a. Apply for guardian or temporary guardian, generally in probate court.

        b. *Saikewicz, supra.* Courts are uniquely qualified to make these determinations which require "detached but passionate investigation." At 435. Judge makes determination concerning treatment upon advice of guardian *ad litem* and other persons or groups, such as medical health personnel. At 434.

        In re Quinlan, supra. Guardian and family, acting on advice of hospital ethics committee and attending physician that there is no reasonable possibility of emerging from comatose state, may exercise substituted judgment for patient. At 671.

    2. Ethics committees.

    Saikewicz, supra. Voluntary aid to assist the court, but not to be transformed into a required procedure: "We take a dim view of any attempt to shift the ultimate decision-making responsibility away from the duly established courts of proper jurisdiction to any committee, panel or group, *ad hoc* or permanent." At 434.

    In re Quinlan, supra. Responsibility remains on health professionals and is not shifted to the courts; ethics committee or like body should be consulted under hospital procedures. At 669.

D. Substituted judgment test.

    1. Permits the guardian and family of an incompetent to exercise their best judgment as to whether the ward would exercise the right to refuse treatment in the circumstances. *In re Quinlan, supra*, at 664.

    2. Best interests of an incompetent does not require submission to noncurative treatment that will increase suffering while not substantially prolonging life. *Saikewicz, supra*, at 428.

    3. Permits court to substitute its judgment in the "best interests of the child" where child's life is threatened by parental decision to refuse medical treatment. *Custody of a Minor*, 379 N.E.2d 1053 (Mass. 1978). Order denying parent full custody. At 1065-66.

IV. Minors have the right to expect ordinary and necessary care and treatment and do not forfeit the right to decline life-prolonging treatment.

A. Common law right to expect ordinary care necessary to preserve life.

Parental right of privacy arises in context of decisions about rearing infants and controlling life styles; *See Wisconsin v. Yoder,* 406 U.S. 205 (1972); *Pierce v. Society of Sisters,* 268 U.S. 510 (1925); *Meyer v. Nebraska,* 262 U.S. 390 (1923).

People ex. rel. Wallace v. Labrenz, 104 N.E.2d 769 (Ill. 1952), *cert. denied,* 344 U.S. 824 (1952). Decision upholds appointment of guardian and authorization of guardian's consent to blood transfusion necessary to preserve life and health of unborn child, due to Rh factor of mother.

State v. Perricone, 181 A.2d 751 (N.J. 1962). Parents are free to become martyrs themselves, but it does not follow that they are free to make martyrs of their children before they have reached the age of discretion to make that choice for themselves; care ordered. At 757, quoting *Prince v. Massachusetts,* 312 U.S. 158 (1944). Allowed the state to prohibit children from distributing religious pamphlets on the street. At 166-67.

Custody of a Minor, 379 N.E.2d 1053 (Mass. 1978). Court order removing legal custody from parents who refused to provide chemotherapy for child suffering from leukemia; chemotherapy only available treatment offering hope for cure (50 percent survival rate beyond five years); fatal if untreated. At 1057-58. Parents offered no substitute treatment consistent with sound medical practice. At 1064. (Parents took child to Mexico for laetrile therapy, in order to escape effects of the order, where child died in October 1979).

Court has inherent equity power to protect those unable to protect themselves. At 1060. Although parents are natural guardians of children and have power to make decisions about child care, family autonomy is not absolute, and private realm of family life will be entered by courts where parental decisions jeopardize safety of child. At 1056, 1062-63.

In the parental relationship, right to control and nurture child carries with it a correlative duty to care for and protect child. At 1063. Parental right of privacy may not be asserted on behalf of children. At 1063.

Cf. Matter of Hofbauer, 411 N.Y.S.2d 416 (Sup. Ct. Appl. Div. 1978). Parents have primary right to determine child's treatment; the issue is whether they provide adequate care, not whether some other form of treatment is better. At 418-19.

Petition of Dennis and Donna McNulty, (No. 1960, Mass. Prob. Ct., Essex County 1978). High risk cardiac surgery ordered over objection of parents to save life of child with congenital rubella, deaf, and mentally retarded; where life-saving procedures exist, quality of life is not an issue.

B. Common law right to expect ordinary care necessary to preserve health.

Muhlenberg Hosp. v. Patterson, 320 A.2d 518 (N.J. Super. 1974). Application for appointment of guardian and order allowing transfusion for infant facing imminent danger of brain damage without a transfusion granted over objection of Jehovah's Witness parents. Threat present warranted protection equally as in threat to life. At 519.

In re Sampson, 317 N.Y.S.2d 641 (Fam. Ct. 1970), *affirmed*, 278 N.E.2d 918 (N.Y. 1972). Transfusion ordered over parental objection incident to surgery to correct severe facial disfigurement and necessary to insure physical, mental, and emotional well-being.

Mitchell v. Davis, 205 S.W.2d 812 (Tex. Civ. App. 1947). Custody removed from parent who was treating child suffering from arthritis or effects of rheumatic fever with prayer and home remedies despite physician's contrary recommendations.

Note: Both the *Sampson* and *Mitchell* cases were brought under state "neglected child" statutes.

Contra, In re Hudson, 126, P.2d 765 (Wash. 1942). Refusal to consent to corrective surgery for a congenital arm deformity not grounds for removal of custody or for ordering surgery since life was not in danger and procedure was risky.

In re Tuttendario, 21 Pa. Dist. 561 (1911). Surgery to correct rachitis not ordered where procedures were risky and life was not in danger.

In re Seiferth, 309 N.Y. 80, 127 N.E.2d 820 (1955). Court refused to order surgery for cleft palate and harelip since family, including the child, preferred to attempt cure through natural therapy, and since surgery could be delayed. (Note: if there had been testimony that the child's prospect for cure would have been jeopardized by delay, court might have ordered treatment).

In re Phillip B., 92 Cal. App.3d (1979). Court refused to order surgery to correct congenital heart defect where surgery was risky and without surgery child might survive from a few to 20 years with progressive physical incapacitation; factors of child's mental retardation and potential for outliving parents may have been relevant.

In re Green, 292 A.2d 387 (Pa. 1972). Court noted that order for transfusion would have been entered if surgery and transfusions were necessary to save life; here merely elective procedure; remanded to allow 17-year-old minor patient to make decision for himself.

C. Statutory right to be free from child neglect.

Hoener v. Bertinato, 171 A.2d 140 (N.J. Super. 1961). Parents who refused blood transfusion for benefit of unborn baby guilty of neglecting to provide child with "proper protection."

People ex rel. Wallace v. Labrenz, supra. Right to practice religion freely does not include liberty to make martyrs of children or to expose them to ill health, communicable disease, or death. At 774, *quoting Prince v. Massachusetts, supra,* at 166, 170.

Typical state statutes:

1. Massachusetts General Laws c.119, §24 grants jurisdiction to consider petitions alleging lack of "necessary and proper physical . . . care" for children " . . . whose parents . . . are unwilling . . . to provide such care." Has been held to include lack of medical care. *Custody of a Minor, supra,* at 1059-60.

2. Michigan Child Protection Law, MCL §722.621 *et seq.,* defines child neglect to include failure to provide adequate medical care, but provides that a parent or guardian who does not provide specified treatment because of religious beliefs shall not be declared a negligent parent or guardian for that reason alone. This does not, however, prevent a court from ordering necessary medical services.

3. Washington Juvenile Court Law, RCW §13.04.010 (12), defines a dependent child as one "who is grossly and willfully neglected as to medical care necessary for his well-being." Serious issues are raised as to whether the terms "grossly and willfully" render statute inapplicable to religious objection cases where child is not otherwise neglected. *See Jehovah's Witnesses in State of Washington v. King County Hosp.,* 278 F.Supp. 488 (W.D. Wash. 1967), *cert denied,* 390 U.S. 598, *rehearing denied,* 391 U.S. 961 (1968).

D. Doctrine of substituted judgment permits courts to implement nontraditional treatment decisions. Traditional "best interest" approach modified to permit transplant of organ from one child to another.

Strunk v. Strunk, 445 S.W.2d 145 (Ky. App. 1969). Kidney transplant from incompetent to brother authorized by court as being in "best interests" of incompetent child.

Hart v. Brown, 289 A.2d 386 (Conn. Super. 1972). Kidney transplant from minor to twin sister authorized by court.

Contra, In re Guardianship of Pescinski, 226 N.W.2d 180 (Wisc. 1975). Kidney transplant from minor to sister denied where no consent given by minor or guardian and no demonstration of benefit to the ward, even though dire need of transfer was established.

E. Right of privacy to decline life-prolonging treatment where no hope of recovery exists.

In re Benjamin C., No. J 914419 (Super, Ct., Los Angeles County 1979). The court allowed physicians to disconnect respirator from comatose minor with irreversible brain damage and no possibility of regaining consciousness, even though minor was not brain dead; disconnection of respirator no homicide, rather merely allowing nature to take its course.

V. Factors to be considered in determining whether the right to be free from unwanted bodily intrusion may be upheld or overcome.

A. Nature of treatment as life-saving or life-prolonging

B. Motivation: suicidal or to be free of bodily intrusion

C. Competence of patient

D. Age of patient

E. Presence or absence of dependent children

F. Quality of life not relevant to question of whether or not to provide treatment

VI. Procedures to be utilized by hospitals and health care providers in dealing with treatment refusals.

A. Checklist of information to be ascertained:

1. Name and age of patient

2. Names, addresses, and relationships of next of kin

3. Religious affiliation of patient or parent/guardian of minor patient

4. Patient's or guardian's response if court were to order treatment

5. Patient's reason for refusing care

6. Patient's mental condition; if in doubt, seek psychiatric consultation when time permits

7. Present diagnosis, prognosis without treatment, prognosis with treatment, whether procedure is emergency or elective

8. Whether patient is parent; if so, names and ages of children; extent of resources, availability of others to care for, nurture, and support children.

B. Procedures for elective surgical cases where possible necessity for blood transfusion exists and patient or parent/guardian has refused to consent.

1. Require prior review of the case to determine degree of risks involved, and whether physicians are willing to perform procedure within patient's constraints; if so, obtain waiver from patient; if not, do not undertake care. If minors, pregnant

women, possible incompetents, or parents of minors are involved, see following sections.

2. Where cases involve children or pregnant women, and potential for necessary blood transfusion is more than remote, seek prior court order.

3. Where cases involve possible incompetents, obtain psychiatric consultation and seek appointment of a guardian to make decisions about patient's care and treatment.

4. Where cases involve parents of minor children, assess potential for risk of liability to children and determine whether to seek prior court order.

C. Procedures for patients who refuse life-prolonging care for non-religious reasons.

1. Competent adults

   a. Assess competence and reasons for refusal

      1. Life motives

      2. Whether patient would accept if ordered

   b. Assess potential for liability to children

   c. If patient is competent and motives are not suicidal, if no potential for liability to children exists, and if patient is adamant in refusal, honor that decision.

   d. If patient's motives appear to be suicidal; if there are dependent children; or if patient would accept treatment if ordered, seek court order. Court will probably uphold refusal unless patient indicates willingness to acquiesce.

2. Minors or pregnant women

   a. Seek court approval. If truly only life-prolonging, court may honor refusal, but only if no prospect for cure or medical advance exists, and in the case of pregnant women, only if life cannot be sustained past birth.

3. Incompetent adult

   a. Seek guardianship and court approval. Court will probably uphold refusal if care is truly life-prolonging.

Selected Bibliography

BRAIN DEATH

Curran, W.J., *The Brain-Death Concept: Judicial Acceptance in Mass*, NEW ENG-LAND JOURNAL OF MEDICINE 298(18): 1008-09 (May 4, 1978).

Curran, W.J., *Settling the Medicolegal Issues Concerning Brain-Death Statutes: Matters of Legal Ethics and Judicial Precedent*, NEW ENGLAND JOURNAL OF MEDI-CINE 299(1):31-32 (July 1978).

Grenvik, A., *et al, Cessation of Therapy in Terminal Illness and Brain Death*, CRITI-CAL CARE MEDICINE 6(4): 284-91 (July-August 1978).

Homan, R.W., *Ethical, Legal and Medical Aspects of Brain Death: A Review and Proposal*, TEXAS MEDICINE 75(6): 36-43 (June 1979).

Horan, D.J., *Definition of Death: An Emerging Consensus*, TRIAL 22-26 (December 1980).

Kennedy, I.M., *The Kansas Statute on Death: An Appraisal*, NEW ENGLAND JOUR-NAL OF MEDICINE 285: 946-50 (1975).

Selby, R., Selby, M.T., *Status of the Legal Definition of Death*, NEUROSURGERY 5(4): 535-40 (1979).

Veith, F.J., *et al., Brain Death: A Status Report of Legal Considerations*, JOURNAL OF THE AMERICAN MEDICAL ASSOCIATION 238(16): 1744-48 (Oct. 17, 1981).

Victor, M.G., *Brain Death: An Overview*, MEDICAL TRIAL TECHNIQUE QUARTER-LY 27(1): 37-62 (Summer, 1980).

Wright, R.K., Ostrow, A.A., *The Role of the Medical Examiner In Determining Time of Death In Brain Dead Patients*, JOURNAL OF FLORIDA MEDICAL ASSOCIATION 67(2): 134-36 (Feb. 1980).

DNR ORDERS

Dunn, *Legal Models For the Terminally Ill*, TRUSTEE 32:7 (1979).

McCarthy, D., *The Use and Abuse of Cardiopulmonary Resuscitation*, HOSPITAL PROGRESS 56(4): 64-68, 80 (April 1975).

Rabkin, Gillerman, & Rice, *Orders Not to Resuscitate*, NEW ENGLAND JOURNAL OF MEDICINE 25:364 (1976).

Schram, R.B., Kane, J.C., Rober, D.T., *"No Code" Orders: Clarification in the Aftermath of Saikewicz*, NEW ENGLAND JOURNAL OF MEDICINE 299(16): 875-78 (October 1978).

No Code Orders vs. Resuscitation: The Decision to Withhold Life Prolonging Treatment from the Terminally Ill. WAYNE LAW REVIEW 26(1): 139-72 (November 1979).

GUARDIANSHIP

Mitchell A.M., *The Object of our Wisdom and our Coercion: Involuntary Guardianship for Incompetents,* SOUTHERN CALIFORNIA LAW REVIEW 52(5): 1405-52 (July 1979).

Paull, D., *The Creation of an Ombudsman: The Guardianship and Advocacy Commission,* DEPAUL LAW REVIEW 29(2): 475-92 (Winter 1980).

Guardianship for the Adult: A Need for Due Process Protections in Vermont, VERMONT LAW REVIEW 4 (1): 95-140 (Spring 1979).

Limited Guardianship for the Mentally Disabled, CLEARINGHOUSE REVIEW 12 (4): 231-33 (August 1978).

HOSPICE

Affeldt, J.E., *Accreditation Clinic: How the JCAH Views the Hospice Care,* HOSPITAL MEDICAL STAFF 9(6): 15-21 (June 1980).

Bodine, G.E., Sobotor, W., *The Hospice: An Integrated Bibliography,* JOURNAL OF HEALTH AND HUMAN RESOURCES ADMINISTRATION 3(1): 29-55 (August 1980).

Brooks, T.A., *Legal and Regulatory Issues in Hospice Care,* HOSPITAL MEDICAL STAFF 9(6): 15-21 (June 1980).

Cassileth, B.R., *Hospice: The Rise and Implications of a New Addition to the Health Care Scene,* HEALTH LAW PROJECT LIBRARY BULLETIN 5(6): 189-95 (June 1980).

Rizzo, R.F., Rizzo, L., *Hospice Program: Law, Guidelines, and Implementation,* NEW YORK STATE JOURNAL OF MEDICINE 79(8): 1244-47 (July 1979).

DuBOIS, PAUL M., THE HOSPICE WAY OF DEATH (Human Sciences Press, New York) (1980).

NURSING—ETHICS

Bandman, Elsie L., *The Rights of Nurses and Patients: A Case for Advocacy* in Bandman, E. and Bandman, B. (eds) BIOETHICS AND HUMAN RIGHTS, (Little, Brown and Co., Boston) (1978).

Bandman, E.L., *The Dilemma of Life and Death: Should We Let Them Die?* NURSING FORUM 17(2): 118-32 (1978).

Murphy, Catherine, *The Moral Situation in Nursing* in Bandman, E. & Bandman, B. (eds) BIOETHICS AND HUMAN RIGHTS (Little, Brown, & Co., Boston) (1978).

Wald, F.S., *Terminal Care and Nursing Education,* AMERICAN JOURNAL OF NURSING 79(10): 1762-64 (October 1979).

NURSING—PHYSICIAN RELATIONS

Aroskar, M., *et al, The Nurse and Orders Not to Resuscitate,* HASTINGS CENTER REPORT 7(4): 27-28 (August 1977).

Dalton, MEN WHO MANAGE: FUSIONS OF FEELING AND THEORY IN ADMINISTRA-

TION, C. 4, *Relations Between Staff and Line* (John Wiley & Sons, New York) (1959).

Gargaro, W.J., *Cancer Nursing and the Law: Assisting Suicide*, CANCER NURSING 3(1): 69-70 (Feb. 1980).

Stein, L., *The Doctor-Nurse Game*, AMERICAN JOURNAL OF NURSING 68:101-05 (1968) (reprinted from ARCHIVES OF GENERAL PSYCHIATRY 16: 699-703 (1967).

TERMINATING CARE—CIVIL OR CRIMINAL LIABILITY

Collester, *Death, Dying and the Law: A Prosecutorial View of the Quinlan Case*, RUT-GERS LAW REVIEW 30:304 (1977).

Foreman, Percy, *The Physician's Criminal Liability for the Practice of Euthanasia.* 27:54 BAYLOR LAW REVIEW (1975).

Giancola, P.J. *The Discontinuation of "Extraordinary" Medical Treatment from a Terminal Patient: A Physician's Civil Liability in New York*, MEDICAL TRIAL TECHNIQUE QUARTERLY 26(3):326-54 (Winter 1980).

Guthrie, L.B., *Brain Death and Criminal Liability*, CRIMINAL LAW BULLETIN 15(1): 40-61 (January-February 1979).

Sharp, Thomas H., Jr., and Crofts, Thomas H., Jr., *Death with Dignity—The Physician's Civil Liability*, BAYLOR LAW REVIEW 27:86 (1975).

Weissburg, C., Hartz, J.N., *Judicial Approach Beginning to Develop for Terminating Life Support Systems*, REVIEW 12(4): 44-48 (August 1979).

Euthanasia: Criminal, Tort, Constitutional and Legislative Considerations, NOTRE DAME LAW REVIEW 48:1202 (1973).

Euthanasia: The Physician's Liability, JOHN MARSHALL JOURNAL OF PRACTICE AND PROCEDURE 10:148 (1976).

TERMINATING CARE—DEFECTIVE NEWBORNS

Duff, R.S., Campbell, A.G.M., *Moral and Ethical Dilemmas in Special Care Nursery*, NEW ENGLAND JOURNAL OF MEDICINE 292:75-78 (1973).

Engerhardt, H., Tristam, Jr., *Ethical Issues in Aiding the Death of Young Children*, in MAPPES, THOMAS, A. & ZEMBATY, JANE S. (eds), BIOMEDIAL ETHICS (McGraw-Hill, New York) (1981).

Freeman, J.M., *To Treat or Not to Treat: Ethical Dilemmas of Treating the Infant with a Myelomenengocele*, CLINICAL NEUROSURGERY 20:134-46 (1973).

Gustafson, J.M., *Mongolism, Parental Desires, and the Right to Life*, PERSPECTIVES IN BIOLOGY AND MEDICINE, 16:529-57 (1973).

Horan, Dennis J., *Euthanasia, Medical Treatment and the Mongoloid Child: Death as a Treatment or Choice?* BAYLOR LAW REVIEW 27:76 (1975).

Mueller, R.A., Phoenix, G.K., *A Dilemma for the Legal and Medical Professions: Euthanasia and the Defective Newborn*, ST. LOUIS UNIVERSITY LAW JOURNAL 22:501-18 (1978).

Robertson, John A., *Involuntary Euthanasia of Defective Newborns*, in MAPPES, THOMAS A. & ZEMBATY, JANE S. (eds) BIOMEDICAL ETHICS (McGraw-Hill, New York) (1981).

Sergeant, K.J., *Withholding Treatment from Defective Newborns: Substituted Judg-*

ment, Informed Consent, and the Quinlan Decision, GONZONGA LAW REVIEW 13:781-811 (1978).

Soskin, R.M., Vitello, S.J., *Defective Newborns: A Right to Treatment or a Right to Die?* AMICUS 4(3):120-27 (May/June 1979).

Tietz, W., Powars, D., *The Pediatrician and the Dying Child: "Physician, Know Thyself",* CLINICAL PEDIATRICS 14(6): 585-91 (June 1975).

TERMINATING CARE—ETHICAL ISSUES

Bayley, C., *Terminating Treatment: Asking the Right Questions,* HOSPITAL PROGRESS 61(9): 50-53 (September 1980).

Beauchamp, Tom L. and Childress, James F., PRINCIPLES OF BIOMEDICAL ETHICS (Oxford University Press, New York) (1979).

Black, P.M., *Focusing on Some of the Ethical Problems Associated With Death and Dying,* GERIATRICS 31(1): 138-41 (January 1976).

Duff, *Guidelines for Deciding Care of Critically Ill or Dying Patients,* PEDIATRICS 64:17 (1979).

Herman, T.A., *Terminally Ill Patients: Assessment of Physician Attitudes Within Teaching Institution,* NEW YORK STATE JOURNAL OF MEDICINE 80(2): 200-07 (February 1980).

McCormick, Richard A., *To Save or Let Die: The Dilemma of Modern Medicine,* in MAPPES, THOMAS A. & ZEMBATY, JANE S. (eds), BIOMEDICAL ETHICS (McGraw-Hill Book Co., New York) (1981).

Nicholson, R., *Should the Patient be Allowed to Die,* JOURNAL OF MEDICAL ETHICS 1(1): 5-9 (April 1975).

Poe, W.D., *The Physician's Dilemma: When to Let Go,* FORUM ON MEDICINE 3(3): 163-66 (March 1980).

Reich, W., *The Physician's 'Duty' to Preserve Life,* HASTINGS CENTER REPORT 5(2): 14-15 (April 1975).

Skillman, J.J., *Ethical Dilemmas in the Care of the Critically Ill,* LANCET 2(7881): 534-37 (September 1974).

Ufford, M.R., *Brain Death/Termination of Heroic Efforts to Save Life—Who Decides?* WASHBURN LAW JOURNAL 19(2): 225-59 (Winter 1980).

Ethical Implications of Investigations in Seriously and Critically Ill Patients (COMMITTEE ON ETHICS OF THE AMERICAN HEART ASSOCIATION) Circulation 50 (6): 1063-69 (December 1974).

TERMINATING CARE—INCOMPETENT PATIENTS

Annas, G.J., *The Incompetent's Right to Die: The Case of Joseph Saikewicz,* HASTINGS CENTER REPORT 8:21 (February 1978).

Annas, G.J., *Quinlan, Saikewicz, and Now Brother Fox,* HASTINGS CENTER REPORT 10(3): 20-21 (June 1980).

Baron, C.H., *Medical Paternalism and the Rule of the Law: A Reply to Dr. Relman,* AMERICAN JOURNAL OF LAW & MEDICINE 4(4): 337-65 (Winter 1979).

Buchanan, A., *Medical Paternalism or Legal Imperialism: Not the Only Alternatives for Handling Saikewicz-type Cases,* AMERICAN JOURNAL OF LAW & MEDICINE 5(2): 97-117 (Summer 1979).

Connery, J.R., *Court's Guidelines on Incompetent Patients Compromise Their Rights*, HOSPITAL PROGRESS 61(9): 46-49 (September 1980).

Carroll, P.R., *Who Speaks for Incompetent Patients? The Case of Joseph Saikewicz*, TRUSTEE 31(12): 19-24 (December 1978).

Glantz & Swazey, *Decisions Not to Treat: The* Saikewicz *Case and Its Aftermath*, FORUM ON MEDICINE 2:22 (January 1979).

Paris, J.J., *Court Intervention and the Diminution of Patients' Rights: The Case of Brother Joseph Fox*, NEW ENGLAND JOURNAL OF MEDICINE 303(15): 876-78 (October 9, 1980).

Ramsey, P., *The* Saikewicz *Precedent: What's Good For an Incompetent Patient?* HASTINGS CENTER REPORT 8(6): 36-42 (December 1978).

In re Quinlan: *Defining the Basis for Terminating Life Support under Right of Privacy*, TULSA LAW JOURNAL 12:150 (1976).

TERMINATING CARE—PVS/COMA

Bai, K., *Around the Karen Quinlan Case—Interview with Judge R. Muir*, THE INTERNATIONAL JOURNAL OF MEDICINE AND LAW 1(1): 45-67 (Summer 1979).

Connery, J.R., *The Moral Dilemmas of the Quinlan Case*, HOSPITAL PROGRESS 56(12): 18-19 (December 1975).

McCormick R.A., (Editorial) *The Karen Ann Quinlan Case*, JOURNAL OF THE AMERICAN MEDICAL ASSOCIATION 234(10): 1057 (December 1975).

Involuntary Passive Euthanasia of Brain-Stem-Damaged Patients: The Need for Legislation—An Analysis and a Proposal, SAN DIEGO LAW REVIEW 14:1277 (1971).

THE RIGHT TO DIE

Bernstein, A.H., *Incompetent's Right to Die: Who Decides?* HOSPITALS 53(17): 39-42 (September 1979).

Brown, R.H., and Truitt, R.B., *Euthanasia and the Right to Die*, OHIO NORTHERN LAW REVIEW 3:615 (1976).

David, P.P., *Psychiatric Considerations for the "Right to Pull the Plug"*, ILLINOIS MEDICAL JOURNAL 155(6): 380-83 (June 1979).

Ettinger, D., *The Texas Natural Death Act*, THE HOUSTON LAWYER 77-87 (November-December 1977).

Kaplan, R.P., *Euthanasia Legislation: A Survey and A Model Act*, AMERICAN JOURNAL OF LAW & MEDICINE 2:41 (1976).

Monagle, J.F., *Living Will Does Not Resolve Medical-Ethical-Legal Dilemma*, HOSPITAL PROGRESS 57(5): 76-79 (May 1976).

Relman, A.S., *Michigan's Sensible "Living Will"*, NEW ENGLAND JOURNAL OF MEDICINE 300(22): 1270-71 (May 1979).

Riga, P.J., *The Impersonal Decision Maker: Courts of Equity and the Right-to-Die Cases*, CATHOLIC LAWYER 24(4): 301-12 (Autumn 1979).

Robitscher, J.B., *The Right to Die*, HASTINGS CENTER REPORT 2(4): 11-14 (September 1972).

Living Will: Already a Practical Alternative, TEXAS LAW REVIEW 55:55 (1977).

Living Will: The Right to Death With Dignity? CASE WESTERN RESERVE LAW REVIEW 26:485 (1976).

Living Wills—Need for Legal Recognition, WEST VIRGINIA LAW REVIEW 78:370 (1976).

The Right of Privacy and the Terminally-Ill Patient: Establishing the "Right to Die", MERCER LAW REVIEW 31(2):603-16 (Winter 1980).

The Right to Die: A Proposal for Natural Death Legislation, UNIVERSITY OF CINCINNATI LAW REVIEW 49(1): 228-43 (1980).

Rejection of Extraordinary Medical Care by a Terminal Patient: A Proposed Living Will Statute, IOWA LAW REVIEW 64(3): 573-658 (March 1979).

Statutory Recognition of the Right to Die: The California Natural Death Act, BOSTON UNIVERSITY LAW REVIEW 57:148 (1977).

Sullivan, W.F., Spinella, N.A., *Death with Dignity Legislation*, THE CATHOLIC LAWYER 23(3): 187-200 (Summer 1978).

Table of Cases

Index

team, health care, 253-65, 267-69,
270, 284
Teel, Karen, 34
terminally ill patients
—treatment, guidelines for, 10
—treatment, medical standards for,
30-31
—treatment, newborns, 236-37
—treatment, ordinary/extraordin-
ary, 5-6, 73, 99-100, 108, 139,
239, 248
therapeutic privilege
—arguments against, 81-82
—generally, 79-82, 88
—in emergency situations, 84-85
Twain, Mark, 28

Uniform Anatomical Gift Act, 68
Uniform Brain Death Act, 66
Uniform Crime Charging Standards,
196-98, 311
Uniform Determination of Death
Act, 67-68
University of California, Los Angeles
Program in Medicine, Law &
Human Values, 228
University of Michigan, Program in
Primary Care Nursing, 273-74

Veatch, Robert M., 19

Werdnig-Hoffmann's syndrome, 40
withdrawing/withholding life sustaining treatment (see also deci-
sion/making)
—difference between, 14-15, 73-74,
243
—for patients in persistent vegetative
state, 72-75
—from defective newborns, 213-25,
216-19, 222-25, 230-32, 240-41,
243, 248-49
—from incompetent patients, 4, 20,
25, 32-34, 100, 115, 117-23, 123-
24, 138-45, 159-61, 166-68, 173,
178, 182, 186-87
—liability for, 6, 25-26, 194-99, 216-
19
—prosecution by district attorney,
26, 169, 187, 194-99, 201-4, 207-
9, 216-20
—reaction of medical profession, 29,
214
—under Jewish law, 94-96

Yale Law School, 191
Yale–New Haven Hospital, 214
Yale University School of Medicine,
94
Yarling, R., 21
Young, Vincent Martin, 8

About the Editors

A. EDWARD DOUDERA, J.D., is executive director of the American Society of Law & Medicine, headquartered in Boston, Massachusetts, executive editor of the AMERICAN JOURNAL OF LAW & MEDICINE, and managing editor of LAW, MEDICINE & HEALTH CARE.

J. DOUGLAS PETERS, J.D., is a partner in the law firm of Charfoos, Christensen, Gilbert and Archer, P.C., Detroit, Michigan, and an adjunct assistant professor of law and medicine at the University of Toledo College of Law and the Wayne State University School of Medicine. Mr. Peters has also served as Chairperson of the State Bar of Michigan Committee on Medicolegal Problems and is the author of numerous articles on the subject of law and medicine. Mr. Peters is on the Board of Directors of the American Society of Law and Medicine and serves as an editor of LAW, MEDICINE AND HEALTH CARE.